Political Power in Alabama

Political Power in # ALABAMA

The More
Things Change . . .

*Anne Permaloff
and Carl Grafton*

The University of Georgia Press ■ *Athens and London*

Designed by Betty Palmer McDaniel
Set in 9.5 on 13 Century Schoolbook
by Tseng Information Systems, Inc.
Printed and bound by Braun-Brumfield, Inc.
The paper in this book meets the guidelines for
permanence and durability of the Committee on
Production Guidelines for Book Longevity of the
Council on Library Resources.

Printed in the United States of America

99 98 97 96 95   C   5 4 3 2 1

Library of Congress Cataloging in Publication Data
Permaloff, Anne.
    Political power in Alabama : the more things change—
/ Anne Permaloff and Carl Grafton.
    p. cm.
    Includes bibliographical references and index.
    ISBN 0-8203-1721-7 (alk. paper)
    1. Alabama—Politics and government—1951–
I. Grafton, Carl.   II. Title.
F330.P47 1995
976.1′063—dc20   94-38515

British Library Cataloging in Publication Data available

To the professors who, both as teachers and as researchers, stimulated our interest in the political world and the study of political behavior, especially

Norman Blume
William H. Flanigan
Donald Kash
Kenneth Kofmehl
and Roberta S. Sigel

Contents

Acknowledgments

We thank the many individuals who assisted in the preparation of this volume, including those who agreed to be interviewed. Governor John M. Patterson, Governor Albert P. Brewer, and Bob Ingram supplied many hours of their time for open and frank interviews. Governor Patterson also allowed us access to portions of his closed personal files.

The staff of both the Alabama Department of Archives and History and the Auburn University at Montgomery Library were especially helpful. Dr. Thomas Vocino supplied both encouragement and assistance. Ms. Susan Cagle and Dr. William Blow with the Alabama Commission on Higher Education supplied information on the educational system that was unavailable from archival sources. Ms. Sujata Singh spent many hours photocopying library materials.

The Research Grant-in-Aid Program at Auburn University at Montgomery supported portions of the research. Some of the materials in chapters 5 and 6 were published in article form by *The Alabama Review,* edited by Dr. Sarah W. Wiggins.

Introduction

This is a book about Alabama politics from 1958 to 1970, a period of almost revolutionary change. Because of Alabama's central place in the history of civil rights in the United States, scholars have tended to focus on such events as the Birmingham demonstrations and the Selma-to-Montgomery march and on such personalities as Martin Luther King Jr. and George Wallace, to the near exclusion of a rich and complex political environment and a host of important but less widely publicized issues. Many of these issues, including property tax equity, school funding, school quality, and economic development, are still leading concerns today, and they are almost unchanged from the forms they took in the 1950s and 1960s.

In many states throughout the country the politics of the 1950s centered on urban-rural disputes, but a different pattern existed in Alabama. The state contained several cities including Birmingham, part of a major steel manufacturing region, and Mobile, a large seaport. These industrial and commercial centers contrasted sharply with the majority of the state's counties, which had largely agricultural economies. Thus Alabama offered a rich environment for urban-rural conflict. Instead, state government was, to a large degree, orchestrated by an elite that bridged urban-rural differences.[1]

As of 1958 Alabama had been wrapped in a stifling cocoon of elite dominance and economic backwardness for more than a half century. State government was dominated by an alliance of the largest industrial and agricultural concerns, often called the Big Mules. The Big Mule Alliance was founded in 1901 on a broad congruence of its members' interests. They wanted low taxes, a school system that provided the minimal education required by farm laborers and factory workers, no effective labor unions, a small electorate, and racial segregation. They won control of state government through disenfranchisement of the electorate (black and white), control of the legislature (especially the Senate), and a refusal to reapportion the legislature.

By 1958 the alliance's industrial and agricultural halves were becoming disaffected with one another, and outside forces were driving them apart. In a few years the legislature and the electorate would be drastically restructured. This period of change in the political system could have been a time to set new policy directions for Alabama. Instead, opportunities offered to the electorate and its representatives were thrown away. The actions taken and the decisions made then established the politics of Alabama today and the seemingly intractable economic, social, and political problems the state now faces.

A large and potentially confusing tangle of forces and events underlies a full account of the alliance's dominance and breakup and their subsequent impact on change in the political system and on discarded (not just lost) opportunities. We were forced by this complexity to select occurrences that warrant especially close examination. We will focus on decisions that had the potential to narrow or close political lags and economic-cultural gaps that dominated Alabama politics in the 1950s. The political lags centered on civil rights, urban-rural disparities and regional differences within the state, the lack of party competition, and the structure of the tax system. The economic-cultural gaps separated Alabama and the South from the nation as a whole in terms of the quality of health and education services available and income levels. These lags and gaps were exacerbated, if not created, by the Big Mule Alliance.

A *lag,* as the term will be used here, is a failure in the responsiveness of the state's political system. It is a falling behind, a disparity that lasts for decades. A lag develops when the general public or a large interest fails to obtain a significant part of what it wants or when a very small group dominates the policy-making process, getting virtually everything it wants.[2] A lag is created and maintained by forces controllable by state government, legally or politically or both.

When interest-group pressures are converted into public policy without significant delay, the political process operates smoothly and quietly, even when resulting public policy is based on compromise and no single interest is fully satisfied. The more completely a group is frozen out of the political process and its interests ignored, the more traumatic will be the later settlement of its claims, especially when that group represents a large portion of the population (for example, blacks in Alabama). In other words, the elimination of a lag, which by definition is a significant, long-term disparity in governmental responsiveness, is bound to be upsetting to the entire political system. It may take years for the system to absorb the changes. In addition, vestiges of the past may remain as parts of the governmental structure and as cultural beliefs.

In 1958 black Alabamians had no direct political representation. They were not permitted to vote in any significant numbers. There were no blacks serving in elected offices in either state or county government. The major interest groups representing blacks had little, if any, direct influence on state policy-making. Many of the same techniques that governmental officials used to bar blacks from political representation and participation were also employed to reduce the representation and participation of lower-income whites.

A *gap* is a difference between a state or region and the nation as a whole. Gaps may also exist among regions within a state. They may be seen in the large differences that separated Alabama and the South from the nation in such measures of economic well-being and quality of life as income, educational spending and attainment, and expenditures on highways. Gaps are created both by political lags and by a host of economic, social, and political forces beyond the control of state government.

There is no question that Alabama's political lags were caused by the Big Mule Alliance. It wrote the 1901 constitution, blocked the Republican party from power, disenfranchised much of the electorate, and maintained the malapportioned legislature. The alliance's role in causing economic and cultural gaps and in preventing them from closing is somewhat more difficult to document, but we will do so. Despite extensive change in the 1960s, including the breakup of the alliance, elements of the arcane political structure inherited from the Big Mules are still in place today, and they remain steep barriers against progress.

Elite Dominance

The Big Mules controlled the legislature, the governor's office, and the Democratic party almost continuously from 1901 until the late 1950s. This is the single most important fact about Alabama politics and government during this period.

The alliance suffered occasional setbacks, but these problems were easily managed. For example, a potent mixture of populism and the Ku Klux Klan appeared in the 1920s. By 1926 the Klan had gained such power that its candidates for the governorship, the office of attorney general, the U.S. Senate, some congressional seats, and many state and county offices defeated Big Mule opponents. U.S. senator J. Thomas "Cotton Tom" Heflin was the most prominent Klan-populist leader. Heflin's virulent attacks on blacks, Jews, and Catholics were taken in stride by the Big Mules, but when he opposed the Democratic party's nominee for president, Al Smith, primarily because he was a Catholic, the Big Mules moved against him. They disliked the northern liberal almost as much as Heflin did, but the Big Mules had fashioned the Democratic party into a key instrument of dominance. It was essential that electoral victories be won for all Democratic party nominees, including presidential candidates. The party's image of invincibility was more important than the election of a repellent Democrat who, after all, would be gone in a few years. So Heflin was expelled from the party, and his career ended. Heflin's defeat was one of several devastating blows that the alliance landed against the Klan.

The Big Mules had the greatest difficulty maintaining continuous control over the governor's office. They were unable to block access to the primary-election ballot. Nor could they prevent direct populist-oriented appeals to the voters. As a result, well-financed but dull Big Mule gubernatorial candidates sometimes lost to more attractive opponents the Big Mules did not control.

Two examples of triumphant populist candidates were the charming Bibb Graves and the charismatic James E. Folsom Sr. Graves, first elected to the governor's office as a Klan-populist candidate in 1926, turned out to be a New Deal liberal, but he was also a spoils politician with whom the Big Mules could make deals through their strong presence in the legislature. Although Graves irritated the alliance, he did not threaten its existence. Folsom was a tougher case. His stated purpose in entering public life was the destruction of Big Mule power by enacting legislative reapportionment on a one-person-one-vote basis and ending voting discrimination against blacks and poor whites. He also campaigned for an expanded governmental role in road construction, education, welfare, and hospital construction.

In Folsom's first term (1947–51) the Big Mules crushed his programs in the legislature. A combination of his inexperience and lack of discipline and the Big Mules' considerable political abilities and majorities in the House and Senate caused his defeat. In his second term (1955–59) a more experienced, if not more self-disciplined, Folsom succeeded in electing House and Senate majorities not beholden to the Big Mules. However, his victory was short lived and moot, swept aside by white reaction against *Brown v. Board of Education*. Folsom won passage of what he referred to disparagingly as "pocketbook legislation," but that was all.

The Big Mules experienced another threat during the Folsom years—the beginning of an effective civil rights movement. They responded by organizing the States Rights or Dixiecrat party in 1948 and "massive resistance" after *Brown v. Board*.[3]

Emerging Alliance Weakness

As far back as 1946, difficulties began to appear in alliance ranks. In the 1946 Democratic primary, Commissioner of Agriculture and Industries Joe Poole, a gubernatorial candidate, experienced serious campaign-funding shortages. In addition, he was an extraordinarily maladroit campaigner. Poole was the candidate of the reactionary rural wing of the alliance centered in that portion of the state known as the Black Belt, which ran east and west near the southern third of the state. Named for its relatively rich, dark soil, it was home to wealthy plantation owners (including Poole) and disfranchised black majorities or near majorities. Both Poole's ineptitude and his funding problems suggested the weakness of the Black Belt.

The sense that the Black Belt was not fielding viable, well-financed candidates diminished somewhat in the 1950 gubernatorial race. Black Belt candidates included the widely respected former governor Chauncey Sparks and the reactionary prohibitionist J. Bruce Henderson, a state senator from Wilcox County. The winner, Gordon Persons, was a Montgomerian. Although Montgomery is in some respects a Black Belt city, plantation owners viewed it as the home of suspiciously progressive elements, and some sensed that Gordon Persons was not entirely trustworthy. During his term, however, he did little to hurt them. Black Belt gubernatorial fortunes were dealt a serious blow in 1954 when not one viable Black Belt candidate entered the Democratic party primary. James E. Folsom Sr. defeated seven opponents without a runoff.

The Black Belt was losing population while urban counties grew. Between 1930 and 1940 Black Belt county populations increased slightly, but the growth rates of the three most urban counties—Jefferson (Birmingham), Mobile, and Etowah (Gadsden)—were greater even though they started from much higher bases. The 1940–50 decade brought a decline in Black Belt population averaging 2.5 percent for the decade; in contrast, the state's three largest counties posted a mean growth of over 31 percent. Even when growing Montgomery County is included, the mean Black Belt county population dropped from 33,000 in 1940 to 32,000 in 1950, while the mean for Jefferson, Mobile, and Etowah increased from 225,000 to 300,000. Throughout the 1950s Black Belt county population continued to decline at a mean rate of 1.6 percent for the decade, while the mean for the state's three most urban counties increased by 18 percent, to nearly 350,000. The net migration out of Black Belt counties in the 1950s was 157,000.

While the Black Belt segment of the alliance was weakening, some Jefferson County interests were becoming restive within the restrictions of the coalition. Despite a requirement in the 1901 constitution that the legislature be reapportioned every decade, no reapportionment occurred. Jefferson County's rapid growth from 1901 meant that its citizens had far too few representatives. Its ambitious young leaders were stifled by the small number of legislative positions to which they could aspire, one Senate and seven House seats. In the first completely reapportioned legislature in 1967, these numbers jumped to seven Senate and twenty House seats, but the Jefferson Big Mules did not lose control of the selection process until the 1970s, when white flight to the suburbs surrounding Birmingham turned the city into a predominately black area.

In addition to the competition for state leadership within the Jefferson County talent pool, there were at least two differences between Jefferson County and the planters that caused strain between them. First, some of the more sophisticated business leaders and young professionals in Jefferson County recognized that improvements in the state's educational system and physical infrastructure would be needed if Alabama were to compete with other states. A reactionary state government dominated by the old alliance perspectives would make such change difficult. The alliance united industrialists and rigid agricultural interests. The industrialists generated change as a by-product of their activities. In the early years of the alliance, this tense coupling was manageable, because the technological change that industry required to keep it competitive could be contained within small managerial-engineering groups. Many in these groups could be imported from other southern and northern states. Most plant jobs required relatively low educational attainments. As the years passed, however, increasingly sophisticated workers were needed. Improved schools were seen as the only way to assure better-qualified workers.

The second cause of strain in the Big Mule Alliance was the civil rights movement: industrialists had much less to lose from a civil rights victory than did agricultural Big Mules. Planters were minorities in Black Belt counties, and the maintenance of their power depended on the continuation of segregation and voting discrimination.

Another force was at work to generate strains in the alliance. The 1950s saw the rise of an urban population, particularly from Birmingham northward. The locus of voter power in gubernatorial elections slowly shifted toward this region. Urban concerns that then found their way into gubernatorial politics profoundly affected executive-legislative relationships. As long as reapportionment could be blocked, the governor needed to maintain a good working relationship with the alliance to pass a legislative program and satisfy the urban constituency. The alliance-controlled legislature could block policy initiatives or attempts to change existing law. Whenever Birmingham/Jefferson County interests aided their rural alliance partners on key votes, tensions between them and other urban areas (especially those in north Alabama) grew.

Changing Times

Near the end of Folsom's second term in 1958, the Big Mule Alliance appeared robust. Although Alabama and like-minded southern states were losing civil-rights court cases, few doubted the Big Mules' ability to maintain fairly complete control of the state legislature. There seemed little danger of electing another radical governor like Folsom. The South was well represented in Congress, and it appeared that a variety of legal and political tactics would stave off the civil rights movement for many years.

Fewer than four years later the alliance was in disarray. Within a decade a drastically different political system was forming in Alabama. The Black Belt–Birmingham partnership was disintegrating, a change that made possible the restructuring of the political system and the closing or at least narrowing of all lags and gaps. The reapportionment of the legislature on a one-person-one-vote basis produced a major shift in power toward the cities and away from rural counties in general and Black Belt counties in particular. The end of state-sponsored voting discrimination and segregation bore the potential for a huge increase in black political power. The beginnings of meaningful ethics standards for government officials altered the rules for interest groups' influence over public officials. The basis of legislative conflict shifted from alliance counties versus other counties to rural counties throughout the state versus urban counties. Medium-sized counties aligned themselves with whatever side gave them the immediate advantage. During this period suburban growth had not yet developed to the extent found outside the South. Legislative politics began to organize around traditional interest groups rather than the Big Mule Alliance. Finally, no continuing legislative coalitions were able to guide the state in new directions or accomplish anything of a consistently constructive nature.

These were large changes. They made important differences in people's lives and in the operation of the political system. Opportunities were opened to many. In addition to blacks, other new voters were suddenly added to the electorate as white politicians encouraged whites to register and as women became more politically active. Urban voters suddenly had substantially greater influence in determining the membership of the legislature. Many of these enormous changes resulted from decisions and forces external to the state; the federal judiciary played an especially important role. Few of the improvements that the state saw resulted from plans and decisions made by its own citizens and leaders.

The alliance's demise deserves attention because of the unusual way the alliance bypassed urban-rural disputes that dominated the politics of so many states with large cities, including neighboring Georgia. The Big Mule Alliance also provides an example of a classic power elite operating within a democracy. Unlike most elites, it was born, matured, and died in relative openness. At the same time, alliance politics laid the political foundation that blocked real policy change in the state for decades to come.

The great tragedy of this period is that even though the alliance's reactionary grip on public policy was broken and the political system made potentially more responsive to the citizens' wishes, state government seemed unable or unwilling to take advantage of these changes to improve the quality of life in Alabama for everyone.

Critical Decisions

In the years 1958–70, amid the disarray of the alliance's breakup, Alabama decision makers—including the electorate, four governors, three legislatures, the pieces of the former alliance, and various interest groups—made many choices, some of which had the potential to produce significant improvements in the state's quality of life. With few exceptions, their choices were bad ones. Decision makers were repeatedly offered two roads to travel. One led to a better future (a narrowing of lags and gaps) and the other to stagnation. Over and over, they chose the latter road.

This fluid, fast-changing period is a mirror through which Alabama can see its future, for the state today looks much the way it did in 1970. Today, Alabama decision makers are faced with most of the same problems they failed to resolve in the period 1958–70. They can see how the future will look if they make the same mistakes as their predecessors, because they are living in the future created by the governors, lieutenant governors, and legislators elected in 1958, 1962, 1966, and 1970.

One of our objectives is to understand what occurred in this period of drastic change. Perhaps by dissecting the actions taken during this period, we can avoid the repetition of at least some of its worst elements. The primary approach we will take will be to identify critical decisions and to try to understand how and why they were made and how they molded the present.

Every aspect of a state's development consists of hundreds and thousands of decisions large and small. But there are points when decision makers are faced with a choice that is clear and that can produce an abrupt departure with the past. Once a choice is made, subsequent decisions or nondecisions tend to be little more than an endorsement of the critical choice.

We will focus only on decisions that had the potential to move the state in new directions (that is, to narrow lags and gaps). For example, tactical maneuvers executed by Martin Luther King Jr. during the demonstrations in Birmingham that forced the Kennedy administration to alter its passive approach to civil rights reform will not be analyzed here. Important and clever as these decisions were and important as the Kennedy administration's implementation process was, they were part of a powerful trend. At most, they accelerated change that would have continued even if the Birmingham demonstrations had never occurred.

This work will focus only on real choices—alternatives actually available to state decision makers, including the Alabama electorate. Some of the decisions to be examined were taken by a governor acting alone. Others involved action by a governor and the legislature, sometimes cooperatively and sometimes not. Still other actions were taken by the electorate. All were affected by the nature of group politics and political lags existent in the state.

Critical decisions that had an enormous impact on the state were made outside Alabama both before and during this period. These decisions included federal civil-rights policies as well as federal decisions in the areas of space exploration, health care, income maintenance, and other social programs. Even though we will describe these decisions and take them into account, our focus is on state-level decisions.

We will either describe or examine closely the following critical decisions:

"Brown v. Board." This path-breaking U.S. Supreme Court decision on school desegregation affected the Black Belt Big Mules more seriously than it did the urban Big Mules. It drove a wedge between them.

The movement of federal troops into Little Rock, Arkansas. President Eisenhower's actions in support of school desegregation weakened nascent southern Republicanism and led to the development of new strategies and tactics for blocking school integration.

Property tax equalization. In 1959 Governor John Patterson attempted to restructure a grotesquely unfair property-tax valuation system. Had he succeeded, primary and secondary school funding and educational quality might have vastly improved, and equity in ad valorem taxes would certainly have been achieved.

Education funding. In the 1959 legislature Patterson proposed mildly progressive tax increases to fund substantial enhancements in education funding. The legislature passed regressive tax increases that generated much smaller totals than Patterson's proposals.

Reapportionment and redistricting battles during the Patterson administration. These conflicts publicly signaled the breakup of the Big Mule Alliance.

"Baker v. Carr" and "Reynolds v. Simms." There would have been no reapportionment in Alabama—possibly for many years—without these federal court decisions.

The growth and development of Huntsville and the University of Alabama Medical Center in Birmingham. Huntsville went from being a cotton marketing hub to a center of engineering research and development. At the end of World War II the medical center in Birmingham barely existed. By 1970 it was rated as one of the top five medical complexes in the nation. Both developments occurred because local leaders assumed responsibility for economic and social growth. They also reflect reliance on federal monies and federal programs as local leaders recognized that the state leadership base would offer them little assistance.

George Wallace's failure to push for property tax reform. Wallace made no effort to modify the unfair property tax system that John Patterson had fought to overthrow.

The fight over a gubernatorial succession amendment and Lurleen Wallace's campaign for governor. These two events tied the state to the past and removed several promising young moderates from the legislature and potential statewide leadership positions. They also damaged Alabama's national image and probably exacerbated Alabama's negative relationship with the federal government.

Federal civil-rights statutes, the 1965 Voting Rights Act, and federal court decisions with regard to civil rights. These policies overthrew de jure and to some extent de facto segregation and voting discrimination.

The founding of private academies. The number of private schools increased abruptly over the years in direct response to federal actions favoring integration. Their founding (and the direct gubernatorial support they received) undercut political support for public schools as more affluent parents moved their children from the public system.

The federal push for mandatory desegregation via forced busing and the weakening of neighborhood schools. Forced busing further reduced political support for public schools and accelerated the growth of the private academies.

The Brewer administration's attempts to reform education. Governor Albert Brewer proposed a set of farsighted education reforms aimed at improving the quality of public schools and increasing funding for them. Most of his reforms were opposed successfully by education interests and the remaining fragments of the alliance.

The Brewer administration's attempts to reform the property tax structure. Brewer tried to achieve property tax equalization a decade after John Patterson had done so. His attempts also failed, and for many of the same reasons.

The 1970 election, which returned George Wallace to power over Albert Brewer. Wallace had no interest in educational or property tax reform or in effective and efficient administration. His reelection signaled a continuation of race baiting and a continuing deterioration of Alabama's national image. It showed that the past would remain more important than the future in the formulation and implementation of public policy.

To understand why these decisions were in fact critical, we devote the next chapter to identifying the political lags and economic-cultural gaps that Alabama suffered in the 1950s. We also examine the origins of these lags and gaps and link them to alliance actions and the governmental structure it created and maintained.

1

Lags and Gaps in Recent Alabama History

In a fully functioning constitutional democracy, everyone possesses equal rights, the one-person-one-vote standard obtains in legislative apportionment, no single political party is kept in power by artificial means, and taxes are paid according to the principles of equal treatment of equals and unequal treatment of unequals. Much of the political activity in Alabama after World War II centered on the efforts of those in control of state government to block the transformation of Alabama government into a democratic and responsive system and to maintain civil rights, urban-rural, regional, and political party lags.

Although lags—defined as long-term failures in the responsiveness of the state's political system—can be compared among states, we will apply the concept to a single political system (Alabama) or to an absolute standard of a responsive constitutional democracy. The existence of the lags will be traced to the Big Mule Alliance's dominance of the state's political system.

These lags, however, were and are not unique to Alabama. The civil rights lag existed throughout the nation in the early decades of this century and continued in the South until the 1960s. Alabama was fairly typical of the South except that the leaders of its urban areas might have been expected to be less intransigent in their opposition to the civil rights movement (in the manner of Atlanta) than they were. The difference lay largely in the relationship between the Black Belt and urban areas both in terms of the alliance and the Black Belt origins of many urban leaders.

Overrepresentation of rural areas existed throughout the nation. Each of the fifty states suffered from a lag the characteristics of which depended in part on demographic and geographic patterns specific to that state. In most states with cities the size of Birmingham, Mobile, and Montgomery, urban-rural relationships took the form of rather pure urban versus rural battles, complicated by the growth of suburban areas. What was unique in the Alabama case was the degree to which urban legislators and their supporters worked with the rural Black Belt interests to defend the representation inequities.

The Black Belt wing of the alliance was also able to maintain an arrangement by which its state senators were reelected repeatedly while senators from many other districts were unable to succeed themselves. These districts were thus perennially represented by freshmen, and as a result the Black Belt enjoyed substantial tactical advantages over other regions.

Alabama's economy and social makeup should have been fertile ground for vigorous two-party competition, but the Democratic party was one of the alliance's major devices for wielding power. The party firmly suppressed the Republican party, thus blocking the responsiveness of the political system.

After exploring the origins and some of the characteristics of political lags, this chapter will turn to a similar discussion of economic-cultural gaps. Quality of life in 1950s Alabama and the South was inferior to that found in most of the nation. Two of the most important and measurable elements of quality of life are income and educational levels. For perspective, these elements will be examined from the 1920s to the present; they will also be compared to other southern states and the nation as a whole. We will show that the education and income gaps narrowed between the 1920s and the early 1980s as part of a regionwide trend, not as the result of actions taken by the alliance-dominated political system. Because of the state leadership's failure to take advantage of this trend and the effects of the 1901 constitution, it is not surprising that the existing gaps widened in the 1980s.

The Civil Rights Lag

The most notable political lag in Alabama and the South during the 1950s (and many years before) was the disparity between minority rights guaranteed in the U.S. Constitution and southern laws and practices. In the 1950s Alabama's blacks constituted one-third of the population. They were not permitted to vote in significant numbers. Their schools were of much lower quality than those attended by whites. Segregation was rigidly enforced in schools, public facilities, and public transportation. For black Alabamians economic opportunity was minimal. The civil rights lag was based on a set of beliefs about the racial inferiority of blacks that much of the nation had shared only a few decades before.

After Reconstruction the imposition of segregation and voting discrimination laws in the South occurred with the acquiescence and even approval of northern progressives.[1] Influential national news and opinion magazines routinely published the work of authors who argued that blacks, because of their weaknesses of intelligence and character, did not deserve the same rights as whites.[2] Even authors friendly to blacks' aspirations routinely assumed their inferiority. For example, in a 1901 issue of the *Century Magazine,* Jerome Dowd, in the course of outlining what he regarded as a progressive educational system, described blacks this way: "It is a well-established fact that, while the lower races possess marked capacity to deal with simple, concrete ideas, they lack power of generalization, and soon fatigue in the realm of the abstract."[3]

Beliefs concerning the racial inferiority of blacks were part of a larger set of issues regarding immigration. For example, an *Atlantic Monthly* writer observed in one of that publication's most scientifically unsound and least prescient articles that immigrants from southern Italy, Hungary, Austria, and Russia "are beaten men from beaten races; representing the worst failures in the struggle for existence. . . . They have none of the ideas and aptitudes which fit men to take up readily and easily the problem of self-care and self-government, such as belong to those who are descended from the tribes that met under the oak-trees of old Germany to make laws and choose chieftains."[4]

In the first decade of the twentieth century, blacks in large numbers sought employment in cities throughout the country. Urban whites feared job losses and were angered by housing shortages. In 1906 white mobs in Atlanta killed and injured defenseless blacks and burned their houses. The rioters were not punished.[5] Race riots also occurred in Philadelphia and in Springfield, Illinois.

During this period there was little sympathy in the federal government for the rights of blacks. For example, in 1906 a group of black U.S. Army soldiers in Brownsville, Texas, killed a white civilian and injured another. President Theodore Roosevelt dishonorably discharged all battalion members. His action, based only on the report of a single inspector, was supported by a Senate investigating committee. Congress waited until 1972 to rescind the discharges.[6]

Roosevelt's successor, the progressive scholar Woodrow Wilson, appointed Josephus Daniels, a North Carolina newspaper publisher, secretary of the navy. Only a few months before his appointment, Daniels had written an editorial advocating nationwide segregation and voting discrimination against blacks.[7]

According to John Hope Franklin, the first Congress of the Wilson administration "received the greatest flood of bills proposing discriminatory legislation against blacks that had ever been introduced into Congress."[8] Few of these proposals became law, but the president ordered the segregation of federal employees' lunchrooms and restrooms and began cutting blacks from the civil service.[9]

During World War I black movement from the South to the North accelerated. After the war more race riots occurred in Tennessee, Nebraska, Illinois, and Arkansas. In the summer of 1919, mobs in Chicago caused twenty-three black and fifteen white fatalities and over five hundred injuries (a large majority to blacks). More than one thousand families, mostly black, were left homeless.[10]

Racist feelings against black, Jewish, eastern European, and Mediterranean minorities grew in the 1920s. For example, Henry Ford's magazine, the *Dearborn Independent,* sought to expose so-called international Jewish conspiracies and promote the superiority of the "Anglo-Saxon-Celtic race."[11]

Racist attitudes were widespread in the 1920s among respected writers and intellectuals who held teaching positions in the nation's finest universities. Intelligence tests, seen as scientific measuring devices, appeared to show that minorities had average scores lower than those of American-born whites. These tests were formulated, applied, and interpreted without regard to even elementary principles of scientific research design. Differences in education, language abilities, and other environmental factors were ignored. Dr. William MacDougall, a Harvard psychology professor whose textbook *Introduction to Social Psychology* was first published in 1908 and reprinted twenty-five times in various editions, argued that intelligence tests and Darwin's theory of natural selection supported the idea that Nordics were inherently superior to other racial groups.[12] He characterized those who disagreed as superstitious and antiscientific.

Immigration policy continued to be an explosive issue in the post–World War I period. Some who favored expanded immigration did so out of idealistic notions of the brotherhood of the world's people; others wanted only cheap labor for their factories. Advocates of reduced immigration were similarly disparate. They included conservatives who feared that foreigners would bring radical ideologies, unions that opposed expansion of the labor market, and progressive racist intellectuals.

Dr. Henry Pratt Fairchild, a sociology professor at New York University and a leader in many professional associations, was a prominent racist of this period. Fairchild maintained that mental traits of southern and southeastern European immigrants made them "difficult if not impossible to

assimilate into the American national life."[13] Dr. Henry Osborn, a paleon-
tologist, was president of the American Museum of Natural History for a
quarter century. A prolific and widely published author, he received many
scientific awards. Like William MacDougall, Osborn believed in the inherent superiority of Nordics. He argued against "the educational sophistry
that education and environment will offset the handicap of heredity."[14]
Theodore Stoddard held both a law degree and a Ph.D. from Harvard and
wrote twenty-two books and numerous articles in such popular magazines
as the *Saturday Evening Post* and *Collier's*. His major theme was that inferior races, because of their higher birthrates, were overrunning Nordics.[15]

Even Vice President Calvin Coolidge wrote in a 1921 issue of *Good Housekeeping* that "there are racial considerations too grave to be brushed aside
for any sentimental reasons. Biological laws tell us that certain divergent
people will not mix or blend. The Nordics propagate themselves successfully. With other races, the outcome shows deterioration on both sides."[16]

Secretary of Labor James J. Davis opined that "the older immigrants to
America were the beaver type that built up America, whereas the newer
immigrants were rat-men trying to tear it down; and obviously rat-men
could never become beavers."[17] Margaret Sanger, a prominent advocate of
birth control, shared these views when she announced that her movement
sought "more children from the fit, less children from the unfit."[18]

This same period saw the resurrection of the Ku Klux Klan. The Klan's
list of enemies included blacks, radicals (Communists), Catholics, Jews,
non-Anglo-Saxon Protestant immigrants, and labor unions (as advocates
for such groups). By 1924 Klan membership nationwide was estimated at
over four million. The majority resided outside the South; Klansmen could
be found in every state.[19] Known Klan members campaigned for and won
governorships in Alabama, Georgia, Colorado, and Indiana. Still others
won state and congressional races with Klan support.

Abruptly, by the late 1920s, leading scientists and scholars began to
reject theories of racial inferiority. As the methodological weaknesses of
"scientific" racism became increasingly obvious, scholarly research began
to focus on the evils of racism and prejudice. Environment and environmental circumstances, not innate personality or intelligence differences,
were viewed as the forces determining human behavior. Scholars such as
Franz Boas, Ashley Montague, Ruth Benedict, and Margaret Mead led the
scientific attack against racism.[20]

A social psychologist named Otto Klineberg reexamined the results of
World War I intelligence tests given to American soldiers, including blacks.
Earlier the results of such tests had been used to show the inferiority of

blacks to whites. Klineberg analyzed the impact of education and socioeco-
nomic background and found that black migrants to the North had higher
IQ scores than southern blacks and southern whites. Klineberg's analysis
of IQ scores for blacks from New York City showed that IQ scores tended to
increase in relation to the number of years a person had resided in the city.
Environment rather than innate intelligence differences accounted for the
variations in test scores.[21]

Political parties quickly responded to the changing perceptions of eth-
nicity and race. In 1924 John W. Davis, the Democratic presidential candidate, and Robert La Follette, the Progressive party nominee, both pledged
that, if elected, they would not discriminate on the basis of race or religion. La Follette criticized the Ku Klux Klan and, in what some viewed
as a direct appeal to Italian and Irish voters, voiced opposition to American entry into World War I and support for an independent Ireland. Only
four years before, James M. Cox, the Democratic presidential nominee, had
questioned the loyalties of immigrant groups and some blacks.[22]

The year 1924 also marked the beginning of a movement by blacks toward
the Democratic party, a shift that accelerated when in 1928 the Republican party, in a move to rebuild GOP strength in the South, seated white
delegates (the Lily-Whites) at the national convention instead of black Republican leaders, who had good reason to expect better treatment. Jewish
and Catholic voters returned to the Democratic party as the KKK and various anti-Catholic, anti-immigration, and anti-prohibition groups attacked
the party's nominee, Al Smith.[23]

By 1929 the Klan's membership and influence had waned. Its violence
and bizarre trappings repelled many Americans and made the group an
easy target for attacks by newspapers and government leaders. In addition, Michael Newton and Judy Ann Newton argue, financial corruption,
alcoholism, and various sexual escapades on the part of Klan leaders persuaded many of the faithful that they were being duped by hypocrites and
thieves.[24]

The rise of Nazism and Hitler focused attention on the use of race and
racial division as political tools for gaining or maintaining power. Communists began to exploit America's racial problems to embarrass the United
States and to recruit new adherents to their cause. Concern over exploitation of the race issue from the far right and far left activated many heretofore silent organizations. American scientists also realized that sound
scholarship alone could not defeat racism. Political action was required,
too. Many scientists who turned to such political activity were liberals or
Jews or both.[25]

The Great Depression intensified racial divisions. Blacks and whites competed for the same scarce jobs. In the late 1920s lynchings increased throughout the nation but especially in the South. The popular media covered the new scholarly studies of race, and religious and civic-minded organizations joined black groups such as the National Association for the Advancement of Colored People (NAACP) in calling for antilynching legislation.[26]

In 1932 an antilynching bill was introduced in the U.S. House of Representatives. The bill called for penalties on law enforcement personnel (generally sheriffs) who failed to prevent a lynching, and the county government in which the lynching occurred would be required to pay a fine of up to ten thousand dollars to the family of the victim.[27]

In February 1934 NBC radio carried the Senate Judiciary Committee's hearing on the antilynching bill. Walter White, executive secretary of the NAACP, mounted a national campaign to secure passage of the legislation. He obtained public endorsements from prominent organizations, individuals, and major publications. Eleanor Roosevelt even persuaded President Franklin Roosevelt to meet with White. In their discussion White not only pushed for the legislation but also presented statistics on the growing Democratic vote among blacks in northern cities. Roosevelt offered no real commitment to the bill because the southern congressional leadership was important to the passage of the administration's legislation. The battle to pass an antilynching law continued for several years, keeping the issue of violence and basic civil rights before the public.

In the 1930s President Roosevelt and northern Democrats sponsored programs that offered new opportunities in housing, employment, and education for blacks as well as poor whites. In addition, blacks held high advisory positions in the Roosevelt administration.

In the middle to late 1920s, southern segregationist leaders felt that their racial beliefs and segregated institutions had the approval of most of the nation's scientific and political elite as well as the mainstream media. A decade later the situation had reversed. As C. Vann Woodward described it, "Quite abruptly and unaccountably—or so it seemed to many Southern white people—an avalanche of denunciation, criticism, and opprobrium descended upon the South from above the Mason and Dixon line. Militant and organized demands from both Negro and white sources of pressure were raised for immediate abolition of segregation. There was a harsh intolerance and aggressiveness about the new agitation that frightened the South."[28]

Blacks continued their massive migration to northern cities, where they were becoming politically mobilized and more influential in determining the national Democratic party's agenda than were southern whites. This was especially evident with President Roosevelt's 1941 creation of the Committee on Fair Employment Practices.

Racist rhetoric became unacceptable for national and nonsouthern political leaders of both parties. A few racist authors continued their anti-black and anti-immigrant rhetoric, but their numbers and influence rapidly dwindled, as did legitimate publication outlets for their writings. Open expression of racist beliefs was no longer socially acceptable anywhere but in the South. By the end of World War II, segregationists, including members of the Big Mule Alliance, were frozen in the 1920s like dinosaurs in a glacier. By the 1950s they were separated from the nation's intellectual mainstream; they were a minority disdained by leaders throughout the rest of the country. After World War II blacks intensified civil rights mobilization. In Alabama nascent weakness in the Big Mule Alliance and pressure from the federal government assisted their efforts. The civil rights lag became the central feature of Alabama state politics well into the 1960s and '70s.

There is no established quantitative scale with which to measure lags, but in a democracy when one-third of the population is segregated, denied the right to vote, and discriminated against politically, a lag exists. When such a lag remains for more than a half century, closing it is not easy or peaceful. By the 1950s the national political system had partially responded to the demand of a large group of citizens for equal treatment. The nation was narrowing its civil rights lag, but Alabama and the rest of the South blocked change.

Equality and the Big Mules

It is essential to an elite's continuance that its authority be respected in some sense. To a considerable extent, respect for authority depends on the role that the notion of hierarchy plays in human relationships.

The alliance's isolation, caused by its separation from the nation over segregation, widened as a generalized tendency away from hierarchical authority spread throughout society during most of the century. This fundamental shift manifested itself in many ways, including changes in family life and in the way business and governmental organizations operated, increasingly widespread educational opportunities, and the dissemination of information through print and electronic media.[29]

The sociologist Ernest W. Burgess, writing in 1948, listed what he viewed as the basic characteristics of the pre–World War I family: "Control was centered in the father and husband as the head of the farm economy, with strict discipline and with familistic objectives still tending to be dominant over its members." After the war the American family was forced to adapt to rapid social changes such as urbanization, secularization, instability (especially in the form of increasing divorce rates), movement by the wife and children into the labor force, and an increasing democratization of family life. Burgess argued that American families were moving toward a model that he labeled the companionship form. The major characteristic of this model was that the central bonds connecting family members were found "in the interpersonal relationship of its members, as compared with those of law, custom, public opinion, and duty in the older institutional forms of the family."[30]

Work relationships and the structure of private- and public-sector organizations underwent significant changes during this century. In the first decade Frederick Taylor, inventor of the time-and-motion study, quite seriously referred to a pig-iron handler named Schmidt as an ideal worker because he had the physique and brain of an ox. Taylor then provided an example of how he addressed Schmidt: "You will do exactly as this man tells you tomorrow, from morning to night. When he tells you to pick up a pig and walk, you pick it up and you walk, and when he tells you to sit down and rest, you sit down."[31] The so-called principles school that represented the most advanced thinking about public management in the 1930s comprehended the administrative process in highly simplified, hierarchical terms not far removed from Taylor's. All organizations were assumed to be pyramidal and were thought to operate according to strict principles of chain of command.[32] The practitioners of the principles school reflected the management practices and societal attitudes of their time.

As business and government organizations found themselves faced with increasingly complex problems, they were forced to respond with ever more sophisticated tools wielded by necessarily better-educated workers. In this atmosphere the usefulness of older conceptions of human interaction and organizational structure diminished.

Human motivation on the job came to be viewed much less in terms of the piece-work pay that was Schmidt the pig-iron handler's reward and more in terms of the creativity of the work itself. Managers could no longer afford to order highly skilled subordinates to pick up a pig and walk, because the pig was increasingly being carried by a complex machine and the subordinate's responsibility was to keep the mechanism in good working order and even improve its operation.[33] The subordinate often knew more about the specifics of the task than the manager. Knowledge was no longer concentrated at the top of organizations but distributed rather evenly throughout. Organizations often could not be viewed as pyramidal entities; instead, they were seen as networks functioning more by consultation than by orders given and obeyed.[34]

These long-term changes were accelerated by World War II and the sense of power it gave returning veterans, and by the widely expanded educational opportunities provided by such programs as the GI Bill of Rights. The 1930s and the post–World War II period also saw a rapid expansion in labor union membership throughout the nation and in Alabama cities such as Birmingham, Gadsden, and Mobile. These changes produced a looser, more fluid society in which workers and voters saw themselves less as cogs in machinelike organizations and more as self-sufficient individuals.

All of this ran counter to views held by alliance members, who saw themselves as ruling their plantations, their companies, and the state according to chain-of-command principles.[35] The alliance became ever more out of touch with the increasingly egalitarian times and felt no need to adapt to change as elites throughout the nation were doing.

Elites and Lags

Elites commonly become disconnected from their environments. Sometimes this happens because the environments change and the elites do not accommodate themselves. Often this rigidity develops because the elites fail to bring like-minded but adaptive outsiders into their fold or, having brought them in, fail to listen to the warnings newcomers bring about a changing world. After the founding of the alliance, the Alabama elite failed to do either. Elites sometimes lose touch because their members become incompetent or corrupt, factors that were not important in Alabama.

Three rather different bodies of social science theory predict essentially identical outcomes when an elite becomes disconnected from its environment. Elite theory does it directly. Interest group theory and systems theory do not examine the activity of the elite directly, but they offer clear predictions about any political system that ceases to respond to environmental change.

Interest group theory originated in the work of Arthur Bentley and David Truman.[36] Its precise formulation varies between these two authors and among their many interpreters, but essentially all who use this concept view government policies as the result of forces emanating from interest groups. In some sense government, which itself consists of interest groups, combines and compromises these forces and produces public policy.

A naive version of interest group theory views the statutes, regulations, and decisions that constitute public policy as resulting, at least in the long term, from pressures exerted by interest groups. Government responds to changing pressure. When it fails to satisfy a particular interest, affected groups often increase their efforts by recruiting new members, raising additional money for campaign contributions, and forming new alliances with other groups. Such increased activity may or may not be successful, depending on the countermeasures of other groups and their leaderships.

David Truman suggests that the outstanding characteristic of politics in the United States is that multiple access points to authority are present, ensuring that in one way or another all organized groups participate in policy formulation. At the state level these multiple access points include the governor, lieutenant governor, legislators, Speaker of the House, chairs of legislative committees, and the courts. Depending on election results and subsequent bargaining, all groups have a chance to influence policy formulation. The resulting responsiveness of the political system is critical to the long-term stability of a society. Without it potentially explosive forces build within the system.

Truman identifies overlapping memberships among interest groups as another stabilizing factor. Because most interest groups contain members of other interest groups, the claims of any one group are kept within boundaries deemed reasonable by the others. This is contrasted with "a situation in which virtually all interaction takes place within social strata and in which there are few or no organized groups whose membership is drawn from more than one class."[37] Such a situation, which describes Alabama in the 1950s with considerable accuracy, could, Truman argues, easily lead to destructive conflict between strata of the society.[38]

Political behavior is also commonly analyzed in the light of systems theory, a perspective most often identified with David Easton. Systems theory views the political system as fueled by public policy demands and electoral and other kinds of supports.[39] In a smoothly functioning political system, government balances conflicting demands and supports and provides compromise outputs (for example, statutes, executive orders, judicial decisions). A political system that fails to respond to significant demands and supports over a long period of time is malfunctioning and is likely to suffer, in the stiff wording of the systems theorist Ervin Laszlo, "a fundamental reorganization of the institutional and value structure," or, in other words, a revolution.[40]

Unfortunately, neither group nor systems theorists provide practical guidance to assist someone trying to forecast or even explain the timing of the destructive conflict described by Truman or the restructuring of the political system predicted by Laszlo.

A branch of political thought often called elite theory addresses the implications of elite isolation directly. Elite theorists usually assume that domination of a political system by an elite is the norm. For them there would be nothing unusual about Alabama's Big Mules except perhaps for the unlikely urban-rural combination.

Elite theorists share with group and systems theorists an interest in isolated and unresponsive government. They argue that one way isolation of an elite can be avoided is through a process called "circulation of political elites," by which representatives of new interests and new groups, perhaps spawned by new technologies or changing economic conditions, are made part of the elite. Kenneth Prewitt and Alan Stone observe that for the social order to remain stable under conditions of change, "outlets are necessary for these new interests and the groups that press them. These outlets are provided by the circulation of elites."[41]

The kinds of elite adaptation mechanisms described by group, systems, and elite theorists occurred in Alabama at the end of the nineteenth century. Black Belt plantation owners took over state government after the Civil War, but they faced a powerful threat in the growth of Jefferson County's iron foundries and steel mills. The Black Belt tacticians could have stood and fought, and ultimately lost, against the growing wealth and power of Jefferson County. Instead, they included industrialist representatives in their high councils. This circulation of elites produced enormous change in elite membership, but the basic system remained in place and was strengthened.

The similar perspectives of the Black Belt and industrialist leadership groups facilitated their merger. The situation in the 1950s was entirely different. It was clear then that the alliance would not voluntarily permit blacks or poor whites to enter white-dominated social, economic, or political circles or join white leadership ranks. The circulation of elites had stopped, and the civil rights lag would be maintained until something exploded.

Malapportionment and the Urban-Rural Lag

Another lag in Alabama and all other states in the 1950s was the overrepresentation of rural areas in state legislatures. This pattern translated directly into rural counties' receiving more state funds than they deserved on a per capita basis. The constitutional mandate for reapportionment each decade was never met. On the basis of 1950 census data, the most extreme cases were Jefferson and Mobile Counties, where each House member represented more than 77,000 citizens, and the Black Belt counties of Henry, Lowndes, and Bullock, which had fewer than 9,500 voters per representative. Senate apportionment was comparably skewed.

Since very few blacks voted in rural Black Belt counties, de facto malapportionment was even more severe than these figures suggest. For example, in 1960 Lowndes and Wilcox Counties had no blacks registered to vote, even though blacks represented 80.7 and 77.9 percent of each county's population respectively. A Lowndes County House member effectively represented only 2,240 registered white voters. In Wilcox County the number was 2,950.[42]

Alabama's malapportionment was not unusual. Every state legislative body was malapportioned. In 1960 the Hawaiian House of Representatives came closest to a one-person-one-vote standard, and even it was malapportioned, with a ratio of largest to smallest single-member district of 2.2 to 1. Forty-seven legislative chambers in the United States were apportioned so that their largest districts contained ten times more people than their smallest districts.[43]

What was unusual in Alabama was the degree to which the legislative delegation from the state's largest counties shared policy goals with the perpetuators of their malapportioned condition. As representatives of the alliance, they and their Black Belt partners sought to block social, economic, and political reforms. In so doing, they separated themselves from and angered political leaders from other urban areas. Together they should have formed the basis of an urban-oriented partnership in opposition to rural domination.

Some Alabama state government funds were distributed equally or nearly equally among the state's sixty-seven counties. For example, 93.8 percent of Alabama's state financial aid to counties for road construction and maintenance was distributed equally among the counties. The remaining 6.2 percent was distributed to cities on the basis of the number of motor vehicle registrations and population.[44] Legislative malapportionment maintained these allocations even as the populations of rural counties diminished and those of urban counties increased.[45]

Another unique aspect of the urban-rural lag in Alabama (and much of the South) was a delay in suburbanization. Although the elite of Birmingham escaped the pollution and heat of that city by settling in areas such as Mountain Brook and Homewood, the central city–suburban growth pattern came to Birmingham and Mobile in a substantial way only in the 1970s and 1980s. Other Alabama cities experienced this movement even later.

The Black Belt Versus North
and South Lag

Legislative malapportionment had a regional dimension that overlaid urban-rural differences. The counties running through the lower middle section of the state compose the Black Belt, originally so named because of the relatively dark, rich soil found there. The Black Belt was the home of cotton plantations and slavery. Black Belt counties still have an agricultural base and large black populations, often constituting majorities. These counties embrace some of the most intense poverty, worst schools, and most dismal living conditions to be found anywhere in the nation.

The city of Montgomery, in Montgomery County, is geographically in the Black Belt. It is also the state capital, a substantial business center, and home of large U.S. Air Force facilities. Over the years Montgomery's political leaders represented various mixtures of these interests.

Birmingham, the state's largest city, is located in Jefferson County. It was the center of the urban half of the Big Mule Alliance. Birmingham was, throughout the period covered in this book, one of the nation's leading centers of iron and steel production because of the concentrations of iron ore and coal in and around the city. Other major businesses located there included the Alabama Power Company, the telephone company, and large insurance companies such as Liberty National. With the 1960s came the expanded development of the University of Alabama at Birmingham and its medical center, bringing a group of educated non-Alabamians to Jefferson County.

Some Mobile shipping companies and law firms were also part of the Big Mule Alliance, as were a number of corporations in Gadsden, located in Etowah County in northeast Alabama. Unlike Jefferson County's legislators, those coming from Etowah County often represented labor unions.

In the 1950s Huntsville (Madison County, near the Tennessee border) was known more for its leading position in the textile industry than for the growing Redstone Arsenal, which in the 1960s, under the leadership of Werner Von Braun, became an important part of the National Aeronautics and Space Administration's rocket research program. As NASA grew, Huntsville's population changed dramatically and with it the nature of Huntsville's legislative representation.

Rural counties located in the extreme north (the counties north of Birmingham, or the top third of the state) and south (below the Black Belt) had relatively poor soil and hilly areas suited mainly to small farms. They were often centers of populist activism.

Black Belt counties had more single-county senatorial districts and fewer multicounty districts than did northern and southern rural counties. Some multicounty districts rotated senators from term to term, so that their senators never succeeded themselves. Meanwhile, Black Belt senators, representing only a single county, tended to serve term after term. Thus a relatively large portion of Black Belt senators were seasoned legislators, and northern and southern senators were more likely to be freshmen. Furthermore, the Black Belt was economically and socially more uniform than northern and southern regions. The alliance served as a network of bridges connecting the homogeneous, experienced, frequently wealthy Black Belt legislators; the often equally experienced Jefferson County legislators, who were supported by wealthy corporate patrons; and lawmakers from Mobile and Gadsden.

The Party Competition Lag

The Alabama Republican party of the 1950s was little more than a ghost. The important elections were Democratic party primaries; Democratic nominees won the general elections. The Democratic party's strength derived from vestiges of feelings remaining from the Civil War, the popularity of the New Deal among the voters (if not alliance leaders), and the fact that the Democratic party was a major part of the Big Mule system of power.

A large segment of the Big Mules declared their willingness to abandon the Democratic party in 1948 for the States Rights party (known more commonly as the Dixiecrats), which had been formed as a protest against the national Democratic party's civil rights program.[46] But the Big Mules quickly returned to the Democratic fold because the Republican president Dwight Eisenhower moved too quickly and effectively on behalf of civil rights to suit Big Mule tastes. In 1954 the U.S. Supreme Court, led by an Eisenhower appointee, Chief Justice Earl Warren, declared segregated schools to be unconstitutional. In 1957 Eisenhower sent federal troops into Little Rock, Arkansas, to enforce school integration.

Even though the national Democratic party became less sympathetic to the segregationist cause than the Republicans, GOP leaders were unable to translate irritation with the national Democratic party into party strength at the state level. Southern Democratic congressmen and senators held leadership positions and were able effectively to block civil rights legislation.

Sarah Morehouse characterizes nonsouthern party differences in terms of "rural and small-town Protestant America represented in the conservatism of the Republican party and the liberal coalition of metropolitan minorities and industrial labor supporting the Democrats."[47] In this context the South should have been predominantly Republican. But change does not come quickly, and Democratic party traditions are strong in the South. To a significant degree, partisanship is learned from childhood. Those raised in a family with strong partisan attachments do not shift their loyalties easily. They are even less inclined to shift allegiances when they control one party's primaries and leadership structure and that party's nominees dominate congressional decision-making structures through the seniority system. As ambitious young candidates contemplate seeking public office, their choice of party will largely depend upon whether they have a chance of victory. As a result, the majority party has the choice of the best leadership talent available.

During the 1950s and '60s the migration of educated, often Republican whites into the urban South diluted the strength of the Democratic party. According to Philip Converse, approximately four-fifths of the decline in southern Democratic partisanship during this period resulted from Republican migration to and Democratic migration from the South.[48] Those moving into the South were little affected by the Democratic loyalties of the region.[49] (The migration of people into and out of the South has been a major factor in explaining many changes in differences between the South and the rest of the nation over time, both political and economic.) Countering the increase in the Republican party's strength was the growing Democratic partisanship of blacks together with their increased voting participation.[50]

The Economic-Cultural Gaps:
Alabama and the Nation

Lags indicate the presence of breakdowns in the political system's responsiveness. Coexisting with and often related to these lags were a number of economic-cultural gaps between Alabama and the nation. By virtually any measure, in the 1950s the quality of life for most Alabamians and other southerners was inferior to that in many other parts of the nation. For example, in 1959, 39.5 percent of Alabama's farms were on dirt or unimproved roads, placing Alabama fortieth in the nation in percentage of farms on paved roads. Most states ranking below Alabama were in the far West, where rural population densities were extremely low.[51]

To understand how Alabama's inferior position came about, one must have some sense of how far behind the nation Alabama was. Data sometimes must be examined as far back as the 1920s or 1930s in order to establish long-term trends. The image of Alabama that emerges from an examination of virtually any quality-of-life indicator is the same. For a number of decades beginning in the 1920s or '30s and running through approximately 1980, Alabama fell far below national averages. With other Deep South states, it occupied a position near the bottom. But throughout this period Alabama and all other southern states gained on the national averages.[52] From 1980 to the early 1990s, however, Alabama's progress stalled in many respects.

Two of the most important quality-of-life indicators are income and education. Income pays for better houses, automobiles, clothing, and other personal material goods. It also buys better health care, education, roads, parks, and even environmental quality, all of which are wholly or partly supplied by government. Honest and efficient government administration can stretch tax revenues; dishonest and inefficient government administration can have the opposite effect. There are, however, clear limits to the effect on quality of life that the efficiency of government administration alone can have. There is a strong but imperfect relationship between personal income measures and quality of life. In the long run good schools are as important to the quality of life as income. Better trained or educated people earn more and enjoy more fulfilling lives. The higher incomes they earn feed directly into the economic system, making it healthier, and higher incomes provide tax revenues by which government can provide improved services.

Education Funding and
Educational Attainment

In 1950 Alabama's educational levels were lower than the nation as a whole by any standard measure. The gap between the percentage of Alabamians completing high school and that of the nation as a whole was 8.4 percentage points in 1940. By 1950 the gap increased to 12.7 percentage points, by 1960 it diminished a little to 10.8, by 1970 it had risen slightly, to 11.0, and in 1980 it was 10.0. In 1989 the gap expanded to 13.7 percentage points. (Regression analysis based on the 1940–80 data suggests that if the state pattern had held, the figure would have been 74.5 percent of the national total in 1989, or a difference of 2.4 percentage points.) Alabama improved in absolute terms (from 15.7 to 63.2 percent) but in comparison to the national average, its position deteriorated, especially in the 1980s. Other standard measures of education paint a similar picture.

For example, Herman Leonard, using complex statistical comparison techniques based heavily on a state's ability to pay, places Alabama's primary and secondary school spending in 1979 as tenth from the bottom. In that year Alabama spent approximately $550 per pupil less than it could have. By 1989 Alabama declined to eighth from the bottom and spent roughly $850 per pupil less than it could have.[53] In 1956–57 Alabama spent $3.25 on schools for every $100 of disposable income after taxes, compared to $3.35 for the South and $3.41 for the nation. In the South, Alabama was ahead of only Florida and Virginia.[54]

Alabama's teachers were paid substantially less than the national average. In 1930 Alabama teachers earned on average 55.8 percent of the earnings of their counterparts in the nation as a whole. In 1940 their position deteriorated to 51.6 percent. By 1950 this figure had improved to 70.1 percent, by 1960 to 73.8 percent, and by 1970 to 79.8 percent. By 1981 the gap narrowed still further, to 87.9 percent, and by 1986 Alabama, at 90.5 percent, appeared to be closing the gap. But by 1990 Alabama's position dropped to 81.7 percent of the national average, an incredible reduction of 8.8 percentage points in only four years. These figures suggest that at some point in the 1980s Alabama's decades-long climb reversed.

Many Alabama teachers were inadequately educated. In 1956–57, 11.6 percent of urban teachers and 22.3 percent of rural teachers did not hold college degrees, but surprisingly, the inadequately prepared teachers were not concentrated in black schools. In rural areas 22.6 percent of white teachers and 22.0 percent of black teachers were not college graduates. In urban areas the spread was considerably greater—14.5 percent of white teachers and 6.1 percent of black teachers lacked college degrees.[55]

The history of education funding in Alabama looks virtually the same when it is examined in terms of state per-pupil expenditures as a percentage of average U.S. per-pupil expenditures. In 1960 Alabama's per-pupil spending was at 63 percent of the national average. This figure fell to 60 percent in 1973. After rising to 70 percent in 1980, it moved downward again, to approximately two-thirds of the national average in 1990. In contrast, from 1960 to 1990 neighboring Georgia grew smoothly from 67.5 to 91.1 percent of the national average.

Comparing Alabama with the nation as a whole and with another southern state is a legitimate way to present data, but it does not convey all aspects of the state's condition compared with others. All averages or means fall along a distribution. Roughly one-half of the cases fall below the mean. It is important to know not just how far Alabama fell below the mean, but where Alabama fell compared to other states. For example, Alabama's average 1961 primary and secondary school teacher salaries, $3,850, fell into the second group from the bottom. Those in the bottom group were South Carolina ($3,725), South Dakota ($3,675), Arkansas ($3,550), and Mississippi ($3,415). The comparative position of teacher salary figures almost three decades later is similar, although Alabama is not quite so near the bottom.

Alabama students' scores on the Scholastic Aptitude Test (SAT) reflect the inadequacies in schools suggested by the above data. The SAT is an examination administered in all states and is widely used for the evaluation of college admission applications. Alabama's raw verbal and mathematical scores increased steadily from 1974 to 1986, both absolutely and in comparison with the U.S. average. Unfortunately, these rankings use raw figures and overstate Alabama's position relative to other states.

There is a very strong relationship between SAT scores and the percentage of students who take the test.[56] In 1982, the most recent year for which data concerning percentages taking the SAT are available, only 6 percent of Alabama high school graduates took the examination, compared to over 45 percent for all the other states whose students scored lower on the mathematics examination. States like Alabama, with 20 percent or lower of their high school graduates taking the SAT, tend to score much higher than states like Connecticut, with higher percentages (30 percent or more) taking the examination. The reason is simple: in the low-percentage states only the best academic performers take the examination, but in the high-percentage states those participating are more representative of high school graduating classes.

In 1979 Alabama's mathematics and verbal scores moved closer to the others in the low-percentage group, but they were still the lowest in this group. By 1981 they were second lowest. Alabama's scores increased sufficiently by 1986 to place it ahead of five states in the low-percentage group. This is roughly where it remained through 1991, although the number of states that had a participation rate of 20 percent or lower had dropped. One could argue that Alabama has crept upward in SAT scores compared to other states since 1974, but that would be the most optimistic interpretation that would be supported by these data. There is no question that Alabama's SAT scores would plunge if higher percentages of its high school graduates were to take the examination.

Another measure of primary and secondary educational achievement (available for only a limited time frame) is the percentage of military draftees failing the selective service's mental requirements. In 1960, 18.8 percent of Alabama draftees failed the examination, a figure exactly equal to the national average. This placed Alabama in thirty-fourth place, ahead of sixteen states, most of which were southern. In 1972 the average national failure rate was 6.7 percent. At 18.3 percent, Alabama's position was far below the national average, placing Alabama in forty-seventh place, ahead of only Georgia, South Carolina, and Mississippi.

These dismal statistics reflect statewide averages and do not adequately portray the educational inequities and inadequacies rooted in economic and racial factors. Wilcox County provides a worst-case example of the effect of Alabama school expenditures on a Black Belt school system. In 1967 a National Education Association team under the supervision of Floyd Hunter, a specialist in community power analysis, studied education and life in the county.[57]

In the 1950s rural Wilcox County's economy was based on the plantation model. Cotton was being replaced as the dominant crop by cattle raising and wood-pulp timber growing and processing, but these crop differences made little change in how people lived. Blacks owned smaller farms and had larger families to support on less efficient holdings. As the 1960s began, Wilcox and six other Alabama counties (Bullock, Greene, Hale, Lowndes, Perry, and Sumter) ranked among the lowest one hundred counties in the nation in terms of per-capita income. In 1959 the median family income in Wilcox County was 39 percent of the state figure as a whole ($1,550 compared to $3,937).[58]

In 1964 Wilcox County's total instructional expenditures were $192.00 per white student and $123.00 per black student. Differences in noninstructional expenditures were even more marked: for maintenance, $18.07 per white student and $.56 per black student; for transportation, $40.00 per white student and $10.00 per black student; for new buildings and sites, $18.00 per white student and $3.00 per black student. Total capital outlay amounted to $26.00 per white student and $6.00 per black student.[59] Expenditures for white students were well below the national average and even the Alabama average. The effect of even lower expenditures for black schools was devastating.

During testimony in the 1966 U.S. District Court civil suit that placed Wilcox County schools under a desegregation order, a graduate of Annie Manie School noted that the school "has no foreign language or physics course. Chemistry is available, but there are only four spots for experiments. Two students work at each spot. There were 48 students in my chemistry class [and] while eight conduct experiments, the other 40 watch and take notes. We had experiments only on Fridays. . . . Textbooks are furnished by the school board. This year is the only year that they were.

We had about 25 chemistry books in my class."[60] White schools were given more textbooks per student and had an average of eight fewer students per teacher. The physical condition of black schools was appalling. A majority of the black schools had no indoor toilet facilities and relied on unsanitary outhouses.

Higher education was another area where Alabama's expenditures were consistently low; the pattern mirrored that for primary and secondary school spending. Herman Leonard ranks Alabama sixteenth from the bottom in higher education expenditures in 1989. Using statistical techniques that consider a state's ability to pay, he calculates that Alabama spent roughly $750 per student less than it could have done.[61]

Unfortunately, even Alabama's relatively low expenditures for higher education overstate its position. Alabama's junior colleges, community colleges, and universities number far beyond the needs of a state of its size. We will document later that many of these campuses were built because of political, not educational, considerations. A number prosper despite ample evidence that they are not providing students with a good or even adequate education. Notable programs flourish in the University of Alabama and Auburn University systems, but Alabama has a great many campuses of mediocre quality or worse absorbing tax dollars and wasting the students' time and money.

The percentages of managerial and professional business personnel educated outside Alabama in 1955 is suggestive of the poor quality of Alabama's schools at that time, although comparative data with other states are not available. In a study performed by the Alabama Business Research Council, 70.3 percent of top management personnel and nearly 45 percent of middle managers in the 1950s were educated outside the state.[62]

Income Gaps

Alabama's economic well-being mirrored its educational condition. From 1930 to 1980 Alabama's per-capita personal income as a percentage of U.S. per-capita personal income climbed rather steadily from 41.8 percent to 78.3 percent.[63] Beginning in 1980 this long-term upward trend leveled or reversed. An extrapolation of the 1930–80 trend would have resulted in a forecast of a 1990 figure of over 85 percent. Instead, the 1990 amount was only 77.9 percent.[64] These data are somewhat different from those published in another U.S. government source, which present a slightly more optimistic image of Alabama's situation.[65] In the years 1970–80 the state was well under the national average but growing from 72.7 percent to 77.7 percent. The first half of the 1980s produced no progress, but from 1980 to 1990 there is a gain of 2.5 percentage points rather than a loss.

Other data from the same source paint a less rosy picture. Average earnings in Alabama as a percentage of those for the entire nation declined in the 1980s by 0.5 percent after substantial increases in the 1970s (from 79.6 percent in 1970 to 84.3 percent in 1975 and 87.4 percent in 1980). Average wages and salaries as a percentage of the national average declined 2.3 percentage points in the 1980s after having increased 7.5 percentage points in the 1970s. And in a recently published study Paul Brace counted Alabama as one of the sunbelt states that suffered a net decline in per-capita personal income in the years 1968–89 when national growth is held constant.[66]

It is sometimes observed that the income gap between the Southeast and the nation is less meaningful than raw per-capita income and similar data would suggest because the cost of living in the Southeast is below the national average. A study conducted by the Advisory Commission on Intergovernmental Relations (ACIR) questions the validity of this argument, claiming that "the appropriate cost of living adjustments are neither conceptually clear nor are good data available on actual cost of living differences among regions."[67] Despite its methodological misgivings, the ACIR attempted to adjust nominal (raw) regional per-capita income figures for the years 1970 and 1975. The results suggest that cost of living adjustments have a fairly substantial effect. For example, in 1970 per-capita income in the Southeast was 82 percent of the national average measured with nominal figures and a full 10 percentage points higher when adjusted for cost of living. In 1975 nominal per-capita income in the Southeast was 86 percent and adjusted per-capita income 93 percent, a 7-percentage-point difference.[68]

Overall Trends

The figures presented above and others like them show Alabama (and the South as a region) steadily improving its situation compared to the nation as a whole from roughly 1920 to 1980. Between 1980 and 1990 this progress slowed or ended, and in some cases Alabama's condition worsened relative to the nation. These data differ somewhat, but they paint rather consistent pictures.

Throughout this period the best Alabama was able to accomplish in most instances was to climb toward the national average, not meet it or exceed

it. The only bright side to this observation is that in the case of income
this meant that Alabama was improving on an absolute scale, because the
national average was increasing. Unfortunately, with educational achievement Alabama also followed national patterns. In this case the quality of
the nation's schools declined, and Alabama's schools dropped with them.

The Origins of Economic and Cultural Gaps

The reasons for Alabama's weak economic condition
and poor quality of life cannot be found in a shortage of natural resources.
The state is endowed with good soil, water for agriculture and transportation, minerals, and other economic building blocks. Instead, Alabama's economic situation in the 1950s (and today) was caused by a complex economic
and political history going back to the Civil War.

Many economic historians place part of the blame for Alabama's backwardness on the Big Mules, who stifled business and educational development beyond their own narrow domains because development threatened
their political and economic hegemony. The authors' earlier work and that
of others has shown that Black Belt planters never wanted state government to promote economic development, either directly or indirectly via
stronger support of education, except for a few highly focused programs that
benefited them.[69] A policy to support educational and economic progress
would increase taxes and introduce new and possibly effective players into
the political process. Because the plantation owners had a tenuous hold on
political power, significant economic change might easily reduce their influence, as in fact it did. Urban Big Mules, who in many instances ran what
might be termed industrial plantations, were scarcely more enthusiastic
about economic growth than their Black Belt brethren.

Early in this century the gaps began to narrow. Many factors contributed
to the diminution, among them federal legislation and financial assistance
during the Great Depression; World War II–related economic growth combined with military contracts and bases; cultural and social changes produced by war; postwar federal funding assistance to states and individuals;
out-migration of poorly educated blacks; in-migration of educated whites;
and a variety of interregional economic factors.

A Big Mule apologist might argue that gaps narrowed because talented
Alabama leaders energetically worked to close them. This seems unlikely,
because practically everything the alliance did worked against the narrowing of gaps (and the closing of lags) and because all southern states

experienced the same effects. Alabama was swept along economically and culturally by federal power, federal financing, and national economic forces, much as it was bludgeoned into civil rights and reapportionment.

As the alliance fell apart, its component parts and other segments of the political system failed to take advantage of the wave of economic and educational progress. Opportunities were wasted, partly because very few leaders were interested in capitalizing on them.

From before the turn of the century to the 1950s, Alabama's political system failed to respond to groups seeking rights guaranteed in the Alabama and U.S. Constitutions. It also insulated rural Black Belt legislators and the Democratic party from competition. In the language of political systems theorists, the Alabama political system failed to translate demands and supports into public policy. The political system remained essentially unchanged from the year 1901, when the Alabama constitution was enacted and a pact between rural and urban Big Mules was sealed. Access was locked and bolted against outside influences—anyone not part of the alliance elite or its few trusted subordinates.

Political systems run by power elites must make a special effort to refresh the membership of the elites by recruiting new members who bring with them new perspectives and the viewpoints of previously unrecognized interest groups. If they fail to do so, they increase their chances of being overthrown.

2

Gaps and State Government Policy-Making

A state's economy is affected by many factors, including its history; natural resources; the relationships over time between its economy and the economies of other states, the nation, and even other countries; and decisions made by the state's political leaders. In this chapter we survey a variety of literatures to examine the relationships between these factors and the economic-cultural gaps between Alabama and the South and nation. We also consider how these gaps changed over time. Our primary concern is whether the actions and inactions of state government are important to the creation and the widening or closing of gaps. The chapter concludes with an examination of how Alabama's Big Mule Alliance, operating in a traditionalistic culture highly conducive to dominance by an elite, affected Alabama's gaps with the South and the nation.

History (for this study, events that occurred before 1958) sets the stage for the main relationships with which this chapter and the entire book are concerned.[1] The state's economy, containing the factors of production (land, labor, capital, and talent), is the engine that drives everything else. The state's natural resources roughly mold the economy. Policies of the federal, state, and local governments affect the nature and health of the economy.[2] The economy produces income, part of which is siphoned off by state government for its purposes. Local governments and the federal government also remove resources from the economy in the form of taxes, but for the sake of clarity these relationships are discussed only peripherally. The question of tax incidence and fairness, or who pays taxes, is an important point to which we will return repeatedly.

Decision makers in state and local government determine how much is spent on education and how efficiently and effectively these funds are mandated. The allocation of education dollars and the skill with which that spending is administered help to determine the level of educational attainment achieved by students. Educational attainment, in turn, feeds back into the economy in the form of trained or untrained workers, professionals, and managers who represent two of the four factors of production, labor and talent. Migration can also add to or detract from labor and talent.

State government revenues are used for capital stock spending, such as bridge and road construction, that enhances quality of life and becomes part of the economy. Land, labor, talent, and capital in turn generate income. Taxation of this economic activity generates the revenue to fund more education, capital expenditures, and other quality-of-life spending.

Civil rights policies emanate from federal and state governments. The need for governmental action in this area is in part determined by how previous governmental and economic-sector decisions have made the opportunity for education or training, income growth, and capital accumulation available to those within the government's sphere of authority.

Origins of the Gaps Between Alabama and the Nation

One reason economic and cultural gaps may occur between a particular state and national averages is that natural resources in the state are inadequate. Natural resources act as a foundation or set of constraints for economic activity. The topography of the land and the availability of rivers for transportation and power generation influence a region's economic health, as do the fertility of the soil, the availability of underground water for agriculture and industry, fuel reserves, minerals, and the structure and stability of the subsoil. Plentiful rainfall for agriculture is immensely valuable, and a moderate climate can attract management personnel associated with new manufacturing plants and other businesses, just as harsh conditions can repel them.[3] The relative importance of these factors can change over time, even though the factors themselves may not. For example, inexpensive water transportation may become less critical than access to an international airport.

In the South as a whole, several important resources are limited. Most soil is of medium or poor quality, and extra effort is required to maintain its fertility and avoid erosion.[4] In 1947 southern farmers used more than one-half of the fertilizer consumed nationally, even though they produced only about one-fourth of the nation's agricultural income. The relatively warm temperatures of the South provide advantages for agriculture, but in the days before air conditioning they also presented serious barriers to industrial and urban development. Rainfall is frequent most of the year.

Compared to many southern states, Alabama's outdoor recreation resources were and are inferior. There are relatively few scenic mountain areas, and the state's share of ocean coast is small. In 1945 Alabama's mineral production was slightly above average for the South if Texas is excluded.[5] The rich veins of coal and iron ore near Birmingham accounted for the city's rapid growth beginning in the last two decades of the nineteenth century. Alabama has rich water resources for transportation, hydroelectric power production (the northern part of the state is served by the Tennessee Valley Authority), and fishing.[6] There is also plenty of water for farming. Ample forest lands are especially well suited for the pulp industry.

Overall, Alabama is not richly endowed in natural resources, but it is far from impoverished. It would be difficult to assign blame for the state's situation to a scarcity of natural resources, and as far as we are aware, no economist has done so.[7]

Alabama's Economic History

Alabama's economic situation in the 1950s was caused in part by complex economic and political forces that heavily influenced the entire South. Southern economic history is described in a huge literature littered with technically difficult and often contentious issues. This chapter can only sketch some of the outlines of that history. For the purposes of this study it is sufficient to think of southern economic history as beginning after the Civil War.[8]

Southern agriculture recovered quickly from the effects of that conflict. Within a decade the region's agricultural production reached new highs.[9] Cotton was the primary crop. Although the South remained committed to cotton for many years, market forces caused a slow shift from cotton to manufacturing, following national trends in the same direction. From the Civil War through 1909 value added by southern manufacturing grew by an annual average of more than 7 percent.[10] Although southern industry developed rapidly, it was not sufficient to counter rapid rural population growth. In 1880 rural population density in the North and South were nearly equal. By 1930 southern rural population was twice as high as that of the North.[11] In Alabama, Birmingham's iron and steel industry was a major source of wealth, but it did not help the state economy as much as it might have done. There were also textile and other small manufacturing plants scattered around the state. Mobile's port and a substantial fishing industry also helped.

It is the consensus of economic historians that post–Civil War southern manufacturing began with a heavy reliance on northern capital from which it did not quickly escape.[12] Birmingham is probably the most often cited example of this phenomenon. Midwestern states at comparable levels of development also imported capital, but over the years in-state interests took control of capital resources. In the South capital tended to remain in out-of-state hands. As a result, nonagricultural wealth owned by out-of-state interests increased from 1880 to 1920.[13] Another difference between the two regions was that the Civil War and its aftermath damaged the South more. When the U.S. government declared debts incurred by the Confederacy void, many holders of Confederate bonds lost a major portion of their capital.

After the Civil War the United States adopted tariffs on imported manufactured goods to protect so-called infant industries from destructive competition from more advanced European economies. These tariffs drained the South financially by increasing the cost of imported manufactured goods and those made in the United States. The domestic products came primarily from the Northeast. Funds that could have gone to capital investment either flowed into the U.S. treasury in the form of tariffs or to northern manufacturers in the form of prices higher than they would have been able to charge without tariff protection. The tariffs were on such a scale that from 1880 to 1910 tariff revenues constituted roughly one-half of total U.S. government receipts.[14]

With the control of some of its largest industries located out of state, the South (and Alabama) developed into an economic island or colony; similes used by economic historians vary. Like most colonies, the South came to specialize in low-wage, low-technology agriculture and industry, and fell far behind the rest of the nation in economic development and the quality of life it could offer its citizens.[15] Thomas H. Naylor and James Clotfelter present a classic image of southern economic development: "Not only did the South fail to develop a pattern of industrialization that would lead it into the economic mainstream of America, but it also failed to develop the type of social, political, and educational infrastructure necessary for sustained economic growth. Much of the industry was exploitative in nature, utilizing child labor and sometimes convict labor. State governments were controlled by coalitions of planters and leading industrialists."[16] Needless to say, the planter-industrialist coalitions using child and convict labor had no interest in improving schools or any other aspect of their communities except those parts that immediately benefited them. Indeed, they had a strong interest in *not* improving the schools because these costly institutions would diminish the pool of untrained people willing to work in plants and on farms at subsistence wage levels.

Northern companies no doubt profited from their ownership of branches in the South and Alabama. The rise in the 1880s through the turn of the century of northeastern trusts such as Standard Oil and United States Steel further weakened the South's economic position.[17] In addition to the normal fruits of capital ownership, nonmarket devices gave northern companies added benefits. These nonmarket devices included a selective pricing technique known as "Pittsburgh Plus." U.S. Steel set the prices of the products in its Birmingham operations equal to those of the same products manufactured in Pittsburgh plus freight costs from Pittsburgh, regardless of the actual Birmingham manufacturing and transportation costs, both of which were often lower.[18]

Discriminatory railroad rates are also frequently included in lists of devices used to victimize the South, although the magnitude of rate discrimination is difficult to determine.[19] Daniel O. Fletcher describes as "formidable" the methodological problems associated with calculating pre-1947 freight rates, for which adequate data do not exist. He finds that "a simple comparison of class rate scales is useless, for the majority of traffic moves on commodity or exceptions rates. Freight tariffs are complex documents made up of many individual rates set between thousands of pairs of individual cities. There is no simple 'price list' that can be set down for comparison purposes." Comparing rates for two equivalent points is also difficult, Fletcher argues, because sets of states similar distances apart may have different costs owing to objective geographical differences such as grades.[20]

After World War I Congress enacted a tariff that, together with a weakening of foreign economies because of the war, reduced the marketability of U.S. agricultural products, including those grown in the South. Expanded cotton cultivation in India, Egypt, and the Sudan further hurt the South, as did increased cotton textile manufacturing in such low-wage countries as Japan, China, India, and Brazil.[21]

The South's status as an economic colony began to change, partly as a result of New Deal programs. The National Recovery Administration and the Fair Labor Standards Act raised wage rates. Although southern congressional opposition to these measures was intense, substantial support for them later developed among the general public and congressmen and senators. The 1938 senatorial elections of Claude Pepper of Florida and Lister Hill of Alabama, supporters of the New Deal, signaled the change. Price supports in the Agriculture Adjustment Act of 1933 encouraged mechanization, and unskilled workers began to leave the farm and the South. Resulting labor shortages encouraged further mechanization of southern farms in the 1940s. Rural electrification via the Rural Electrification Administration and the Tennessee Valley Authority also accelerated southern modernization.[22]

State industrial-promotion activities are often described as beginning in the 1930s. Mississippi's "Balance Agriculture with Industry" program is usually credited with being a pioneering attempt, although efforts in Alabama and other southern states predated it. In 1923 Alabama created the Department of Commerce and Industries to promote agriculture and manufacturing, and in 1927 the state formed an Industrial Development Board for the purpose of attracting new manufacturing facilities.[23] Clarence H. Danhof observes that in the South, state government agencies charged with the task of attracting industry were not very effective in the 1930s because they did not understand the informational needs of businesses considering relocation. Gavin Wright argues that many in southern state governments did not want success because of their desire to remain isolated.[24] In the 1940s state agency strategies became somewhat more aggressive and sophisticated.

All of these tendencies—the reintegration of the South's economy with the nation's, increases in wages relative to the North, the exodus of low-wage unskilled workers, and increased mechanization of agriculture and industry—were reinforced by World War II. The military absorbed enormous numbers of low-wage farm and factory workers; their departure further accelerated mechanization.[25] World War II also brought an increase in federal spending in the South, which already enjoyed a disproportionate number of military bases. The population of Mobile rose by 61 percent between 1940 and 1943 because of ship building, and the east south central states' percentage of total U.S. production increased from 3.4 to 5.8 in the years 1940–45.[26] The war years also brought road building assistance to the South in the form of the 1941 and 1944 Federal Aid Highway Laws.[27] In addition, the war experience helped to accelerate the South's cultural reintegration into the rest of the country.

Agricultural employment in the South plummeted in the 1940s. In 1940, 35 percent of southern employees were in agriculture; by 1950 that figure had dropped to 22 percent. In 1940, 15 percent of total southern employment was in manufacturing; in 1950 the figure was 18 percent. Between 1940 and 1960 the South shifted from 65 percent rural to 58 percent urban. During the same period tenant farming decreased dramatically.[28]

Between 1940 and 1950 the South continued to experience a loss of poorly educated blacks and an in-migration of whites. The percentage of blacks in the South dropped from 24 in 1940 to 21 in 1960. During the same years U.S. national figures show blacks at 9.9 percent of the population in 1940 and at 10.5 percent in 1960. In Alabama the black percentage of the population dropped between 1920 and 1970. In 1920, 38.4 percent of Alabama's population was black. In 1940 it was 34.7 percent; by 1960 blacks composed less than one-third of the state's population. Since 1970 Alabama's black population has stabilized at around 25–26 percent.

Southern states also continued to promote industrial development after the war. Ralph Gray and John M. Peterson suggest that some states and localities were very successful with these newer programs.[29] Alabama's efforts were not as sophisticated as those in and around Atlanta and the Research Triangle in North Carolina, but later, in conjunction with the Redstone Arsenal and then NASA, Huntsville made substantial progress.

Alabama and other southern states began to make use of municipal industrial-development bonds in the later 1940s and early 1950s. In Alabama the Cater Act of 1949 authorized the formation of municipal industrial-development corporations that could issue bonds to finance, build, and equip manufacturing or other industrial plants for lease to private firms.[30] In 1951 the Wallace Act allowed cities to construct industrial plants financed by municipal bonds. Either way, the companies paid rent to the cities to fund interest and principal on the bonds and perhaps the maintenance of facilities.[31] Facilities constructed under either act were considered municipal property and therefore free from property taxation. The Wallace Act passed the 1951 House by a vote of fifty-five to four; two of the dissenting votes came from representatives of Jefferson County. The act passed by a vote of twenty-four to seven in the Senate, with Senator Albert Boutwell of Jefferson County leading the opposition, which included the senator from Mobile. Counties such as Jefferson and Mobile already had an industrial base, and their legislators feared the impact of the act on existing industry.

When the Senate passed the Wallace Act, Boutwell introduced a formal protest that was placed in the Senate *Journal*.[32] Boutwell had three major objections. First, the bill discriminated against old businesses and industries by giving tax assistance to new industries and ignoring those that had been shouldering the tax burden. Second, the use of municipal bonds for the development of new plants might lead to federal taxation of all municipal bonds, because "no one can claim that the purchase of land and building for private business is . . . a normal function of municipal government." Boutwell referred to such action as "a socialist venture."[33] Finally, he called the revenue bond issuable under the act "dangerous" for municipal financing, arguing that hard economic times might result in plant closings, which would leave the municipalities without rent to collect and thus possibly lead to default in the payment of the interest and principal on the debt. Such action would lower credit ratings for future municipal bonds and result in increased costs to the municipality. Boutwell's criticisms were repeated in 1993 in North Carolina and Alabama when both states provided hundreds of millions of dollars to lure Bavarian Motor Works (BMW) and Mercedes-Benz plants to their respective states.[34]

Peter K. Eisinger points out that economic development, and the accompanying population growth, carry drawbacks: "higher public service costs, housing shortages, service shortfalls, traffic congestions, and environmental damage."[35]

Economic Mechanisms as Forces of Change

The operations of state, national, and international economies affect one another and are influenced by such forces as migration, technological change, and history. Even discussions of relatively recent economic developments require references to the past. Gray and Peterson argue that, largely because of population settlement patterns and differences in natural resources, many regional divisions of labor established before the Civil War remain part of the economy even today.[36] Once industry and capital were firmly established in the Midwest and Northeast, economic inertia inhibited economic growth elsewhere in the country. Because it was efficient for many kinds of manufacturing firms to be close to other manufacturing firms, it made more sense, for example, to manufacture automobile window glass in Toledo, Ohio, close to Detroit's auto plants, than in Huntsville, Alabama.[37]

Economies of scale were also important. Up to a point, the larger a city is, the more efficient it is. Larger cities can afford better mass transit systems, taller office buildings, and other devices useful only in an urban environment. Thus, local market demand—businesses developing to serve the employees of other businesses—further reinforced the economic dominance of the Midwest and Northeast.

If the U.S. economy were a pure market system, labor, capital, and talent would move freely among states, and the economic gaps documented above would diminish or disappear (at least among states with adequate natural resources) as a result of the trading of economic goods and the migration of these factors of production.[38] Technology and demand change over time, causing dominant industries in a region to wax and wane. For example, the substitution of aluminum and plastic for steel hurt cities like Pittsburgh and Birmingham. In the 1950s and 1960s, new southern textile plants run by nonunion workers operated at lower cost than older, unionized New England factories.[39] In more recent times, competition from abroad damaged southern plants as they had hurt those in New England a generation before.

Gray and Peterson point out that the economies of scale that originally worked in favor of the Midwest and Northeast topped out or were weakened by changing transportation and communication technology. Transportation costs were reduced and service improved by decentralizing plant locations, including placement of some facilities in the South.[40] Locating new plants in the South triggered local market demand.[41] Just as proximity to northern and midwestern customers produced growth in those regions in earlier decades, so too southern customers in a growing economy produced industrial movement to the South. Glenn E. McLaughlin and Stefan Robock estimate that roughly 45 percent of immediate post–World War II plant construction fit this category, and that "market oriented plants in general add more to employment than do labor oriented or material oriented units."[42] Martin A. Garrett Jr. shows that between 1947 and 1958 market-oriented industries such as beverages, baked goods, newspapers and other printed media, fertilizers, cement, and structural metal products represented a major component of the South's disproportionately rapid economic growth.[43] Northern unionization also aided southern economic growth. Labor unions expanded much more slowly in the South, and this made the South more attractive to many industries.[44]

C. James Sample observes that a shift from primary output such as agriculture and extractive industries to more profitable manufactured goods and services to a substantial degree caused southern per-capita income to grow in the years 1950–66.[45] He reports that between 1950 and 1960 southern agriculture had a 48.5 percent loss in employment, forestry and fisheries a 25.9 percent loss, and mining a 32.4 percent loss. Big percentage gainers for this time period included more profitable activities such as food processing (52.2), textiles (103.6), nonelectrical machinery (360), transport equipment (144.2), fabricated metals (129.6), and the armed forces (81.5). Alabama is represented in every one of these growth industries.[46]

From 1940 to 1960 all southern states made strong gains in numbers of people employed in relatively high-paying occupational categories. Gaps between the southern and national averages diminished in such areas as the percentage of people employed in skilled crafts, as supervisors and professionals, and in sales, service, and management.[47]

The historical narrative presented earlier in this chapter noted that migration from the South by poorly educated blacks occurred in the 1930s, '40s, and '50s, and that there was an opposite movement into the South of educated whites. According to Wright, "In the rubber tire industry, for example, where a major southward move occurred between 1947 and 1960, the new plants were highly automated and had few openings for blacks."[48] Migration is the kind of market force that closes gaps, and migration has been a powerful economic adjustment mechanism in the United States throughout the nation's history.[49]

From 1950 to 1960 Alabama experienced a total population growth of only 6.7 percent, compared to 18.5 percent for the nation as a whole. Forty-four of Alabama's sixty-seven counties lost population in the 1950s. The population changes included growth in the urban population (Birmingham, 4.6 percent; Mobile, 51.0 percent; and Montgomery, 25.2 percent) and a loss in rural population. The rural loss was especially great in the Black Belt counties (for example, Lowndes, 14.4 percent; Macon, 12.6 percent; and Wilcox, 20.2 percent). These are dramatic population changes for a ten-year period.

Even Sample, who documents the importance to the South of changing business structures (from agriculture and extractive to manufacturing and service), emphasizes that the most important factor in explaining changes in southern per-capita income from 1950 to 1960 was migration. He focuses on out-migration, but in-migration from the North of relatively skilled and higher paid people would reinforce his findings. According to Sample, in this period economic development was related to "the accumulated stock of private, public, and human capital investment. Positively related to this higher level of stock accumulation are higher levels of agricultural and manufacturing productivity."[50] If unskilled, poorly paid labor leaves one state for another (for example, from Alabama to Michigan), the first state's per-capita income statistics will improve and the second one's will decline. Such movement will produce changes in economic statistics even if no substantive economic changes occur. The tendency is for such migratory patterns to narrow interstate gaps.[51]

The South's improved economic condition resulted from the movement of businesses as well as people. Some companies are not sensitive to location and are able to move with relative ease into areas with labor-supply surpluses. Labor surpluses allow such companies to pay lower salaries.[52] In the

1940s and '50s northeastern states regarded the South the way low-paying foreign countries are viewed by the United States today. Northern labor unions and politicians resented southern workers because their willingness to work for low salaries attracted businesses away from northern regions. Southern rural areas remained attractive to such companies as long as the educational requirements associated with the work they required were not very high.

A major source of post–World War II southern development was the growth in the number of branch plants that northern companies opened in the South. This development had the effect of continuing the South's colonial status. Garrett lists typical branch plant (or multiunit firm industries) operations: meat products; grain mill products; pharmaceuticals; soap; chemicals; rubber products; stone, clay, and glass; blast furnaces and steel mills; primary metals industries; machinery; and instruments.[53] Many of these were well represented in Alabama.

The Federal Government

The federal government affects Alabama's economy directly (for example, in the operation of military bases) and via capital stock spending (for example, highway construction funding). In 1956 southerners led by Senator Lyndon Johnson of Texas won support to fund the interstate highway system authorized by the 1941 Highway Act. They raised the federal government's share of funding from 50 to 90 percent. Bruce J. Schulman argues that the system of interstate highways that resulted further accelerated the South's economic development: "The new highways connected the South with the industrial Midwest, forging the first economical trans-mountain links between the Southeast and areas like Ohio, Pennsylvania, and Illinois. The interstate network also offered prospective southern manufacturers the locations they most desired. It allowed businesses to locate away from cities with their regulations, taxes, crowded conditions, and unions, without sacrificing access to distribution centers."[54] Schulman also demonstrates that the South succeeded in winning more than its share of federal highway monies during the heyday of U.S. highway construction.

Schulman argues that the Federal Airport Act of 1946 followed a similar path. The South received more than its share of airport dollars. This allowed the region to catch up to the size and quality of facilities offered by the North and made it easier for southern manufacturing plants and businesses to connect with other sections of the country and the world. As one would expect, Schulman's analysis of the Senate vote in favor of the program shows overwhelming southern support.[55]

Statutes enacted in this era that distributed funds to states using need-based formulas also benefited the South disproportionately. Such laws included the Public Works Acceleration, Community Health Services Grants, and the Hospital and Medical Facilities Construction Program. Alabama's Senator Lister Hill was especially influential in winning passage of the Hill-Burton and Ferguson-Hill Acts, widely used to expand health care facilities. Federal dollars were critical in developing the world-renowned University of Alabama Medical Center in Birmingham. In 1946 the center and its medical school base barely existed. The center's first long-term development plan was established in 1952 as part of the requirements for federal monies. By 1967 the *Journal of the American Medical Association* rated the medical school as the second best in the nation.[56]

Schulman calculates that in 1940 federal funding constituted 14 percent of government revenues in southern states, an average amount compared to other states. By 1955 the amount of federal support to southern states had grown to 20 percent, and Alabama was at 22.4 percent. The national mean was almost unchanged at 14.1 percent.[57] A study conducted by the Advisory Commission on Intergovernmental Relations (ACIR) came to a similar conclusion. For the years 1974–76 Alabama's share of federal government expenditures was far above average. The ACIR expressed state shares of federal expenditures in terms of an index, with the national average represented by 1.00. Alabama and Maryland, tied at 1.31, were exceeded only by Alaska (1.82), Mississippi (1.65), Hawaii (1.56), New Mexico (1.47), Virginia (1.46), South Dakota (1.33), and North Dakota (1.32). Alabama fared even better in terms of federal expenditures in the state compared to federal taxes paid by state residents. Again, with the national average represented by 1.00, Alabama was at 2.03. Alabama was in fourth place, behind only South Carolina (2.30), Mississippi (2.16), and Tennessee (2.15). ACIR calculations for 1952–76 show similar federal beneficence to Alabama.[58]

The South's share of rapidly growing military expenditures also rose during this period, and Alabama did not miss out. During the 1950s, '60s, and '70s, the South's share of prime contracts increased from 7 percent to 25 percent.[59] Alabama benefited from substantial expenditures at Forts Rucker and McClellon, Maxwell-Gunter Air Force Base (formerly two separate installations), Redstone Arsenal, and NASA's Marshall Space Flight Center, all of which still inject great quantities of money into local economies. During the period covered in this book, Craig Field near Selma and a naval air station near Mobile also contributed to Alabama's economic well-being.

Although it is difficult to compare states in terms of federal military expenditures, an analysis performed by Andrew Kirby suggests that in 1988 Alabama was in the third quartile of states in terms of defense contracts and bases.[60] Some NASA expenditures not included in Kirby's figures would probably add to that standing.

State Government and the State Economy

Alabama's economic history strongly suggests that government can help or hurt the performance of the state's economy. Of the four factors of production (land, labor, capital, and talent), only the first, land or natural resources, is created by forces completely outside government influence. The exploitation of these resources is determined by market factors, including the availability of labor, capital, and talent, and by governmental actions and regulations.

Governments, especially at state and local levels, can substantially affect the quantity and quality of labor and talent through their control of primary and secondary schools, community and technical colleges, and universities. Governments are greatly but not totally dependent on the performance of the economy for what can be spent on schools. Other things being equal, a poor state or community cannot spend as much as a wealthy one. But large amounts of money can be wasted, and small quantities can be spent efficiently. State governments can also affect the labor market by establishing rules under which work is performed. Examples include child labor, convict labor, and right-to-work laws. The latter prohibit employer-labor contracts that make union membership a condition of employment.

Governments at all levels can help the economy by building capital stock in the form of an infrastructure. In the time period covered here, road and bridge construction was probably the most important infrastructure work occurring. Immediately after World War II many Alabama county seats were not connected to each other by paved roads. In addition to improving transportation, paving often permitted the installation of electrical and telephone lines that could not be economically strung along mud roads. The 1950s saw the beginning of construction of four-lane roads and the interstate highway system.

Unfortunately, government spending must be financed by taxes and other revenue sources, and, as will be seen below, government revenue collection can have a detrimental effect on the economy. Two questions immediately arise: Which kinds of taxes have the least detrimental effect? Do the beneficial effects of infrastructure construction and other economically useful spending counterbalance the harmful effects of government revenue raising?[61] A government's tax structure can directly affect the economy and quality of life. For example, high business taxes or extremely progressive income taxes can discourage investment and business activity and therefore employment. At the other extreme, regressive taxes are unethical and economically unsound.

The effect of state political systems on state economic well-being was analyzed by Thomas Dye in a classic study that covered the period 1954–64.[62] Economic well-being essentially means how much the economy is producing and how rapidly that production is growing from year to year.[63] The most common measures are per-capita income, median family income, value added by the economy, and the year-to-year changes in each statistic.

Dedicated members of the Democratic and Republican parties argue that a state's economy performs best when their party controls state government. Dye and others have found that partisans of both persuasions are incorrect; state economies tend to do equally well or badly under both.[64] Dye also examined the relationship between party competition and economic performance. Broadly speaking, he found state governments evenly distributed between the extremes of noncompetitive one-party government (such as Alabama's) and highly competitive two-party systems such as California's, Colorado's, and Indiana's. Political scientists have long theorized that vigorous party competition is beneficial to the quality of government, arguing that competition in the political marketplace benefits the citizen-consumer. Dye found income measures related to party competition. The simple correlation coefficients between income and party competition in the lower and upper legislative chambers and the governor's office were .52, .51, and .66.[65] In other words, 27 percent, 26 percent, and 44 percent of the variation in income could be explained by the existence of party competition in the lower and upper legislative chambers and the governor's office respectively.

Since Dye's measures do not indicate the causal direction of the relationship, we can also say that significant variations in party competition can be explained by income measures. It seems likely that cause and effect operate in both directions simultaneously. Intense party competition may improve the quality of governmental decision making, which in turn would help the economy. Looking at cause and effect in the opposite direction, variations in income might also explain part of the variation in party competition. For example, high-income states tend to include relatively large numbers and varieties of interest groups. This greater heterogeneity might lead to more intense party competition.

Dye also explored connections between levels of economic development and political participation. By economic development he meant urbanization, industrialization, income, and education. Dye's measure of participation was the percentage of voting-age population casting votes. He analyzed gubernatorial elections in the period 1954–64 and congressional elections in 1958 and 1962 in the continental United States. He found simple correlation coefficients of .52, .61, and .66, which meant that 27 percent, 37 percent, and 44 percent of the variation in voter participation could be explained by variation in economic development or vice versa. Consistent with Dye's findings, Alabama, with its low level of economic development, had virtually no party competition and a very low voter-participation rate. Studying the connection between state legislative malapportionment and economic development, Dye found no significant relationships. In other words, more affluent states were as likely to be as malapportioned as less affluent states.

Business Climate, Taxes, and Expenditures

The claim is often made that a state or locality has a positive (or negative) business climate. The business climate is usually viewed as the product of local and state government actions. When this concept is narrowly defined by public officials, it means low taxes, low wage rates, and little more.[66] However, businesses vary widely in the kinds and amounts of taxes they must pay and in the types of workers they employ.[67]

A particular locality might offer a positive climate for a pulp mill and a much less attractive locale for a helicopter manufacturing plant. Low taxes that attract a pulp mill may provide inadequate funding for schools, which in turn generates an insufficient pool of skilled and educated workers for the helicopter plant. Poor schools might make it necessary for the helicopter plant to import workers, but those same poor schools and other negative quality of life factors might make it difficult for the helicopter plant to import workers from other states.

Eight surveys of state business climate performed by four organizations in the years 1975–85 rank Alabama in first, second, fourth, nineteenth, seventeenth, nineteenth, twenty-third, and thirty-seventh place. A 1987 study that graded the states from A to F on four separate indicators of business climate gave Alabama failing grades on all four.[68] Perhaps the most important reason for the differences in these rankings is that the surveys use varying standards, some of which are more appropriate to pulp mills, others to helicopter plants, and still others to a service-based economy.

Thomas R. Plaut and Joseph E. Pluta studied the relationship between four groups of business climate variables and three measures of industrial growth. The central question they addressed was "whether regional industrial expansion is more the result of traditional market factors (such as market size and wage rates), newly emergent market factors (such as energy costs), environmental factors, or tax/expenditure and other business climate factors."[69] Plaut and Pluta focused on two business climate rankings. One, performed by Alexander Grant and Company, was prepared for the Conference of State Manufacturers' Associations (COSMA).[70] The COSMA report conceptualized "business climate" in a narrow fashion, confining itself to such variables as union membership, state expenditures and debt per capita, state and local taxes per capita, average weekly manufacturing wage, energy cost per million BTUs, and manufacturers' pollution abatement expenditures per capita. According to COSMA, a state with a healthy business climate would have no union membership and low wages, taxes, and other costs.

The second ranking of business climate was done by the Fantus Company, an industrial-site-location consulting firm.[71] Fantus viewed business climate more broadly, ranking states in three categories: legislative climate, facilities for living, and population characteristics. Legislative climate included taxes, public expenditures, public debt, and labor law. Facilities for living referred to education, recreation, and health care. Population characteristics included skill level (such as average school years completed and selective-service registration rates), income characteristics, and union membership (with the absence of unions being most desirable). The Fantus conceptualization of business climate is considerably more sophisticated than COSMA's because it balances factors that should be kept small (for example, taxes) with others, such as education, in which an increase is desirable but attainable only with higher taxes.

Plaut and Pluta used industrial growth measures encompassing two periods, 1967–72 and 1972–77. At least for the years studied, a state's economic performance was related to its business climate as measured by both ranking studies.[72] Correlations between the Fantus and COSMA rankings and economic performance measures were surprisingly consistent given the different ways the two studies defined business climate. In all cases the correlations were negative, because a state with a good business climate had a low-ranking number (for example, 1 for first place), and a state with a poor business climate had a high-ranking number. The simple correlations between percent change in value added and the Fantus and COSMA rankings for 1967–72 were −.65 and −.67, respectively. (Value added is the value a business adds to the goods and services it purchases from other firms. It is the difference between sales or gross receipts and the cost of materials, labor, and other purchases.) The correlations between percent change in real capital stock and the two rankings were −.47 and −.57, respectively. Correlations for 1972–77 were comparable. Overall, the highest variance explained was for the COSMA rankings and percent change in capital stock in 1972–77. In no instance did business climate explain more than 49 percent of the variance in an economic variable. Plaut and Pluta also performed a more comprehensive analysis including all the variables listed above; it produced even higher correlations.[73]

Traditional market factors were more important than business climate in explaining differences in industrial expansion. The factors that explain growth in real value added were, in order of declining importance, energy cost and availability; labor cost and union activity (which are strongly affected by state government policies); land cost and availability; climate (with the southeastern climate a negative factor); business climate, taxes, and government expenditures; and proximity to markets.[74]

Growth in capital stock was explained by energy; land; proximity to markets; business climate, taxes, and government expenditures; labor; and climate, in that order. Growth in employment depended most on climate and labor factors, with business climate, taxes, and government expenditures third most important. Studies of the economics of plant location that approach the topic from the perspective of the business decision-maker arrive at remarkably similar conclusions.[75]

According to Plaut and Pluta, corporate profit tax, personal income tax, and sales tax rates "have little effect on state industrial growth." Property tax rates are *positively and strongly* related to growth in value added, capital stock, and employment. Plaut and Pluta argue that this unexpected outcome is caused by the fact "that high property taxes are indicative of a locally-dominated state and local tax system." Their analysis revealed "two distinctive state and local tax systems—a state-dominated tax system characterized by high corporate and personal income taxes and a locally-dominated tax system characterized by high property taxes." They hypothesize that industry is strongly attracted to those states with a locally-dominated tax system because firms are able to avoid high overall state taxes, pick a community with low local taxes, and/or choose a community with the tax/expenditure system that best meets their needs." Their description of the relatively undesirable state-dominated tax system (high corporate and personal income taxes) does not fit Alabama, nor does their description of the more desirable locally-dominated tax system with high local property taxes and low state taxes.[76]

Industry is also attracted to states with high education expenditures.[77] In a state such as Alabama where corporate and personal income taxes are relatively low and serve as the major source of educational funding, funding for education is also low. When, as in Alabama, local property taxes, which can be used to augment state funding, are capped by state limits and reinforced by a traditional-agrarian culture, the funding levels stay low.

Robert J. Newman examined two major components of business climates, the power of labor unions and corporate income-tax rates. He related them to industry-by-industry employment changes in the states and the District of Columbia. The fifteen industries in his analysis included textiles, chemicals, fabricated metals, electrical equipment, and transportation equipment. Newman measured union power by the existence of right-to-work laws and union membership as a percentage of nonagricultural employment. As of 1970 nineteen states including Alabama had right-to-work laws or constitutional amendments. Alabama's was passed as a statute in 1953. Between 1953 and 1964 Alabama's union membership as a percentage of nonagricultural employment followed national trends, declining from 24.9 percent to 19.9 percent. Only New York, Delaware, the District of Columbia, and Kentucky experienced an increase. Using regression analysis, Newman concluded that the existence of right-to-work laws or constitutional amendments contributed heavily to the movement of industries south. There was a positive relationship between increases in employment and right-to-work laws or constitutional amendments for all fifteen industries in the years 1957–65. In eleven of the industries, the relationship was statistically significant at the .05 level. With regard to the relationship between corporate income-tax rates and employment changes, the relationship was in the predicted direction (increased tax rates lead to diminished employment) and statistically significant in seven of the fifteen industries. The effect of corporate tax rates was weaker than the effect of right-to-work laws or constitutional amendments and stronger than union membership. Newman's findings are consistent with most recent studies and with business-climate rating services that regard union strength and corporate taxes as negatively affecting business climate.[78]

L. Jay Helms focused on the balance between taxes that depress economic performance and productive government expenditures that enhance it. Using a complex time series analysis covering 1965–79, Helms concluded that "state and local tax increases significantly retard economic growth when the revenue is used to fund transfer payments [for example, unemployment compensation and welfare payments]. However, when the revenue is used instead to finance improved public services (such as education, highways, and public health and safety) the favorable impact on location and production decisions provided by the enhanced services may more than counterbalance the disincentive effects of the associated taxes."[79]

Alaeddin Mofidi and Joe A. Stone also studied the balance between taxes and expenditures. Their conclusions were similar. They found significant negative relationships between tax levels on the one hand and net investment and employment on the other. They also discovered significant positive relationships between expenditures for health, education, and highways, but not for transfer payments such as welfare.[80] Reinforcing these findings, Steve Eller and Kenneth A. Wink found a strong positive relationship between increases in per-capita income and infrastructure spending in North Carolina counties. They found no relationship between increases in per-capita income and county/city development expenditures (total spending on transportation, garbage, planning and zoning, economic and community development, and the like), state highways expenditures, or city/county spending for culture and recreation.[81]

Bruce L. Benson and Ronald N. Johnson provide further reinforcement for the thesis that taxes inhibit economic activity. They found that between 1966 and 1978 capital formation was negatively affected for an average of 2.2 years after new taxes were levied. Capital formation was measured by per-capita capital expenditure for new plant and equipment.[82]

What are we to conclude from these studies in terms of a prescription for high levels of economic growth? First, government policies can help or hurt a state's economic prosperity, although economic, technological, geographical, climatological, and similar factors over which governments have no or only partial control are more important.[83] No single set of government policies will attract all kinds of new businesses and encourage growth of existing ones. Many businesses, including many that employ highly paid workers, are not repelled by relatively high taxes, especially property taxes, if those taxes are devoted to purposes useful to them, such as education, highway construction, and other public services. A logical extension of this observation is that businesses that require low taxes and do not need public services such as education are likely to be businesses that require only manual laborers and pay low wages.

The quality of life enjoyed by a community or state will be influenced by the tax and public-service profile it adopts. These considerations assume that higher taxes buy efficiently and effectively administered schools and roads built economically and over functional routes. In other words, these considerations assume that public resources are handled according to high standards of public administration. We will see in later chapters that this description does not fit Alabama's state government.

Economic Development and Education

When Thomas Dye examined the relationship between economic development and spending for education, he found them to be tightly connected. For example, he discovered a strong relationship between economic development and per-pupil expenditures. The most substantial relationship was a simple correlation of .83 between median family income and per-pupil expenditures in the 1961–62 school year. In other words, 69 percent of the variation in one was explainable by the other. This relationship may mean that wealthier states can afford to spend more on education than poorer ones, or that higher spending on education produces higher earnings, or both.[84] Economic development and education probably reinforce one another in a loop, although in this book we theorize that the link is not direct.

Despite the obvious strength of the relationship between economic development and education (wealthier states tended to spend more than poor states), variations in educational spending at particular levels of income are dramatic. In 1960 near the $1,510 per-capita income level, where Alabama is found, per-pupil expenditures varied from $112 (Alabama) to $149 (South Carolina), a 33 percent difference. The fact that South Carolina's per-capita income was $114 less than Alabama's makes the contrast even more dramatic. Although Alabama probably could not have afforded $250 or more per pupil, it could have managed $150 or $160 with little strain. By 1970 Alabama was still near the bottom in primary and secondary school support. Several states near Alabama's per-capita income level of $2,903 were spending more for schools. Most notable was Louisiana, with a per-capita income of $3,041 and per-pupil expenditures of $372–54 percent more than Alabama's $241.[85] Davis and Lucke, looking at spending in 1979–80, also found large variations in the relationship between state wealth and education spending. The correlation between revenue capacity and spending for primary and secondary schools was .65 (32 percent of variance explained) and .34 between revenue capacity and spending for postsecondary education (12 percent of variance explained).[86]

What is important about educational spending is what it buys in terms of educational attainment. Following Powell and Steelman, our own analysis found a strong relationship between expenditures for education and normalized SAT scores.[87] Specifically, we found a correlation of .53 between per-pupil expenditures and average teacher salaries on one hand and a measure of SAT score differences among the states. Per-pupil expenditures are a much stronger predictor of a mean SAT score than average teacher salary. Teacher pay and per-student expenditures accounted for only about one-fourth of the variation in student performance. Three-quarters of the variation was *not* accounted for by these somewhat deterministic factors. Additional indicators of educational attainment such as the percentage of the state's population over twenty-five with four years of high school and median number of school years completed also correlate with teacher salaries and per-capita expenditures at approximately the same level as normalized SAT scores.

Other things being equal, in terms of student performance it is better to be a wealthy state that can easily afford to spend more on schools. Relatively modest increases in spending appear to produce substantial improvements in student performance. Dye found little independent relationship between per-pupil expenditures on the one hand and party competition, political participation, and legislative malapportionment on the other.[88]

Low Pay, Low Tech

Since education and income are positively related, it should follow that states that try to attract low-tech industries that require only rudimentary skills among workers will not do well economically. To some degree this describes much of the South, including Alabama,[89] and this thesis is reinforced by most business climate studies. Stephen McDonald describes southern states that "attract industry largely on the basis of cheap labor; industries such as textiles, apparel and furniture and fixtures, for instance. . . . Large numbers of workers may be employed in such industries but the total economic impact is relatively small."[90] Danhof adds: "These considerations suggest that industrialization as it has been carried out in the past is no longer a way in which the region can hope to claim its part in the Nation's future. The Nation's future is on the technological frontiers. . . . the locality in which technological developments occur is the locality which will enjoy the fullest benefit of the product."[91]

Southern-owned businesses have been relatively simple and small, but more sophisticated branch plants often rely on foreign (that is, trained outside the state) management.[92] In the case of a city such as Birmingham, much of that management group has lived outside the city limits. During the heyday of the steel industry, corporate executives found the neighboring cities cleaner and cooler, and there they established properly funded school systems for their children. They physically abandoned Birmingham, and it has been argued that they abandoned the city psychologically as well.[93]

Capital Stock Spending and Economic Development

Well-administered state and local government spending on capital stock or infrastructure can attract new industry and enhance economic development in many ways.[94] Amenities such as good roads, cultural facilities, and attractive parks draw new businesses and high-quality employees to work in existing concerns. Amenities may also reduce labor costs because potential employees are willing to accept lower pay in return for the opportunity to live in a desirable location. Capital development can reduce a business's operating costs. For example, good roads and convenient airports represent a production input for which a business is not required to pay on a per-unit basis as it would raw materials or labor.[95]

Economic Development Programs of State and Local Governments

Most studies of state economic development that cover the period between 1920 and 1950 suggest that a majority of state and local government efforts to attract industry were largely unsuccessful because they were implemented ineptly and because some political leaders did not want them to succeed. More recent work indicates that many industrial development programs cost governments more than the benefits provided to the community by the new business.

Before World War II the most popular incentive used was direct tax (especially property tax) concessions. In the postwar period states kept tax incentives and developed additional techniques that promised to attract new industry or permit expansion of existing operations. These included state loan-guarantee programs and direct state loans, both of which New Hampshire pioneered.[96] As of 1965 Alabama had not adopted either technique.

Local industrial development bond (IDB) financing was first authorized in 1936 in Mississippi and first used in Alabama in 1949. By 1959 thirteen states had adopted it. Under this approach, local governments typically issue tax-free bonds to finance plant construction. Since the facilities are publicly owned, they are not subject to property taxation. Firms pay rent sufficient to cover interest, principal, and maintenance costs.

From 1956 to 1968 Alabama had the second largest number of IDBs and was by far the heaviest user in terms of dollar amounts. In this period the dollar value of Alabama IDB issues as a percentage of the national dollar value ranged from 3.3 to 53.7, with a mean of over 15 percent. In 1967, the year during this period in which Alabama issued the largest dollar amount of these bonds, the total was almost $240 million. No trend is apparent in the percentages, but the absolute dollar figures show a strong upward trend for Alabama and the nation.[97]

According to an Alabama Business Research Council study of six south-eastern states during 1958–59, new plants and plant expansions financed with IDBs "accounted for 20 to 35 percent of the total capital investment in new production capacity and approximately the same percentage of the related gains in manufacturing employment." (The Alabama figure was roughly 20 percent.) Among the firms responding to the study, "approximately two-thirds of the firms using IDBs indicated that they probably would have located somewhere in Alabama even had IDB financing not been available. However, the remaining one-third which would have located elsewhere accounted for almost 80 percent of the dollar volume and 43 percent of the new manufacturing jobs."[98]

New England pioneered another inducement technique in the post–World War II period: Maine's widely copied development credit corporation. Development credit corporations are state chartered but privately financed through stock sales, borrowing, and retained earnings. Funds raised this way are used to make loans to businesses. Alabama did not use this technique. As of 1965 Alabama still used the local development corporations authorized by the Wallace Act. They operated in a manner similar to state development credit corporations. By 1965 Alabama had created 19 such entities, but many other states had several times that number. For example, Georgia had 139 and North Carolina 152.[99]

In the early 1950s southern states began to reduce corporate tax rates as another way to attract industry. Corporate tax rates in the South were above the national average in 1950, but by the late 1970s they were below.[100] Michael Kieschnick estimates that as of 1980 Alabama had the fourth lowest tax burden for manufacturing corporations of all fifty states and Washington, D.C. In that year a hypothetical average manufacturing corporation with gross sales of approximately $7 million paid $65,770 in Alabama taxes and $387,630 in Massachusetts, which had the highest tax rate.[101]

Alabama established corporate franchise taxes and corporate income taxes in 1935. The corporate franchise tax was originally set at $2.00 per $1,000 of capital stock and applied equally to domestic and foreign (out-of-state) corporations. In 1955 the tax rate on domestic corporations increased to $2.50 per $1,000 of capital stock. Out-of-state corporations were raised to that level in 1963 and then to $3.00 in 1971. Further increases followed in the 1980s. The corporate income tax was initially set at 3 percent of net taxable income. In 1963 it was raised to 5 percent. Current rates for both taxes keep Alabama in line with or below the tax rates in the neighboring states of Florida, Mississippi, Georgia, and Tennessee.[102]

Evaluations of Economic Development Programs

William J. Stober and Laurence H. Falk analyzed the efficiency of property tax exemptions (a form of direct tax concession) used to attract new industry in Alabama and six other states, mainly southern. They concluded that "the property tax exemption is an extremely inefficient subsidy in the sense that the value to a firm receiving an exemption falls far short of the dollar cost to the state or its political subdivisions." Stober and Falk are joined in this conclusion by most other observers.[103]

Benjamin Bridges Jr. analyzed property tax exemptions in Wisconsin. Performing detailed cost studies comparing dollar savings for businesses produced by exemptions to other cost factors, he found it difficult to generalize about this relationship because the ratio of property tax to a business's output increases with the business's size and property tax rates vary widely among localities. He tentatively concluded that property tax exemptions do not usually affect a business's choice of region, but that they could be an important factor in determining a location within a region. In six of thirty cases, property tax exemptions were sufficient to overcome Wisconsin's relatively high labor costs compared to six other states in the region. In approximately twenty-five out of thirty-one cases, property tax exemptions were equal to or greater than tax differentials between Wisconsin and neighboring states. Bridges did not report whether these or other inducements actually affected business location decisions. According to Bridges, low-interest loans made by state or local finance authorities could have made a difference in some cases. Out of a total of thirty cases examined, interest cost reductions equal to 1, 2, 3, and 4 percent of company assets would overcome Wisconsin's labor cost disadvantages in 3, 8, 11, and 14 cases, respectively. Bridges does not report whether Wisconsin's relatively high labor costs reflect greater skill levels in its labor force.[104]

Deciding whether industry location inducements are worth while is not easy. Each type of inducement carries benefits and costs. One benefit to a state and locality is "the present value of the increase in income of 'original' residents."[105] But if a given investment blocks another by using capital that might have been otherwise used, this benefit is reduced. A cost not mentioned by Bridges but apparent to Albert Boutwell more than thirty years ago and still being studied by economists and the Alabama legislature is that new residents attracted by a new plant often demand new or improved governmental services. It is easily possible for these services to cost more than the additional taxes paid by new residents.[106]

Bridges argues that for a revenue bond program not funded by tax exemptions, benefits probably exceed costs in most instances. This is especially true if the bonds are sold outside the state. Even if they are sold in state, they may not substantially reduce the state capital pool, because in some instances the businesses would not seek the loans in the private sector if market interest rates had been charged. Bridges argues in a similar manner that loan guarantee programs are probably cost-beneficial. Like virtually all writers in this field, he is much less sanguine about property tax exemptions.

State industrial-promotion activities that focus on tax exemptions, loan guarantees, and other finance-oriented inducements suffer from the fact that these factors are relatively insignificant when business decision makers are surveyed about location factors. Markets, labor, raw materials, and transportation are listed as far more important than taxes or financial inducements.[107] Robert Ady, president of PHH Phantus Corporation, says: "What companies find most desirable in looking for a site is a qualified workforce."[108] We saw earlier that many businesses are willing to pay for such a workforce.

Alabama has emphasized industrial development bonds and property tax reduction and other tax breaks. Analysts who specialize in industry promotion programs, as well as scholars who study the effect of taxes and other business climate factors on economic activity, agree that tax breaks are ineffective and inefficient tools with which to attract industry. And devices such as industrial development bonds, also used by Alabama, are rarely helpful, although businesses will take advantage of them if they offer attractive interest rates.

The Economy, State Government, and Taxes

Dye found a strong and unsurprising positive relationship between per-capita taxes paid to state and local governments and median family income (r = .76 and variance explained = .58). In other words, state and local governments in wealthier states tend to receive more revenues per capita than those in poorer states, but these wealthier states vary a great deal in taxes received per capita. Among the eight poorest states with 1959 median family incomes around $3,000–$4,000 per capita, taxes hovered just below $50. In a large group of states bunched between roughly $5,000 and $6,500 in median income, per capita taxes varied from $50 to almost $250.[109]

Tax burden (also called tax effort) is measured by the ratio of taxes paid to personal income.[110] Dye arrayed the states on scales of per-capita taxes versus tax burden and found substantial variation. Alabama was a low-burden, low-tax state. In other words, compared to other states, Alabama could afford higher taxes, which could bring improvements in schools and other quality-of-life programs. Norman Luttbeg, using 1986 data, also categorized Alabama as one of the ten lowest tax-effort states.[111] Dye and Luttbeg represent the majority view.

A study conducted by the Advisory Commission on Intergovernmental Relations indicated very tentatively that Alabama's tax effort for the years 1975–83 exceeded its tax capacity. In 1983 tax revenue exceeded tax capacity in only one category, general and selective sales taxes. Tax revenue and tax capacity were very close in licenses, personal income taxes, severance taxes, and corporate net income taxes. Property tax capacity was far ahead of revenue.[112] In other words, the property tax was underutilized.

Tax incidence is also important to economic development issues. Questions of incidence concern which classes, races, economic groupings, such as landlords and tenants, and legal entities including corporations and partnerships, pay taxes. We will explore these matters in detail in later chapters. At this point it is sufficient to say that Alabama's tax system was regressive in the 1950s and remained so in the 1980s. Because it has changed little since the 1980s, it is still regressive today.[113]

Alabama State Government Leadership

In Alabama, as in most states, the governor, lieutenant governor, and state legislators are the most important governmental decision makers. Since part of our concern is the effect of their leadership, it is important to explore the nature of leadership. Above-average economic progress will not come about unless state leadership is both effective and constructive.

Effective leaders are those who move their constituents in directions they would not ordinarily take on their own. This definition assumes that effective leaders have vision. They must have ideas about what needs to be changed and how those changes can be brought about. Effective leaders must be able to communicate that vision to the public, members of their team, and other members of the executive and legislative branches. Vision and the ability to communicate that vision are necessary but not sufficient conditions of effective leadership.

Effective and constructive leaders are concerned with improving the social, economic, and/or political life of their constituents. They have a strong moral sensibility—a clear set of ideas about right and wrong and an ability to apply those standards to situations at hand. The presence of a moral sensibility might be thought of as part of a leader's vision, but it deserves independent treatment. Having a strong moral foundation gives depth and power to a leader's positions. It provides direction, and it adds to a leader's effectiveness. Effective and constructive leaders are usually open-minded and often unconventional. They are frequently experts in at least some aspects of state government. They also possess strategic and tactical skills.

Alabama's Big Mules were effective but *not* constructive leaders. Through most of the first half of this century, the core of their world view was a variant of Social Darwinism: life was a competitive struggle, and those who won—that is, those who struggled to the top of the societal heap or were born to the best families—had the right to rule.[114] For the Big Mules, blacks occupied the bottom of the social hierarchy because they belonged there. For example, John B. Knox, in his opening address to Alabama's 1901 constitutional convention, said: "There is a difference . . . between the uneducated white man and the ignorant negro. There is in the white man an inherited capacity for government, which is wholly wanting in the negro."[115] To the Big Mules this relatively fixed hierarchy was as natural as gravity. In their view nearly everyone was satisfied with the roles assigned them by their personal and racial capabilities. Dissatisfaction originated not with southern blacks, who understood their place, but with northern agitators.

To a limited extent, the Big Mules were democrats. Leaders, at least those who occupied governmental positions, were to be elected. The electorate, however, should be restricted to propertied, literate whites, and those seeking office should have the appropriate economic and political philosophy.

Big Mules often spoke of their obligation to provide leadership for the lower classes, but in practice their leadership was entirely self-serving. By assuming that certain groups were uneducable beyond minimal levels, the Big Mules could justify low school expenditures. Graduates of institutions such as the black schools in Wilcox County were fit for employment only at a minimum wage in coal mines, steel mills, and plantations owned by the Big Mules. Opportunities for more rewarding employment were limited to the graduates of public and private schools attended by Big Mule family members and the sons and daughters of managers and other professionals who directly supported and served the Big Mules.

Political Culture Influences

Daniel J. Elazar suggests that the most important factor shaping a state's political structures, electoral behavior, and methods of organizing for political action is its political culture. Political culture represents a state's "particular pattern of orientation to political action."[116]

Two contrasting views of the political order are at the heart of political culture distinctions in the United States. The first views political order as a marketplace. In the marketplace "the primary public relationships are products of bargaining among individuals and groups acting out of self-interest." The second or commonwealth view centers on the public interest. Here, individual citizens cooperate "to create and maintain the best government in order to implement certain shared moral principles" (85–86). According to Elazar, the emphasis on one view versus the other has resulted in three major cultural patterns—moralistic, individualistic, and traditional. These patterns in turn are mixed in various ways. The mix is largely the result of migration patterns, which in turn are affected by such forces as immigration, war, and economic crises (86).

The individualistic political culture emphasizes the marketplace. Here "government is instituted for strictly utilitarian reasons" and handles "functions demanded by the people it is created to serve." Private motives are paramount. Community intervention in private activities is minimized. Government "is restricted to those areas . . . which encourage private initiative and widespread access to the marketplace." Politics is "another means by which individuals may improve themselves socially and economically" (87). Mutual obligations based on personal relationships are at the heart of the individualistic system. Generally, these obligations are coordinated through political parties staffed by professionals. The public views politics as a dirty business; political corruption is expected and viewed as normal (88). Public policy initiatives occur only as the result of direct public demand expressed through political parties and interest groups. As the alliances between groups shift and new groups enter the governing coalition, policy changes result.

The moralistic political culture is built on the commonwealth concept. Both the citizens and the politicians seek the public good and govern in the public interest. In this culture the most highly held personal values are "honesty, selflessness, and commitment to the public welfare" (90). Government work is viewed as public service carrying with it moral obligations. Using political office to enhance one's economic position is frowned upon, as is the rewarding of one's political friends and allies. Political parties are tolerated but not highly valued, and amateur participation in politics is encouraged. In such a system governmental intervention in economic and social life is encouraged (91–92).

The traditional political culture exists in areas heavily dominated by an agrarian history. Its base is "an ambivalent attitude toward the marketplace coupled with a paternalistic and elitist conception of the commonwealth. Reflecting an older, pre-commercial attitude, it accepts a substantially hierarchical society as part of the ordered nature of things, authorizing and expecting those at the top of the social structure to take a special and dominant role in government" (92–93). Government limits its actions to preserving the existing social order and its control over the system. This includes the view that only those with the right social and economic background should serve in government or participate in any way in the political life of the community. Reliance on personal ties and self-interest are important influences on governmental actions (93).

Elazar categorizes Alabama's culture as traditional but suggests that in a few areas moralistic and individualistic elements have been grafted onto the traditional base. North Alabama, including the Huntsville area, has a traditional-moralistic culture, and the areas around Jefferson and Mobile Counties blend traditional and individualistic elements. In both instances, the traditional aspect dominates.

The importance of this traditional cultural base is the high correlation between it and specific characteristics of the political system and public policy. Elazar and others find that traditional states such as Alabama discourage the participation of citizens in politics through stiff registration laws, tend toward one-party politics, and are highly unified on issues internally but at odds with national policies. Policy is not determined by competing group forces or shared concerns for the public interest, but by self-interested individuals seeking to maintain their social, economic, and political positions of power.[117]

Leadership, Political Culture, and
Economic Development Efforts

On the basis of Elazar's work we would not expect to
find aggressive, imaginative economic-development campaigns in a traditionalistic state dominated by a political elite such as the Big Mule Alliance. In fact, Alabama's industrial promotion efforts were dismal bores,
whether conducted at the state or local level. They droned along through
the decades with sporadic special campaigns. These operations popped up
here and there with press conferences and announcements of new public
relations campaigns with new slogans. After a year or two of intermittent
activity and few results, they slumped into inactivity. Reading the booster
materials and news releases produced by the state, local chambers of commerce, and similar organizations, one senses a constrained "going through
the motions" quality. It is as if their authors understood that they really
did not have much to offer incoming industry and that they did not have
a chance of competing with other states. "Alabama, the state of surprises,"
one of many booster slogans, seemed to translate into "Alabama: it's not as
bad as you think."

Like all state chief executives, Alabama governors acted as salespersons
for their state. They and their industry promotion agencies mounted advertising campaigns in major city newspapers, made appearances at trade
shows, and met with corporate executives considering plant construction.
These campaigns were notable only for how ordinary they were.

A basic cause of the weakness of Alabama's efforts to promote industry
was that the Big Mules, suspended in a predominantly traditional culture,
did not want development campaigns to succeed or at best did not care. Like
their rural brethren in other southern states, Black Belt Big Mules wanted
no new industry or very low-level agriculturally oriented industry such
as textile mills.[118] Another part of the problem lay in the colonial nature
of many of Jefferson County's largest businesses. The out-of-state owners
of those businesses had no interest in promoting Jefferson County or Birmingham. The urban Big Mules had no objection to modest promotional
activities, but they were not committed to them. New industry might mean
expanded employment opportunities for "their" subsistence-paid workers.
The wrong kind of industry might demand expanded governmental services.

In both the Black Belt and Birmingham, there were genuine boosters of
industrial development, small-business people who occasionally launched
new industry-hunting campaigns but without the support of the Big Mules

and often against their direct opposition. Irving Beiman traced part of Birmingham's problems of economic retardation to Big Steel's dominance of the Chamber of Commerce until well into the mid 1940s. In the 1940s much of the industrial development activity came from the Junior Chamber of Commerce and its younger members. According to Beiman, the larger steel companies financed this group, and they threatened to terminate their financial support unless efforts to search for industry were stopped.[119] Hence, one observes a dreary, tired quality in the resulting campaigns, compared to the campaigns that came out of Atlanta. The Atlanta campaigns exhibited an unapologetic enthusiasm and optimism combined with an energy that did not flag. From the perspective of the 1990s, it is difficult to believe that Birmingham and Atlanta were once regarded as nearly equal competitors in the economic development race.

Sheldon Hackney's definitions of Alabama's major turn-of-the-century groups help us to understand the origins of Alabama's anemic economic boosterism. In addition to the Big Mules (Hackney called them the Bosses), there were the progressives, primarily small businessmen. Their votes in the 1901 constitutional convention reflected "a compound of humanitarianism, concern for clean government, a felt need for government regulation of powerful concentrations of wealth and a desire for increased public services. That the Progressives knew the cost of progress and were willing to pay it was reflected in their distinctive advocacy of higher debt, taxation and spending levels."[120] The progressives were the main boosters of business growth and economic development, but they lacked the political power base from which to make their efforts successful. The very state constitution they helped to forge would be used to block and hinder the growth and development they sought.

In a widely read article, William H. Nicholls takes a somewhat different slant, but one that largely reinforces the perspective presented in this book. Nicholls associates the South's economic backwardness with southern tradition, somewhat in the manner of Elazar. In Nicholls's rendition the key southern value was agrarianism and a rejection of the "progress at any price" orientation of industrialism. Agrarianism "perpetuated a strong love of the land" and "made a tradition of leisure, which has discouraged economic enterprise on the part of the wealthy class and has produced, and even given sanction to, laziness and lassitude on the part of poor whites and Negroes."[121] Closely related to agrarianism and inhibiting economic progress still further was a rigid social structure combined with a weakness in the elite's sense of responsibility to the rest of society. The feeling of noblesse oblige that might have been associated with the aristocracy's presence was corrupted by slavery and further undermined by a spirit of individualism that allowed blue bloods to ignore the plight of the poor with equanimity.

Nicholls also describes undemocratic southern political structures very much along the lines portrayed here. In his view, widespread conformity protected the political power elite:

> The South's extreme cultural and ethnic homogeneity was transformed into strait-jacket conformity and intolerance of dissent. . . . [In] rejecting Yankee thought and the Yankee mind, Southerners closed their minds on every other important social doctrine as well. The results were a general intolerance of intellectualism, an acceptance of violence as an ultimate weapon against nonconformity and dissent, and a corruption of higher education as it too increasingly repudiated innovation and novelty in thought and behavior.[122]

We differ little with Nicholls's views except that Alabama's Big Mules, including the Black Belt planters, were as a whole extremely hardworking. Their written correspondence suggests that, far from making a tradition of leisure, they embraced hard work as part of the individualism that Nicholls associates with them and that we describe in terms of Social Darwinism.

The critical difference between Alabama's Big Mules and their northern or Atlanta counterparts was not hard work or ambition. Rather, it lay in the Alabamians' tradition-bound narrowness and lack of vision concerning their own enterprises and something approaching total blindness with regard to society as a whole. Nicholls also fails to capture the spirit of many, if not most, Black Belt Big Mules. When J. Bruce Henderson, a planter and state senator, telephoned his agricultural extension agents before dawn, a common practice for him, it was to obtain advice concerning how to expand the existing farm operations he had inherited from his father. His was the kind of ambition that sought to own all his neighbors' property, not the kind that produced large improvements in productivity or opened new markets for his products. The extraordinarily wealthy, Oxford-educated Earl McGowin was an energetic leader in the field of forest conservation and scientific timber raising. Yet toward the end of his career he, like many other owners of timberland, sold his holdings to out-of-state corporations that made large parts of the Black Belt rural equivalents of Birmingham in their colonial status.

In this century Alabama has had few effective leaders not of or controlled by the Big Mule Alliance. Indeed, in state government overall, there were few effective leaders of any description. This served alliance interests because the Big Mules' primary objective in state government was inaction. Although few would gainsay the importance of leadership, it is best to be suspicious of placing too much weight on leadership when trying to explain the quality of the Alabama state government's decision making because an exclusive focus on leadership is too obvious and too easy. It is akin to saying, "If only politicians cared about the public interest instead of themselves, the state (or city or country) would be a better place." The equivalent statement regarding leadership is "If only we had better leaders we would have a better state government." This sentiment alone will not carry our understanding very far.

Traditional approaches to enhancing the economic development of a state or locality stressed financial incentives, especially tax breaks. It is probably not accidental that many of these programs as they applied in Alabama directly benefited the Big Mules. It would be easy to overstate this point, because the kinds of financial incentives used in Alabama were found in other states not dominated by a tightly knit power elite. Also, using financial incentives to produce industrial growth represented the conventional wisdom of the 1950s and '60s. Nevertheless, a large political science literature and common sense suggest that political power can frequently be found at the origin of tax breaks. The largest industry group receiving tax breaks was timber, and given the state's rich forest lands, the timber industry would have had a presence in Alabama regardless of tax breaks.[123] Traditional cultures prefer incentives that reinforce existing patterns of economic domination—tax concessions, capital subsidies, right-to-work laws.[124]

At every point in Alabama's economic history this century something seemed to be suppressing the state's progress. The "something" in question, we contend, was the nature and quality of political leadership operating in the context of an elite-dominated traditional culture. Critical decisions made by the state's political leadership and the state's electorate could have narrowed the lags and gaps we have documented, but all too often they did not.

3

The 1958 Campaign and the Organization of State Government Under John Patterson

The year 1958 marked a watershed in Alabama electoral politics. The campaigns of that year set the pattern for many elections to come as race openly became a major issue. The efforts of the federal government to integrate the public schools of the South and its initial examination of the voter registration process eventually led the political elite to view an expanded electorate of white, working-class, and lower-middle-class Alabamians as a potential force for blocking unwanted political and social change. White registration offset black registration, and as the winning candidate for governor soon pointed out, voter registration lists determined the composition of juries. An establishment that once disdained political participation by the lower orders now mobilized them for defensive purposes by playing on their racial fears.

After the 1958 election the Big Mule Alliance briefly enjoyed legislative success. Within two years, however, the alliance would begin to unravel, but the termination of formal cooperation would extend for more than a decade. Because of their parallel interests, the attitudes they implanted in the electorate, and the government structures they created through the 1901 constitution, components of the alliance continued as a major force in state policy-making long after formal cooperation ended.

The 1958 Primary Election Campaign

Fourteen candidates faced each other in the 1958 gubernatorial race. Many were well-known current or former officeholders. From the beginning, political insiders and newspapers singled out three candidates as most likely to win. They were George C. Wallace, a former legislator and now a circuit judge; Jimmy Faulkner, a millionaire newspaper publisher and former legislator; and Attorney General John M. Patterson. All three candidates devoted more time to the segregation issue than their counterparts had in past campaigns, but race did not take their full attention. They committed more space in speeches and campaign literature to schools and industrial development.

Jimmy Faulkner was from Baldwin County in south Alabama. He conducted a lackluster, country club–style campaign similar to his unsuccessful 1954 effort. He criticized the other candidates for "making big promises" and observed: "I can't do anything alone. I've got to have the cooperation of the people and of the legislature and everybody else to make a good governor."[1] Such wisdom did not win elections.

Faulkner tried to dispel his bland, aloof image with populist rhetoric. The distinguished, gray-haired, somewhat prissy-looking Faulkner would say: "You won't have to have an appointment to see me. You just walk right in. In fact, I'm gonna knock the hinges off that door to the governor's office. Why you can come right in, take a seat and put your feet on my desk if you want to. That is unless you are a lady."[2]

Many wealthy Alabamians backed Faulkner. Because of their support his campaign was financially sound, but it lacked workers willing to devote the grueling hours necessary to win in what was still mainly a pretelevision race. His county campaign managers were often difficult to reach, and he himself took a two-week vacation during the campaign and, incredibly, made a point of announcing that fact.

George Wallace was from Barbour County, in the Black Belt along the Georgia border. Wallace's pronouncements in favor of segregation were restrained. In one speech he promised that "segregation shall be preserved with dignity and respect."[3] In another he traced his efforts on behalf of segregation back to 1947, "long before any other candidate was thinking about the problem." Using blunter language, he said he would out-litigate and out-legislate "those punk politicians" who would destroy southern customs and traditions. He promised that if federal courts ordered integration of any school, he would close the school immediately and transfer the students and teachers to another. Federal troops would then be pointing "their fixed bayonets" on an empty building.[4] He often softened his segregationist bombast by observing, "I've never made a derogatory remark about one of God's children and I never will. If I am governor, I am going to treat all fairly."[5]

In a half-page newspaper advertisement that focused on segregation, Wallace pointed to his record as a staunch defender of racial separation. In reality, his record consisted entirely of empty symbolic acts such as his threat to arrest any "member of the FBI or other federal police" who might attempt to investigate Alabama's grand-jury selection procedures.[6]

Another half-page newspaper advertisement concentrated on education and listed two accomplishments in that field: his sponsorship of the Wallace Trade School Act and the Alabama GI and Dependents Scholarships Act. The advertisement stressed his interest in raising the "over-all status of teachers and students in Alabama." It also dealt with industrial development, segregation, law enforcement, health, welfare, and agriculture, in that order.[7] Reflecting his political beginnings as a supporter of Big Jim Folsom, Wallace placed considerable emphasis on programs to aid the needy. "I respectfully submit that we owe a debt to our elders that I intend to help Alabama pay," he intoned.[8]

At rallies the presence of the perennial candidate and political jokester Ralph "Shorty" Price continually plagued Wallace. In a typical performance Price suggested that Wallace had been overly lenient with black defendants in his court in an effort to woo the "colored vote." He referred to his target as "Wishy-Washy Wallace" and baited Wallace by saying that he walked "the same road with Big Jim." On this occasion Wallace responded to Price's remarks by glaring at him pugnaciously and growling through tight, thin lips, "All my public life I have worked to help the mentally ill. I will continue to do so."[9] As the campaign developed, the Patterson camp paid Price's incidental travel expenses.[10]

The Patterson Campaign

John Patterson's campaign was unique among the leading candidates in its hard-edged, grim tone. He stood foursquare in favor of segregation and against "gangsters." Patterson was justified in emphasizing the second point. On June 18, 1954, his father, Albert Patterson, who had won the Democratic party primary for the office of attorney general, was murdered by Phenix City vice leaders. The Democratic party executive committee then selected John Patterson as the nominee for attorney general.

Patterson was born in Tallapoosa County. During his youth his parents were schoolteachers in Cullman and Tallapoosa Counties, and his father was principal of the Coosa and Clay County high schools. This gave him several "home" counties. His own political base was Phenix City, in Russell

County near the Georgia border and Fort Bragg. There he had shared a law practice with his father.

Patterson combined his central themes of segregation and crime in statements such as "Crime and corruption is making a last desperate attempt to invade the state. Huge sums of money from outside sources are being used in this governor's race to reestablish such crime capitals as existed in Phenix City. Gangsters and the NAACP have sent in large sums of money in an attempt to defeat me."[11] The short-haired, tough-looking Patterson liked to be characterized as a white knight, a nonpolitician intent on eliminating waste and halting corruption. An ad in the *Greenville Advocate* called Patterson a political amateur and proud of it. It claimed that he had accepted no campaign funds from organized interest groups and had been forced to make a "poor man's race." As a result he had "made no promises of jobs or favors to any self-seeking groups or individuals and . . . pulled no punches on vital issues." He was "a morally clean man. He was raised to be one by God-fearing parents who put right principles above all else." He was "fighting John Patterson," "fearless in thought . . . resolute in action . . . and friendly with all who believe with him that good Government is Alabama's greatest need."[12] Patterson's approach was underscored by his brilliant campaign slogan: "Nobody's for Patterson but the people."

The Black Belt planter and former state senator J. Bruce Henderson had won Patterson an interview with the Jefferson County Committee of 100 (a group of prominent business leaders), but that august group did not support Patterson in any way. During the interview they evidenced great enthusiasm for Patterson's cause. He believes that they attempted to fool him into relying on financial assistance they never intended to supply.[13]

As attorney general Patterson had demonstrated that he was not satisfied with the kinds of empty gestures that provided the bulk of George Wallace's responses to the civil rights movement then and later. In 1956 Circuit Court Judge Walter B. Jones had issued a restraining order at Patterson's request barring the NAACP from operating in Alabama. The legal reasoning behind Patterson's request was that the NAACP had not registered as an out-of-state corporation as required by Alabama law. Patterson later won court support for his demand that the NAACP produce a list of its members. When the organization failed to comply, Judge Jones (on July 25, 1956) declared the association in contempt and imposed a one-hundred-thousand-dollar fine. The Alabama Supreme Court refused to review the contempt citation or the fine. An NAACP appeal to the United States Supreme Court was still pending during the 1958 primary campaign, so Patterson could rightly claim that he had been responsible for the only ban against NAACP operations in the nation.

Patterson had also filed suit against the Tuskegee Civic Association, which was leading a boycott against white merchants in Tuskegee. The boycott began in 1957 as a protest against the passage of a statute that changed the boundaries of Tuskegee to remove four hundred potential black voters from the city. Under the old boundaries blacks outnumbered whites seven to three. During the primary campaign Patterson sought a contempt of court ruling against the black leaders W. C. Patton and William P. Mitchell for disobeying the injunction against Alabama NAACP operations.

In campaign speeches Patterson advocated a bill to require the closing of public schools should the federal government attempt to integrate them.[14] Given his courtroom successes against the civil rights movement and his ongoing legal harassment of some of its leaders, such legislation probably appeared to be a realistic option to some voters.

A large Patterson newspaper advertisement asked voters to "Elect Fighting John Patterson." Directly under his photograph the caption read: "His ACTS for Segregation Speak Louder Than Words."[15] Another advertisement announcing the time and location of a rally had as its headline "Integration in Alabama? 'NEVER' Says Attorney General John Patterson Candidate for Governor."[16] A third read: "John Patterson Will maintain segregation. Will uphold law and order. Will eliminate graft and corruption. Will see that organized labor gets fair and square treatment."[17] These promises were followed by the standard pledges to increase old-age pensions, improve hospitals and schools, and aid farmers. Patterson's campaign materials featured an unusually positive treatment of labor unions. The *Anniston Star* characterized him as promising a "pro-labor administration." Generally, however, labor did not support the Patterson campaign, preferring Wallace and the dark horse candidate George Hawkins to the attorney general.

According to columnist Bob Ingram, Patterson began the campaign as a "dull, listless" speaker, and Charles Meriwether, his campaign manager, paints a similar picture. But Patterson warmed to the task, and his public speaking gained "force and enthusiasm," according to Ingram.[18] For the entire campaign, Patterson basically gave versions of the same speech. He relied heavily on emotional appeals. In every appearance he referred to his slain father and stressed that the state's traditions and its system of government were being destroyed by forces internal (graft, corruption, and waste) and external (the federal courts, NAACP, and northern politicians) to the state. An example of his best performances is the following:

> I will see to it that there is no mixing of races. . . . The NAACP is the
> No. One enemy of Alabama. . . . They're trying to force integration on
> us. . . . But we [the attorney general's office] drove them out of the state.

I've lived in a place where the gangsters and the corrupt politicians got together and took the government away from the people . . . a place where I had to carry a pistol down to get my mail in the morning . . . a place where every time I take down a law book, I get smut on my hands from the time the gangsters tried to burn me and my father out. . . . When I'm governor there'll be no room for gangsters to operate in this state. . . . I offer you an administration which will enforce the laws of the state, maintain segregation without violence, and get your money's worth from every tax dollar.[19]

Patterson devoted little attention to specific opponents in his campaign, leaving this task to his supporters. For example, Walter Craig, later hired as the chief assistant to the highway director in the Patterson administration, wrote a long letter to the editor of the *Centreville Press,* a pro-Patterson newspaper. The published letter consisted of eleven "questions" from Craig with extended "answers" from the editor. One question was "Is it true that Judge George Wallace voted against one of the first segregation bills ever introduced in the Alabama legislature?" The editor's answer read: "Yes this is true. The Legislative record in Montgomery will show that while a member of the Legislature in 1951 Judge Wallace voted against a segregation bill. Rep. Sam Engelhardt of Macon offered an amendment specifying that if the U.S. Supreme Court should invalidate Alabama's school segregation laws then the appropriation set out in the education appropriation bill would automatically terminate." Craig asked: "Is it true that Judge George Wallace reduced the fine and sentence on a Negro man who appealed a case to his court, and this Negro was represented by a Negro lawyer by the name of Fred Gray?" The editor replied:

In the March 7, 1957 issue of the Union Springs Herald, . . . the following article appeared in reference to a case tried in Judge Wallace's court: "Judge George C. Wallace placed Eddie Lee Jordan, 17, a negro boy who was defended by Fred Gray, a Montgomery negro attorney, on probation last Friday. Charged with reckless driving, Jordan . . . was arrested by the highway patrol after he had caused Circuit Solicitor Seymore Trammell to drive his vehicle into a ditch to avoid a collision on a dirt road. . . . He was fined $25 and given three months by the Justice of the Peace Court at Midway. Young Jordan appealed the case to the Circuit Court. . . . At the end of the trial, Judge Wallace found Jordan guilty, but deferred sentence until March 1. Friday he fined the boy $25 and gave him three months, but placed him on probation."[20]

Although George Wallace was the primary target of this question-and-answer ritual, one of Craig's questions concerned Jimmy Faulkner's position with regard to racial separation. The editor's responses suggested that the Baldwin County newspaper publisher was "soft" on segregation.

The widely mistrusted political professional Charles Meriwether managed Patterson's campaign. In an attempt to undermine Wallace's segregationist credentials, Meriwether used handbills and other informal communication channels to publicize antisegregation votes Wallace cast while in the legislature. The Patterson campaign tried to place the blame for the handbills on the Faulkner camp. The same techniques were used to paint Faulkner as a liberal.[21]

Endorsements

The *Montgomery Advertiser, Montgomery Journal, Florence Times, Selma Times-Journal,* and *Tri-Cities Daily* endorsed Wallace. The *Selma Times-Journal* saw Wallace as defending the interests of the Black Belt.[22] Many editors writing in support of Wallace argued that he had more experience than his closest rival, John Patterson. They often tried to characterize the thirty-six-year-old attorney general as a boy rather than the major statewide officeholder that he was. The editor of the *Montgomery Advertiser,* Grover Hall Jr., went so far as to assert that if elected Patterson would be the least experienced person to be governor in the state's history, apparently forgetting that only twelve years before James E. Folsom Sr. won without ever holding an elective public office. According to Stephan Lesher, Hall was Wallace's "principal campaign and political strategist" in 1958 and would remain so until Hall's death in 1973.[23]

The *Centreville Press* supported Patterson, giving as its sole reason the candidate's strong segregationist position.[24] The *Greene County Democrat* endorsed Patterson because of his opposition to "loan sharks, political grafters, and influence peddlers."[25] The *Birmingham Post-Herald* endorsed him, somewhat balancing its sister newspaper's support for Faulkner. And, of course, Patterson's hometown *Phenix City Citizen* as well as the nearby *Columbus Ledger* supported his candidacy.

Although the *Anniston Star* suggested that the governorships of Wallace and Faulkner would be compromised by the presence of Folsomites on both their staffs, it made no endorsement in the first primary. Wallace had the active support of Folsomites W. LaRue Horn, Frank Boswell, Broughton Lamberth, and E. C. Boswell; Faulkner was assisted by Pitt Tyson Manor, Bill Drinkard, Knox McRae, Pleas Looney, Rex Trubey, and Fuller Kimbrell. The *Star* chose to ignore the fact that these political professionals could shift to a new leader as readily as they could buy new shoes but with a shorter breaking-in period. Whatever problems the state would experience with them would have nothing to do with ties to Folsom or populist sentiments.

The *Huntsville Times* and *Dothan Eagle* made no endorsements in the first primary. The *Tuscaloosa News, Birmingham News, Lee County Bulletin, Limestone Democrat,* and *Demopolis Times* endorsed Faulkner. The *Lee County Bulletin's* reasons were vague clichés about progressive government, dignity, honor, a stout heart, and a firm resolve.[26] Faulkner shared the AFL-CIO's endorsement with Wallace and three other candidates.

The Creek tribe, numbering sixty thousand, endorsed Patterson and actively worked for his election. The group supported "segregation, states' rights and liberties of the individual," according to Chief Calvin McGee.[27] The tribe's support resulted from Attorney General Patterson's legal assistance in a long-standing land dispute with the federal government.[28] The Ku Klux Klan also tended to favor John Patterson, but the large Bessemer chapter preferred George Wallace.

These fragmented and often dispirited endorsements were reflected in the inability of the state's political commentators to discern a clear image of major interest groups decidedly supporting any one candidate. The Black Belt was split between Wallace and Patterson. Major industrial leaders were undecided or just unenthusiastic. Perhaps the only clear pattern was that few county political rings endorsed Patterson, who tended to be viewed as an outsider.

The Campaign for Lieutenant Governor

The Alabama office of lieutenant governor resembles that of vice president of the United States and might therefore be dismissed as a relatively unimportant position by the casual observer. Aside from the fact that the lieutenant governor assumes the office of governor in case of the governor's death, removal from office, resignation, or prolonged absence from the state, there is little similarity in terms of power. One point of dissimilarity is that candidates for governor and lieutenant governor run independently of each other. It is therefore possible for them to be members of different political parties, as happened when a Republican governor, Guy Hunt, and a Democratic lieutenant governor, James E. Folsom Jr., were elected in 1990.

Alabama's lieutenant governor *actively* presides over the senate whenever it is in session and by custom selects and appoints all committee members and committee chairs. He makes these choices unencumbered by seniority. The degree to which the lieutenant governor consults with the governor regarding committee assignments varies depending on their personalities, political parties, party faction, and interest group affiliations.

Five men ran for the Democratic party nomination for lieutenant governor in 1958. The three serious contenders were state senators and men of substantial ability.

E. W. Skidmore (Tuscaloosa)[29] ran as a staunch prolabor union liberal. In 1953 he had dramatized his prolabor position by filibustering against the right-to-work law that later passed the legislature.

Sam Engelhardt (Macon), a plantation owner and a leading Black Belt Big Mule, supported passage of the right-to-work law. Before he started the campaign, Engelhardt resigned as executive secretary of the Alabama Association of White Citizens Councils. The organization's members were segregationists who were not sufficiently extreme to join the Ku Klux Klan. Engelhardt made clear that his resignation was just a way for him to devote full time to the campaign and not a renunciation of the councils.[30]

Albert Boutwell was born in Montgomery but brought up in Black Belt Butler County. After graduating from law school he practiced law in Birmingham and represented many Big Mule companies. Ordinarily a dependable supporter of Birmingham's Big Mule interests, Boutwell sided with Skidmore in voting against the right-to-work statute, but he reversed himself in 1958. Boutwell was completing his fourth term as state senator. His campaign highlighted his legislative career, which consisted partly of opposition to Folsom and his policies and a championing of good-government reforms such as low-bid laws. In the area of civil rights Boutwell pointed to his authorship of a segregation-preservation constitutional amendment guaranteeing "freedom of choice." He was also chairing a fourteen-member legislative committee to maintain segregation. The *Greenville Advocate* claimed with no little justification that state senators and representatives as well as private citizens "believe that the Jefferson county senator has been the greatest single contributing factor in this state's so far successful fight to keep the schools, parks and other places segregated."[31]

The Campaign for the Democratic Party Executive Committee

In 1948 many Alabama Democrats had abandoned the Democratic party for the Dixiecrat party, and in response a loyalty oath

had been required of Democratic candidates. In 1958 those who had supported the Dixiecrat split and other diehard segregationists campaigned
to put onto the executive committee of the state Democratic party people
who would overturn the loyalty oath. They believed that this would allow
the state to be more independent and to deal more effectively with both
national parties. At this time President Dwight Eisenhower's appointment of Earl Warren as chief justice of the Supreme Court and his use of
troops to support school integration in Little Rock prevented any significant movement toward the Republican party. Segregationists also viewed
the national Democratic party's activities as dominated by a liberal wing
seeking to destroy states' rights and the southern way of life.

In virtually their only participation in the 1958 campaign, U.S. Senators John Sparkman and Lister Hill strongly endorsed supporters of the
loyalty oath. So too did Congressman George Huddleston Jr., who represented Jefferson County. In a radio speech Lister Hill combined references
to the Eisenhower administration's civil rights policies with old populist
themes: "I believe the people of Alabama now recognize more clearly than
ever that the Republican Party is the ancient enemy—the party of bayonets in the South, the party of farm distress, the party of unjust taxation,
unfair tariffs, and discriminatory freight rates—the party of hard financial policies, of depression and economic disaster."[32] The outgoing governor,
James Folsom, continued his unending support of the loyalty oath.

Democratic Primary Results and the Runoff Campaign

When the primary votes were counted, John Patter-
son enjoyed a fairly substantial lead over George Wallace (31.8 percent to
26.3 percent). Jimmy Faulkner ran a distant third. Patterson's greatest
strength lay in the Black Belt, the central area, and southwestern Alabama. This result reflected his direct appeal to segregationists and the fact
that he was born and reared in and near these areas. Wallace held his home
region of Barbour and surrounding counties. Neither did very well in most
of north Alabama, because of the geographical distance of their homes from
that region and the presence of north Alabama candidates.

In the lieutenant governor's race Albert Boutwell held a substantial lead
over E. W. Skidmore, although Boutwell did not reach the majority required
to win without a runoff. Reflecting the importance of home county support
in Alabama elections, Boutwell's greatest strength was in his Jefferson
County base, Huntsville, Etowah County (Gadsden), and several north Ala-

bama counties. He was weak around Tuscaloosa, Skidmore's home. Boutwell also was strong in the Black Belt and south Alabama, where one might have expected Sam Engelhardt to do better, but Boutwell had been born and brought up in the Black Belt and had maintained his personal ties to the region.

None of the state's newspapers had a coherent explanation for the Patterson or Boutwell victories beyond the usual post-hoc observations that both ran effective campaigns and neither was associated with Folsom. The Folsom explanation gained credence as the result of perhaps the most unusual and surprising outcome in the 1958 primary—House Speaker Rankin Fite's defeat by three votes (3,992 to 3,995).[33] Other Folsomites also lost, including senate leader Broughton Lamberth, Fuller Kimbrell, Ed Brown (Folsom's press secretary), Senator Garet Van Antwerp III, Representative Otto E. Simon of Mobile, and Bryce Davis. Ruby Ellis, Folsom's sister, lost in her bid for secretary of state. Folsomite Richmond Flowers was defeated in the attorney general's race. Senator Harlan G. "Mutt" Allen of Cullman lost a race for probate judge, and Murray Battles failed in his attempt to win a circuit judgeship. Association with Folsom was a liability in 1958. Many observed that this phenomenon hurt George Wallace, who had been a Folsom regional campaign manager four years previously. Wallace was never able to shake the suspicion that he harbored some of Folsom's populist tendencies, and in 1958 he experienced considerable difficulty convincing the electorate that he was a true-believing segregationist. At the same time, his Black Belt ties worried many in north Alabama.

It was more advantageous to be associated with the Phenix City story. Patterson's chief assistant attorney general, MacDonald Gallion, won the primary race for attorney general. Gallion had played an important part in the Albert Patterson murder investigation and was an outspoken segregationist then involved in establishing a private-school funding scheme to avoid forced integration. Circuit Judge Walter Jones, who presided over the NAACP cases and had been the presiding judge in the Phenix City trials that resulted from Albert Patterson's murder, was renominated by a large majority.

In the runoff the *Dothan Eagle,* a reactionary publication, endorsed Patterson, as did the *Marion Times-Standard.* Sam Engelhardt announced his support for Patterson. The *Birmingham News* continued to support Wallace in the runoff. As was common for the *News* at that time, its coverage was exceedingly biased in favor of the candidate it endorsed. Typical headlines read: "Patterson rolls with Klan's wave—Wallace," "Wallace hurls new broadside at Patterson," and "Wallace urges tax relief for senior citizens."[34] The few headlines that mentioned Patterson were in much smaller type.[35]

Gessner McCorvey, a reactionary Mobile lawyer and former chair of the state Democratic party's executive committee, supported Wallace, as did the Birmingham Big Mule instrument James A. Simpson, but so did the liberal judge Roy Mayhall of Jasper and Clyde W. Anderson of Florence.[36]

The *Anniston Star, Southern Star* (Ozark), *Greensboro Watchman, Enterprise Ledger, Brewton Standard, Lee County Bulletin, Union Springs Herald,* and *Tuscaloosa News* endorsed Wallace. The Lee County newspaper's reasoning was that Wallace was a supporter of education and without ties to Big Mules. Wallace was also endorsed by the liberal *Florence Times,* the *Tri-Cities Daily,* the moderate *Huntsville Times,* and the Black Belt Big Mule *Selma Times-Journal.* However, the *Mobile Labor* may have lost credibility with knowledgeable readers when it described George Wallace as "a man in whose veins flows the warm blood of humanitarianism."[37]

The *Huntsville Times* claimed that Wallace's record was better than Patterson's in the areas of education, reapportionment, and support for the Tennessee Valley Authority. A railroad brotherhood local in Mobile supported Wallace while repudiating the endorsement of Patterson by the Alabama Joint Legislative Council of Railroad Brotherhoods.

The *Montgomery Advertiser* attacked Patterson's campaign manager Charles Meriwether's connections with E. H. "Boss Ed" Crump of Memphis. Meriwether's relationship with the infamous Crump was never made clear, and even cloudier was what difference it made in Alabama. Nevertheless, as the *Advertiser* and other newspapers told the story, Meriwether was a dark eminence manipulating the inexperienced boy candidate.

Meriwether had managed Admiral John G. Crommelin's 1950 senatorial campaign against Lister Hill. Crommelin later dived into racist politics so extreme as to embarrass Meriwether and Patterson even in the context of 1958 Alabama. Meriwether had also managed Birmingham City Commissioner Wade Bradley's 1953 campaign and had helped the Birmingham attorney Albert Rosenthal direct Albert L. Patterson's winning campaign for the attorney general nomination.

The media tied anti-Meriwether stories to Patterson's low profile during the runoff campaign. He refused to appear in joint candidate forums, made few speeches, and focused on a handshaking tour of the state. Many in the press attributed these actions to Meriwether's "pulling the strings," and a series of political cartoons (many paid for by Wallace supporters) reinforced the imagery. Typical ads pictured Patterson as either a marionette or a ventriloquist's dummy on Meriwether's knee.[38]

Patterson's runoff strategy was in fact designed to minimize verbal misstatements by the front-runner. The plan also focused the candidate's activity in areas where he had not previously campaigned and in the counties of his greatest strength.[39] According to one Patterson aide, this allowed "Wallace to hang himself." By calling attention to Patterson's absences from the stages on which he appeared, Wallace kept Patterson's name in the headlines.[40] It was "a deliberate stall, killing as much time as possible, shaking hands and making no statements."[41]

Reinforcing the innuendo concerning Meriwether, a *Birmingham News* reporter spotted the Alabama Ku Klux Klan leader Robert Shelton in John Patterson's campaign headquarters in Birmingham. Shelton was seen talking to Patterson's brother Maurice. When a *News* photographer approached, Shelton ducked into Meriwether's office. Meriwether denied any knowledge of Shelton's identity, as did Patterson.

The day after the Shelton story broke, Bob Ingram of the *Montgomery Advertiser* discovered that a form letter written on official stationery of the attorney general's office was being widely distributed.[42] The letter read as follows:

Dear Mr. ——:

A mutual friend, Mr. R. M. (Bob) Shelton, of ours in Tuscaloosa has suggested that I write you and ask for your support in the coming Governor's race.

I hope you will see fit to support my candidacy and I would like to meet you when I am next in ——.

With warm personal regards, I am

Sincerely your friend

Ingram called Patterson about his connections with the KKK leader, reaching him in the television studio where the national television program *This Is Your Life* was being filmed. Patterson, who later claimed that he was distracted by the hectic and unfamiliar surroundings, denied knowing "anybody named Shelton." Ingram pushed on and Patterson replied: "I know two or three Bob Sheltons, but I think you are referring to the Bob Shelton in Tuscaloosa who works at the rubber plant and is a union member. I know him quite well. I have met with him a number of times during the campaign, but I didn't know he was the grand dragon. In fact, I didn't know he was even a member of the Klan." When asked if he repudiated Klan support, Patterson responded that he did not.[43]

The editor of the *Montgomery Advertiser*, Grover Hall Jr., and other editors whose papers supported Wallace launched a series of articles and columns that kept the story alive, often quoting Wallace's attacks on Patterson. Hall and his reporter Bob Ingram thought the Klan connection would have "disastrous consequences" for Patterson's campaign. They were surprised to discover that it did not hurt and may even have helped him by demonstrating he was "the one true segregationist in the campaign." It caused "not a ripple."[44] Charles Meriwether believes that the Klan membership in Alabama was not very great in 1958, but that Klan "fellow travellers were a major force. The Klan was far stronger electorally than its small membership would suggest."[45] In his view the stories thus served to help the campaign, not hurt it.

Meanwhile, George Wallace had difficulty maintaining consistency. While he accused Patterson of "rolling with the new wave of Ku Klux Klan and its terrible tradition of lawlessness,"[46] he tried to characterize Patterson as weak on segregation![47] Wallace's specific criticism was that as attorney general Patterson had failed to intervene in the Autherine Lucy case. (Lucy sought to integrate the University of Alabama.) Wallace claimed that the university had been obliged to employ outside attorneys to defend itself when in fact that was the preference of the university's independently constituted board.[48] Wallace also halfheartedly complained about Patterson's failure to prosecute a single member of the Folsom administration, a dangerous ploy considering how many Folsomites were supporting Wallace.

Patterson, satisfied with his lead, continued to associate his opponents with "law violators, professional politicians, and the NAACP."[49] In mid-May the attorney general asked the Alabama Supreme Court to speed up a 1957 suit against state officials accused of misspending more than one hundred thousand dollars. The suit was directed against three Folsom appointees— Bill Drinkard, director of the Conservation Department; Comptroller John Graves; and Finance Director Fuller Kimbrell—and a contractor named J. W. Gwin.

Before the runoff the *Muscle Shoals Sun* commented cruelly but accurately that the only candidate who could defeat John Patterson would be one "whose mother was shot in Phenix City."[50] Patterson swept most of the state except for Wallace's home county and those surrounding it in the extreme southeast corner and five counties in the northwest corner. Albert Boutwell also enjoyed an overwhelming victory, but his areas of greatest strength shifted to the Black Belt and the southern part of the state, and of course he did very well in Jefferson County. Boutwell's weakest area was northwestern Alabama. States' rights, anti–loyalty oath candidates won a majority of seats on the Democratic party executive committee.

The Republican party meeting in convention nominated thirty-three-year-old W. L. Longshore Jr., a Birmingham attorney, as its gubernatorial candidate, and James H. Jones of Centre for lieutenant governor. Of course, neither had the slightest chance of winning. Claude O. Vardaman was reelected party chairman. One of the planks in the Republican platform endorsed continued segregation.

Reapportionment and Regional Issues

During both the primary and the runoff campaigns, reapportionment issues periodically surfaced. North Alabama and urban areas were growing rapidly. They suffered from a tax system that extracted taxes from the more populous counties and then divided much of the revenue equally among the sixty-seven counties. The malapportioned legislature and Big Mule Alliance prevented readjustment of these allocation formulas.

Early in February an editorial in the *Huntsville Times* had pointed out:

The population of North Alabama is increasing, that of the middle and southern portion—except for Mobile and one or two nearby counties—either is standing still or declining.

In North Alabama, especially the Valley, there is pulsing advance, growth; new industries, great plans for the future. . . .

South of Birmingham—always excluding Mobile, which is much like the Valley in its progress and spirit—the farming depression, racial problems, lack of industry to employ those leaving the farms have put a damper on politics as well as on economic and other matters.

Where most of these counties cast 1,000 to 2,000 or 3,000 votes, the registration is far higher in most North Alabama counties. Jefferson, of course, heads the list, but Madison, Etowah, Calhoun, Lauderdale, Colbert, DeKalb, Marshall, Cullman, Franklin, Jackson, Limestone, Morgan and Walker have registrations as much as 10 or 15 times larger, in some cases.

Up here is where the votes are, and here is where the South and Central Alabama candidates for all state offices, especially governor, are going to spend most of their time.[51]

All three of the front-runners in the gubernatorial primary had claimed in north Alabama speeches that they supported reapportionment, but all of their statements were viewed as suspect. An April *Times* editorial reflected this view:

South Alabama candidates may give lip service to reapportionment, but it is doubtful whether they wish to be pinned down on this issue. . . . From the south side of Jefferson (Birmingham) County to the Tennessee line on the north, between 70 and 75 per cent of the votes in all Alabama are cast.

Central and South Alabama—and that includes the Black Belt—vote only 20 to 25 per cent of the total.

Naturally, therefore, only lip service is likely on the reapportionment issue from all South Alabama candidates.[52]

The newspaper's editor also found no outstanding issue (with the possible exception of segregation) in the campaign. He argued that education, reapportionment, and the Tennessee Valley Authority—in order of importance—were the most vital issues to north Alabama.[53]

The regional representation issue was important to urban areas as well. For example, during the runoff the *Lee County Bulletin* noted: "We have no doubt that John Patterson wants to do right by the schools. But his inexperience and his naivete . . . would be grist in the mills of those who would surround him. We mean the big corporate representatives from Birmingham and the reactionary pinch pennies such as Bruce Henderson from the country districts. Their principal aim is to collect as little tax money and spend as little as possible."[54] North Alabama and urban interests carefully watched the new governor, paying particular attention to the staffing of his cabinet and key legislative positions as indicators of his regional loyalties.

After the Runoff

Once nominated, Patterson seemed intent on continuing to demonstrate that he was a vigorous and effective opponent of the civil rights movement. In June he returned to court to mount further attacks on the NAACP. He tried to prove that the civil rights organization was still actively operating in the state but under a different name (the Alabama State Coordinating Association for Registration and Voting) despite the court injunction that he had obtained two years before that banned the organization. Patterson also continued his push for contempt citations against W. C. Patton and William P. Mitchell. In October, when agents of the United States Civil Rights Commission asked to see Macon County voting records, Attorney General Patterson advised the Macon County Voter Registration Board not to allow it.[55]

On June 30 the U.S. Supreme Court countermanded the contempt citation and one-hundred-thousand-dollar fine levied against the NAACP, but the court refused to dissolve the restraining order barring NAACP operations in Alabama. It ordered the Alabama Supreme Court to grant a hearing on the merits of the restraining order, because the NAACP had never received a hearing.

In 1957 Patterson had won a temporary restraining order prohibiting Tuskegee blacks from using force or intimidation to support their boycott against white merchants. On June 21, 1958, Circuit Judge Will O. Walton dissolved the injunction that he himself had granted. Judge Walton ruled that Patterson had failed to show that the Tuskegee Civic Association was sponsoring an illegal boycott or that it had used force to support a boycott. He upheld a person's right to "trade with whomever he pleases."[56]

Albert Boutwell also was active after winning the nomination for lieutenant governor. He suggested the reestablishment of a special legislative committee on segregation similar to the one he had chaired as state senator. One of Boutwell's objectives was to ensure the passage of legislation that was not too obviously segregationist. A statute with a blatantly segregationist objective or history would be more likely to be struck down by federal courts.[57] Boutwell typically fought the civil rights movement through subtle and quiet legal strategies and tactics.

The day after proposing the creation of the special legislative committee on segregation, Boutwell spoke before a rally sponsored by the Dallas County Citizens Council. He was introduced by the influential state senator Walter Givhan, a longtime Farm Bureau leader who was chairman of the Dallas County Council and president of the Alabama Councils. Boutwell outlined a two-pronged strategy for the defense of segregation. First, the South should attempt to take back powers removed from it by the federal government. Second, the state of Alabama should relinquish some authority to the localities. He argued that this would make federal action and litigation more difficult by forcing the Department of Justice to bring action against multiple authorities rather than at just one point. Boutwell also criticized Governor Folsom's lack of support for the defense of segregation and praised Patterson as much more likely to serve the segregationist cause. In a later speech he suggested the creation of a permanent organization to facilitate a unified southern fight.[58]

Legislative Leaders in Alabama

Given the Big Mules' domination of the legislature in the pre-reapportionment period, one might expect that committees would be stacked in favor of legislators from the Black Belt, Jefferson County, and to a lesser degree Mobile and Etowah (Gadsden) Counties. Other regions, especially north and south Alabama, would be expected to have little or no representation on committees. And, given the importance of governors in organizing the House and lieutenant governors in organizing the Senate, one might also expect to see them rewarding counties that supported them in the Democratic primary.

These conventional views miss the subtlety with which the Big Mule alliance operated.[59] Many central leadership offices, positions on key House and Senate committees, and committee chairs and vice chairs were held by those from outside Big Mule circles throughout the post–World War II era.[60] House speakers came mainly from north Alabama and the Black Belt, although Speakers pro tempore included some midstate members. Presidents pro tempore of the Senate had a regional pattern mix similar to the Speakers pro tempore. Overall, the Black Belt *and* north Alabama dominated the leadership of the House and Senate. The central region was represented in later years.

The House leadership committees during this period were Ways and Means, Rules, and Judiciary; the Senate leadership committees were Rules, Finance and Taxation, and Judiciary. The chairs and vice chairs of the three major committees in each house represented a mix of regions. From 1947 to 1963 north Alabama, the central region, and the population centers of Mobile and Jefferson Counties shared chair and vice chair duties with the Black Belt. South Alabama was represented only as part of a Black Belt/ south district.

Black Belt and Jefferson County legislators tended to be personally wealthy or in the employ of large corporations. In the 1950s Albert Boutwell, who represented many corporate interests; Hugh Kaul, with large timber holdings; and wealthy plantation owners like Sam Engelhardt and Walter Givhan were typical.

Patterson's Legislative Leaders

The Speaker of the House is elected by the members of the House, but in the 1950s traditional practice still called for the governor-elect to voice his preference and for that preference to be respected by members of the new House. In effect, the governor selected the Speaker. John Patterson's choice was Charles Adams, a veteran legislator and insurance salesman from Patterson's original home county of Tallapoosa. He was elected without a dissenting vote. Adams had been an opponent of the Folsom administration in the previous legislature, and he was an active

Patterson backer in the election.[61] The balding, jowly Adams was frequently described as quiet-spoken and fair-minded. Following standard practice, the Speaker chaired the critically important Rules Committee. Representative E. K. Hanby (Etowah), a Patterson supporter, became vice chair.

House committee members and chairs were selected by Patterson with relatively little input from his Speaker.[62] Joseph W. Smith, a longtime friend and supporter from Patterson's adopted home county (Russell), was named chair of House Ways and Means. Eight members of that fifteen-person committee were freshmen. This caused veteran legislators to grumble, but a large majority of these established House members had not supported Patterson, and they understood the implications of that. Virgis Ashworth of Bibb County in central Alabama became chair of the House Judiciary Committee. Ashworth was a Patterson supporter, and Bibb County had voted for Patterson in both primaries.

By tradition the lieutenant governor makes committee selections in consultation with the governor. Patterson would not have been able to dictate committee chairs and members to the independently elected and highly experienced Boutwell the way he had to his Speaker.

Tradition also requires that the governor name the president pro tempore (a position filled by vote of the Senate). The president pro tempore serves as the governor's Senate floor leader.[63] Patterson chose an influential Montgomery attorney named Vaughan Hill Robison, an able parliamentarian and sometimes fiery speech maker. Robison also became chair of Finance and Taxation. Montgomery County had voted for Wallace in the first primary and was one of the few to also give him a majority in the runoff, but Robison had supported Patterson.

Albert Boutwell was known as a clever tactician, and Patterson wanted to be prepared for his meeting with the future lieutenant governor regarding committee chairs and members. Before the meeting Patterson met several times with Robison, Engelhardt, Floyd Mann, and Virgis Ashworth to plan his Senate choices. Said Robison: "We had no idea what Albert was going for. We picked our people we wanted on the committees, tried to speculate on who Albert would select. We wanted majority control on the committees. We had an easel with poster boards for each committee. We'd go through the Senate roster, see who would best serve to carry out John Patterson's programs, try to figure out Albert's connections to each man."[64]

Patterson handled the actual negotiations with Boutwell. They met behind closed doors and worked out a mutually satisfactory division of committee assignments. The supposedly inexperienced Patterson gained a majority on each committee. The prominent attorney Larry Dumas of

Jefferson County was named Judiciary Committee chair. Patterson lost Jefferson County in the first primary but won it overwhelmingly in the run-off. Dumas was not a Patterson supporter but was named chair of Judiciary because of Boutwell. Bob Gilchrist of Morgan County, who had coordinated the Patterson campaign in north Alabama, was named vice chair. Morgan had supported Patterson in both the primary and runoff. E. O. Eddins of Marengo County, in the Black Belt, was appointed to ten standing committees and as vice chair of Finance and Taxation. Marengo County had supported Patterson in the primary and runoff. Dave Archer, the newly elected senator from north Alabama's Madison County, which Patterson had lost in the first primary and won in the runoff, became chair of the senate Rules Committee. Archer had not worked in the Patterson campaign but considered himself a Patterson supporter. The chairs of the leadership committees included two from central Alabama, two from the Black Belt (including Montgomery), one from Jefferson County, and one from north Alabama. None came from south Alabama.

In interviews Patterson confirmed that he followed the usual pattern of basing his choices on a legislator's support in the primary, his personal ability, and support from his home county. In several instances Patterson selected individuals with outstanding leadership capabilities who had supported him but whose counties had not. Vaughan Hill Robison was the most notable example.

The editors of the *Birmingham News* complained that key committee chairmanships and other important legislative positions had gone disproportionately to south Alabama.[65] The editors were especially disappointed by this, they said, because it would hurt chances for reapportionment. Analysis of Patterson's appointments shows there was no basis for their complaint.

Patterson's Executive Branch

Most of Patterson's cabinet choices came from the Black Belt or from large cities in the Big Mule–Black Belt alliance. The breakdown was 19 percent Jefferson County, 24 percent Montgomery County, 33 percent Black Belt counties other than Montgomery, 14 percent south Alabama, and 9 percent north Alabama. The north Alabama press carefully studied the regional breakdown of the appointments, worried that their region was again underrepresented and that the Black Belt and south Alabama would again control the decision processes of the state. Newspapers from other areas often joined in these concerns, viewing Jefferson and Montgomery County people as part of the Big Mule Alliance.[66] It was also their perception that the legislative leadership appointments did not appropriately reflect north Alabama's voting impact.

The strategy and tactics used by a governor in the legislative arena were very different from those required in the statewide electoral arena. Cabinet appointees would have to shepherd their programs and budgets through a malapportioned legislature where north Alabama's voting impact was much weaker than in gubernatorial elections. The press did not appear to grasp the distinction.

Only four of Patterson's appointees had high-level administrative experience in the legislative or executive branch. Ten were new to state government.[67] Earl McGowin (Butler) was one of Patterson's most experienced cabinet officers. He was appointed state docks commissioner. He had been Governor Frank Dixon's House floor leader and the commissioner of conservation under Governor Gordon Persons. McGowin was a Rhodes scholar, with an Oxford degree in economics and political science, and a wealthy timberland owner. Grover Hall Jr. once described him as the most cultured person in Alabama.

Sam Engelhardt, a wealthy Macon County cotton grower, former legislator, segregation leader, and unsuccessful candidate for lieutenant governor, became highway director, one of the two most important cabinet positions. After his appointment Engelhardt maintained close and active ties with the White Citizens Council. He corresponded regularly with its new president, Walter Givhan of the Alabama Farm Bureau, as well as council members from other states.[68] As highway director Engelhardt maintained a list of contributors to the Citizens Council Educational Fund. Out of ninety-four contributors only seven were not highway department employees.[69]

Harry N. Cook was a former *Birmingham News* reporter who had covered Albert Patterson's murder and subsequent Phenix City investigations and cleanup. He then served as assistant to Congressman George Huddleston Jr. Cook had not worked in the Patterson campaign, but he applied for the position of press secretary after hearing that the governor-elect was searching for someone to fill that post. Partly because Patterson remembered his *Birmingham News* work, he got the job.[70]

Harry H. Haden, one of Patterson's professors at the University of Alabama School of Law, was named commissioner of revenue. Haden had not sought this appointment and accepted it only after securing a promise from Patterson that the governor would support reform of the state's poorly administered and inequitable property tax system.[71]

Joseph G. Robertson, a Birmingham native, was Patterson's executive secretary as attorney general, and he remained in that position when Patterson became governor. The two had been close friends for many years, and Robertson had been Patterson's driver and assistant during the campaign.[72] He looked like a slightly shorter version of Patterson himself.

Patterson's campaign manager, Charles M. Meriwether, was named finance director, the single most important appointive position in Alabama state government.

Mixed Signals

In 1958 the voters selected the most effective champions of segregation for both lieutenant governor and governor. The Big Mule newspapers disagreed concerning Wallace and Patterson, but Wallace was generally viewed as the more moderate candidate on racial issues. No major daily appeared enthusiastic about either candidate. Both were clearly committed to maintaining segregation, but their campaigns also featured unwelcome populist components.

Very little in the election signaled the end of the Big Mule Alliance. Support for the two winners came from both geographical segments of the alliance. Candidates for governor and lieutenant governor who espoused reapportionment as centerpieces of their campaigns were thrashed, but the fact that editorial coverage of the campaign, particularly in north Alabama, examined a candidate's stand on reapportionment began to suggest the growing importance of the issue.

4

The Enigmatic
John Patterson and
the Alliance at Work

A set of vexing and expensive-to-repair problems in public education faced Governor Patterson as he took office. His attempts to deal with these problems activated the Black Belt–Big Mule Alliance in opposition. When he also sought to reform the tax laws of the state, alliance opposition further solidified. These battles drained the administration's resources, weakened Patterson's ability to achieve other policy goals, and gave the alliance partnership its last major victories.

In 1958 Alabama's public education system suffered from a profusion of financial, political, and demographic problems that threatened to erode the quality of already-poor schools or even destroy them. Funding levels were too low, and property taxes, a major source of support, were collected inconsistently, inefficiently, and unfairly. Financial shortages were exacerbated by a nationwide recession and steel industry strikes. Federal court pressure on segregation was certain to increase financial burdens further while diminishing the electorate's support for public schools. Population movements from the Black Belt placed added pressure on city schools. Students were barely being prepared for the industrial revolution, let alone the space age that had begun with the October 1957 launch by the Soviet Union of the world's first artificial satellite.

In January 1958 Austin Meadows, state superintendent of education, announced that 105 schools had been placed on probation because they fell below accreditation standards. Schools that failed to meet those standards by the beginning of the next school year would lose their accreditation, and graduates would find it difficult to secure college entry. Two engineering programs at Auburn University (then called Alabama Polytechnic) had lost their accreditation, and the University of Alabama had been warned of possible loss of accreditation for its engineering school. Two state-operated black colleges and Troy State Teachers College were also on the verge of losing accreditation.

In March 1958 the state board of education took the unprecedented action of passing a resolution asking Governor James E. Folsom Sr. to call a special legislative session to deal with the education problems. Coming at the height of the Democratic gubernatorial primary contest, the resolution reinforced the importance of the educational issues that had already surfaced in most candidates' speeches.

Alabama Education Commission

A campaign to increase funding for education had begun in August 1957, when the Alabama legislature passed the Lackey-Edwards bill creating the Alabama Education Commission. This blue-ribbon group was to conduct a survey of the educational system and to recommend improvements that were "within the reasonable capacity of the people to support."[1] The commission's work was timed to coincide with the election campaigns for state offices, and its formal report was to be presented near the time the new governor and legislature would take office in January 1959. The commission was to examine programs, policies, and financial needs for the next ten years.

The twenty-one commission members were selected as prescribed by the Lackey-Edwards bill. The governor named three from the field of public education. The Senate picked four from its membership and the House five of its own. Senators and representatives from each of the nine congressional districts met to select one person to represent each district. They chose the leaders of some of the state's major interest groups.

The commission selected its own chair, Representative Joe Dawkins of Montgomery, a Folsomite and labor union supporter. Its instructional program committee was chaired by Senator Joseph W. Smith of Phenix City, who returned to the legislature in 1959 as a member of the House and part of the Patterson leadership team. The personnel committee was chaired by Earl C. Pippin of Montgomery, vice president of the Alabama Labor Council and a member of the Communications Workers of America. Hayse Tucker of Tuscaloosa, a former senator and former state finance director, chaired the buildings and transportation committee. The organization and administration committee was led by Representative Virgis Ashworth of Centreville, who would serve as a Patterson floor leader and in 1961 be Patterson's choice for speaker. The financing education committee was chaired by the Birmingham investment banker Mervyn H. Sterne, a bona fide Big Mule, and the higher education committee by the attorney C. B. Gillmore of Grove Hill.[2]

One part of the commission's work documented and reported to the public the poor condition of the state's schools. For example, commission member Hayes Tucker, in a presentation that received widespread newspaper coverage, announced that Alabama had 1,081 schools with no sewage facilities, 183 with no electricity, 194 without water, and 430 with no central heating. He maintained that the schools needed $340 million immediately just to meet construction costs.[3] The commission also publicized the poor quality of education provided in many schools and offered the promise that improved education would generate better jobs and a more vigorous economy.

The commission's committee on educational finance reported that in 1956–57 per-pupil expenditures for public schools in Alabama were $165. To close the gap with the national average of $300 per pupil would have required an increase of $100 million per year. The committee indicated that the $300 target could be met in ten years but acknowledged that because other states would also be increasing their expenditures, Alabama would still fall below the new national average.[4]

The finance committee based part of its findings on a 1957 report by the Legislative Interim Committee on Revision of State Tax Laws. That interim committee had been chaired by Representative Joe Dawkins, chair of the Alabama Education Commission, and Senator Albert Boutwell, lieutenant governor–elect, was its vice chair.[5] Its report lamented that low property-tax levels were undermining Alabama schools, noting that in 1953 school districts received only 18 percent of their revenues from this source compared to a mean of 68 percent for school districts nationwide. This "neglect and virtual abandonment of the property tax has developed out of restrictive effects of Constitutional rate maximums and completely unrealistic assessment levels."[6]

Partial solutions recommended by the finance committee included improving the board of equalization (a mechanism for standardizing property taxes), establishing a "strong" property tax division of the Alabama Department of Revenue to provide assistance to the counties, and requiring counties to maintain inventories of real estate. The committee placed major emphasis on increasing the salaries of public school teachers and staff and higher education faculty and staff. It recommended an increase in the state income tax to a flat rate of 5 percent and a rise in the corporate income-tax rate to 5 percent.

Construction bonds were to be authorized for higher education and for public schools. Local school districts were to match state bond monies on a fifty-fifty basis. Over $3 million would be reserved for systems with rapidly rising enrollments. Each county would receive a guaranteed allocation of $250,000, and the remaining $30 million was to be divided among the state's 113 school districts. The fifty-fifty match would be feasible if a recommended increase in property taxes was also approved.

The finance committee asserted that local school districts would raise assessments more willingly if property tax receipts were locally assessed and collected. The state collected 6.5 mills—3 mills for schools, 2.5 mills for the general fund, and 1 mill for Confederate pensions. The 3 mills for schools were distributed to the counties on the basis of the school-age population. The committee recommended that the state relinquish its property taxes. To compensate for the resulting revenue loss, the state sales tax would be increased by one percentage point, but only if the state relinquished the property tax.

The full commission overruled the committee recommendation that the state turn property taxation over to the localities but retained the committee's sales tax increase. This classic regressive tax had long been supported by the Big Mules as the only way to ensure that blacks and other poor Alabamians paid their "fair share" of the tax burden. Since the finance committee and the commission had learned that some school systems used construction funds to build noneducational facilities such as lunchrooms, auditoriums, and administrative offices, the commission recommended that the new bonds fund only "classrooms and those rooms in constant daily use at full capacity."

Support for the commission's recommendation for a sales tax increase came from the Alabama Education Association (AEA), the white teachers' organization.[7] The AEA also supported removing exemptions on sales and use taxes, a property tax increase, and a gross receipts tax on services such as those offered by barber shops, electricians, lawyers, and doctors.[8] Joe Dawkins, the commission chair and a supporter of the populist-liberal Folsom administration, opposed the sales tax increase, as did representatives of organized labor and the League of Municipalities.[9]

Representative Hugh Kaul, a Birmingham lumberman and a Big Mule Alliance member, fearing that urban-labor-liberal interests would recommend higher property taxes in place of the sales tax increase, warned against attempts to sabotage the committee's good work and thereby undermine the cause of quality education in Alabama.[10] Kaul's dual representation of Birmingham-industrial and rural lumber interests was one of many human bridges between the two parts of the Big Mule Alliance.

The Alabama Farm Bureau Federation, the most powerful component of the Black Belt–Big Mule power structure, made its position clear at a meeting in mid-January 1959. It called for a lowering of the sales tax on farm equipment to the same level as that on automobiles. Walter Randolph, president of the Farm Bureau, also announced the organization's opposition to the removal of sales tax exemptions for farm raw materials.[11] A typical Black Belt newspaper editorial concerning increased taxes for schools argued with apparent seriousness that taxes were already so high that there was hardly anything left to tax.[12]

Meanwhile, the representatives of some counties near state borders expressed their opposition to a sales tax increase because such a levy put their merchants at a disadvantage relative to those in adjoining states.

Segregation and School Funding

Supporters of public education feared that opponents might use public sentiment against *Brown v. Board* to block increased funding for public schools. In July 1959 Superintendent of Schools Austin Meadows issued a statement that warned, "The enemies of public schools and those who did not want to pay the school bills timed sharp and deep threats at public schools in with the fear of integration to choke education in this state." Their attacks, according to Meadows, were not direct: "They oppose the means for providing education."[13]

In the fall of 1958, MacDonald Gallion, the Democratic nominee for attorney general, drafted papers to create a private segregated school system if the public schools were to close in response to court-ordered integration. The private school system would be funded by private endowment, a fanciful notion given the enormous sums required to run public school systems. It would be run by a board of trustees headed by Walter J. Hanna, who operated a steel company and served as a major general in the Alabama National Guard. Gallion acted as a private citizen. He had resigned from Attorney General Patterson's staff to campaign for the post of attorney general. Given Gallion's and Hanna's close ties to Patterson (Gallion had been a special investigator and prosecutor in the Phenix City cleanup after Albert Patterson's murder, and Hanna commanded the National Guard units that ran the city), some speculated that he was acting in concert with the gubernatorial nominee.[14]

Albert Boutwell, the nominee for lieutenant governor, and legislative leaders worried that Gallion's efforts could undermine their attempts to coordinate all efforts to block school segregation. They believed that carefully crafted legislation would produce separate but equal educational facilities and ultimately the federal courts' acceptance of Alabama's segregated public schools.

These views were encouraged when the U.S. Supreme Court ruled unanimously that Alabama's school placement law was valid. This statute allowed school boards to assign pupils to schools for a variety of reasons but did not mention race. The court upheld the decision of a three-judge district court that the law "furnished the legal machinery for an orderly administration of the public schools in a constitutional manner by the admission of qualified pupils upon a basis of individual merit without regard to color." [15] It noted that actual administration of the law might result in other litigation and the voiding of the act.

Legislators led by then Senator Boutwell in 1956 had removed from Alabama law all references to compulsory segregation. In 1956 and 1957, school boards were also given the power to close public schools and donate funds and property to private schools. [16] The legislators believed that substantial additions to these carefully thought out statutes would do more harm than good. [17]

The Patterson Position on Education

The newly elected governor, John Patterson, had campaigned on a platform of no tax increases. As a result of meetings with Austin Meadows, the highly respected outgoing superintendent of education, President Ralph Draughon of Auburn University, President Frank Rose of the University of Alabama, C. P. Nelson and Zeke Kimbrough, incoming and outgoing AEA presidents, and Patterson's legislative leaders Joe Smith, Ira Pruitt (who was especially interested in education), and Vaughan Hill Robison (the Montgomery School District's attorney), the governor realized that his no-new-taxes position would have to be reversed.

Patterson had received no significant support from education forces in his gubernatorial campaign. This did not prevent education interests from vigorously lobbying him. He was responsive because they might back him in a reelection attempt, and he did not like to burn bridges. Patterson also believed that although the AEA hierarchy had been against him, many rank-and-file members had voted for him.

In a personal interview Patterson observed that it did not take much to convince him of the difficulties faced by the schools. His parents had been schoolteachers. He had delivered many campaign speeches in schoolhouses, and he knew how ramshackle many of them were. He remembered seeing the ground through holes in the floor of one.[18] In addition, strong public sentiment favored greater school funding.

In his inaugural address Patterson promised:

> I will preserve and promote the cause of public education in Alabama. I want to see every child in this state afforded the best education possible irrespective of race or color.
>
> The white and Negro pupils should have equal school facilities, but they must be segregated. I will oppose with every ounce of energy I possess and will use every power at my command to prevent any mixing of the white and Negro races in the classrooms of this state.[19]

Governor Patterson opened his first regular session of the legislature by calling for a large increase in appropriations for public schools. He simultaneously asked for the authority to close schools threatened with integration.[20]

A charitable and probably correct interpretation of his school-closing proposal is that it disarmed segregationists who opposed public school funding because of the possibility that the schools soon would be integrated. Patterson maintains today that very few state leaders seriously entertained the idea of closing public schools if they became integrated.[21] However, Charles "Pete" Mathews, a longtime legislator and lobbyist, argues that as the threat of integration intensified, legislative enthusiasm for funding public schools sharply diminished.[22]

An articulate and effective defender of segregation, John Patterson was also a liberal Democrat by firm personal belief. Outside of civil rights issues, Patterson was quite consistent in this regard, both in his election campaigning and the policies he favored as governor. His beliefs are also clearly displayed in recent personal interviews. Patterson, like many state leaders and citizens, believed in the virtues of public education. He also shared the white consensus belief that public schools would be destroyed by integration. In this view inferior black students would diminish the quality of schooling and whites would leave the public schools, thus reducing educational quality still further.

Special Legislative Sessions on Roads and Education

Before wrestling with the school funding problem, Patterson called a special legislative session on roads. He wanted road construction dollars with which to induce legislators to support other programs, including increased funding for education. According to Patterson, "A fellow hunting a bridge in the legislature—it's going to be costly for him."[23] Alabama also needed more and improved roads, and the federal government matched state appropriations by a formula highly favorable to the states. Patterson asked the legislature to approve a $60 million revenue-bond issue to be funded by a one-cent-per-gallon gasoline tax enacted during the Folsom administration. The legislature approved the bond issue without a dissenting vote.

A special session to deal with education issues was held during the recess of the regular legislative session. Patterson opened the special session on June 24, 1959, with an address in which he argued the case for schools. Even though the "dark cloud of school integration hangs heavily over our heads," he said, "we cannot afford to crawl back in a hole as far as public education is concerned. . . . We have a duty to provide the best education possible for all our people, both white and black. We must provide equal school facilities for the Negro children, but they must be segregated. . . . I am opposed to giving one penny of money to support an integrated public school."[24] Patterson was once more suggesting that if the federal government refrained from implementing integration, black schools would be significantly improved; otherwise, black schools and public education in general would be destroyed.

Basing his comments on the report of the Legislative Interim Committee on Finance and Taxation, Patterson noted that $42 million per year would be needed over and above the current spending levels for education. He recommended a four-part tax package to produce the additional revenue. He proposed a 3 percent tax on contracts over $25,000, an increase in the sales tax on automobiles from 1 to 3 percent, a reduction of the state income tax exemption for individuals from $1,500 to $1,000 and from $3,000 to $2,000 for couples, and an increase in the maximum state income tax rate on corporations from 3 to 5 percent, with the requirement that the rate be graduated on the same scale as the tax on individuals. The first two policies needed only legislative action; the latter two required legislative passage of constitutional amendments, which then would be submitted to the voters. He also asked for a $75 million bond issue for school construction ($25 million to higher education and $50 million to the public schools on a fifty-fifty match).[25] Overall, Patterson's tax package could be characterized as progressive in the sense that those with higher income would pay higher tax rates.

Patterson's bond issue for education allocated dollars among county and city school districts, junior colleges, and universities. Most education interests found the plan acceptable. The allocations had been well publicized throughout the state before the special session began in order to build public pressure on legislators. Even the typical Black Belt legislator could ill afford to oppose the bond issue when it meant voting against a new school building in his county.[26]

Because education's funding needs were so widely understood and teachers represented a lobby of substantial strength, much of the debate that followed Patterson's proposals accepted the premise that new taxes of some sort would be enacted. But the specific nature of the levies was very much open to question. By the end of its third week, the special session amounted to little more than groups positioning themselves for battle. A barrage of proposals would levy taxes on beer, liquor, cigarettes, advertising, soft drinks, and divorces, and there was continuing support for an increase in the sales tax.[27] Patterson opposed all of these taxes on the grounds that they were regressive.

Newspaper reporters and legislators sometimes described Patterson as naive in the ways of the Alabama legislature, but his actions during the special session and archival files suggest otherwise. A June 12, 1959, memorandum from Highway Director Sam Engelhardt to Patterson reads: "The attached sheet will show you or give you the names of the counties we are giving extra road money. Thought you might need this along with the hammer."[28] Copies were sent to Speaker Charles Adams and Patterson's floor leaders, Senator Vaughan Hill Robison and Representative Joe Smith. Engelhardt had orders to spend a minimum of one hundred thousand dollars in every county as a basis for building legislative support. Monies over that amount, such as these funds, were allocated to reward legislators for their assistance on specific programs.[29]

Engelhardt continued to firm support for the governor's programs by using road construction projects. A July 1, 1959, memo from the highway director provided another list of counties with which road construction arrangements had been made. Engelhardt noted, "Thought this might be beneficial to you in use of the hammer."[30]

During the education fight Patterson telephoned legislators and local community leaders such as county commissioners, board of education members, mayors, and bankers. He reminded the community leaders of how their areas would benefit from the reform package and encouraged them to call their legislators.

Borrowing from Governor Folsom, Patterson liked to make the calls after ten o'clock in the evening to give them "maximum emotional impact." He began using this tactic before the special session to encourage community leaders to pressure their legislators into cosponsoring the education legislation. After receiving a seemingly endless stream of such calls all weekend, one legislator rushed into the governor's office declaring it the worst weekend of his life. He then signed on as a cosponsor.[31]

In the fourth week of the special session the administration-dominated House Ways and Means Committee reported out a bill that called for a one-half-percent reduction in the sales and use tax, combined with the removal of approximately thirty exemptions.[32] The tax applied to everything except agricultural commodities, raw materials (interpreted as parts or ingredients in the manufacturing of products), and oil and gasoline (which had long been taxed separately for highway purposes). Patterson endorsed the bill, but it came under attack by the Alabama Chamber of Commerce, the Associated Industries of Alabama, and the Alabama Farm Bureau Federation, the three most powerful lobbying organizations in the Big Mule Alliance.[33]

The House passed the bill on July 15 by a vote of sixty-two to one. This overwhelming vote did not necessarily reflect actual legislative sentiment. It is common in the Alabama legislature for the losing side to abstain or switch to the winning side once the outcome of the vote is clear. In such instances the outcome is determined by earlier actions such as votes on amendments or apparently innocuous procedural matters.

Analysis of the fifty-one-to-forty-six vote on a procedural motion that would have delayed consideration of the bill reveals a classic Big Mule lineup opposing the tax—a majority of Black Belt and some other rural counties together with Birmingham and Mobile (fuel and supplies for ships would be taxed).[34] Although the overall pattern of these votes is predictable, several counties do not fit. We reviewed this vote with Governor Patterson in 1992 and asked him to explain it. Patterson devoted an hour to poring over vote printouts and a map depicting the voting patterns of county delegations. An analysis of road construction money flowing to some counties supplements information provided by Patterson.

During our archival search we discovered another valuable source of information about the Patterson legislature. In the 1950s the former governor Frank Dixon (1939–43) worked as a lobbyist to keep labor unions from overturning a right-to-work statute passed during the administration of Gordon Persons. Dixon maintained a card file on members of both chambers in all three legislatures of the 1950s.[35] The cards were usually incomplete only for legislators he knew well and the few about whom he could not find information. Dixon's notations contain few references to John Patterson except when individual legislators were his administration floor leaders. They characterize legislators almost entirely as for or against Folsom or as for or against labor unions. While Dixon's files focused entirely on the likelihood of an individual's favoring or opposing labor unions and the right to work, they serve as a useful check on Patterson's memory. There were no inconsistencies between the two.

In his analysis of the votes, Patterson regarded as valid the basic model of Black Belt, Jefferson County, Mobile, and south and south central rural counties' opposition to additional school funding except for support generated by highly regressive taxes. In his mind only counties that did not fit this pattern required explanation.

Twenty Big Mule and rural counties voted for the Patterson position:

Baldwin. Given Baldwin County's proximity to Mobile and its dependence on the shipping industry, one would expect its representative to side with those from Mobile and oppose the tax package. According to Patterson, however, L. W. Brannan, the Baldwin County representative, "connected politically" with the governor and tended to support him. Brannan was also a member of the Democratic party's executive committee and supported Sam Engelhardt's election as chair.

Washington (due north of Mobile). Patterson did well there in the election, but he would have predicted that it would oppose him on this vote because it was rural, and Washington County received none of the extra road construction money. Dixon's notes do nothing to clarify this vote.

Monroe (northeast of Mobile and Baldwin). Monroe County follows the same pattern as Washington, except that Patterson described the vote of Monroe County's representative Ralph Jones as a matter of principle and called Jones a "team player." Monroe County also voted for Patterson in the Democratic primary.

Escambia (east of Baldwin). Escambia was rural and would have been expected to oppose the tax, but Representative Hugh Rozelle was originally from Clay County, where Patterson had personal ties. He was a longtime friend of the governor's and had supported him in the election. Escambia also received two portions of extra highway money.

Houston (southeast corner). Houston County contained Dothan, a small city, which would make it slightly more inclined to support Patterson than the neighboring counties would have been. In addition, Charles H. Adams (not to be confused with Speaker Charles C. Adams) was a member of the Rules Committee, and Houston County received two batches of extra highway money. Dixon listed Adams as "close to Foots," meaning U.S. Senator Lister Hill's confidant Marc Ray "Foots" Clement.[36] This suggests some orientation toward education.

Crenshaw (south central, between two Black Belt counties). Crenshaw would be expected to vote against the tax, but it received one batch of highway money. According to Dixon, Crenshaw's representative, Guy Owens, was a businessman and farmer with an Alabama Farm Bureau Federation orientation, but he had served on the school board, which perhaps indicated greater than average knowledge of and sympathy for education.

Pike (Black Belt). Pike was comparable to Crenshaw in terms of county orientation and highway funds, except it is home to Troy State University. One of the county's two representatives, A. L. Boyd, served as a Patterson floor leader. Dixon's sources were divided concerning Boyd's sentiments toward right-to-work laws, even though he had been on Dixon's side in 1951. They noted that his son-in-law was a school principal.

Montgomery. Montgomery's legislators often did not vote with other Black Belters because of Montgomery's urban status and the fact that it housed many institutions that employed professionals interested in education. In addition, Joe Goodwyn, one of three Montgomery County representatives, was a strong and able advocate of education. The county also received one extra batch of highway money.

Autauga (northwest of Montgomery). One would expect this Black Belt county to vote against the tax. Representative E. A. Grouby was a personal friend of Albert Patterson, the governor's father. In addition, he sought an expensive plot of state land as a construction site for a new high school, but the county could not meet the state's price. Patterson sold the land to the school district for one dollar, and, according to Patterson, Grouby remained loyal throughout the remainder of Patterson's term. Dixon's notes characterized Grouby as "to the left. Supported by Folsom. . . . Former school teacher."

Elmore (north of Montgomery). Elmore is a rural county on the edge of the Black Belt. Patterson was on good personal terms with both Elmore representatives via his ties with Speaker Adams, and the county received two batches of highway money. Representative Leonard Johnston was, according to Dixon, "supposed to be OK" on right-to-work but also a "Folsomite."

Coosa (central Alabama). Another rural county, Coosa received no extra highway money, and Patterson had no explanation for the supportive vote. According to Dixon, the Coosa representative was very conservative.

Chilton (central Alabama). Another rural county, this one received one batch of highway money. In addition, Patterson had personal ties to Chilton County by way of his wife. Dixon identified the Chilton representative, Francis Speaks, as an attorney for the University of Alabama and a Folsomite. He ended his description of Speaks with the terse comment: "How to reach: No way."

Russell (east central). This positive vote does not look right geographically, but it was Patterson's home county.

Lee (east central). Lee's supportive vote also looks odd geographically, but Auburn University is located there, and both representatives were strong Auburn supporters. One also ran a business selling school supplies.

Sumter (Black Belt, west border). Ira Pruitt, one of the two Sumter County representatives, was a Patterson leader. Patterson described him as "an odd Black Belter." He was an Alabama Power Company attorney and a friend of the Jefferson County Big Mule leader Albert Boutwell, but he liked Patterson on a personal level and had been a friend of his father. Jesse Harvey, the other Sumter representative, was a former teacher whom Dixon described as "on the liberal side." Sumter County also received extra highway money.

Pickens (north of Sumter). Patterson had no explanation for this positive vote, and Pickens received no extra highway money. There is nothing in Dixon's notes that relates directly to education, but they list the Pickens County representative as on the union side on right-to-work.

Tuscaloosa (west of Jefferson). Home of the University of Alabama, Tuscaloosa would be expected to support the tax package, and its representatives did.

Bibb (south of Jefferson). Bibb County's representative, Virgis Ashworth, was a Patterson leader, and, according to Dixon, his wife was a teacher. Dixon also wrote: "Difficult to analyze. Rather count on our side than Folsom's, but needs indoctrination."

Lawrence (north central). Lawrence's representative had strong AEA support. This, together with its northern geographical location, outweighed the rural makeup of the county.

Etowah (northeast). Over the years Etowah County sent both extremely liberal, labor-oriented individuals and conservative Big Mules to state government. In this instance, both were in the former category. One representative wanted to be named to a state regulatory board and saw this vote as a way to ingratiate himself with the governor.

There were three votes against the tax bill that Patterson believed needed explanation:

Fayette (west of Jefferson). According to Patterson, Fayette's representative, James Branyon, was an old Folsom supporter who was never friendly to him. In addition, Fayette is a rural county and received no extra highway money.

Winston (northwest of Jefferson). Patterson could not explain this negative vote. No highway money was provided Winston County. Dixon's index card simply listed the Winston representative's name.

Lauderdale (northwest corner). Patterson was on bad personal terms with one Lauderdale representative and had a poor relationship with the other's labor union supporters. No highway money was provided Lauderdale.

Patterson's explanations, together with Dixon's notes and the road monies distributed by the Patterson administration, explain all but four counties if abstentions and splits are ignored. The closeness of the vote (fifty-one to forty-six) indicates that Patterson bought only a few more votes than he needed. It also suggests the strength of the hard core Big Mule Alliance even in the face of a public relations blitz and the entire weight of the governor's office plying counties with road construction money.

After.House passage the bill moved to the Senate. In hearings before the Senate Finance and Taxation Committee, corporate leaders appeared in force. They included Arthur V. Weibel, president of the Tennessee Coal and Iron Division of the United States Steel Corporation (Jefferson County), and William Engel, a Birmingham industrialist and chairman of a Birmingham business group called the Committee of 100. Forrest Castleberry, writing for the *Montgomery Advertiser,* characterized Weibel as the major industry leader with regard to legislative matters and remarked that his style was to avoid public settings: "As far as anyone around there now knows, it was his first appearance in the state's legislative halls."[37] Weibel and Engel argued that taxing machinery that a company needed for its manufacturing operations would have a detrimental effect on Alabama business. Hugh Comer, chairman of the board of Avondale Mills (and son of the former governor B. B. Comer), characterized the bill as a tax on money "before you earn the money." R. C. Palmer, an executive of Ingalls Iron Works and Shipbuilding Company of Decatur, and W. Cooper Green, a vice president of Alabama Power and former Birmingham mayor, also opposed the bill, as did the state's auto dealers, who were represented at the hearings.[38] It was no small matter that five senators were automobile dealers.

The business witnesses received rough treatment at the hands of Senator Ryan de Graffenried Sr. and Howell Heflin, president of the Tuscumbia school board and a member of the Alabama Education Commission. Heflin observed that Georgia, Louisiana, Arkansas, and Tennessee had sales taxes on heavy machinery, and all showed faster industrial growth than did Alabama. The Patterson-dominated Senate Finance and Taxation Committee reported out the House version virtually intact.[39]

Patterson also analyzed a critical Senate education-tax vote similar to the House vote discussed above, but space limitations do not permit a complete description of it.[40] The Senate vote consisted of the same mixture of interests and motives affecting individual votes—association with parts of the alliance, universities, public schools, or the AEA, personal animosity or friendship toward the governor, logrolling, and favors, especially in the form of highway money.

Statements concerning the incidence of taxes paid by businesses can be tentative at best, but a plausible argument can be made that the House version was less progressive than Patterson's and that the final version was less progressive than the House version. Furthermore, the final version would raise only half the revenue that Patterson's original proposals would have generated. Agriculture escaped almost unscathed. Education received more funding, but the overall result was a substantial·victory for the alliance, even though the governor applied all the resources at his disposal.

Today Patterson remembers what he calls "the education fight" with mixed feelings. He does not regret the positions he took, but he is irritated that it "required that we use every conceivable form of patronage—roads, bridges. It practically wrecked our administration—we had to forgo a lot of what we wanted to do."[41]

This alliance-managed critical decision promised little more than to maintain the education spending gap between Alabama and the nation (its actual effect will be analyzed later) while maintaining or even exacerbating the regressivity of the Alabama tax system. When property-tax equalization issues were added to the political debate, the recalcitrant alliance through its actions further ensured that the gap would not close. These decisions followed a pattern typical of many others extending back to the turn of the century.

Property Tax Equalization

In 1959 property tax assessments throughout the state were grossly unfair. A *Montgomery Advertiser* editorial observed: "No field of taxation in Alabama so abounds with inequities as the property tax. It has been possible to find land on one side of the fence assessed at 75 cents an acre, on the other at $10 an acre—with neither coming close to a reasonable assessment."[42]

In a personal interview Patterson described the case of a young couple "just starting out in life" who would buy a house assessed at 25 to 30 percent of fair market value because it had just been purchased. Their neighbors who had lived in their houses for a long time and whose houses had not been reassessed since they had been purchased would be paying property taxes that were effectively 5 percent of fair market value. Many mining, timber, and agriculture properties were also assessed at 5 percent of fair market value or even less.

The corrupt property-tax system that Patterson inherited was the accidental product of reforms carried out in 1939 by forces backing Governor Frank Dixon. The pre-Dixon reform system had property-tax review boards elected at the county level. Dixon and many others believed these bodies too inclined to maintain low assessments that provided inadequate support for school districts and municipalities.

Frank Dixon, a Jefferson County Big Mule, was an elitist in the best and worst senses of the word. He was a leader of enormous talent, imagination, and energy. For his distinguished service in World War I, the French government had awarded him the Croix de Guerre with palms and had made him a chevalier of the Legion of Honor. His background helped to make him an impressive vote getter. He first ran for governor in 1934, losing to the popular Bibb Graves by only 21,831 votes. In that campaign he advocated a program to equalize school funding that he included as part of his successful race four years later.[43] In the 1930s he led and participated in a good-government reform movement that appeared to be centered in Birmingham.[44]

Dixon's property tax assessment reform, which was introduced by Hayse Tucker of Tuscaloosa, chair of the Senate Finance and Taxation Committee and a member of the 1958 Alabama Education Commission, supplanted locally elected boards with three-person boards. These board members would be chosen by the governor from names submitted by the county commission, the county board of education, and the largest municipality in the county. Each would submit three names.

The seriousness of Dixon's intent was indicated by his support for a second proposal, which would have limited the distribution of state funds among counties to the ratio of a particular county's tax assessments to the total taxable valuation of property with the county. Such a distribution formula was intended to provide motivation to county board members to treat assessments professionally. A county that continued its old patterns would lose state money. Dixon abandoned this idea on advice from his legislative leaders, who assured him that it had no chance of passing. (In 1969 Governor Albert Brewer would advance a similar proposal.) Dixon's ideas about property tax reform received support from the Alabama League of Municipalities, education forces, and some urban Big Mule interests such as the *Birmingham News*.

The Senate voted nineteen to fourteen for Dixon's bill, although the actual division was probably more accurately shown in an earlier procedural vote of seventeen to sixteen.[45] The vote pitted much of north Alabama, centered around Jefferson County, plus Mobile and south central Alabama, against most of the Black Belt. This division looked a great deal like splits in the alliance that occurred two decades later. The bill passed the House sixty-three to thirty-four.[46] A one-sided Senate vote three weeks later had many Black Belt counties joining the majority. By this point many realized that Dixon's forces would win and that the changes would be open to manipulation.

In 1959 Revenue Commissioner Harry Haden led the Patterson campaign for property tax equalization. The revenue commissioner enjoyed considerable latitude in setting tax obligations, and true to his good government orientation, Haden created a hearing board to set liabilities in disputed cases. Chaired by the commissioner, the board consisted of senior merit-system employees. Haden believed that the board reduced the influence of politics.

The Alabama constitution required that property be assessed at 60 percent of its fair market value, but assessments were generally in the 5–15 percent range. In 1950 the Supreme Court of Alabama held that assessment at 60 percent could not be enforced because virtually no property was in fact assessed at that amount. Haden calculated that uniform assessments at 30 percent of market value would satisfy the court and would generate an additional $40–50 million per year. Higher-population counties already assessed property at levels near this rate. Their officials increasingly expressed their irritation that their counties contributed most of the tax monies to the state treasury but did not receive comparable amounts of state assistance.

Each county had a board of equalization that accepted appeals from property owners who believed that the assessments of their property were unfair. The state commissioner of revenue chose members from nominations submitted by boards of education, county commissioners, and county commissioners of revenue. Board members served four-year terms and could be removed only by impeachment. In practice the boards did little, and they almost never increased taxes, especially if a wealthy and powerful person or organization owned the property. The revenue commissioner had the authority to set aside assessments and reassessments made by county boards of equalization.[47]

Patterson actively recruited county board of equalization members who would help to implement Haden's tax equalization plan. He telephoned school board members, again using the late-night ploy, asking them to find nominees with enough fortitude to participate. Education groups and League of Municipalities members whose cities would benefit were also canvassed. Locating individuals willing to serve proved difficult because property tax increases of the magnitude advocated by Haden and Patterson generated enormous ill will, and in small towns and rural counties, revenge, including physical threats to person or property, could be rendered easily.[48]

The Haden-Patterson equalization plan had barely begun when the Senate Finance and Taxation Committee summoned Haden to testify before it. Bob Ingram provided a vivid report of what occurred:

> Haden went into painful detail citing the inequities which exist in assessments. Especially was this the case, the non-political Haden observed, in the assessing of timber land, industrial property and farms.
>
> Sen. E. O. Eddins of Marengo, like Haden a Patterson man, nearly had apoplexy. Rep. Ira Pruitt of Sumter, also a Patterson man, appeared on the verge of a stroke. . . . [Pruitt] picked up a pencil and began to do a little figuring, obviously calculating what it would cost him (and his clients) if Haden's program was carried out. When he completed his multiplying a look of sheer terror flashed across his flushed face.
>
> Haden, nobody's fool, wasn't long in sensing the effect his words were having on some of the Patterson people. But this only seemed to encourage him to new heights.
>
> Sen. Eddins finally broke in to voice a complaint. After all, he reasoned, assessments in Marengo County had been increased 106 per cent in the past 10 years.
>
> "You ought to give some credit to counties who have done a good job like that," Eddins complained.
>
> Had he been very politic Haden could have agreed to this thinking and in doing so reduce Eddins' rocketing blood pressure. But he didn't.
>
> "The assessments are still too low," Haden retorted. "I can show you instances right now in your county where some property is assessed at 3 percent of its value while other property is assessed at 30 per cent."[49]

Senator Alton Turner (Coffee, Crenshaw, and Pike), a Patterson ally who was the attorney for some large timber interests, was also vocally unenthusiastic about Haden's testimony.

In a tensely worded letter, Senator E. B. Haltom Jr. (Limestone and Lauderdale) described how Haden was applying pressure to county equalization boards to increase assessments. According to this letter, sixteen hundred assessments had been increased in the city of Florence alone.[50] If true, this would have been an enormous achievement for a program only six months old.

Bills to strip the revenue commissioner of his equalization powers were introduced in the Senate, but by Patterson's request they were locked up in the Finance and Taxation Committee. During one committee hearing, Albert Davis (a former senator from Pickens County) and other Farm Bureau speakers drew applause as they tried to characterize equalization as a power grab by the revenue commissioner. The *Montgomery Advertiser* described the scene: "Davis, his white hair cut in a senatorial sweep, pumped out his indictment in orotund language. At one point, he got carried away and addressed the committee as 'gentlemen of the jury.'"[51] His arguments had a well-used ring about them: "The power to tax is the power to destroy." "That's too much power for one man. The only man I would trust with that much power is the man who walked up Golgotha's hill." "My God, the sins that have been committed in the name of education."[52]

Anti–property tax legislators launched a filibuster that stopped the general appropriation bill. Filibuster participants included the Black Belt leader J. Roland Cooper; Walter Givhan, a veteran Farm Bureau, Citizens Council, and Black Belt power-wielder; and Bob Kendall, a frequent Black Belt supporter. While the hard core of filibusterers came from the Black Belt, the extended debate enjoyed support far beyond their ranks and included Senator Larry Dumas of Jefferson County.

The major foes of property tax equalization were rural, but Larry Dumas's active opposition, plus that of Associated Industries, individual mining companies and the Alabama Mining Institute, the Committee of 100, U.S. Steel, and Alabama Power, indicate that the alliance was still functioning. John Patterson regards this explanation as valid, saying that opposition to equalization came from a "classic Black Belt–industrial coalition (with some exceptions) with a lot of other help and little enthusiasm on our side."[53]

The Alabama League of Municipalities favored equalization, but Patterson believes that Ed Reid, the organization's politically astute head, regarded equalization as a lost cause even before the fight began and expended little effort on its behalf. "Even school people didn't support us much," Patterson says today, shaking his head in disbelief.[54]

Patterson and the anti–property tax reform group finally agreed to end the filibuster. Under the truce, as reported in newspapers, Patterson would allow the bills that would strip Haden of his equalization powers out of the Senate Finance and Taxation Committee once the regular session resumed. The actual terms of the truce were different from those made public. Patterson promised to end widespread equalization in return for the legislature's abandoning the anti-equalization bills that would have stripped the revenue commissioner (Haden) of his authority.[55]

According to Patterson, the leader who most effectively represented anti-equalization interests was Dallas County's Walter Givhan. J. Bruce Henderson, a former senator from Wilcox County, also played an important role behind the scenes. Both men had supported Patterson's gubernatorial candidacy because of his civil rights position, and both enjoyed support in Jefferson County. Givhan was always associated publicly with Black Belt agricultural interests, but he received campaign money from Jefferson County contributors even when he had no opponents.

Patterson finally gave up the fight in order to avoid damaging the revenue commissioner's authority and, less important, because he did not want to further antagonize the many legislators who opposed equalization but favored increased spending for education.[56] "It became obvious that they would win. We felt that it was better to have the power and not exercise it than not have the power. If we hadn't done this, the power would have been stripped."[57]

In describing his defeat on equalization and his partial victory on school taxation, Patterson sketched out the basic technique by which Big Mules developed long-term legislative support. A young man fresh out of law school would put up his shingle in a rural county as one of perhaps fifteen or twenty attorneys in the county. He had no business. Then a representative of Alabama Power Company would offer him a five-hundred-dollar-a-month retainer. A railroad company would offer another five hundred, an insurance company another five hundred, and so forth. Soon the young lawyer would have a steady two-thousand-dollar monthly income and have done little or nothing to earn it. Then he might get into the legislature, perhaps with additional support from his benefactors. "Do you think he will be reminded of those retainers?" Patterson asked rhetorically.[58]

Segregation and Voting Rights Issues

           The legislature continued the impassioned support of segregation that began immediately after *Brown v. Board* in 1955. For example, Senator Larry Dumas (Jefferson) sponsored a successful bill that allowed any public school to operate outside the state system. Patterson lost in his attempt to win passage of bills that would empower him to close schools threatened with integration. In stopping these bills the legislature was not acting on sudden civil-libertarian urges. The bills were opposed by segregationists who felt that they would undercut the pupil placement law crafted by Albert Boutwell in 1955.

In 1958 the U.S. Commission on Civil Rights demanded to see voter registration records in Barbour, Bullock, and Macon Counties. After much rhetorical bombast, a compromise agreement gave the federal officials access to the records.[59] The most important point conceded by the commission concerned whether registration officials could be forced to answer questions about the performance of their duties. Voting officials were supported in their refusal to testify by an Alabama law that designated them judicial officers. Their position was defended by perhaps the largest and most able legal team ever assembled in Alabama. The team of at least nine attorneys included John Patterson, former governor Chauncey Sparks, and state senator L. K. "Snag" Andrews.[60] Federal officials retreated on this point.

Responding to the federal government's intervention in the voter registration process, state senator Walter Givhan won Patterson's backing for a bill that empowered boards of registrars to destroy records of rejected voter applicants after thirty days.[61] Both chambers quickly approved the bill, and the governor signed it. Near the time he signed the Givhan bill, Patterson spoke in New Orleans. He said that federal officials and the Republican administration, having failed to integrate the South by force, had decided to register blacks to vote en masse regardless of their qualifications.[62]

A few weeks later, in a speech before the Alabama Association of Citizens Councils (with Patterson, Boutwell, and Givhan at the head table), Patterson recommended a no-compromise, no-retreat approach to the voter registration fight. He said whites should present a united front against blacks, organizing a massive white-voter registration drive and white bloc voting "against them as they do against us."[63]

The State Democratic Party
Executive Committee

Early in 1959 the executive committee of the state
Democratic party elected Highway Director Sam Engelhardt as its chairman. In an acrimonious fight, Engelhardt, Patterson's candidate, defeated
Montgomery attorney Frank Mizell Jr., a virulent segregationist, by a vote
of thirty-six to thirty-five. The losers, many of whom were Engelhardt's old
Citizens Council allies, were known as antiloyalists because of their desire
to remain uncommitted with regard to national Democratic presidential
nominees. With his newly converted loyalist in the chairmanship, Patterson crushed the candidacies of two other antiloyalists for the offices of vice
chairman and secretary.

All of this occurred after Patterson told antiloyalists in August of 1958
that he would take no part in the elections for party officers. Any governor-
elect's preference for the Democratic party head was highly influential, so
Patterson's stance was considered odd. Either because they believed him or
because they interpreted his statement as veiled support, the antiloyalists
caucused to select a slate headed by Mizell, and the executive committee
voted twenty-three to thirteen for the slate during a fall caucus. After the
initial vote all but three of the thirteen turned their support to Mizell.

In January 1959 a majority of executive committee members reaffirmed
their support for Mizell. In a letter to Patterson, Gessner McCorvey, a Dixiecrat and a former chair of the Democratic executive committee, described
Patterson's aide Charles Meriwether as "going all around the State con-
tacting members of the States' Rights, Anti-National Loyalty Oath Group
of the State Democratic Executive Committee, who are in honor bound to
support Frank J. Mizell, Jr., . . . and requesting them to violate the solemn
pledge they made to support Mr. Mizell."[64]

The *Union Labor News* took a realistic position on the fight:

Engelhardt is NO identified friend of LABOR. Nevertheless, his opponents
in this fight are the known enemies of organized labor, starting with
the notorious [*Birmingham News* columnist] John Temple Graves the
Third, and other scalawag Republicans masquerading in the Democratic party, right on down through the ranks of the Ku Klux Klan
and the NAACP—all of them are FOR Frank Mizell. . . . Most independent unions and many rank and file members including this newspaper
supported John Patterson in the campaign.[65]

Patterson favored staying with the national Democratic party because
he believed pragmatically that the state's interests could be effectively put

forward only via one of the major parties. In 1959, just two years after Eisenhower sent troops into Little Rock, he considered the Democratic party the only realistic alternative.[66] Patterson opposed Mizell because the combative and abrasive racist might encourage Alabama delegates to walk out of the 1960 Democratic national convention.[67]

There may also have been a powerfully felt personal reason for Patterson's opposing Mizell. He declared that "Mizell didn't stand up with us" at a critical juncture of the Phenix City cleanup. Mizell and five other Democratic party executive committee members had voted against voiding party nominations for corrupt Russell County officials. Patterson believed that voting fraud had been committed, among other possible crimes, and that "when we needed help more than any other time in our lives, Mizell just didn't stand up with us."[68] Some contemporary observers believed that Patterson's Russell County explanation smacked too much of a post-hoc justification for axing Mizell, but the passion in Patterson's voice three decades later as he described the Phenix City "cleanup" suggests that his feelings about Mizell's behavior were genuine.

The tacticians who engineered Patterson's executive committee victory were Fuller Kimbrell, a solid Folsomite, and Circuit Judge Roy Mayhall, an early supporter of George Wallace and sometime backer of Folsom. A great many of the antiloyalists on the committee had been Patterson supporters. They included Lukin Anderson (Escambia County campaign manager for Patterson), Alston Keith, Senator Walter Givhan, J. Bruce Henderson, and O. P. Lee. In defeating the antiloyalist slate, Patterson surprised a great many people by turning against his supporters and siding with some former opponents.[69]

Summing Up 1959

With the exception of the handling of reapportionment, 1959 can be characterized as the alliance's last year of successful, cooperative effort. Legislative voting analyses, newspaper accounts, and interviews with Patterson, Vaughan Hill Robison (Patterson's Senate leader), Dave Archer (the Senate Rules Committee chair), Bob Ingram, and Pete Mathews all contribute to a portrait of alliance dominance.

Patterson's education tax proposals were discarded and replaced by tax increases far smaller and less progressive than his original proposals. His attempts at property tax equalization were crushed. This was the last year of politics as usual as it had been practiced since the constitutional convention of 1901 that had sealed the Big Mule Alliance.

The 1960 Presidential Race

Despite his reactionary approach to civil rights, Patterson had revealed a liberal side with his support for school funding, progressive tax reform, and the defeat of the Democratic party antiloyalists. Many Alabamians believed his liberalism went too far when he became an early and avid supporter of John F. Kennedy's bid for the presidency in 1960. This was probably a major reason for his decision to take control of the Democratic party machinery.

Many considered the Massachusetts senator extremely dangerous. In an April 1959 note to Sam Engelhardt, the secretary of the Association of Citizens' Councils of Mississippi, Robert B. Patterson, wrote, "Here is the man who the South will be asked to support." He attached a copy of an editorial from the April 28, 1959, *Pittsburgh Courier* that characterized Kennedy as "on the right side and adopting the right tone" with regard to "the problems of the Negro and their relation to the future of the United States." The story noted that Kennedy advocated appointing blacks to government positions.[70] Given the close relationship between Sam Engelhardt and Governor Patterson, Engelhardt had to have been transmitting information of this sort to Patterson.

Oddly, Patterson's assistance was the second instance of Alabama support for John F. Kennedy's national aspirations. At the Democratic party's 1956 national convention, presidential nominee Adlai Stevenson threw the choice of the party's vice presidential nominee open to the convention without indicating his preference. The resulting contest quickly resolved into a fight between the extremely liberal Tennessee senator Estes Kefauver and the lesser-known Kennedy, whose father was easily as reactionary as most Alabama Big Mules and whose brother Robert had served on the staff of the Red-baiting Senator Joseph McCarthy.

Pete Mathews, who attended the convention, remembers Kennedy's sister Eunice lobbying the Alabama delegation. In an interview he nastily mimicked her harsh Boston accent, making the point that there was little real communication between the nouveau-riche northeastern Democrat and the Alabamians he described as a "bunch of rednecks." He ended the story, "And we voted for Kennedy," but then corrected himself, saying that the Alabama delegation really voted against Kefauver.[71] Many interview subjects speculated that Patterson favored Kennedy because he saw a rising star. Mathews said, "John Patterson was young and Kennedy was young . . . , and John Patterson had ambition." Some believed that Patterson identified on an emotional level with the wealthy and glamorous Kennedy.

In April 1960 the *Montgomery Advertiser*'s Grover Hall Jr. expressed his sense of presidential politics:

JP ought to be red ashamed of himself for the fraud of his assurance to Alabamians that Senator Kennedy is a pal of the South.

Like all other candidates for President, Elephant or Donkey, Kennedy is out to reform JP himself and all other Alabamians.

Kennedy said it once again in Detroit March 26:

"We have not yet secured for every American, regardless of color, his right to equal opportunity at the polls, in the classroom, in the 5-and-10-cent store, and at the lunch counter." [72]

Hall understood that Patterson could be an embarrassment to Kennedy nationally. In a June 26, 1960, editorial entitled "Kennedy Delouses Self of Dixie Ticks," he wrote: "Kennedy is beginning to handle the Governor's adoring support as a goatish intrusion." [73]

Apparently Patterson did not see himself as a tick or a goat. He and his chief aides, Charles Meriwether, Sam Engelhardt, and Engelhardt's assistant Walter Craig, actively participated in the presidential campaign. [74]

The central presidential political battleground was the selection of presidential electors and delegates to the Democratic party's national convention. With regard to the presidential electors, the fight was between loyalists who were pledged to vote in the electoral college for the Democratic nominees for president and vice president and antiloyalists who refused to commit themselves because of the likelihood that the nominee would be an enemy of the South. Central Big Mule members or their spear carriers constituted the antiloyalist slate. [75]

The loyalists made clear that they too were segregationists, but that the first priority for segregationists was to remove the Republicans from the White House. [76] Loyalist statements stressed the virtues of Democratic progressivism and presented long lists of such party accomplishments as social security, rural electrification, and the minimum wage, as well as programs that more specifically benefited Alabama, such as the Tennessee Valley Authority and the Redstone Arsenal in Huntsville. Senators Lister Hill and John Sparkman (who was running for reelection) strongly endorsed the loyalists.

Big Mules disagreed on how to deal with presidential and national politics in 1960 or whether it mattered much what they did. Grover Hall Jr. also seemed to be of two minds on the matter: "Although friendly to the spirit that motivates the revolt of the independent slate of elector candidates, *The Advertiser* has repeatedly emphasized that this undertaking is to some extent a walk in the dark. For if the independents are elected, the voters have relinquished control over the state's 11 electoral votes. . . . It should be undertaken only in highly exceptional circumstances."[77]

Hall summarized the loyalist position as a pledge to vote for the Democratic party's nominee no matter how obnoxious he might be to Alabamians. He quoted a loyalist statement: "The Republican programs of the last seven years have brought bayonets to Little Rock, sitdowns to the South and a civil rights bill through Congress, as well as high interest rates, disastrous farm programs." Hall continued: "This is uninspired, hack contention. And it would be misleading if Alabamians did not remember that Democratic leaders said they would have gone farther sooner at Little Rock; that the civil rights fuse really commenced to burning in the 1948 days of Truman; that the Democratic presidential candidate, Lyndon Johnson, is chiefly responsible for the civil rights bill."[78]

In retrospect it is easy to understand why the Big Mules were in disarray over their 1960 presidential choices. Given the information available and the events of the preceding few years, there were no good choices from their perspective.

Patterson seemed to have no difficulty picking sides. He and some of his cabinet members worked actively on behalf of loyalist candidates in the runoff. His support for the loyalists once again put him in opposition to people who had supported him for governor and in league with former opponents. The antiloyalist, or states' rights slate as it came to be called, ran ahead in the first primary. Only one elector candidate, antiloyalist J. Bruce Henderson, was elected in the first primary without a runoff.[79] The runoff produced six victories for loyalists and four for states' righters, resulting in a total of five states' rights electors.

With regard to the Democratic party convention, there was little clarity until nearly the time of the primary. Originally, Patterson claimed that he would take no part in delegate selections, but behind the scenes he distributed a list of preferred candidates. The list included

Charles Belew of Fairhope, who spent money in 1958 for Patterson; John F. Britton, a right-voting member of the State Democratic Executive Committee and a Patterson appointee to the Prison Board; Fred Davis of Centreville, chief of Patterson's military staff; A. F. (Dick) DeVan of Mobile, the first state Committee member to switch from Mizell to Engelhardt a year ago; Joe Elliott of Decatur, another state committee member who voted right; Ed Estes of Gadsden, one of the biggest Pattersonites; E. C. (Sonny) Hornsby, a '58 campaign worker and honorary colonel; PSC member Ralph Smith, ex-cabinet member, appointed to the PSC by Patterson, etc; Newt Rains, a relative of Mrs. Ralph Smith and, ironically, as big a Patterson man today as he was a Folsom man in the past. There are some others on the list for reasons not so well known—Frank E. Dixon (not the ex-gov); Raymond Weeks, J. C. Henderson of the Alex City Outlook, Secretary of State Bettye Frink, Waymon Benson of East Tallasee and Robert H. King of Gadsden.[80]

Everyone assumed that the chairman of the delegation would be Attorney General MacDonald Gallion. In yet another last-minute move, Patterson intervened the day before the vote and practically forced the election of Probate Judge T. C. "Cliff" Almon of Decatur instead.[81] Patterson also pushed for maximum support for Kennedy at the convention.

When Kennedy was nominated, despite a strong Democratic civil rights plank, Patterson worked for his election.[82] Patterson even campaigned for him out of state,[83] and he and Charles Meriwether collected money for the Kennedy campaign, often personally delivering cash to Kennedy in brown paper sacks. According to Patterson, neither he nor the state gained anything from his support for Kennedy, and he withstood considerable abuse for his support.[84]

Kennedy's selection of Lyndon Johnson as his vice-presidential nominee did little to assuage the anger of states' righters about the civil rights plank and Kennedy's efforts to distance himself from the South.[85] Even those states' righters who had favored Johnson as the presidential nominee did so only out of desperation. But Alabamians and the South as a whole were not inclined toward a systematic, organized revolt against the Democratic party nominee.[86]

A political scientist named Donald Strong published a pamphlet before the 1960 elections entitled "Urban Republicanism in the South."[87] In it he described voting studies that indicated that Deep South cities showed signs of splitting from the Democratic party. Strong concluded that both Eisenhower elections (1952 and 1956) represented "an early step in a long-run trend toward an enduring presidential Republicanism accompanied by a lesser grass-roots variety."[88] But, he accurately added, this development did not foretell "the speedy growth of a full-fledged Republican party that will run candidates from governor down to sheriff."

Strong argued that the Democratic party would remain dominant because southern opposition to the national party leadership did not translate into opposition to state and local Democrats. Furthermore, even Democratic officeholders who voted for Eisenhower wanted no Republican competitors at the state and local levels.

The 1960 Republican state convention nominated virtual political unknowns for the U.S. Senate and for president of the Public Service Commission. Only two candidates were nominated for the state's nine congressional seats. The Republican party lag continued.

The Alliance's Last Good Year

John Patterson tried to restructure a grotesquely unfair property tax valuation system. Had he succeeded, primary and secondary school funding and educational quality might have vastly improved, and property tax equity certainly would have been achieved.

The Big Mules' evisceration of the Patterson reforms resulted from a congruence of Black Belt and other rural interests with those of Jefferson and Mobile businesses. Two years after the events described here the Big Mule Alliance flew apart over congressional redistricting and legislative reapportionment. Even if the occurrences of 1959 and 1961 had been reversed in time, it is doubtful whether significantly improved education funding or any property tax equalization would have been achieved. Few changes in the underlying interests of the alliance partners would develop in the 1960s. All that would occur would be a surprisingly small shift in the balance of their formal legislative powers because of reapportionment.

5

The Alliance in Disarray

A malapportioned legislature was one of the cornerstones of the alliance's power. Although the 1901 Alabama constitution required reapportionment every ten years and charged the legislature with this responsibility, no reapportionment occurred. Black Belt legislators and those from Jefferson County and other industrial centers controlled approximately one-half of the votes in both chambers, and this partnership repelled all reapportionment attempts over the years.

Black Belt legislators were highly unified and well organized. They came largely from one- or two-county districts, and many returned to Montgomery year after year, developing a mastery of procedural rules and experience in legislative maneuvering.

North Alabama legislators represented more diverse interests. They divided along urban and rural lines as well as varied economic interests. North Alabama House legislative districts tended to include two or three counties, and some Senate districts contained four or five counties. Many districts followed informal rotation agreements that produced perpetually inexperienced legislators who stood little chance against parliamentary veterans from the Black Belt.

Jefferson County stood apart from north Alabama. The Jefferson legislative delegation worked with the Black Belt to block tax and education reforms and maintain the status quo economically. The delegation undertook little in the way of policy initiatives, concentrating instead on the passage of local legislation. Jefferson County representatives were financed and hand picked by the major business interests in the county.

One reapportionment attempt was championed by Governor Frank Dixon, a Big Mule from Jefferson County, in 1939. Dixon was part of a Big Mule "good government" reform movement centered in Jefferson County in the 1930s. It shared with many similar urban-based movements around the country a desire to achieve reapportionment.

Dixon's proposal (HB10) contained a powerful enforcement mechanism. It provided that if the legislature failed to reapportion itself in the session immediately following publication of the results of each decennial national census, the task would be taken over by a board consisting of the governor, secretary of state, and attorney general. Both chambers would be reapportioned on a one-person-one-vote basis to the degree possible with districts that were compatible with county lines.[1] Had the bill been enacted and implemented, the Alabama legislature would have been the closest in the country to the one-person-one-vote standard.

The major push for HB10 came after passage of a sweeping Dixon-backed reorganization of the executive branch and passage of the controversial property tax equalization bill described in the previous chapter. Reapportionment received a cooler reception. According to the *Birmingham News,* some of Dixon's own legislative leaders refused to support it.[2]

HB10 was defeated sixty to thirty-one. The winners were a coalition of Black Belt and rural counties. Urban counties tended to support reapportionment, but Montgomery County opposed the bill. A Senate vote to postpone the bill followed a similar pattern. Jefferson, Mobile, Houston (Dothan), and most north Alabama counties voted against postponement (that is, for the bill) or did not vote.

The alliance again repulsed reapportionment in 1947 and 1949, when it opposed Governor James E. Folsom Sr.'s modest proposals to give each county one senator.[3] Even an imperfectly reapportioned state government under Folsom promised to be overtly hostile to Big Mule interests. The threat from Folsom's policies drew the alliance's members back together.

The alliance's solidarity continued in Folsom's second term. On January 18, 1956, the Senate defeated reapportionment by a vote of eighteen to fifteen.[4] On February 3, 1956, a House vote of seventy-four to twenty-three passed a constitutional amendment that drastically increased the size of the legislature. A peculiar coalition of Black Belt and Folsom administration supporters backed this proposal. Essentially, Folsom and his people wanted any reapportionment bill, and the Black Belters feared being blamed for opposing progress, especially when there was no chance that the amendments would be passed by the electorate. The Senate killed the bill.

Reapportionment Attempts in 1959

One of the earliest mentions of reapportionment in John Patterson's term came in June 1959. While Senator Roland Cooper of Black Belt Wilcox County filibustered against property tax equalization,

Patterson remarked, "The people who are filibustering are the greatest advertisement for reapportionment. When a handful of people can stall the state government, something should be done. Reapportionment is the best answer."[5]

Four months later, Patterson launched a reapportionment fight in the House Judiciary Committee over a bill sponsored by Bert Haltom and supported by the administration. It included a 40-member Senate and 120-member House. On three separate votes, the ordinarily administration-controlled committee split six to six.[6]

Supporters of the measure came largely from north Alabama. Three representatives from urban areas voted against it. Senator Hugh Locke, a Jefferson County Big Mule, attempted to justify his opposition by saying that the bill did not create a pure one-person-one-vote reapportionment. He added that he also feared that the bill would prompt a fight that would jeopardize other legislation.

The lineup of counties looked different on an important House floor procedural vote concerning reapportionment in 1959. Thirty-four Black Belt representatives voted against reapportionment, two voted for it, and six abstained or were absent. All the representatives from Jefferson County voted for reapportionment. The three Mobile representatives split their votes three ways: for, against, and abstaining. This vote did not signal a divorce of Black Belt, Birmingham, and Mobile interests, but it was an indication of growing divisions over reapportionment. On most other concerns, such as sales tax increases and race, most Black Belt representatives joined with every Jefferson County and Mobile representative in opposition.

Reapportionment Strategy in 1961

Traditionally, attempts to reapportion the legislature involved the introduction of constitutional amendments. But in 1961 several lawmakers argued that since the legislature had a constitutional obligation to reapportion itself, reapportionment could be enacted by statute, a relatively easy method that required only a simple majority vote of each chamber and no popular referendum.

Since the constitution fixed the size of the House and Senate and guaranteed at least one representative per county, the statutory approach required restructuring district boundaries. Black Belt legislators opposed statutory reapportionment, for it would not only decrease their relative strength in each house because of the declining population base in their counties, it would also force incumbents into the same districts. Most proposals to achieve reapportionment through constitutional amendment increased the number of legislators in the more populous counties while leaving district boundaries intact. Such boundaries followed county lines and therefore did not pit incumbents against each other.

There was another reason Black Belters considered the constitutional-amendment approach less objectionable. Constitutional amendments required passage by an extraordinary majority in each house, and Black Belt legislators and their allies generally commanded enough votes to stop such amendments outright. Even if their efforts to block passage failed, constitutional amendments faced a second hurdle, a popular vote. With their resources, restrictions on voter registration, and manipulation of vote counts in rural counties, they often controlled such referendums.

The Tennessee reapportionment case *Baker v. Carr*, which was before the U.S. Supreme Court, added another dimension to Alabama's reapportionment politics. It raised the issue of whether qualified voters in a state had a legal right to challenge state legislative reapportionment that failed to give them equal protection under the law.

In 1961 forces favoring reapportionment shifted their attack from the Judiciary Committee to the House Constitutions and Elections Committee and successfully gained approval of three bills. Representative Albert Brewer, a north Alabama advocate of reapportionment, moved to permit the committee to report the legislation out of order. This would allow the reapportionment bills to get ahead of many others that were competing for attention at the end of the session. His motion lost.[7]

This vote came after alliance members had eviscerated Patterson's efforts to equalize property taxes and had totally rewritten his school tax proposals. It signaled the beginning of breakdown in the Big Mule Alliance; north Alabama, including Birmingham and Etowah County, *and* Mobile County voted for reapportionment. Of the state's large city delegations, only Montgomery's representatives voted against reapportionment. Black Belt and other rural mid-state counties lined up against northern and urban counties.

Complicating reapportionment politics, Alabama lost one congressman as a result of the 1960 census. The legislature had to produce a redistricting plan or run statewide at-large congressional elections in 1962. Black Belt legislators had a stake in preventing at-large congressional elections. More than 50 percent of the state's population lived in Jefferson County and north Alabama. In at-large elections these counties had the potential to elect all eight congressmen, leaving the Black Belt without congressional representation. Before the 1961 legislative session, Black Belt legislators threatened to filibuster any reapportionment measure, but they wanted congressional redistricting. North Alabama legislators threatened to filibuster congressional redistricting unless a satisfactory reapportionment measure passed.[8]

Other political concerns were tied to congressional redistricting. By law many state commissions and boards, including university boards of trustees and the state Democratic executive committee, were organized on the basis of congressional districts.

The Speaker's Vote

The first order of business in the May 1961 House was the election of a Speaker to replace Speaker Adams, who had been named a judge. The constitution required election by a voice vote, with fifty-three votes needed for election. By custom the governor named his choice, and that candidate usually won without difficulty. In 1961 there were two contenders, Virgis Ashworth (Bibb), the Speaker pro tempore and Governor Patterson's choice, and Albert Brewer (Morgan). Brewer stressed the need to establish a speakership independent of gubernatorial influence and to return legislative power to the legislative branch.

As testimony to his continuing importance in a legislative liaison role, Sam Engelhardt received major responsibility for organizing the vote. In a January 29, 1960, letter to Patterson, he described a typical mixture of opportunists and Patterson loyalists:

> In accordance with your instructions to call certain men regarding Virgis Ashworth for Speaker and Ira Pruitt for Speaker Pro Tem, I would like to report the following:
>
> Barnett of Perry will let me know
> Bevill—yes
> Brannan—yes
> Brewer—no. He doesn't think Ashworth will be fair.
> Camp—will vote for Ashworth if we build a $150,000 bridge and 20
>   miles of roads. I would like to say that our budget will not stand this.
> Dickson—yes. Will vote for anybody the Governor wants.
> Gilmer—yes
> Hardy—yes
> Long of Perry will let me know
> McLendon of Bullock—probably, but wants to talk to the Governor
> Mead—yes

Nettles—wants to talk to Ashworth

Oakley—yes

Owens—will let me know. Would rather have Pruitt, but in the end will
vote with the majority.[9]

A motion to recess served as a test vote. Brewer sought a recess to call
a Democratic caucus and hold a secret-ballot election in the caucus.[10] The
recess motion failed sixty-three to forty-one. After the test vote several
representatives jumped to the winning side, increasing Ashworth's election margin to eighty-two to twenty-two.[11] Brewer attributed his loss to
pressure from the governor. He argued that twenty-four of his forty-six
pledged votes deserted to Ashworth in return for gubernatorial promises of
bridges and roads.[12] Clear regional divisions were not evident in the vote,
but Brewer's north Alabama base was stronger than Ashworth's.[13]

Survival of the Fittest

The law of the jungle applied in the 1961 Alabama
legislature. Given the loss of a congressional district, it would have been
safe to predict that the district to be eliminated would be the weakest in
some sense. A district occupied by a congressman about to retire would be
a prime candidate for elimination, but Alabama had none in that category.
The next most likely to be eliminated would be the district of a freshman,
and Congressman George Huddleston of Jefferson County's District 9 was
a freshman. Another possibility would be to target a lawmaker who had
fallen from public favor. Congressman Kenneth Roberts was probably the
least popular Alabama representative in 1961.

Governor Patterson's opening message to the legislature decried the
legislature's failure to reapportion itself and pointed to recent evidence that
the federal courts would step in and take action. Patterson outlined the
administration-sponsored reapportionment bill. It raised the Senate membership from 35 to 40 and House membership from 105 to 120. Patterson
characterized the measure as giving more populous counties the greater
representation they deserved while protecting the interests of rural areas.
If the legislature failed to reapportion itself, he challenged it to give the
people the right to vote on whether they wanted a constitutional convention
to accomplish the task. The governor said very little about congressional
redistricting.[14]

Patterson's proposal gave Jefferson County eleven House members compared to its current seven. Since Jefferson County had one-fifth of the state's

population, it was entitled to one-fifth of the House membership, or twenty-four seats. And Jefferson County received the same Senate representation as Houston County, even though their 1960 populations were 634,864 and 50,718 respectively.

The Black Belt response to Patterson's proposal came quickly.[15] Following Hugh Locke's example, the Black Belt focused on the fact that the Patterson plan did not follow constitutional guidelines requiring apportionment based on population—this after spending a half century violating the Alabama constitution's reapportionment requirements. According to Representative M. D. Gilmer (Dallas): "The governor's reapportionment bill is just an arbitrary thing. It does not go according to the constitutional requirement of apportioning according to population." And Senator E. O. Eddins (Marengo) noted piously: "The governor's reapportionment bill is not adjusted to population. If the governor's bill was in line with the Constitution it wouldn't be necessary to submit it to the people. They want reapportionment, but everybody wants to reapportion to suit their own tastes."[16]

Meanwhile, two bills became the major focus of House debate with regard to congressional redistricting. HB1, sponsored by E. A. "Bud" Grouby (Autauga) and others, affected the southern part of the state (Districts 2 and 3). Congressmen George Grant of Troy and George Andrews of Union Springs were placed in the same district. Not surprisingly, the bill had the support of northern representatives.

HB244, sponsored by Representative Ferguson and others, combined two northern districts (4 and 5). It pitted Congressman Albert Rains of Gadsden against Congressman Kenneth Roberts of Anniston. The bill received widespread support from Black Belt and southern representatives. On the second legislative day Senator Walter Givhan (Dallas) and several Black Belt cosponsors introduced the Senate version of the Ferguson redistricting plan.

The governor's reapportionment plan (HB129) was also introduced on the first legislative day.[17] It had strong north Alabama support. Senator Haltom (Lauderdale) later introduced a similar bill in the Senate. Haltom's bill came to dominate most of the reapportionment debate.

The press reported strong support for the Ferguson-Givhan redistricting bill. Bob Ingram of the *Montgomery Advertiser* indicated that the House bill had forty-three signatures (ten short of a majority) and eleven cosponsors in the Senate, only seven votes away from a majority.[18]

Ingram described the Ferguson-Givhan legislation as "a relief bill for Congressmen Armistead I. Selden and Carl Elliott." He noted that Elliott took an active but behind-the-scenes part in drafting the legislation and that a Selden staffer was "mistaken several times during the past week as Ferguson's shadow. He's here and busy."[19]

A *Birmingham News* reporter, Charlie Grainger, wrote that Ferguson openly declared his interest in protecting Selden's seat. (Ferguson and Selden were both from Tuscaloosa.) Grainger argued that survival of the Grouby plan depended on support from the Montgomery delegation, since the plan shifted Montgomery County into the Fourth Congressional District.[20] The delegation basically supported the Ferguson-Givhan plan.

A May 5 *Birmingham News* editorial characterized the congressional redistricting battle as a simple power struggle between two groups having small but significant liberal-conservative differences on some but by no means all issues.[21] It identified Rains, Roberts, Elliott, and Jones as the liberal block and Boykin, Andrews, Grant, and Selden as the conservatives. Congressman Huddleston of Jefferson County (District 9) was a swing man who tended toward a conservative voting pattern.

According to the editorial, the Ferguson plan targeted Roberts's district for two reasons: his support for President Kennedy's plan that realigned House Rules Committee membership in order to ease the movement of civil rights legislation to the House floor, and the "wandering" nature of his district. Roberts's district extended from St. Clair County (bordering Jefferson County) to Dallas County in the Black Belt. It contained so many voters with opposing political views that it was an easier redistricting target than the more homogeneous districts. The Ferguson-Givhan bill placed Dallas County in the Sixth District, where it was more at home economically and politically. The editorial also noted that Etowah County might be physically closer to Jefferson County, but that philosophically it was closer to Dallas County.[22]

It was conceivable that the relationship between legislative reapportionment and congressional redistricting could have taken the form of an even distribution of pain. Thus, with stable factions facing each other (for example, north versus south Alabama), one group could have taken a reapportionment loss and the other a redistricting setback. However, Black Belters believed that if they could control the timing of the two issues, they would be able to manipulate the votes from the North and South and win on both bills.

North Alabama representatives wanted reapportionment voted on before redistricting. They believed that once south Alabama achieved redistricting, north Alabama would no longer have any leverage to force compromise on reapportionment. The north Alabama effort received support from

Fourth Congressional District representatives, who feared passage of the Ferguson bill because it eliminated their district.

South Alabama and Black Belt legislators viewed the makeup of the congressional delegation as crucial to their social and economic survival. Their congressional representatives held key committee positions. Combining or eliminating their districts could affect civil rights legislation and agricultural policy, because new members would have no seniority and thus no clout. And many viewed north Alabama as too liberal on economic matters. Reapportionment of the state legislature would also assist north Alabama more, because south Alabama and Black Belt counties tended to be less populous. Thus, alliance representatives could play on regional fears to achieve their own ends.

There followed weeks of jockeying for position in both chambers with regard to both redistricting and reapportionment.[23] The entire repertoire of legislative tricks was applied, including subtle amendments, timing, and filibusters.

Chop-Up

On the ninth legislative day (May 30), Representative John Guthrie of Cullman County (James E. Folsom Sr.'s adopted north Alabama home) introduced a redistricting bill (HB653) that came to be known as Chop-Up. It divided Jefferson County into four sections and placed each section in a different existing congressional district. The bill was sent to the House Judiciary Committee.[24]

The existence of the plan was known well before its introduction. At first Jefferson County legislators refused to take it seriously. Senator Larry Dumas described the bill as "a jest." He seemed to have faith in the legislature's ability to recognize that Jefferson County was entitled to its separate congressional seat and in fact deserved two seats, not one.[25] Echoing Dumas, a *Birmingham News* editorial dismissed the Guthrie plan as "tom foolery."[26]

According to Guthrie, the Chop-Up bill had several positive features. First, Jefferson County, which then controlled one congressional seat, would share in the selection of four congressmen, which would help the county in the long run.[27] Today Albert Brewer dismisses this argument, saying that the real effect would be to ensure that Jefferson had no decisive voice in any of the districts.[28] Second, Jefferson County was voting Republican in presidential races and offered that party an organizational base in the state. Diluting the area's impact on congressional decision-making would weaken the Republican threat and thereby strengthen the Democratic party at a time when states' rights Democrats and loyalist Democrats weakened the party by competing for control.[29] This second argument was inconsistent with the first: if Jefferson County was strengthened by Chop-Up, it could not also be weakened. Third, Congressman George Huddleston of the Ninth District was the only freshman in the Alabama delegation. Guthrie portrayed the elimination of his district as an equitable way to handle the loss of a seat. To Jefferson County legislators and residents, Guthrie's rationales were just a coverup for attempts to dilute Jefferson County's power and influence.

At the beginning of legislative day eleven (June 6), supporters of the Ferguson redistricting bill (HB244) and the Haltom reapportionment bill (HB129) seemed to gain a small advantage with a favorable House Rules Committee report. Supporters and opponents of the two bills jockeyed for position throughout the day.[30] Finally, fourteen representatives (Albea, Smith of St. Clair, Cabiness, Hanby, Meade, Hardaway Johnson, Leonard Johnston, Grouby, Harris, Vickers, Camp, Casey, McClendon of Chambers, and Ingram) offered a variant of the Guthrie Chop-Up plan. It structured the districts differently but also divided Jefferson County into four parts, placing each section in a separate congressional district. A motion to table the new amendment passed, sixty to thirty-one.[31]

During the floor debate Albert Brewer argued that the bill would give control of the Democratic party to the Dixiecrats, "whose political philosophies are as Republican as Tricky Dick Nixon." He charged that the Democratic executive committee would include sixty-four members from just three north Alabama counties. He told the House that passing the bill would "do more harm to the Democratic Party in Alabama than all the walkouts and independent electors could ever do." Brewer also argued that the Alabama congressional delegation, working against the governor, had established "devious schemes in dark corners."[32]

Tempers ran high during the debate. Representative Broadfoot charged Congressman Boykin with engineering the bill and called it a snake. He then pulled out a live snake to illustrate his point. Representative Albea claimed the bill represented an "unholy alliance." Gilchrist warned the representatives from Jefferson County and the Fifth and Seventh Congressional Districts that if they passed the Ferguson-Givhan bill "you've lost your chances for any reapportionment bill."[33]

On the twenty-sixth legislative day, Senator Larry Dumas offered an amendment to the special order calendar report that put three reapportionment bills at the top of the calendar. The bills included those written by Senators de Graffenried (Tuscaloosa) and Caffey (Mobile). They kept the current House and Senate numbers and reshuffled districts to the disadvantage of Black Belt and rural counties.[34]

Dumas proposed the changes in the special rule because such an amendment required only a majority vote. His amendment also shifted the emphasis to reapportionment. Rural south Alabama senators joined Black Belt senators in a move to stop reapportionment and focus on redistricting. They were willing to filibuster the Dumas motion.

Ferguson-Givhan proponents believed that the Jefferson County delegation had agreed to support their bill partly as a way to stop Chop-Up and that Dumas's action broke the agreement. They further believed that by emphasizing reapportionment over redistricting, Dumas and Jefferson County wanted it all, because if redistricting efforts failed, the at-large election process would still favor that most populous county in the state. Proponents also knew that there was little chance of breaking the filibuster.

Chop-Up Takes Hold

Ferguson-Givhan opponents used Dumas's move as a wedge to open the way to build an alliance with counties outside Jefferson. In addition to protecting their own counties, these legislators wanted redistricting, not at-large elections. And many wanted to end the filibuster and return to routine activities such as budgeting.

Chop-Up was a perfect mechanism through which north and south Alabama gained most of what they wanted. Since the bill eliminated the Ninth Congressional District (Jefferson County), the other districts were protected. And it punished "Imperial Jefferson," as Black Belters and many in north Alabama called the county, for its attempt to manipulate the legislative process.

The actual compromise (backed by two-thirds of the Senate) called for adoption of the Rules Committee's special order placing reapportionment, redistricting, and the appropriations bills at the top of the calendar in that order. Then Chop-Up, with minor changes granted in exchange for voting support, would be introduced as a substitute for Ferguson-Givhan when that bill came up for a vote. The changes reduced the number of Jefferson County residents in Congressman Selden's district and moved Dallas County from the Fourth to the Sixth Congressional District and Chambers County from the Fourth to the Third.[35]

When word of the agreement became known, a new filibuster erupted. It was led by Senators Dumas (Jefferson), de Graffenried (Tuscaloosa), and

Haltom (Lauderdale) with brief assistance from Senators Caffey (Mobile) and Archer (Madison).[36] Chop-Up supporters acted to grind down the filibustering members by voting to adjourn the August 3 session at midnight and then reconvening the Senate immediately.

Senator Dumas threatened to filibuster until the end of the legislative session if necessary. He accused the former governor James E. Folsom Sr. (to whom Guthrie was very close) of pushing the Chop-Up compromise, saying, "Folsom conceived of the bill as a spite measure against Jefferson for the poor showing he has made there during his two successful campaigns for governor."[37] He argued that former senator Neil Metcalf (Geneva), another Folsom supporter, played a key role in the compromise and that Folsom planned to run for reelection in 1962 and had made phone calls to legislators in an effort to increase the opposition to Ferguson-Givhan.[38] Dumas also reminded the public that Senator L. K. Andrews, an active member of the compromise group, was Congressman Andrews's brother and claimed that the congressman played a key role in the decision-making.

John Guthrie has denied that Folsom played any part in writing the bill or achieving the compromise and claims that Folsom's participation was limited to giving tactical advice.[39] North Alabama legislators were notorious for in-fighting and their inability to maintain a cohesive front. As a result, Folsom told Guthrie to avoid cosponsorship of the legislation. Co-sponsors would, he felt, inevitably jump off the bill when pressures were applied. In addition, lawyers would be especially vulnerable to offers of retainer fees from the Birmingham corporations.[40] Folsom also advised backers of the bill to pay off loans from Jefferson County banks and warned that banks, the power company, Birmingham newspapers, and other interests would direct their lobbying efforts against them.

Guthrie received reports of pressure directed at the bill's backers, including warnings from Birmingham-based friends that supporters traveling through Jefferson County would be carefully watched for legal violations, especially traffic, as a means of embarrassing and discrediting them. Birmingham-based distributors called on their agents to pressure them to lobby their representatives to vote against the bill. The agents received implied threats of supply problems should they fail to act. There were direct threats and reports of individuals trying to provoke fights and other confrontations.[41]

On August 4, after seventy-eight hours of continuous debate and in a state of exhaustion, the three filibustering senators agreed to a compromise. Senator Dumas offered an amendment to the special order calendar that placed Ferguson-Givhan (HB244), reapportionment (SB1), and appropriations legislation, in that order, at the top of the calendar. His amendment passed. In return, Chop-Up supporters agreed that the Senate would hold the bill for one week before sending it to the House. This would give Jefferson County forces time to organize.[42]

Ferguson-Givhan came to the floor for a vote, and Senator Cooper offered the Chop-Up bill as an amendment. It passed, twenty-nine to six, with Senators Berryman, Caffey, de Graffenried, Dumas, Haltom, and Wilson voting no.[43] The vote for the Haltom reapportionment bill was seventeen to fifteen.[44] Since twenty-one votes were needed for passage, reapportionment was dead in the Senate. Later House action also blocked reapportionment.

As agreed, Chop-Up sat in the Senate for the next week. Since the Ferguson bill had passed the House and the Chop-Up bill had passed the Senate as a substitute for it, the House faced three options: accept the change; reject it but accept creation of a House/Senate conference committee; or accept neither the bill nor a conference committee and thereby kill the legislation.

During the one-week recess, the press reported that a plan proposed as a House Judiciary minority report weeks before might serve as a compromise to Chop-Up. Generally called the "9-8 plan," it required Democratic and Republican primary nomination of one congressional candidate in each of the nine existing districts followed by at-large statewide run-off elections four weeks later to select the eight nominees for the general election ballot. The advantages cited for the plan were that incumbents would be the major candidates, that the procedure would be less objectionable than at-large elections, and that the 1963 legislature could deal with the issue when personalities were removed from the problem. The Jefferson County delegation, and Senator Dumas in particular, pushed the plan as a way to prevent Chop-Up.[45]

On a special edition of a Birmingham public affairs broadcast, Representative Perry called Chop-Up "a product of a defeated Black Belt who couldn't get their own bill and a foolish Fourth District who even while they were making this obscene alliance with the Black Belt got outfigured." Representative Turner saw a positive aspect to the Black Belt action: "If there is anything good that can come out of this legislation it is that the alliance between the Black Belt and Jefferson County is forever dead. I honestly believe that before this fight is over Jefferson County will find where its true friends are—from the populous areas of this state and in north Alabama."[46]

A front page *Birmingham News* editorial blasted Chop-Up as a Black Belt and small-county defensive tactic, claiming:

The future of Jefferson County, its welfare, its political entity, its ability to continue as a good, strong force for all Alabama welfare is at stake on the Senate floor in Montgomery today.

The situation is of maximum seriousness. Senate forces have nakedly cut loose from the Ferguson-Givhan "get-Roberts" bill to sink Jefferson. They are dangerous. They plan to put a new and heavy burden on this county and its people.

There is not time to lose. Jefferson leadership and rank and file must do whatever they can to make their anger known. Here are legislators once more trying to use Jefferson as a legislatively weak pigeon to be plucked. . . .

The matter is of absolute maximum seriousness. Jefferson County is about to be pilloried unless the wisest and most emphatic action is taken to bring to the for front of all Alabama legislators' minds the horrors which could emerge from this legislative Pandora's box, the disunity in the state, the weakening in a multitude of ways of the keystone county of the State of Alabama.[47]

Governor Patterson confined his public responses to Chop-Up to statements opposing at-large congressional elections. He described such contests as "a very unwieldy and unsatisfactory way of electing our congressmen. There would be upwards of 100 candidates in the race, there would be smear campaigns, and it would be too expensive."[48]

The Jefferson County delegation, Birmingham elected officials, and Jefferson County–based organizations actively lobbied House members. Jefferson County representatives focused their efforts on north Alabamians. Labor groups were especially active but often working for, not against, Chop-Up. The head of the AFL-CIO's Political Education Committee in Alabama argued that Chop-Up would increase labor's access to and assistance from the Alabama congressional delegation.[49]

The head of the Birmingham Bar Association promised a federal court fight, if necessary. Claiming that such a fight would lead to reapportionment of the state legislature, he said:

If the senators from the Black Belt and other parts of Alabama succeed in destroying Jefferson County as a congressional district . . . it is absolutely certain that an attack will be made in federal court questioning the constitutionality of the redistricting bill by reason of the failure of the legislature to put in reapportionment since the Constitution of 1901.

And it seems to be certain that this will bring federal reapportionment, which no one wants.[50]

House debate on the Chop-Up substitute for Ferguson-Givhan began on August 11. An early procedural vote demonstrated that Chop-Up supporters enjoyed a fifty-seven-to-forty-seven majority. When Chop-Up opponents realized the weakness of their position, they began a filibuster and also attempted to get the House to adjourn. Supporters of the bill held back numerous adjournment attempts. The speaker called the session to an end at 11:59 P.M. and then immediately reconvened the House. Finally, in the twenty-first hour of the filibuster, a cloture motion passed (fifty to forty-three) and ended debate.[51] By a vote of fifty-six to thirty-nine, the House finally accepted Chop-Up as a substitute for the Ferguson-Givhan bill.[52]

Jefferson County forces then turned their attention to persuading the governor to veto the legislation. Business and legal interests in Birmingham mounted an all-out campaign for the veto, as did the Birmingham press. The *Birmingham News* charged that Congressmen Andrews, Roberts, Selden, and Elliott were in close touch with those advocating Chop-Up and that representatives of Congressmen Boykin, Grant, and Jones were working on their behalf.[53] A *News* analysis of the House vote showed that members from Congressman Andrews's district voted solidly against Jefferson County and that the key figure in the district was the congressman's brother, a state senator. The strongest support for the county came from Congressman Rains's district; the others were split, with Grant's and Elliott's districts largely for Chop-Up and the other districts more evenly divided.[54]

The *News* claimed Governor Folsom was working behind the scenes against Jefferson County and noted that "by design or accident" Folsom was in a Montgomery hotel the night before the House vote and that several legislators close to him voted against Jefferson County on all the key Chop-Up votes. The newspaper also charged that the "Black Belt high command was gunning for Jefferson."[55]

Charlie Grainger's analysis of the situation reminded Jeffersonians that it was largely representatives of the urban and northern counties that stood by them. He quoted a north Alabama ally, Albert Brewer, who welcomed Jefferson County "into its true geographical area—the political alliance of North Alabama." Brewer called the Jefferson County–Black Belt alliance "sixty years of marriage of the Imperial Queen and a scoundrel."[56]

On August 14, 150 business and civic leaders met in Birmingham to discuss Chop-Up tactics. They argued that the bill sent a message to industry that said Alabama's political climate was unfriendly to business and industry. Letters and telegrams sent to the governor to urge a veto of the legislation expressed similar sentiments.[57]

The columnist Hugh Sparrow claimed that Chop-Up supporters misled

House members when they argued that legislators in other states had chopped up and divided big congressional districts. Sparrow wrote that a check of the *Congressional Directory* for 1960 showed no large populous area divided as Jefferson County had been. Some areas had a divided district but had a district of their own as well; other cities had more than one district within their boundaries. A few areas extended beyond the boundaries of one county, sharing districts with those areas. Sparrow concluded that Chop-Up was the first time on record that a county with population great enough to have one or two congressmen of its own had been divided.[58]

Various Jefferson County groups and the Birmingham press urged county residents to flood the governor's office with letters and telegrams calling for a veto. Opponents of the legislation from other counties pushed their followers to join the letter-writing campaign, and hundreds of letters descended on Montgomery.[59] The *Birmingham News* even wrote a letter to the governor in the form of a front page editorial.[60]

North Alabama newspaper editors met with Governor Patterson on August 23. He called the Chop-Up legislation "spur-of-the-moment," "hasty," and based on "political, personal and regional considerations."[61] He indicated that he would not sign the bill; thus his options were to let it become law without his signature, veto it outright, or use executive amendment procedures to suggest changes. He mentioned the 9-8 plan as a possible executive amendment, but he expressed concern that should he send an executive amendment to the legislature, a filibuster could stop his administrative program, including appropriations measures.

On August 25 Governor Patterson signed and transmitted to the House a message outlining a proposed executive amendment to Chop-Up (HB244). The amendment called for conducting the 1962 congressional elections (and those thereafter until the legislature redistricted the state into eight districts) within the existing nine-district structure. Democratic and Republican primaries would be held in each district, and the candidate receiving the largest number of votes in each primary would enter into a statewide runoff primary held four weeks later. Each voter would be able to cast eight votes in the runoff. The eight candidates receiving the most votes in each party runoff would then achieve their party's nomination.[62]

Governor Patterson considered Chop-Up "not a fair and equitable answer to our redistricting problem." He cited two central problems. First, it hurt economic development and the business climate by destroying an economically progressive congressional district. Second, though admitting that in the future a large county might have to be divided into more than one district, he argued that dividing Jefferson County, "having enough population to warrant a congressional district of itself and in fact being the most populous county and congressional district in the state, into four separate parts and parceling these out to surrounding congressional districts so as to divest the citizens of that county of direct representation in Congress, is to me unthinkable, unwise, above all wrong, and therefore unconstitutional."[63] The House voted against the executive amendment fifty-five to thirty-nine. It then voted sixty-one to thirty-five to override the governor's veto.[64]

Throughout the House debate, representatives of the congressmen seeking to avoid at-large elections actively lobbied members. The *Birmingham News* reported that House members received warning that friends and relatives would lose their federal jobs should they vote to sustain the governor's veto.[65]

In the Senate complex parliamentary maneuvering, including a Dumas-led filibuster, followed the House action. Members charged Lieutenant Governor Boutwell with assisting the filibustering senators through his handling of recognition rights, especially by not recognizing point-of-order motions from antifilibuster senators.[66] Senator Alton Turner, who led the Chop-Up supporters, unsuccessfully sought recognition more than thirty times.

As the Senate entered its last legislative day (September 1), only a cloture vote could stop the filibuster. Since Chop-Up supporters could not sustain a cloture vote, they brought a state health officer into the Senate to examine the filibustering senators and the lieutenant governor to determine if they were fit to continue. When all were declared fit, the only hope of ending the filibuster died.[67] The legislative session ended without passage of a reapportionment or redistricting plan, and for the first time in the state's history, the regular session failed to pass the general appropriations bill.

Governor Patterson called a special session to handle the appropriations crisis. He first polled legislators to get their assurances that they would limit themselves to a five-day session and would not introduce any redistricting plan other than the 9-8 proposal he had offered in his executive amendment to Chop-Up. The special session passed the appropriations bill and a modified version of the 9-8 plan, which withstood a federal court challenge. Both the 1962 and 1964 Democratic primaries and the Republican conventions used this plan to select their congressional nominees, but only the 1962 general election votes for Congress were cast on an at-large basis.

Jefferson County's Revenge

On August 12, shortly after the House passed the Chop-Up bill, fourteen Birmingham residents filed a class action suit in District Judge Frank M. Johnson's court on behalf of all the residents of the state of Alabama. Their suit asked that all members of the Alabama legislature be elected at-large until the legislature abided by its constitutional mandate to reapportion itself. It asked that the at-large races be required beginning in 1962. It also requested that a three-person district court panel hear the case.[68]

The suit claimed that the failure of the legislature to reapportion itself denied Alabamians equal protection under the law in the areas of voting and taxation. It noted inequities in legislative representation, citing the legislative representation of Jefferson and Lowndes Counties and the maintenance of an "arbitrary, unreasonable and discriminatory formula" for allocating taxation and revenue to the counties. Later the claimants asked the federal court to prevent the legislature from making token changes in the structure of the Alabama legislature and to block any constitutional amendments that would allow reapportionment without regard to population.[69]

The plaintiffs based their suit on the 1957 and 1960 Civil Rights Acts and the Fourteenth Amendment to the U.S. Constitution. The suit named as defendants three county probate judges (standing in for all sixty-seven such officials), the secretary of state, attorney general, and the chairs and secretaries of the state Democratic and Republican parties who ran the state's election machinery.

A Birmingham attorney, Charles Morgan Jr., filed the suit. He had the assistance of George P. Taylor, Robert M. Loeb, and Kenneth Howell in preparing the case. The Young Men's Business Club of Birmingham, composed of young businessmen with progressive political and economic views, supplied the financial backing and sanctioned the use of some of its members as plaintiffs. Others later joined as interveners and broadened the financial and geographic support base for the suit. They included leaders in the United Steel Workers in the cities of Birmingham and Mobile and in Etowah County, the Jefferson County Democratic Campaign Committee, and the Citizens Committee for Representative Government on a Fair Basis, which had a Mobile base.

A three-judge district court panel took no action until after the Supreme Court issued its March 1962 *Baker v. Carr* ruling, which declared that the federal courts had jurisdiction in legislative reapportionment cases. The district court panel then ordered the legislature to reapportion itself by July 16, or the court would do it instead. Governor Patterson responded by calling a special session of the legislature in June.

The legislature passed two reapportionment bills before the court deadline and then adjourned. With both bills the rurally dominated legislature attempted to limit reapportionment to a minimum level. One was a con-stitutional amendment that provided for one senator from each county (Folsom's original and often-ridiculed sixty-seven-senator bill) and a 106-member House to be reapportioned after each census by the method of equal proportions so that each county received at least one representative.[70] The other reapportioned the two chambers under existing constitutional provisions but increased the House representation of several larger coun-ties by reassigning thirteen seats from smaller counties and eliminating five small one-county districts in the Senate.[71]

The federal court voided these plans on July 21. It then ordered im-mediate use of its own plan based on portions of the two legislative bills. The size of the thirty-five-member Senate remained unchanged, but five small one-county districts were converted to two-county districts, and one new two-county district and one new one-county district were also cre-ated. In the House, Jefferson County received seventeen representatives, ten more than it had before. Recognizing that this represented only partial reapportionment, the court ordered the legislature taking office in 1963 to undertake a more thorough reapportionment.[72]

End of the Alliance

The Birmingham–Black Belt coalition finally split publicly and bitterly over Chop-Up. The split was not the simple result of coalition building between Jefferson County and north Alabama. North Alabama legislators were fearful of Jefferson County's potential power, given its large population. Through the linking of redistricting and reappor-tionment issues, several defensive positions were united. Chop-Up gave the north, the south, and the Black Belt continued congressional representa-tion. Only Jefferson County lost. The compromise stopped state legislative reapportionment, which would bring more representation to all of north Alabama but benefit the Birmingham area most. And smaller population counties throughout the state realized that the large tax revenues gener-ated in Jefferson County and redistributed throughout the state might be redirected should the county and other major population centers receive their fair share of representation.

In interviews Chop-Up supporters readily admitted that Black Belt as-sistance was essential for the passage of their legislation, but they denied a deal on reapportionment as the condition for such support. Still, the Chop-Up bill was the major way Black Belters could maintain their impact on congressional politics and the wedge they could use to get assistance in stopping reapportionment.

To a substantial degree, the Big Mule coalition had been sustained by a coincidence of interests between its two member groups, rural planters and big industry. From the time of the coalition's formation at the turn of the century, its members wanted little more than that classic objective of so many elites, maintenance of the status quo. The functioning of the coalition toward that end was facilitated by the common Black Belt origins of many Birmingham power brokers.

As the degree of urban-rural malapportionment increased because of expanding urban populations (including migration from outside the state as well as from the state's rural counties), pressure grew within Birmingham and other populous counties to adjust the terms of the coalition relationship. The first significant public manifestation of this pressure appeared in 1939. The pressure was inadvertently contained by James E. Folsom Sr.'s attacks on the elite and its policy preferences, especially with regard to taxation and education issues, and by federal civil rights action. Later, inevitable differences with regard to the civil rights movement and the economic impact of segregation on Birmingham and its rate of economic development forced reapportionment and congressional redistricting issues to the fore. These underlying tensions combined to destroy the Birmingham–Black Belt alliance. They became public over the redistricting issue and Chop-Up.

A significant part of John Patterson's term went contrary to what alliance members wanted, even though he favored their segregation stand. They came to view Patterson as at least a partial enemy. Through his veto of Chop-Up, he indirectly helped to destroy the Black Belt–Birmingham alliance, but the external federal court pressure was the most important proximate cause of the split.

What was left of the alliance in 1962? The rural counties had been shrinking for decades while Jefferson County and Mobile County had been growing. Nevertheless, the Black Belt agricultural interests and Birmingham industry still shared some common views (for example, opposition to increased taxes) even though their formal partnership was at an end. Their perspectives had not changed much, although the Birmingham contingent had perhaps become more realistic about being unable to ignore national public opinion and political and court pressure regarding civil rights.

Politicos and reporters from Jefferson County and north Alabama hoped for a new alliance between Jefferson County and north Alabama. For example, Morgan County's Albert Brewer claimed that it would be "completely foolish" for Jefferson County to return to alliance with the Black Belt. He felt that the county needed to reevaluate its position and recognize its common ties to north Alabama:

> We in North Alabama have been called liberal, when in fact we are just progressive. The progress we seek and advocate is the same progress Jefferson County seeks and advocates, but we are accused of doing it under a different name.
>
> We believe the interests of Jefferson County and ours are the same and we believe that the future progress of this state is going to reflect an alliance that will embrace all of Alabama.[73]

A Jefferson County representative echoed Brewer's sentiments but from another perspective.

> I was told my first session as a freshman member . . . that we could count on the Black Belt for help. But when the going got rough—on the aviation gas tax reduction bill when we needed only a few more votes to eliminate a six-cent tax and make Birmingham one of the outstanding airport facilities in the South—they were not there.
>
> That, coupled with their primary leadership in the chop-up . . . fight, left me a certain feeling about the Black Belt.
>
> I think the alignment in the future is moving to the northern part of Alabama.[74]

The formation of a new alliance seemed likely.

6

Racial Conflict and the Politics of Race

The early 1960s brought an increase in civil rights campaigns in such areas as voter registration, interstate public transportation, and public accommodations. Alabama's largest cities and several Black Belt counties were targeted. Local and state government counterattacked, producing waves of damaging national news coverage and editorial comment. Many white politicians used racial conflict to further their political careers, and some found it a convenient tool for hindering social, economic, and political change.

Sit-Ins and Freedom Riders

In February 1960 approximately thirty black Alabama State College (ASC) students asked for service at the segregated Montgomery County Courthouse cafeteria. A larger group from the same institution assembled on the capitol steps, sang a hymn and the national anthem, and then departed. ASC, one of Alabama's two public black colleges, fell under the jurisdiction of the state board of education, which was chaired by the governor. The college's president, H. Councill Trenholm, irritated Patterson by failing to discipline the students. The governor even suggested that Trenholm might be dismissed.

Under heavy pressure from Patterson, the board of education ordered Trenholm to expel nine ASC student-demonstrators and place twenty others on probation "pending good behavior." Hundreds of students protested the board's decision in a mass meeting, which was followed a few days later by a prayer service–demonstration on the capitol steps, attended by 750 blacks. Four hundred police, including some on horseback, stopped the demonstration while simultaneously holding back an estimated 5,000 whites.[1]

On May 14, 1961, "freedom riders," civil rights activists attempting to integrate the interstate bus system, were attacked and beaten in Anniston, approximately sixty miles northeast of Birmingham. Their bus was stopped on the road and burned, and the freedom riders were beaten. Hospital staff in Anniston refused to assist the injured, who were then taken in an automobile caravan for treatment to Birmingham. Another bus arrived in Birmingham only to be greeted by a well-armed mob. The mob's attack continued for fifteen minutes uninterrupted by the Birmingham police.

Governor Patterson prefaced a press conference on the subject by observing that "Alabama isn't the Congo." Then, commenting on the beatings, he said: "When you go somewhere seeking trouble you usually find it. I lay full blame on the agitators who come in here for the express purpose of stirring up just such a thing. We can't act as nursemaids to agitators. They'll stay at home when they learn nobody is there to protect them. The state of Alabama can't guarantee safety of fools, and that's what they are."[2] Patterson evaded efforts by reporters to get him to condemn the attacks. The strongest statement he would make was "I don't condone that." As the reporters persisted, Patterson snarled, "Are you people in sympathy with the agitators?"

On May 20 a mob numbering some one hundred attacked freedom riders and bystanders when their bus reached the Montgomery bus terminal. Mob members wielded baseball bats and bottles and threw bricks. As in Birmingham, the police response to these attacks was intentionally slow and ineffectual. The federal government sent four hundred marshals to Alabama to prevent further violence.[3]

A transcript of a taped conference on May 21, 1961, provides insights into the relationships between Alabama and federal officials and the decision making of Alabama officials. Present at the conference were Governor Patterson, Attorney General Gallion, Director of Public Safety Floyd Mann, and Assistant U.S. Attorney General Byron White.

Patterson asked White what instructions had been given to the marshals. White responded that they were going to "patrol the streets." The governor and Gallion asserted that outside agitators were the only problem, that everything was peaceful before the freedom riders came. Patterson then asked what the federal government was doing to discourage outside agitators from coming to Alabama: "Couldn't you publicly ask these students to stay at college and attend to their lessons and their business and not come into the State of Alabama for the purpose of getting embroiled in fights?" White replied: "Well, people in this federal union have a right to move among the states."[4] Patterson ended the conference with a speech telling White that the federal presence in Alabama was unwarranted and unneeded.[5]

That night Martin Luther King Jr. and Ralph Abernathy held a rally at the First Baptist Church. A white mob attacked the church, throwing rocks and smoke bombs through windows and threatening to break in. The federal marshals brought the mob under control, but blacks prudently stayed in the church all night. There were also numerous shootings into black homes and acts of vandalism by whites against black-owned property. These actions, together with pressure from the Kennedy administration, were too much for Patterson, who declared martial law while continuing to denounce the presence of the federal marshals. The governor also accused an official of the U.S. Department of Justice of encouraging the freedom riders and told him that they were Communist-inspired.

Meanwhile, former governor James E. Folsom Sr. telephoned Attorney General Robert Kennedy and endorsed the marshals' presence. He essentially reversed this act of bravado the next day, saying that because law and order had been established, the marshals could leave.[6]

Confrontations with the National Media

In April 1960 Governor Patterson and other public officials began an attack on the *New York Times*. On March 29 the *Times* had published a full-page advertisement soliciting funds to support the activities of Martin Luther King Jr. It was supposedly signed by over sixty prominent individuals, including Eleanor Roosevelt, entertainers, and religious and civil rights leaders such as the black Alabama ministers Fred L. Shuttlesworth, Ralph D. Abernathy, S. S. Seay Sr., and J. E. Lowery. (The Alabama clergymen had not in fact given permission for their names to be used.) Governor Patterson objected to the advertisement's description of the March demonstration on the capitol steps and its aftermath. That account read:

> After students sang "My Country 'Tis of Thee" on the State Capitol steps, their leaders were expelled from school, and truckloads of police armed with shotguns and tear-gas ringed the Alabama State College campus. When most of the student body protested to state authori-

ties by refusing the re-register, their dining hall was padlocked in an attempt to starve them into submission.

Again and again the Southern violators have answered Dr. King's peaceful protests with intimidation and violence. They have bombed his home. . . . They have assaulted his person. They have arrested him several times—for "speeding," "loitering" and similar "offenses." And now they have charged him with "perjury."[7]

On May 9 the governor demanded that the *Times* retract the paragraphs quoted above. He argued that they implied that he was guilty of "grave misconduct and . . . improper omissions as Governor of Alabama and Ex-Officio Chairman of the State Board of Education of Alabama."[8] ASC officials claimed "there was not a modicum of truth" in the description of actions taken at the school.[9]

The *Times* retracted the two paragraphs and apologized to the governor but basically admitted no error. By repeating the offending paragraphs and listing the names of the individuals who had signed the advertisement, the retraction was virtually a free re-publication of the advertisement.[10]

On May 30 Governor Patterson filed a $1 million libel suit in Montgomery against the *Times,* the four Alabama ministers who had signed the ad, and Martin Luther King Jr. Montgomery's three city commissioners had already filed similar suits asking $500,000 in damages from each defendant.[11]

In July the newspaper appeared before Judge Walter B. Jones of the Montgomery Circuit Court to argue that the subpoenas served on the *Times* were invalid and that the Alabama courts had no jurisdiction over the commissioners' suit (and by implication the governor's) because the newspaper was not an Alabama corporation. The plaintiffs' attorneys argued that because the *Times* carried wire service stories originating in the state, state courts had jurisdiction.[12] Judge Jones agreed with the plaintiffs' position. He cited the facts that both regular and part-time reporters worked in the state, that the paper solicited advertising in Alabama, and that it sold its newspapers in the state.[13]

While these events were unfolding, the *Times* became embroiled in other Alabama-based libel suits. Harrison E. Salisbury filed a story from Birmingham that appeared on the front page of the *Times* on April 12 under the headline "FEAR AND HATRED GRIP BIRMINGHAM." A second front-page story ("Race Issue Shakes Alabama Structure") appeared the next day.

According to Salisbury,

From Red Mountain, where a cast-iron Vulcan looks down 500 feet to
the sprawling city, Birmingham seems veiled in the poisonous fumes of
distant battles. . . .

But more than a few citizens, both white and Negro, harbor growing
fear that the hour will strike when the smoke of civil strife will mingle
with that of the hearths and forges. . . .

The reaction [to lunch counter sit-ins] has been new manifestations
of fear, force and terror punctuated by striking acts of courage. . . .

Every channel of communication, every medium of mutual interest,
every reasoned approach, every inch of middle ground has been fragmented by the emotional dynamite of racism, reinforced by the whip,
the razor, the gun, the knife, the mob, the policy and many branches of
the state's apparatus.

In Birmingham neither blacks nor whites talk freely. . . .

Telephones are tapped, or there is fear of tapping. Mail has been
intercepted and opened. Sometimes it does not reach its destination.
The eavesdropper, the informer, the spy have become a fact of life.[14]

The remainder of the story described events related to the sit-ins and the
harassment of black students and black leaders. It also outlined the career
and actions of Birmingham Commissioner of Public Safety Eugene "Bull"
Connor.

Salisbury's second article charged:

Under the corrosive impact of the segregation issue, Alabama's political and social structure appears to be developing symptoms of disintegration.

The lines between legality and extra-legality are becoming blurred.
. . . The distinction between exercise of state power and mob power is
being eroded.

. . . demands are raised more and more frequently for the conventional apparatus of the state—the educational system, the political
machinery and governmental organs—to be dissolved, deliberately
paralyzed or distorted beyond recognition.[15]

The article then discussed the passage of legislation allowing for the dissolution of the public school system should integration be ordered. It pointed
to the open discussion of proposals to eliminate county governments rather
than allow blacks to control them, to dissolve the legislature and substitute
a convention in its place to prevent the seating of black legislators, and
to name only unpledged presidential electors to the Democratic ballot. "In

this kind of political atmosphere there is little or no barrier to the growth and influence of organizations and movements dedicated to hate, intolerance, and terror."[16] Salisbury noted the development of horse patrols—"the rough equivalent of vigilantes"—in five counties, the expanding activities of the Ku Klux Klan, growing anti-Semitism, and increasing violence.

Examining the power structure of the state and Birmingham and the extreme malapportionment of the state legislature, Salisbury concluded that even with malapportionment in place,

the Black Belt counties would not be able to maintain their stranglehold on state government and their retro-grade influence on state policy were it not for a powerful ally, the big industry of Birmingham. The biggest of Birmingham's so-called "big mules" is United States Steel, whose subsidiary Tennessee Coal and Iron, dominated the city economically and, to a considerable extent, politically.

The "big mules" and the Black Belt cooperate and, together, usually run the state. The long years of big-company dominance have stultified Birmingham's political development.[17]

The Salisbury articles outraged Birmingham government officials and the business community. The Birmingham Chamber of Commerce offered to pay the expenses for a *Times* reporter to come to the city and develop an article on race relations that would meet "the highest journalistic standards." It recommended that Birmingham reporters write an article for the *Times* describing race relations in the city and that the *Times* send anyone of its choosing to check the story's accuracy. Finally, the chamber voted to establish a publicity committee to develop "a positive public relations program to publish nation-wide the true facts about the Birmingham community."[18]

Birmingham's three city commissioners (Mayor James W. Morgan, Commissioner of Public Safety Eugene "Bull" Connor, and Commissioner of Public Improvements J. T. Waggoner) wrote to the *Times* and to Harrison Salisbury demanding a retraction of the April 12 article and particularly the following paragraph: "Volunteer watchmen stand guard twenty-four hours a day over some Negro churches. Jewish synagogues have floodlights for the night and caretakers. Dynamite attempts have been made against the two principal Jewish temples in the last eighteen months. In eleven years there have been twenty-two reported bombings of Negro churches and homes. A number were never officially reported." The commissioners argued that this paragraph invited "the false inference that the undersigned has encouraged or condoned racial hatred or religious intolerance."[19] Bull

Connor also demanded a public retraction of defamatory remarks made about him. He cited nineteen specific statements.

Turner Catledge, managing editor of the *Times,* refused to retract the story, but he invited William T. Engel, chairman of Birmingham's Committee of 100, to prepare a rebuttal for publication in the *Times.*[20] The Committee of 100 and the Birmingham Chamber of Commerce together wrote a statement that was published on the May 4 front page. It called the Salisbury stories "biased, warped and misleading" and his "facts" "in most cases either outright misstatements or, which is worse, half truths." The statement continued: "Certainly we have extremists—but what city does not have? Yes, we have isolated cases of violence—but what city does not have such?"[21] The statement also described rapid improvements in the lives of blacks, citing family income, home ownership, automobile ownership, and spending on black school construction and salaries of black teachers. It then asked: "Could Negroes, or anyone else for that matter, have made such rapid progress under conditions such as those described by Mr. Salisbury?"

The statement was followed by another from the managing editor of the *Times;* it supported Salisbury and his stories. The editor noted that Salisbury's work was based on interviews conducted in Birmingham, personal observations, and news items from Alabama newspapers: "He did not go to Birmingham 'seeking sensationalism' or anything else but the facts in a situation that involves Birmingham as well as other cities. We are only sorry that his findings had to be unpleasant to anyone."

On May 6 the Birmingham commissioners filed libel suits against the *Times* and Harrison Salisbury. Big Mule James A. Simpson, "Bull" Connor's mentor and longtime state senator, acted as counsel for the plaintiffs. According to Simpson, he filed the suits in federal court to forestall charges that the commissioners were trying "to lynch them with local prejudice in state court."[22] The newspaper attempted to get the suits dropped, claiming the court had no jurisdiction and that Salisbury did not do business or perform any work or service in the state.[23] At the end of May three city officials from Bessemer, Alabama, filed their own libel suits. The first Salisbury article had compared conditions in Bessemer unfavorably to those in Birmingham. On July 20 a Birmingham city detective also filed suit.

In September a Jefferson County grand jury meeting in Bessemer began an investigation into the Salisbury articles. Preliminary inquiries had developed a list of Salisbury's contacts in Birmingham and a list of the telephone calls he had made.[24] The grand jury eventually indicted Salisbury on forty-two counts of criminal libel.[25]

On September 2 U.S. District Judge H. H. Grooms ruled in Birmingham that the federal court had jurisdiction over the libel suits filed in the federal system because Salisbury worked in the state to gather information for the story. The *Times* appealed the decision to the Fifth Circuit Court.[26]

From the perspective of the *New York Times* and the press in general, the libel suits were attempts to muzzle a free press. An Associated Press reporter wrote a lengthy review of the cases, pointing out that the logic of Judge Groom's decision on federal court jurisdiction would make all out-of-state reporters operating in Alabama accountable in Alabama courts.[27]

The first libel trial was held in November in state court in Montgomery. The attorneys for L. B. Sullivan, commissioner of police in Montgomery, attempted to show that those who read the Salisbury material on the ASC demonstrators associated the statements made with the city government of Montgomery. Grover Hall Jr., editor of the *Montgomery Advertiser,* testified in support of the plaintiffs' contention.

The *Times* argued that the advertisement named no specific persons and could not be considered libelous of any individual. Employees testified that normal procedures were followed in publishing the advertisement and no problems were seen with its content. An employee who accepted the advertisement testified that an original copy did not contain the names of the Alabama ministers, and that they were added later by a member of the committee that submitted it on the assumption that because they belonged to the Southern Christian Leadership Conference, they would have no objection.[28] Attorneys for the black defendants contended that none of them had given anyone permission to use their names.

After two hours and twenty minutes of deliberation, the state court jury found the *New York Times* guilty of libel and awarded Police Commissioner Sullivan the entire amount he had requested from all defendants.[29] The case was appealed to the Alabama Supreme Court, which let the lower court decision stand. It was then appealed to the U.S. Supreme Court, which overturned the state court's decision. The U.S. Supreme Court ruled that under the First and Fourth Amendments to the Constitution a public figure could recover damages for "defamatory falsehood relating to his official conduct" only if the statement was made with malice—that is, with the knowledge that the statement was false. The court also stated that the advertisement did not attack Commissioner Sullivan personally.[30]

This suit and the other libel cases represent only a small portion of the terrible images of Alabama projected in the national media during the Patterson years. On balance, attempts to redress journalistic misstatement or interpretation backfired because every charge of libel or bias was met by a restatement of the original story (or advertisement) and little or no apology. After George Wallace's inaugural, a steady stream of stories describing Alabama public officials (and by extension white Alabamians in general) as racist cretins expanded from a steady stream to a torrent. Negative images were reinforced by each denial and retelling.

Education Funding and Civil Rights

After the 1959 education tax battle, an economic downturn and labor strife decreased the revenues available for education. The public schools did not receive as much funding as had been projected during the school tax fight. The Alabama Education Association (AEA) pressured Governor Patterson to raise taxes still further and proposed a constitutional revision allowing for higher property taxes. Having spent almost all his political capital on the original tax battle and remembering AEA's uninspired support when his nose was bloodied over property tax equalization, Patterson refused to act.[31]

Despite the tensions caused by civil rights politics, support for public schools remained strong. For example, on September 18, 1961, the South Marengo (Black Belt) Civitan Club passed a resolution deploring "the dire financial conditions forced upon the school system of Marengo County and the State of Alabama by proration" and resolving that "the Governor and legislature be urged to alleviate the immediate financial condition and make sure that the public schools will have funds to improve the educational program of Alabama."[32]

The impression one gets from reading the Patterson education files in the Alabama Department of Archives and History is that the Patterson administration tried to keep the public schools running. The files contain few references to the civil rights movement and none to reducing funding because the schools might soon be integrated. Instead, Patterson continued his efforts to improve black schools as a way to delay integration. For example, in a February 1, 1962, letter, Patterson urged State Superintendent of Education W. A. LeCroy to "take all action necessary to improve the administration and teaching programs at both our State Negro colleges so as to make them outstanding educational institutions and to get them accredited. I think the idea of getting competent assistance from the other State colleges to get this job done is excellent."[33]

In a special session the legislature passed an act authorizing a constitutional amendment that would allow modest property tax increases at the local level. The voters ratified the amendment. Had all counties and cities increased property taxes to the maximum permitted by this change a mere

$14 million per year would have been provided schools. In fact, only three large cities and eight urban counties passed increases.

Academic Freedom

When Patterson threatened to expel the students who staged the February 25 lunch counter sit-in at the Montgomery County Courthouse, the general secretary of the American Association of University Professors (AAUP) warned the governor in a telegram that expelling the students would constitute a "gross violation of academic freedom."[34] The general secretary asked for a response from either Patterson or President Trenholm of Alabama State College, but Patterson directed that no response be sent.

On March 3 the state board of education, acting on the governor's request, ordered the expulsion of nine students and placed approximately twenty others on probation. The governor also ordered Superintendent of Education Frank R. Stewart to conduct a full-scale investigation of the college.[35] The *New York Times* reported these and subsequent decisions, reinforcing Alabama's already dismal reputation.

The state board of education met again on March 25, 1960. Governor Patterson assumed the chair and informed the board that pamphlets published by the Congress of Racial Equality (CORE) instructing students on sit-in techniques had been distributed at ASC. At the same meeting Superintendent Stewart informed the board that he had uncovered at least eleven ASC faculty who had been disloyal to the college.

Doubtless Lawrence D. Reddick was one of the allegedly perfidious educators on Stewart's list. Reddick was a full professor of history and head of the history department. He held B.A. and M.A. degrees from Fisk University and a Ph.D. in history from the University of Chicago. Reddick's work had appeared in *The Nation* and *Saturday Review,* and his biography of Martin Luther King Jr. had been published by Harper and Brothers. By any criteria Reddick's academic record was quite good; by the standards of Alabama universities in the 1960s it was outstanding.

Reddick had not played a role in the Montgomery bus boycott, nor was he a leader in subsequent civil rights activities, but he had participated with ASC students in antisegregation demonstrations in February and March of 1960.[36] Patterson ordered Reddick investigated. A file on Reddick assembled in the governor's office included allegations from law enforcement authorities in New York and Georgia that before coming to Alabama in 1955 he had been involved in Communist activities. The evidence for these allegations was very slender. A report from the House Committee on Un-American Activities contained five items. The most damning one reads, "An advertisement in the September 26, 1951 issue of the Daily Worker, page 8, announced that Dr. Lawrence Reddick, Atlanta University, was to speak at a meeting of the National Council of the Arts, Sciences and Professions . . . in honor of W. E. B. DuBois, calling for the right to advocate peace, in New York City on September 28 (1951)."[37] He was also listed in a *New York Times* story as having participated in a Communist rally in 1946.[38]

In an April 12, 1960, letter to President Trenholm, Reddick wrote, "I would have more confidence in the immediate future if I had something better than an annual job contract."[39] After a conference with Trenholm, he wrote a letter of resignation. According to an investigative report written by representatives of the AAUP, Reddick resigned out of "a sense of insecurity and discouragement with respect to the future of the institution."[40] No evidence was presented, nor were allegations made that Reddick had abused his academic position.

The AAUP report concluded that as with the students, "the requirements of academic due process were completely disregarded."[41] It continued, "Whatever the terms of his appointment at Alabama State College, Professor Reddick appears to have been entitled, under the *1940 Statement [of Principles on Academic Freedom and Tenure]*, to continuous tenure status, since he had served five years at Alabama State College and seven years at other institutions of higher learning."[42]

At the June 14 board of education meeting, Governor Patterson accused Reddick of having past associations with Communist groups and urged that Reddick be fired despite the fact that he had already resigned. The board and President Trenholm complied.[43] In a statement published in the *Alabama Journal* the next day, Reddick denied being a Communist.[44] In a June 30 memorandum to Trenholm, he charged that he had been fired without a hearing or any other way to respond to his accusers.[45]

At the July meeting of the state board of education no acknowledgment was made of Reddick's request for a hearing. Instead, President Trenholm described what had been done to end the civil rights activities of students and faculty. Trenholm reported that three professors had submitted their resignations and that additional resignations would be forthcoming.

Dozens of telegrams sent to Patterson from around the country protested the dismissal of Reddick. Only one in the governor's files supported the firing. It was written by Kenneth Adams, who identified himself as the Alabama grand dragon of the Dixie Klans, Incorporated. He wrote, "We congratulate you on your manly decision in discharging that Negro agitator at Alabama State College. We feel as you do that he was guilty of communist activities."[46]

On August 4, 1961, the U.S. Court of Appeals for the Fifth Circuit held illegal the expulsion of six of the nine ASC students for participating in the sit-ins, ruling that due process had not been followed.[47]

Patterson maintained his vigil against civil rights activities in Alabama's black universities throughout most of his administration. For example, in February 1962 he wrote to Superintendent of Education LeCroy:

> I am very much concerned about the activities of certain of the Negro students at the college in Huntsville. An organization known as CORE has been operating in the Huntsville area and organizing and carrying out sit-in demonstrations at the lunch counters in several department stores in Huntsville. . . . They are also conducting an illegal boycott of the businesses of some of the merchants of Huntsville. It appears that these demonstrations will continue unless something is done about them. The actions of these students at Alabama A. & M. bring discredit upon the college and our State.
>
> . . . over the years the people of Alabama have been proud of this college and have backed and supported it in every way possible. I would hate to see the general public which supports this college lose interest in it and lose respect for it because of the bad behavior of some of the students. . . . we, as Governor, Superintendent of Education, and the State Board of Education, have a duty to see that students that go to State colleges behave themselves and obey our laws and study their books.
>
> I now have men in the Huntsville area who are investigating these demonstrations and in due time will give me the names of the students of A. & M. who are involved.[48]

Patterson's Personal Leanings and Style

Was John Patterson a racist? His office published a racist pamphlet written by Wesley C. George entitled *The Biology of the Race Problem*. At the bottom of the pamphlet was the notice "This Report Has Been Prepared by Commission of the Governor of Alabama"; it was dated 1962.[49] The pamphlet was still being distributed by the Wallace administration in the latter months of 1963. Wesley George listed himself as professor emeritus of histology and embryology and former head of the Department of Anatomy, University of North Carolina Medical School.

George's thesis was that blacks were biologically inferior to whites. Typical of the tone and quality of research in this document is an approving quote from a book published in 1892 concerning the "incapacity of savages for civilization. . . . The labor of such men is neither constant or steady. They work, except for a short time, when urged by want and encouraged by kind treatment." George then equated these characteristics to contemporary blacks in the United States.[50] He also argued that the IQs of blacks were considerably lower than those of whites, totally ignoring the more recent scholarly research on the relationship between race, environment, and intelligence tests.[51]

The nature of memoranda sent from Highway Director Sam Engelhardt to the governor and others adds more to the image of beliefs and discourse in and around Patterson. In an August 25, 1961, letter to Patterson, Engelhardt referred to a high-ranking member of the Arkansas judiciary as a "long time nigger killing friend of mine."[52] Patterson would not have tolerated such language, nor would his close associate have used it, had Patterson not shared the sentiment to some degree.

In a March 1960 letter to a friend, Engelhardt wrote, "I believe that the near race riot we had here on Sunday, the 6th [the demonstrations following the expulsion of ASC students], and the quick action by State and local law enforcement people have the coons on the run. One of the most joyful sights I have seen was [Ralph David] Abernathy and a group of his cohorts running like hell with their ecclesiastical robes up over their butts."[53]

Not surprisingly, the Engelhardt files reveal that the segregationist views of Black Belt whites were frequently tied to anti-Semitism. A circular printed by the Elmore County White Citizens Council in a 1961 file folder among Engelhardt's personal papers reads: "The biggest 'big-lie' of all is the colossal fraud that the modern-so-called-Jew is a white man. . . . The jew's mongrel background is undoubtedly responsible for his abysmal inferiority complex and motivates him to do everything in his power to communize, mongrelize and destroy the Great White Christian Race."[54]

Outside of racial matters, Patterson's political philosophy was populist or liberal. This is clearly evident in his most difficult legislative fights in 1959—educational funding and property tax reform. It is apparent in many less widely publicized examples as well. For example, early in 1961 under Patterson's direction Engelhardt adopted pay scales for highway workers that were equal to pay levels in a 1957 contract agreement between the Heavy and Highway Contractors Association of Alabama and local unions having jurisdiction over highway construction in the state. This move irritated a relatively affluent lobbying group called the Committee of Contractors.[55]

It is difficult to gauge Patterson's relationships with other members of
the political community, such as the legislature and reporters. His choice
of legislative leaders was by and large sound, and he skillfully lubricated
the legislative process with patronage. Nevertheless, he appeared naive to
many. One participant described him as inaccessible to legislators and im-
mature: "He is different now. He was an arrogant kid then. He and his staff
made a big show of the fact that they all wore pistols in shoulder holsters.
He had that black limo and always a security force around him. He was
just playing cowboys and indians. His limo would race around preceded by
two motorcycles with sirens. He would roar into a small town. The limo
would come to a halt and his security people would jump out looking in
all directions for potential assassins."[56] Even frequent trips to his favorite
restaurant followed this showy routine.

Patterson truly regarded himself as in a continuing war with the gangsters who killed his father. His precautions were not entirely fanciful, but
it appears that he enjoyed noisy, exaggerated security procedures. Those
procedures and the evident pleasure he took in them irritated the relatively
low-key, countrified legislators with whom he needed to work.

Industrial Development Under Patterson

Under Patterson the Alabama Planning and Indus-
trial Development Board did the usual things to attract industry. There
was no lack of commitment to industrial growth, although none of the
efforts appeared particularly inspired, and doubtless they were equaled or
exceeded by most other states.[57]

Despite civil rights violence and demonstrations, the governor's office
files relating to industrial development contain little evidence that the governor and his staff were worried that these events and official responses
toward them would create a negative attitude toward the state and ham-
per its economic growth and industrial development. Most of the economic
growth problems found in the files are technical, concerning barge traffic
backups, adequate roads, and so forth.

Advocates of growth from the larger cities and among the younger professional classes increasingly viewed racial unrest in the state as a major
barrier to growth and development. For example, a May 1961 telegram to
Patterson from the prestigious Committee of 100 said:

Birmingham's Committee of 100 has worked for 11 years solely to create new jobs in industry and commerce for Alabama citizens. To succeed

in this task an absolute requirement is the creation of an atmosphere of peace and harmony in our state. The events of the past week [attacks on freedom riders] have severely shaken the nation's confidence even in the ability of constituted authority to maintain the peace in Alabama, and it has been especially noted that some authorities seemed deliveratly [*sic*] to have evaded their responsibilities. We respectfully urge, earnestly, that you use every means in your power to assure the people of Alabama, the federal government, and the rest of the nation, both by word and particularly by actions that you have the will, the desire, the ability to preserve law and order.[58]

Strike-related violence also marred the process of attracting industry to the state. A letter written to Director Floyd Mann of the Department of Public Safety in April 1961 referred to a strike at an Anniston General Electric plant during which a considerable amount of violence occurred. The letter stated that representatives of a large manufacturer of metal office equipment had visited Anniston and other southern cities to scout a new plant location. Anniston made the short list, but it was removed because of the labor violence.

Attached to the letter was a description of Anniston written by a nationally known firm that prepared surveys of cities for industries seeking to relocate or build new facilities. The description began: "The shocking spectacle of recent weeks has done incalculable damage to Anniston's future as an industrial community. The sordid stories reported in the 'Anniston Star' add up to picket line intimidation, vandalism and even gunplay to prevent workers from exercising their legal right to work. These accounts have not gone unnoticed in the national press."[59]

Birmingham attempted to improve its execrable image through dull advertising campaigns, by revitalizing the business district, and through expansion of the University of Alabama Medical Center area, which was tied to the medical school, an institution that, against all odds, was rapidly developing an outstanding reputation. The latter two efforts depended upon the use of federal urban-renewal funds for the demolition of older, derelict buildings and improvement of traffic patterns. In the medical center area this largely meant the removal of black housing. The objectives were to attract new businesses, to encourage established businesses to remain, and to bring more affluent citizens back to the downtown area for shopping and medical services.

The expansion of the medical center also depended on the assistance of Senator Lister Hill and others in the Alabama congressional delegation. Funds from the Ferguson-Hill and Hill-Burton Acts aided in hospital construction, and research funding came from the National Institutes of Health and other institutions.

Mayor James W. Morgan established a committee of prominent local businessmen to oversee the downtown revitalization. A handwritten letter from one of the committee members reveals a great deal about the city. The tone of the letter suggests that the author and mayor were on close terms:

I don't think we in Bham like to face the truth about our city, we dread stepping on important toes, we lack confidence in our economy & people and our optimism is more whistling in the dark than in genuine confidence & enthusiasm about our city.

Albeit Bham is the countriest town in the US over 200,000, I can easily prove it is the very best town in the nation & many in the world. No town has had cleaner or more conciencious [*sic*] government, or free from organized crime, rackets & graft—no city has any better year around climate . . . none is better laid off, none has better residential areas (metropolitan), good transportation, reasonable traffic conditions, (on the whole) good productive labor despite over unionization, great natural resources and the *very most important* of *all:* good people (ask anyone who has traveled widely). . . .

But, mayor, we are complacent and ashamed to admit that some things are not good: smoke, congested traffic arteries, to the suburbs which could encourage people to "come to town," too few multi-story parking facilities (perhaps inadequate downtown transportation or taxi system—very inferior & high priced—that would make it less necessary to bring your car to town), smog that keeps many people (including me) from having a downtown office & runs up laundry bills & gives a dirty look to our town. *Please* don't quote me but we need a really modern show piece hotel . . . and our shops with few exceptions are just not as attractive & well stocked as in many similar cities.

. . . I am sure that a real comprehensive, *really* realistic survey of this vast area . . . could completely revitalize downtown & bring the people back—maybe even encourage wide municipal consolidation—if the other merchants could be made to see that competition & service & transportation facilities in this area would "bring 'em back" to town from not only the suburbs but from a wide area in the state.[60]

Birmingham's political leadership periodically attempted to annex two of the city's most affluent neighbors, Mountain Brook and Homewood. The process required state legislative action authorizing a vote among the citizens of the affected areas. A 1959 attempt failed. The city leadership patterned annexation attempts after Atlanta's annexation of affluent Buckhead. The goals were to enlarge the city's tax base and to recommit business leaders who lived in the annexed areas to preserving the city and building a more prosperous future. In addition, the potential voting strength of the black population would be diluted.

Overall, these and similar efforts to promote industry in Alabama were dull and marred by anti–civil rights violence perpetrated by white thugs who were cheered on by state and local government officials. The narrowing of the economic gap between Alabama and the nation that occurred at this time resulted from basic market forces, not governmental action.

The Elections of 1962

Of the nine candidates running for the 1962 Democratic gubernatorial nomination, the most prominent were Eugene "Bull" Connor, former Wilcox County senator J. Bruce Henderson, Lieutenant Governor Albert Boutwell, former governor James E. Folsom Sr., the progressive senator Ryan de Graffenried, Attorney General MacDonald Gallion, and George C. Wallace. The constitutional restriction against governors' succeeding themselves prevented John Patterson from seeking reelection.

Once again, the Black Belt could not field a viable candidate true to its world view. J. Bruce Henderson was in the race but was now seventy years of age and had never been an effective state-level campaigner. Black Belt leaders suspected that George Wallace, the most electable gubernatorial candidate from the region, might be a moderate on segregation, and they were fairly certain that he was untrustworthy with regard to taxing and spending matters. Their Birmingham ally Albert Boutwell had shown himself unreliable during Chop-Up.

In 1961 Highway Director Sam Engelhardt had actively explored the possibility of a gubernatorial race. He and his assistant Walter Craig, his de facto campaign manager, received many letters of support, primarily from automobile dealers (promising cars for the campaign), paint dealers, contractors, and other small-business owners living in the Black Belt. Engelhardt and Craig took many scouting trips during this time, but, like the letters of support, these trips were confined mainly to the Black Belt.[61]

Engelhardt's first correspondence from north Alabama regarding his campaign came from a small construction company in Gadsden. No contacts with major corporate leaders are recorded in his files. By August 1961 Cecil Word of Scottsboro, chair of the Engelhardt for Governor Committee, was sending out mailings using the slogan Stop All Mixing.

Engelhardt's knowledgeable father-in-law, J. Miller Bonner, a reactionary former Wilcox County state senator who had been Governor Frank Dixon's legal advisor, noted this narrow base of support. In a September 23, 1961, letter to Cecil Word, Bonner observed that his son-in-law would make a fine governor, but, he cautioned, competence was not enough to elect a governor. "I have not advised and do not plan to advise him as to running. The consequence of defeat is too disastrous. Defeat means bankruptcy. I call to mind two men who ran for Governor from Wilcox. One died with judgments against him; the other still lives with a heavy mortgage on his plantation."[62] A few days later Engelhardt made the decision not to run. There is nothing in his files beyond Bonner's letter to indicate why.

Schedules published in the newspapers suggest that the 1962 gubernatorial candidates traveled extensively. The leading candidates ran on cliché-ridden platforms of improving schools, attracting industry, maintaining segregation, and promoting tourism. The differences among the candidates were mainly small variations on these basic themes.

Albert Boutwell supplemented the basic school-industry-tourism litany by highlighting his authorship of much of the new legal structure that supposedly protected segregation from federal incursion. A newspaper story, however, quoted a Birmingham lawyer who respected Boutwell but was not supporting him: "He's great on the telephone, talking to some politician, to get something done." But, the lawyer continued, Boutwell is an inept campaigner. "It's a shame. Boutwell knows more about government than any man in the race."[63] Frequent newspaper comments about Boutwell's deteriorating physical condition caused by the heavy pace of the campaign and his diabetes further undermined his credibility as a state-level candidate.[64]

The moderate Ryan de Graffenried's central themes were leadership and reapportionment. He approached the segregation issue by characterizing the U.S. Supreme Court's *Brown v. Board* decision as a "legal travesty" but then adding that "standing up . . . and hollering about the Supreme Court—and I've done some of it myself—is fine. But it doesn't accomplish anything."[65]

Folsom played down the other candidates' frequent emphasis on segregation by observing sarcastically that his opponents were still fighting the Civil War. He promised more road construction in the form of four-lane highways connecting county seats (a reasonable platform plank given his career-long emphasis on highway construction) and increased pensions for the elderly, another longtime concern. "I'm the same old Big Jim Folsom," he would say, "but it used to be wine, women, and song. Now its Metrecal [a diet drink], the same old gal—and sing along with Big Jim."[66] Many who observed him in personal appearances noted that he regularly consumed beverages stronger than either wine or Metrecal.

Folsom's popularity had been severely damaged by a widely publicized meeting with the notorious black New York congressman Adam Clayton Powell during the Montgomery bus boycott in Folsom's second term.[67] His opponents played up this meeting in the 1962 campaign. They simultaneously tagged Folsom as sympathetic to blacks and integration and as a drunk. An advertisement paid for by the Committee for Truth and Honesty in Government, chaired by Elbert P. Jeter of Mobile, read in part: "He said . . . 'Y'ALL COME' but who came . . . ? ADAM CLAYTON POWELL (Negro Congressman from New York)." All the ellipses were in the original advertisement.

George Wallace effectively merged the Powell incident and Folsom's drinking in the public's mind with his crafty promise that alcohol would never be served in the governor's mansion if he was elected. Wallace had served in the House during Folsom's first term, and he then became a circuit judge in Barbour County, where he used his position to build a record defending segregation. Just a few weeks before his term as circuit judge ended in 1958, agents working for the U.S. Commission on Civil Rights asked to see the voting records in his district. Taking advantage of the situation, Wallace gained possession of the records and announced, "If any agent of the Civil Rights Commission comes down here to get them, they will be locked up."[68] The agents then obtained a federal subpoena.

Wallace loudly proclaimed he would never surrender the records. When the threat of a contempt citation loomed, however, he quietly transferred the records to grand juries in Bullock and Barbour Counties and phoned the federal agents to tell them they would be available from the grand juries. Justice Department lawyers still insisted that he be cited for contempt. Appearing before U.S. District Court Judge Frank M. Johnson Jr., Wallace tried to plead guilty. The judge acquitted Wallace, and in an attempt to counter the "fighting judge" image Wallace cultivated for himself, Johnson's opinion described how Wallace used the devious methods explained above to assist the federal agents in obtaining the records.[69]

A newcomer to Alabama observing Wallace's 1962 primary campaign might have concluded that his leading opponent was the federal court system rather than de Graffenried or Folsom. Of the U.S. Supreme Court he said, "I don't think they have the legal brains to try a chicken thief." He accused the federal courts of exercising judicial dictatorship and judicial tyranny.[70] Neither Boutwell's crafty legalistic stratagems nor the conciliatory approaches advocated by Folsom or de Graffenried were for Wallace. He reveled in harsh rhetoric and promised dramatic confrontation with federal officials.

Wallace declared that he would block federal officials at the "school house door" and challenge them to arrest him. The logic behind this tactic was that the federal officials would not have the nerve to use force to remove and jail a state governor.[71] He also began using what would become his central slogan, "Stand Up for Alabama," but it was buried in the small print of advertisement copy. Later, as a presidential candidate Wallace modified the slogan to "Stand Up for America."

"Bull" Connor specialized in tough-sounding quotes such as "All it takes to break up the biggest sit-down demonstration is two good police officers and a couple of police dogs."[72] He was not very successful at attracting people to his rallies. Attorney General Gallion never discovered a theme that distinguished him from the other candidates.

The most prominent candidate for the office of lieutenant governor was James B. Allen, who had served as lieutenant governor in the Gordon Persons administration, between the two Folsom administrations. He had run an unsuccessful race for governor in 1954, but that loss did him little harm because he was just one of a large group defeated by Folsom.

None of the other candidates enjoyed as much statewide name recognition as Allen, although John Guthrie, who was ending his first term in the House, was well known for a relative newcomer because of his sponsorship of Chop-Up. His central campaign theme seemed to be an advocacy of sin. He favored legalized dog and horse racing and more liberal county-option liquor laws.

Bert Haltom, another north Alabama candidate (Lauderdale and Limestone), was ending a term in the Senate. Before that he had served one term in the House. Like Guthrie, he was a vigorous advocate of reapportionment. He and de Graffenried had joined Senator Larry Dumas of Jefferson County in filibustering the Chop-Up legislation. Several politicians active in that era argue that Haltom and de Graffenried had based their Chop-Up actions not on principle but on political necessity—Jefferson County votes could determine the outcome of a statewide election.

Another candidate, J. Daniel Hand, was the immediate past president of the powerful AEA. He had run unsuccessfully for other elected offices.

The Montgomery lawyer Frank Mizell rounded out the list of serious candidates for the lieutenant governor's office. Widely considered the leader of the states' rights faction of the Democratic party, in 1955 he had narrowly lost the chairmanship of the state Democratic party to Sam Engelhardt.

In reading the newspaper coverage of the 1962 Democratic primary, it is easy to forget that Lister Hill was running for reelection to the U.S. Senate. His advertising emphasized his Senate committee work and legislative accomplishments, especially in health care. He devoted little space to segregation issues. Typical was the sentence in one advertisement: "I have always worked and fought to protect our Southern rights and traditions."[73] This limp rhetoric was strongly buttressed by his active participation in anti–civil rights filibustering.[74]

The failure of congressional redistricting meant that a statewide "musical chairs" primary (the 9-8 plan) would be used to reduce the number of congressmen from nine to eight.

Civil Rights Activity During the Primary

In January 1962 a federal court ordered an end to the segregation of Birmingham's parks and recreation facilities. To avoid complying, the city commissioners closed them.

A *Wall Street Journal* reporter described a "significant realignment of forces" in Birmingham in which "conservative business and civic leaders who formerly kept silent on racial questions now find themselves speaking out in favor of open parks and against the bitter segregationists who would close them."[75] The reporter unfavorably contrasted Birmingham's racist city government officials with Atlanta's growth-oriented, pragmatist leaders. On the other hand, he identified the Birmingham Chamber of Commerce, Downtown Improvement Association, and League of Women Voters as public advocates for open parks. And, although many in the business community favored segregation, they also believed that civil rights discord would hurt the city in its competition for new industry.

In March, with Birmingham's public parks and golf courses still closed, a black boycott of white Birmingham businesses began. It had modest objectives, such as the removal of segregation signs, integration of lunch counters, promotion of black employees, and the hiring of additional ones. (A similar boycott began in Huntsville in early April.) The Birmingham commissioners responded by ending the city's financial support for the Jefferson County surplus-food program, the majority of whose recipients were black. "Bull" Connor observed of the food cutoff, "Let 'em root hog or die."[76]

Primary Results and the Runoff

All nine U.S. House incumbents and Senator Lister Hill won their primary races. The congressmen would face each other in the runoff election that would determine the eight finalists.

George Wallace and Ryan de Graffenried moved into a runoff, with Wallace in the lead at 32.5 percent of the vote and de Graffenried second with 25 percent. The gubernatorial primary cleanly divided north and south Alabama. Folsom and de Graffenried shared the north, where both had home counties; they also shared the populist attitudes of the north. Wallace dominated the middle and southern counties. Unencumbered by an effective segregationist opponent like Patterson, Wallace found ready ideological and interest-group support throughout the middle and southern counties. Although Wallace won Montgomery County and de Graffenried took Madison County, neither had clear victories in Jefferson, Mobile, or Etowah Counties, the other major urban centers.

In the lieutenant governor's race, Jim Allen won a 33.3 percent plurality against Bert Haltom's 32.7 percent. They were separated by only 3,200 votes in an eight-person race. Allen won most counties in middle Alabama and northern portions of the state surrounding his home, Etowah County. Haltom's main strength centered in his native northwestern corner of the state, but it also included Jefferson County.

Six blacks were elected to the executive committee of the Jefferson County Democratic party for the first time. Another moved into a runoff election.

Desperate tactics and vacuous rhetoric dominated the runoff campaigns. Ryan de Graffenried sought in vain to tie Wallace to Folsom. This was not entirely farfetched, given Wallace's political origins in the Folsom camp and his occasional populist rhetoric, but Wallace had separated himself from Folsom with regard to race. De Graffenried's views on segregation were closer to Folsom's than Wallace's were, a fact demonstrated by Folsom's endorsement of him.

Wallace campaigned energetically, if routinely, addressing large and enthusiastic crowds that sometimes numbered over five thousand. Wallace's speeches were full of clichés like "I shall be governor of a united Alabama and not the governor for any particular section" and "I will be an honest, sober, and an efficient administrator." He mixed these high-toned sentiments with extravagant criticism of the federal courts.[77]

Meanwhile, in a heretofore quiet race for attorney general, Willard Livingston charged that his opponent in the runoff, former state senator Richmond Flowers, had received a "solid bloc" of black votes.[78]

The statewide congressional runoff revealed a great deal about changing power relationships and continuing regional and urban animosities. The *Montgomery Advertiser* advised voters in south Alabama congressional districts to concentrate on eliminating Congressman George Huddleston of Jefferson County. *Birmingham News* editors chose to take this tactic personally, interpreting it as a reflection of the *Advertiser*'s anger because the *News* had publicized the true nature of the gubernatorial race: "The Black Belt v. North Alabama and OTHER larger-population counties—including the *Advertiser*'s own Montgomery County which suffers from rotten apportionment."[79]

A *News* editorial defined the Black Belt as both a geographical location and, more important, a state of mind: "It includes an alliance of those who don't want Alabama to do much to meet its needs, who fail to pay attention to new jobs for the unemployed and for the growing number of young people wanting employment and an Alabama future."[80] The editorial made no mention of Jefferson County's decades-old alliance with these enemies of progress or the role of the *Birmingham News* in supporting the Jefferson–Black Belt partnership.

George Wallace swept to victory, winning fifty-seven of the state's sixty-seven counties. De Graffenried won significant majorities only in his home county of Tuscaloosa and three north Alabama urban counties—Jefferson, Madison, and Morgan. James B. Allen gained the nomination for lieutenant governor with 54 percent of the vote. In the congressional primary, seventy-seven-year-old Frank Boykin of Mobile was the odd man out.

The Birmingham Elections

Birmingham's business leaders and its growing professional community realized that the city needed to revamp its governmental structure. Its three-person commission was inefficient and unsuited to a city its size. It also gave too much power to "Bull" Connor, who supervised the police and fire functions, and to Commissioner and Mayor Arthur Hanes, whose attitudes toward race were only marginally different from Connor's.

Reform-oriented young professionals and businessmen drafted a proposal for a mayor-council form of government and fought an intense campaign for its enactment. They hoped that the new system would prove attractive enough to influence future annexation votes positively.

In the November general election Birmingham voters seemed to reverse their long-standing support of diehard segregationist city leaders by approving the restructuring of the city government. Mayor Hanes had refused to call this referendum, but Probate Judge J. Paul Meeks had forced it.

The Republican Party

Claude Vardaman, chair of the state Republican party's executive committee for twenty years, ran for reelection. His opponent was John Grenier, a thirty-two-year-old Birmingham lawyer who was often characterized by the press as a Young Turk. In June the Alabama Republican convention selected Grenier. The *Birmingham News* interpreted Grenier's victory as a sign of the Republican party's resurgence in Alabama. It argued that his impressive leadership skills and energy, Alabama's fundamental conservatism, and increasing resentment against the Democratic party, as well as fading memories of Little Rock, could lead to growth in the Republican party.[81]

At the Republican convention a fight occurred over whether the GOP should nominate candidates for governor and lieutenant governor. Because a great many of the delegates liked Wallace and sensed that he was unbeatable, the convention nominated no one for governor. Furthermore, the gathering nominated only three congressional candidates, including Evan Foreman, a Mobile businessman and a segregationist who received national news coverage by accusing the Kennedy administration of "getting ready to register the monkeys to vote."[82] A businessman named James "Jim" Martin received the nomination for the U.S. Senate. The Republicans fielded relatively few state legislative candidates.

The Republican nomination of only a few candidates may have been sensible in the short run. There was no question that the Republicans would have lost virtually all the races they in fact chose to ignore. But running for all offices from the top to the bottom is an important step in building the strength of a minority party in the long run. A minority party cannot just coyly linger hoping that the national party will produce a presidential, senatorial, or gubernatorial victory and that this will somehow translate into lower-level triumphs. Instead, the minority party must run full slates of candidates in election after election, establishing itself in the public's mind and gaining campaign experience so that when an opportunity presents itself, the party is ready to take advantage of it. Given the national Democratic party's rush to embrace the civil rights movement, it was not difficult for Alabama Republicans to foresee, as many did, that such an opportunity might appear in the near future.

Alabama Republican activists, like their counterparts elsewhere in the

South, were inclined to keep their numbers small so that large percentages of them could benefit from patronage and positions available in the Republican administration in Washington or hold national party offices. Attracting newcomers to their ranks would only make competition for these plums fiercer, an especially unappealing prospect for country club Republicans.[83]

Beginning with his acceptance speech, Jim Martin's campaign for the Senate represented a break with this traditional approach to Republicanism, if not Alabama politics in general. He bade Alabama to "return to the spirit of '61—1861, when our fathers formed a new nation."[84] It is significant that Martin had been president of Associated Industries of Alabama, a position reserved for Big Mules.

The General Election Campaign

Senator Lister Hill found Jim Martin to be a surprisingly effective opponent. Hill's last general election fight occurred in 1950, when his opponent, the Independent candidate John G. Crommelion Jr., garnered only 23.5 percent of the vote. The senator neatly bracketed Martin's anti–civil rights thrusts by condemning John F. Kennedy's attempts to desegregate the University of Mississippi while at the same time claiming that a Republican administration would have taken a similar action.

Hill won as expected, but the narrowness of his victory (201,937 versus 195,134) shocked Democrats and signaled the presence of growing GOP strength. Martin won in Jefferson, Montgomery (Hill's home), and Mobile Counties as well as most counties in the southern half of the state. Although Jefferson County voted for Martin, it failed to elect any of the three Republicans nominated for state legislative positions. Republicans won state legislative seats in only Montgomery and Winston Counties.

A *Birmingham News* editorial speculated about the meaning of the election for the Republican party. The editorial correctly observed that the election was a step forward for the GOP, but not a very large one. The campaign represented a "failure to display a genuine sense of Republicanism," an observation that could be made three decades later.[85] By avoiding a race against George Wallace, the Alabama Republican party had suggested that there was no significant difference between it and the state's Democratic party.

The modest Republican showing in Alabama was mirrored in other southern states. North Carolina added one Republican to the single Republican already part of its congressional delegation. Tennessee also added one Republican. In South Carolina the Republicans lost two legislative seats, and the Republican U.S. Senate candidate won only nine of forty-six counties. In Georgia, Republicans nominated nineteen candidates for the state legislature; only four won.

The 1962 election sent out a conglomeration of mixed signals. The Republican party moved almost imperceptibly forward. The Black Belt–Birmingham split was confirmed. Birmingham voters threw out an old-fashioned governmental structure and prepared to evict diehard segregationists in favor of a leader who had built much of his career on defending segregation but now took a more moderate stance. And, although Black Belt leaders considered the newly elected governor too moderate for its tastes, he had won his position as the result of his willingness to defend segregation without compromise.

Patterson's Legacy

John Patterson presided over the breakup of one of the most effective political machines in the nation's history, the Big Mule–Black Belt alliance, which had ruled state government for six decades. In its last gasp it eradicated his attempt to equalize property taxes, a tragic loss for the future of education in Alabama, and it gutted his education tax package, leaving it smaller and less progressive. Patterson did not cause the breakup; it certainly would have occurred, perhaps a bit later, had he never been governor. When he assumed office, the partnership had been strained for more than a decade. He pressed in the same direction as demographic and economic changes. These changes, together with the civil rights movement, would break the alliance's back.

Patterson's actions as governor contributed to the state's quality of life in areas outside the realm of civil rights. He pushed road construction plans that he willingly admits were begun by Jim Folsom. He improved the funding base for schools, even though the alliance gutted his original plans and a depressed economy did not allow for as much increased funding as he would have liked. And he tried to reform a corrupt and destructive property tax system.

His actions did harm in the area of civil rights and to the state's national image. In interviews he defended his policies by saying that he was fighting a holding action to allow emotions to cool. This argument is fallacious. His actions were too effective and too brutal to sustain it.

Those who wanted progress for the South and for state government in general had high hopes for reapportionment. They believed that by making the legislature more representative, the one-person-one-vote standard, which the partially reapportioned legislature would have to put into place for the 1966 elections, would enhance governmental responsiveness and the quality of government. Furthermore, the previous two decades were ones of dramatic narrowing of the gaps between Alabama and the rest of the nation. There would be rough times ahead in the area of civil rights but, overall, at the end of the Patterson administration there was reason for optimism—except for the election of George Wallace.

Breakup of the Alliance

The birth and disintegration of a successful political elite operating in a democracy is an uncommon sight. It is also unusual to see a successful elite founded on an alliance of interests as apparently dissimilar as those of the industrialists and the Black Belt plantation owners. In virtually all states with significant urban areas, state politics centered on urban-rural conflict, but not in Alabama.

The plantation owners built a system that could not remain in power on an equal footing with urban interests. They denied a majority of their citizens the opportunities that most Americans took for granted. As a result, many departed, reducing county populations and making the malapportioned legislature look more grotesque with each passing census. Most relocating companies wanted no part of the Black Belt with its uneducated workers, lack of amenities, and antediluvian political elites. The largely agricultural economy of the Black Belt counties stagnated and weakened the economic basis for political power. Slowly the large landholders began to sell off portions of their holdings, particularly timber lands, to large business entities. These corporate landholders also had a vested interest in maintaining the status quo on taxes.

When the alliance was sealed in 1901, there was little difference between attitudes in the Black Belt and in Birmingham toward blacks and those of many national political leaders, scholars in leading northeastern universities, and authors who wrote for popular national magazines. By the mid-1920s the nation as a whole began to part with its racist past, but Black Belt leaders, dominating counties with large black majorities, could not do so. They saw nothing wrong with their ruling position, and they could not imagine a time when it could be undermined. So they hung on. For a while their industrialist allies stayed with them, opposing progress throughout the state that would not benefit them directly. The plantation owners were widely admired for the creativity of their guerrilla warfare against the future, but it was the narrow creativity of a skilled technician. They were entirely lacking in vision.

Finally, the inability of plantation owners to contribute sufficient money or growing numbers of voters to the political power of the alliance, their increasingly embarrassing behavior under the pressure of the civil rights movement, and most important of all, the authority of the federal courts and the U.S. Constitution encouraged the industrialists to strike out on their own.

Even in a reapportioned legislature the plantation owners would be a power impossible to ignore. They had many interests in common with rural landowners elsewhere in the state, forming a rural coalition new to Alabama but common in other states. Furthermore, the similarity of some interests between the Black Belt and Jefferson County that had originally cemented the alliance and then held it together for six decades had not completely disappeared. The industrialists who dominated Jefferson County did not suddenly see the light and become friends of the common person. Their paternalistic attitudes did not disappear. And, although outsiders with differing political philosophies moved into places like Birmingham, with its medical complex, or Huntsville, with its large federal rocket facility, the older traditional culture base still dominated.

7

Wallace's Leap to National Prominence

George Wallace's inauguration speech presented a blistering defense of the status quo and featured the often-quoted battle cry "Segregation now, segregation tomorrow, segregation forever." Wallace also noted that the South "will determine in the next election who shall sit in the White House."[1] At least one anonymous *Birmingham News* reporter believed that in his inaugural address Wallace began bidding for leadership of the southern opposition to integration.

Attorney General Richmond Flowers's inaugural speech appeared to be a direct point-for-point contradiction of Wallace's. He too was staking out a position for future races. Some charged that Flowers had obtained an advance copy of Wallace's speech, but in a personal interview he denied that accusation. He did not need to see the speech, he said, because "Wallace never gave any other speech."[2]

Appointments and Patronage

Wallace's administrative appointments were spread evenly around the state. He selected James Folsom Sr.'s boyhood friend Phillip Hamm as revenue commissioner. Hamm had served as revenue commissioner and state conservation director under Folsom, and he enjoyed a well-deserved reputation as a prudent administrator and team player. A Birmingham lawyer named Earl Morgan became Wallace's executive secretary (an extremely influential position), and a Jasper (north Alabama) newspaper editor, Bill Jones, was named press secretary.

Wallace's choice as finance director was Seymore Trammell of Montgomery, an attorney and longtime friend. Engineer Ed Rodgers, also of

Montgomery, became highway director, a post he held under Governor Chauncey Sparks in the early 1940s.[3]

Wallace's selection of Albert Brewer as Speaker, Rankin Fite as House floor leader, George Hawkins as Senate president pro tem, and Charles "Pete" Mathews as administration floor leader in the Senate reinforced the impression that leadership positions were being widely and fairly distributed. The first three came from north Alabama, and Mathews was from the north central part of the state, near Birmingham.

Brewer and Hawkins were as far from the Black Belt spiritually as they were geographically. Hawkins was quoted as saying: "Extreme racism will speed rather than deter integration. . . . I have children of my own, and I dread integration, especially for their sake. I find it distasteful. But like it or not, the courts have ruled, and to refuse to abide by these decisions—at the risk of mob violence—is to have no government at all. It is anarchy."[4] This was the statement of one of the most forward-thinking of Alabama's government officials in the 1960s. Not surprisingly, Hawkins and Wallace had a falling out early in the first administration; despite his formal position, Hawkins is rarely described in newspaper stories and never by interview subjects as assisting in the passage of administration-sponsored bills.[5]

Rankin Fite was a legislative operator whose political skills were possibly unrivaled in Alabama history before his time and certainly unequaled since. He was a cynic whose primary and almost exclusive objective was to gain the most patronage for himself and his county. Aside from his hostility to labor unions, he was unconcerned with social issues or the public interest except insofar as such matters would affect his power or the flow of construction projects, jobs, and contracts into his home county of Marion.[6]

Albert Brewer was highly intelligent, introverted for a politician, and fascinated with the intricacies of government. Although he represented a rural north Alabama county, he is usually regarded as closely allied with the more progressive elements of big industry. Since Wallace and his Speaker differed in virtually every way imaginable except that both were white male Alabama attorneys, many observers wondered why Brewer was chosen. According to Brewer, there were three apparent contenders for Speaker. One was Hugh Morrow, but he was never seriously considered because he was not a team player and was rather abrupt in style. Fite was another possibility. No one questioned his ability, but because he had been close to Folsom, Wallace was wary of him. Brewer had been a Wallace supporter in 1958 because he viewed Wallace as more progressive than John Patterson. Brewer had also established himself as independent of Patterson and as politically ambitious (a strong positive for Wallace) two years before when "in a fit of insanity" he ran for the speakership.[7]

Albert Brewer organized the House in 1963 with little direct input from George Wallace. Brewer took the customary position as chair of the Rules Committee; Fite became vice chair. Fite chaired the Ways and Means Committee, and Hugh Merrill of Calhoun County in north Alabama, the Judiciary Committee.

In the Senate Charles Adams of Henry (Black Belt) and Houston (Dothan) Counties became chair of the Rules Committee. Larry Dumas of Jefferson County chaired Judiciary. Pete Mathews, the Alabama Farm Bureau Federation's attorney, became chair of the Finance and Taxation Committee in addition to being Wallace's floor leader. According to Vaughan Hill Robison, "Pete Mathews was 100 percent Farm Bureau and a big George Wallace supporter because the Farm Bureau was a Wallace supporter. That includes the Farm Bureau insurance unit."[8]

Vice-chair positions on the most important committees in both the House and Senate were also distributed broadly, except that none went to Mobile or Montgomery County representatives or senators. In allowing executive and legislative leadership appointments to be spread widely with little reference to which counties supported him in the primary, Wallace followed customary practice.

In 1963 the reapportioned House included seventeen Jefferson County representatives elected at-large. According to Albert Brewer and others, the new delegation differed from the preceding one only in number. Jefferson County House members were recruited by and remained loyal to the Big Mules.[9]

The Wallace administration energetically devoted itself to satisfying the patronage demands of its supporters. Each state contract, regardless of size, received high-level attention. One of literally hundreds of examples that could be cited is the following memorandum to Richard Stone, assistant director of the Finance Department, from Wallace's executive secretary, Earl Morgan:

> I talked to Seymore [Trammell, the finance director] about this matter several days ago and he said that we wanted to follow through on it.
>
> Grant Woodham is Representative for Monroe Calculating Machine Company here in Montgomery. Grant was one of the Governor's very loyal workers in both campaigns and is deserving of the utmost consideration. The Company has another man that handles all of Monroe's business with the State and he refuses to step aside and let Grant

handle any of this business with the State. Please give your attention to this matter and we want to get word someway to the Company that we want Grant Woodham to be able to represent the Company in their dealings with the State of Alabama.[10]

Another typical example is a March 18, 1963, letter to Governor Wallace from L. J. Hays Jr., parts manager of the Tuscaloosa Motor Company: "This is to confirm the agreement with Mrs. W. H. May . . . one of your strong supporters, in regards to the commission on all parts purchased by the State of Alabama from Tuscaloosa Motor Company during your administration. We have agreed to give Mrs. May 5% commission on all State purchases, the larger the purchases the more she will receive."[11]

Similar letters and memos concern such matters as which auto wrecker services were to be given state business and placed on state highway patrol lists for recommendation to accident victims,[12] which banks would receive deposits of state funds (on which the banks paid no interest),[13] and which lawyers would perform Highway Department condemnation work.[14]

Many memos in the Wallace office files promised highway construction projects. One of hundreds from George Wallace was sent in March 1963 to Bob Kendall. It read: "Please discuss with Senator Julian Lowe and Representative Gus Young their road problems. I am very interested in helping them in any way we can."[15]

Wallace left little doubt about his road-building priorities, as illustrated in the following 1963 memo to Highway Department administrator Ed Rodgers:

> I want a crash effort made on this and I want this done if at all possible. In other words, I want this completed during this four years. In fact, I am as interested in this as I am any road in Alabama. . . .
> cc: Rep. Henry Steagall
> Rep. Gardner Bassett
> P.S. This is a project that I would like to make a crash effort on during this Administration.[16]

In a letter to Joe Shaw, editor of the *Cherokee County Herald,* Wallace made his standards for highway project location quite clear. He wrote that Representative Ralph Meade and Senator Kenneth Hammond "were very cooperative with this Administration" and have been rewarded with "extra money for the cities of Cherokee County and also for the County for road and street building."[17] Another standard form of patronage control was giving or denying lawyer-legislators state legal work and other rewards tied to their livelihoods and ambitions.[18]

Patronage concerns are also reflected in Wallace's (and all other governors') attempts to influence the legislature. One of many examples is a January 17, 1963, letter from Representative E. A. Grouby to Wallace:

> In Conference with you on September 17, you asked me what Committees I would prefer to serve on. I told you at that time it did not make much difference and wherever I could be most helpful would be satisfactory. You told me at that time you had to take care of the North Alabama boys in an effort to do away with the sectionalism of North and South Alabama, which I agreed.
>
> In this Conference there was only one earnest and sincere request that I made of you, and that was to retain J. Edward Jones, who was a per diem worker as helper in the Warehouse at the Highway Shops near Kilby, at $1.22 per hour.[19]

This letter also illustrates the care that governors took in selecting geographically representative legislative leaders.[20]

According to all interview subjects who addressed the topic, Wallace's support from interest groups came first and foremost from the Farm Bureau. As the years passed, big business interests also supported him, partly because some of their concerns coincided with his but more out of fear. He commanded such impressive electoral strength that they realized the futility of opposing him. One interview subject recalled with evident distaste how obsequious corporate leaders were in their personal dealings with Wallace. They flattered him whenever possible, and "if they didn't like one of his proposals, they sought to blunt it, not oppose it outright."

Civil Rights Issues in Washington

A month after Wallace's inauguration, President John Kennedy sent the United States Congress a written "Special Message on Civil Rights." In it he observed that "the harmful, wasteful and wrongful results of racial discrimination and segregation still appear in virtually . . . every part of the Nation."[21] Accompanying the message were watery proposals for changes in voting laws and an extension of the essentially powerless Commission on Civil Rights.[22]

According to Robert Loevy, Kennedy's proposals were so modest because the president believed that civil rights legislation ending segregation and other forms of racial discrimination had no chance of winning congressional approval. Kennedy was undoubtedly correct in this assessment. Howard Smith, the Democratic chairman of the House Rules Committee, was a Virginian who was unequivocally opposed to civil rights legislation. At that time the Rules Committee chair could obstruct a bill almost indefinitely even against the wishes of a House majority, and it was impossible to slip a major civil rights bill around the Rules Committee.

In the Senate the chairman of the Judiciary Committee, James O. Eastland, was a Democrat from Mississippi who had blocked over one hundred civil rights bills in previous years. Making Eastland and other southern senators even more powerful, Senate rules allowed wide latitude for filibustering. A small group of senators could paralyze the upper house unless a two-thirds vote invoked cloture.

Loevy points out that Kennedy needed to maintain a coalition in support of his economic, education, and social welfare programs. That coalition included many southern Democrats whom Kennedy could not afford to alienate. He faced a reelection campaign in 1964, and given his narrow victory against Richard Nixon in 1960, it would not have been advisable to further offend an already edgy South.

Legislative Activity:
Roads and Education

Wallace wanted funding for road construction, if only because of its potential for patronage. At the same time, he recognized that additional spending for education would be necessary. Education funding sources opened in the Patterson years had proved disappointing because of strikes and a depressed economy, so education interests pursued new or expanded revenue.[23]

Wallace did not want to raise taxes for both road building and education. Bond issues for capital spending represented normal financial practice, and hundreds of millions of dollars in federal money would be lost if the state did not produce matching funds. He called a special session in March 1963 to pass a $100 million road-bond issue.

A few legislators associated with John Patterson, most notably Senator Bob Gilchrist of Morgan and Lawrence Counties, a former Patterson House floor leader, unsuccessfully fought the bond issue. Allies of past and future governors generally opposed such bills during this period, when governors could not succeed themselves. Patterson loyalists expected that their counties and/or the businesses and law firms with which they were associated would receive below-average shares of the proceeds. This was politics as usual, with the federal matching funds as an extra motivator. Wallace had no more difficulty winning passage of the road bond issue than Patterson had four years earlier.

Wallace brought the legislature back for a second special session on March 19 to deal with education.[24] Once again, Wallace followed the pattern established by Patterson. In his legislative call the governor suggested that his industrial development activities would generate increased tax revenues that would better support education. He made the reverse connection (education supporting accelerated industrial development) less explicitly.

In 1963 Alabama's schools were still, with the exception of a few affluent districts, bleak and undistinguished institutions. Alabama ranked forty-eighth in the nation in per-pupil expenditures, spending $255 per student per year while the national average was $432.[25] Property taxes, a traditional source of funding for primary and secondary schools, were the lowest in the nation. The state also had more children per teacher (29.3) than any other state. Alabama ranked forty-seventh in teacher pay. The average Alabama teacher earned $3,988 per year, compared to $5,735 for the nation. In 1951–52 the average pay of Alabama teachers ($2,531) was $919 below the national average. In 1963 it had slipped to $1,696 below.[26] Only 5.7 percent of Alabama residents were college graduates; the national average was 7.7 percent. Alabama ranked forty-second by this measure. The average Alabamian twenty-five or over had completed 9.1 grades; the national average was 10.6 grades. Between 1956 and 1962 education had lost $50 million to proration—across-the-board spending cuts required to balance the state education budget.[27]

In 1963, unlike many past years, school funding increases were popular among legislators. A *Montgomery Advertiser* editorial provided several explanations, including especially active lobbying by teachers. The editorial justified this activism by citing the kinds of statistics displayed above. Education forces wanted a constitutional amendment that would allow a five-mill property tax increase.[28] They also pushed for a sales tax increase, as they had done at the beginning of the Patterson years.[29] They wanted $50–60 million in increased annual revenues, amounts which, though seemingly large, would have resulted in only a marginal improvement in the state's schools. In favoring a regressive sales tax, educators followed the path of least resistance around business and agriculture interests. Organized labor maintained its traditional opposition to the sales tax and sales tax increases.

Once again, the members of the former agricultural-industrial Big Mule Alliance were in agreement because of a congruence of interests if not team play.[30] They favored the sales tax because it was inherently regressive. They believed that since the poor (often translated blacks) benefited the most from public education (a fallacious proposition), it was fair for them to pay disproportionately for it. They knew that they could probably add exemptions favoring industry and agriculture as they had done in 1959 and many other years. Wallace's inclination as a legislator had been to oppose a sales tax increase, and interview subjects agree that this opposition was part of a tendency toward liberalism that surfaced occasionally.

There were several important votes in a long and complex legislative session. In April the House gave Wallace a two-cent-per-bottle beer tax he wanted.[31] This essentially regressive tax was earmarked for junior colleges. Opposition to the beer tax centered in Jefferson and Mobile, primarily because in those counties the most beer was sold. Dry counties and their often prohibitionist representatives tended to support beer and liquor taxes because they benefited from them even though they were not involved in the collection. The tax passed, sixty-six to thirty-three.[32]

In the second week of April the House voted down an estimated $51.5 million set of education tax bills proposed by the administration. One measure, which would have imposed a 3 percent sales tax on domestic utility bills, was defeated seventy-two to twenty-eight.[33] Opponents of the administration package favored a more or less equally regressive one-cent sales tax increase (from 3 to 4 percent) with retention of existing exemptions.[34] The most important round in this fight was a procedural vote on a motion offered by Representative Sam Nettles of Wilcox County, a leading advocate of the sales tax. Wilcox County legislators had been leaders of the most reactionary Black Belt forces for decades. The vote, which had the effect of killing the Wallace utility tax, was sixty to thirty-eight.[35]

There was a strong negative relationship between a county's support for Wallace in the Democratic primary and this fairly important vote. Chi-square analysis shows that the negative relationship is statistically significant beyond the 1 percent level (.003). Virtually the only counties on Wallace's side in this vote were in the extreme north and the extreme southeast corner. Nearly all of the Black Belt counties plus Mobile, Jefferson, and Montgomery opposed the tax, lending strong support to newspaper analyses indicating that the former alliance partners still were capable of running the legislature. The Big Mule–oriented *Birmingham News* favored the sales tax over Wallace's tax package.[36]

In the third week of April the Senate Finance and Taxation Committee voted out two Wallace bills that increased corporate income taxes, the first even remotely progressive proposals to show signs of life. One of them,

HB90, disallowed corporate deduction of federal income tax payments in determining state income tax liabilities. The committee approved it by a vote of nine to six. The second measure was an enabling act tied to a constitutional amendment increasing the corporate income tax rate from 3 to 5 percent. The committee approved it by voice vote. On the same day, the Senate Constitutional Amendments Committee voted favorably on the constitutional amendment. The only dissenting vote came from Neil Metcalf of Geneva County. Representatives of industry, who had never exhibited shyness about seeking tax exemptions for business or regressive tax increases, charged that these bills were examples of class-based legislation.

While the Senate abused industry, the House voted against another relatively progressive Wallace-supported tax bill that placed a 10 percent levy on road construction contracts and a 1.5 percent tax on all other construction contracts. The vote was fifty-one to forty-one.[37] Jefferson, Mobile, and Montgomery Counties opposed the legislation, and Etowah and Madison were neutral. Thus, on balance urban counties were strongly opposed. The Black Belt split, but a majority of Black Belt counties were opposed. Legislators voted their interests, which coincided to a substantial degree with the old alliance position.[38]

In June the session ended, marked by more than the usual filibustering and maneuvering. By then the legislature had passed tax bills estimated to generate more than $40 million annually. It increased the sales tax to 4 percent. The Wallace administration opposed this bill, as did legislators from counties bordering neighboring states and from counties where local sales taxes were levied. Rural, small-county, and agricultural interests heavily supported the sales tax. This array of forces represented another classic political pattern.

Wallace's two-cent-per-bottle beer tax, earmarked for junior college and trade school construction, passed. The constitutional amendment increasing the corporate income tax to 5 percent passed. Like all constitutional amendments, this one had to be approved by the voters. The legislature also passed the bill that disallowed corporate deductions of the federal income tax in calculating the state income tax. The latter would go into effect only if the voters approved it but rejected the increased corporate tax rate amendment.

Overall, these measures represented a mixture of success and failure for Wallace. Their legislative histories indicate that Wallace leaned toward progressive taxes to improve education.[39] The reader is cautioned not to read into this or any similar observation in this volume the idea that Wallace possessed strong ideological tendencies. The point on which interview subjects agree more than any other is that George Wallace was devoid of a coherent set of beliefs. Some claim he has no principles of any sort. Most typically, he is called an opportunist who adopted populism, progressivism, segregation, or any other political stand only as a means to the end of being governor. One interviewee summed up the consensus by saying: "George Wallace was for George Wallace 1,000 percent." Another put it even more strongly: "Wallace was for Wallace 100%—no, 1,000% self-serving. Elect George Wallace. If things began to go smoothly, he would stir things up."

Asked what legislation was most important to Wallace, the veteran legislator and lobbyist Pete Mathews answered, "Whatever legislation affected him politically." He also observed that the great tragedy of Wallace's time as governor was that he could have done a great deal to improve the state, but he did not care about improving it. He either ended up doing nothing or doing harm.[40] The Birmingham legislator George Lewis Bailes Jr. described Wallace's terms as governor as "all disasters. He sold everything to his cronies so they could make money and give him big campaign contributions."[41] Bailes, like many other informed observers, described Wallace as uninterested in government except insofar as it had implications for his personal political power.

There is ample evidence in the Wallace office files, as there was in Patterson's, that many people in and out of government viewed public education and segregation as two separate concerns, even though a few favored strangling public schools because of forthcoming integration. Personal interviews with legislators and other government officials of this period suggest stronger race-based opposition to public school funding than do these files.

People who wrote to Wallace, whether ordinary citizens or influentials, favored segregation, but they also wanted good schools. To some degree, so did Wallace.[42] His advocacy of increased school funding in the legislature supports this contention, as do small but convincing administrative actions. For example, Wallace, the Mobile legislative delegation, and Superintendent of Education Austin Meadows actively engaged in the creation of "a documentary film on the need for additional support for the Alabama public school system."[43] Wallace promised that his office would contribute two thousand dollars toward the film's production if other bodies such as the universities and the AEA supported it also.

Two-Year Institutions

Although Wallace supported primary schools and universities in 1963 and later years, his only energetic work for public education was in the area of trade schools and junior colleges, often called technical colleges and community colleges, respectively. Collectively they are referred to as two-year colleges or two-year institutions.

By the end of the Patterson administration the state had twelve two-year institutions. The first was established in Randolph County in 1922.[44] Legislation designed to encourage the establishment of similar schools had been championed by Representative George C. Wallace in 1947.[45] That statute provided for the construction of four additional state vocational schools and for a state takeover of a fifth school in Decatur. Further legislation passed during the Patterson administration authorized creation of two junior colleges.

Albert Brewer credits Rankin Fite with starting what came to be an avalanche of community college and technical college construction during the Wallace administration. According to Brewer, Fite wanted a technical college in his home town of Hamilton, and he wrote a bill to accomplish this objective. To facilitate passage he fit his technical college into a bill creating five junior colleges and five technical colleges. Construction would be funded by a two-cent beer tax. These policies were encompassed in three bills introduced by Fite.

University and primary-secondary school representatives fought Fite's bills. Their strength was greatest in the Senate, where the rules made minority opposition more effective. A Senate filibuster on the issue began on April 23 and lasted 107 hours. Although the new schools were very popular, several senators questioned the need for ten. They altered the legislation to remove the reference to ten schools and gave the state board of education the power to decide on the appropriate number of two-year institutions and the responsibility for operating all two-year institutions.[46]

Albert Brewer recalled that the senators responsible for changing the bill expected the board of education to reduce the number well below the original ten. The lawmakers believed that the education community's opposition to the two-year colleges would translate into authorization of only three or four institutions. Instead, removal of the ten-school cap resulted in the creation of more than ten schools.

In June 1963 the state board of education (Wallace as governor was an ex-officio member) appointed a committee of eight educators and instructed them to recommend geographical areas where the first five institutions should be built. Subsequent decision making ignored its work.

One of Fite's community and technical college bills created the Alabama Trade School and Junior College Authority and gave it the responsibility to issue bonds and otherwise oversee construction of trade schools and junior colleges.[47] The authority's members consisted of the governor, state superintendent of schools, director of finance, and state treasurer.

The authority became nothing more than a mouthpiece for Wallace with regard to the location of new junior colleges and trade schools. This accounts for the quickness of the decision making. The sites of eleven institutions were set in the authority's October 9, 1963, meeting, and another five in the October 29 meeting.[48] Minutes of the meetings contain no hint that these decisions were made according to any plan, nor is there any indication from any source that analysis was used to determine locations, sizes, or curricula for these institutions. Newspaper accounts and interview subjects agree that political concerns, especially those of George Wallace, were the only criteria used.[49]

Nine of the first eleven sites were located in the home counties or adjoining counties of the nine members of the state board of education. By inflating the number of institutions that were required, board members were able to build a patronage base of their own and gave George Wallace a pool of patronage jobs and contracts that he could and did exploit. Analysis reveals that legislators received their rewards not through campus sites but through the jobs and contracts awarded. Speaker Fite and Lieutenant Governor Brewer, however, won the two additional sites for their home counties.

The Tuscaloosa Chamber of Commerce wrote a proposal for a trade school for blacks in Tuscaloosa and submitted it to Wallace on October 22. The main justifications for the new school were increasing pressure for admission of blacks to Shelton Trade School plus the great numbers of blacks in the area. Supporting documentation, in its entirety, consisted of one page of population data and letters from Tuscaloosa officials.[50] The authority approved the school one week later. At least three other black schools were created, in Mobile, Montgomery, and Birmingham, with a "separate but equal" status and consequent waste.

As of 1966 Alabama had thirty-two two-year colleges operating or under construction, a 167 percent increase within a span of four years.[51] Three more were created during the Brewer administration (1968–71) and George Wallace's second administration (1971–75).

An examination of the county locations of two-year institutions raises further suspicions concerning the educational rationality of decision making in the Wallace administration. Thirty-five two-year institutions existed at the end of 1970. Today there are thirty-four such institutions, some of which operate branch campuses.

In 1970 eleven of the two-year institutions were located in counties with population densities ranging from 15 to 36 persons per square mile. These were very rural counties. Jackson and Escambia Counties, the most densely populated of this group, contained as their most prominent cities Scottsboro and Atmore. The counties with population densities of 37 to 70 persons per square mile housed six two-year institutions. Most of these counties were rural with one small city. Walker County, the most densely populated of this group, adjoins Jefferson County to the northwest, and its largest city is Jasper. Counties with 71 to 169 people per square mile were mainly rural with one prominent small to medium city. The most densely populated was Calhoun, the home of the city of Anniston and of Fort McClellan. Ten institutions were located in this category of counties. Only five counties, with 170 people per square mile and above, approach what most readers would regard as urban centers. Each contained a relatively large city. These counties and cities were Etowah (Gadsden), Montgomery (Montgomery), Madison (Huntsville), Mobile (Mobile), and Jefferson (Birmingham). These counties housed eleven of the two-year institutions, with three each in Etowah and Mobile and two each in Birmingham and Montgomery.

Perhaps the least administratively rational site placements were in the strip in the southwest and south central areas of the state. Mobile County, as the second most densely populated county and the county third in the state in population, deserved one and perhaps even two institutions. Instead it had three. The decision to grant Mobile three two-year institutions is even more dubious when the University of South Alabama, also located in Mobile, is considered. The seven-county strip to the east of Mobile and stretching from Baldwin and Clarke to Coffee County in the southeastern portion of the state included eight two-year institutions. In this group it is incredible that Covington County received two of these institutions. Covington had a population density of only 35 persons per square mile. Conecuh County, another part of this group, had a population density of only 18 (fourth lowest in the state), and Monroe, next to it, only 20. Five of the seven counties fell into the lowest population density category. The eight campuses in this strip of counties could easily have been four or five if carefully placed near county borders so that residents of two or three counties could attend a single institution. When the three institutions in densely populated Mobile are added to this block, the counties show an excess of five to seven campuses. The wide west central area of the state completely lacked public two-year colleges and technical schools. Similar logic and resulting savings or more uniform geographical distributions could have been applied to the other three major blocks of campuses located in the east central, northeastern, and north central areas. Alabama could have been saved the cost of seven to ten campuses, and the remaining campuses could have been somewhat larger and presumably more efficient with little, if any, loss in quality or accessibility.

Low enrollment figures also suggest that the process of locating the two-year institutions fell well short of any standard of administrative rationality. By 1979 only six campuses had enrollments of 2,000 or greater; six had enrollments of less than 1,000.[52] What is worse, these are head counts and not full-time equivalent (FTE) figures. The Carnegie Commission on Higher Education recommended that high quality, economical community colleges should range from 2,000 to 5,000 FTEs. Fall 1994 enrollment figures supplied by the Alabama Commission on Higher Education show that among the nineteen community colleges, seven still had fewer than 2,000 students, enrollment in five was between 2,000 and 4,000, and seven had more than 4,000 students. The highest enrollment was in Decatur (7,249) and the lowest (1,144) in Brewton. The three institutions still called junior colleges had between 1,096 and 2,118 students, and the twelve technical schools had enrollments that ranged between 190 and 1,773, with only three of the twelve having more than 1,000 students.

Wallace directly and closely involved himself in selecting contractors to build the junior colleges and trade schools and in deciding which banks would be used as depositories by the schools. As they were being constructed, Wallace interested himself in their staffing. A Wallace office file dated 1964–65 contains directives and letters of recommendation written by the governor to board of education members and college and school officials on behalf of prospective administrators, teachers, and even custodians. One example is a letter from Wallace to Olin Smith, director of the Eufaula Trade School: "Marshall Williams talked to me about a relative of his who is highly qualified in welding. I want you to talk with Marshall about this matter and I would like for you to employ him in the school." Another example is a letter, quoted here in its entirety, from Wallace to W. Byron Causey, president of Alexander City Junior College: "Dear Byron: I want us to be sure to look after Paul Jackson." This was followed by a June 1, 1965, letter from Wallace to Causey, also quoted in its entirety: "Just a note to tell you that I hope you will look after the Paul Jackson matter."[53]

A system developed with such explosive speed, without a plan or objective criteria, and with the governor intervening in staffing at all levels was bound to develop imperfectly. Even J. F. Ingram, the state director of vocational education, recognized that there were problems. In a letter to George Wallace he wrote:

There is a growing need for a coordinating authority for the colleges and universities in Alabama. There is also a growing need for the establishment of function of trade schools and colleges. At present some of the junior colleges are needlessly and expensively moving into some occupational areas already being served by the trade schools . . . at considerable expense for buildings and equipment. There is dire need for a clear division of functions by the two types of institutions.[54]

George Wallace's stated objective was to put two-year institutions within driving distance of everyone in Alabama.[55] This seems an odd goal considering that many K–12 public schools were so poor, but almost any knowledgeable observer in Alabama would argue that for Wallace the appropriate standard to be applied in this situation and all other situations is political, not administrative, rationality.

Instances of duplication of effort and wasted resources also can be found in the system of higher education. Two examples from the 1960s are the creation of the University of Alabama at Huntsville (UAH) and Auburn University at Montgomery (AUM). Both institutions were created in response to community efforts, and both were located in cities with a four-year state institution already in place. The existing institutions were black, and their faculties and student bodies were active in the civil rights movement.

The University of Alabama opened an extension center in Huntsville in the winter of 1950. By the 1957–58 academic year student enrollment was at over two thousand, with students coming from a seven-county area. In April 1958 the University of Alabama Board of Trustees voted to build a permanent center in Huntsville on an eighty-three-acre site set aside for this purpose by the city. The university supplied $750,000 of the building costs, and the remainder was supplied by the city and county governments.[56]

Almost immediately city officials, working with administrators from the Redstone Arsenal and NASA, began a drive to expand the center into a four-year and graduate-level institution. They argued that the facility was vital for the economic development of the city and surrounding areas. The commanding general at Redstone Arsenal appeared before a joint session of the Alabama legislature to press for the four-year college. He told the legislators that technological advancement was the way to future growth and prosperity and that Alabama did not have "enough fully prepared manpower available . . . to support new industry."[57]

In 1961 Dr. Werner von Braun, director of the Marshall Space Flight Center, appeared before another joint session of the legislature to solicit $3 million for a newly formed research institute at UAH. He argued that Alabama and the space facility could face a loss of funds and programs unless the state took immediate action. He said that engineers with bachelor's degrees wanted to complete advanced degrees and that they were leaving the Alabama facility to do so. He also pointed to the fact that not enough engineers and scientists were being produced in-state and that Huntsville's academic, cultural, and research environment had to be improved immediately in order to attract people from outside the state and keep them and native Alabamians in Huntsville.[58]

Bills authorizing a vote on a bond issue for building the facility passed immediately. The public then ratified the bond issue. Efforts such as these resulted in awarding four-year and graduate status to the Huntsville facility. Today it offers work through the doctoral level. Just a few miles away is Alabama A & M, a largely black institution, which also offers graduate and undergraduate degree programs.

Auburn University at Montgomery (AUM) was created in 1967 by an act of the legislature.[59] In 1968 Morris Dees and Fred Gray, representing the Alabama State Teachers Association (the black National Education Association affiliate), headed by Joe Reed, filed suit to prevent a bond issue to fund construction of AUM. They contended that Alabama State could be expanded to meet fully Montgomery's higher education needs in an integrated environment. They alleged that the creation of AUM represented an attempt to perpetuate segregation at the college level and "to keep whites from attending Alabama State College."[60] Judge Frank M. Johnson Jr., writing for a three-judge district court panel, ruled that the Auburn branch would offer a wider variety of more advanced programs than Alabama State was providing, and that as long as the Auburn branch did not discriminate, its creation did not violate federal law. In effect, AUM represented a completely "new institution" rather than a white duplicate of ASC. In January 1969 the U.S. Supreme Court affirmed the ruling by refusing to accept the case on appeal.

In 1983 federal lawsuits were filed by the U.S. Justice Department and a group of blacks representing Alabama State University (formerly Alabama State College) and Alabama A & M. The suits were combined under *Knight et al. v. State of Alabama et al.* The Knight plaintiffs charged that the effects of segregation remained and emanated throughout the higher education system.

This suit encompassed much more than the AUM-ASU dispute or even the counterpart situation in the Huntsville area. The most significant charges were that historically white institutions duplicated programs available at ASU and A & M, that ASU and A & M were denied adequate funding, including federal land-grant funds for A & M, and that ASU and A & M had been denied the right to conduct advanced programs.

After nearly a decade of complex legal maneuvering, Judge Harold L. Murphy of the Northern District of Georgia, sitting by special assignment, issued in December 1991 a 360-page opinion in which he found in favor of the plaintiffs in many respects, including the issues of funding and duplication of programs. Murphy ruled in favor of the defendants regarding the missions of ASU and A & M and land-grant funding, among other matters. The judge found no indications of overt racial discrimination at AUM, which in the winter 1994 quarter had a black enrollment exceeding 20 percent. The white enrollment at ASU was estimated at between 1 and 3 percent.

Six months after the Murphy ruling, the United States Supreme Court decided *United States v. Fordice,* a case dealing with similar issues in the Mississippi higher-education system. On the basis of *Fordice,* the Knight plaintiffs appealed those parts of the Murphy decision that were decided against them. On February 24, 1994, the U.S. Court of Appeals for the Eleventh Circuit remanded the case to the district court for further consideration. Its decision affirmed the Murphy decision in part, reversed it in part, and vacated it in part.

While the district court reconsiders the issues outlined by the appeals court, ASU and AUM operate under guidelines established by the Murphy decision. For example, the Murphy ruling required the creation of a joint ASU-Auburn committee that included representation from their boards of trustees, the governor's office, and the Alabama Commission on Higher Education. The purpose of the committee is to reduce duplication of programs and bring about exchanges of students between the campuses—in effect, to make AUM more black and ASU more white.

As of this writing, mandatory and voluntary exchanges are being implemented on a trial basis under court scrutiny. Small numbers of students from each campus in one master's-level education program and one undergraduate program in business are obliged to take two courses required in their degree program on the other campus. All students may cross campuses to take courses on a voluntary basis. In the winter 1994 quarter a total of only sixty-one students were involved in these cross-campus exchanges. The small number is explained by the mechanical difficulties involved in meshing a semester schedule on one campus and a quarter schedule on the other.

In a cooperative effort with Maxwell Air Force Base, Troy State University also had entered the Montgomery community. By contract with the air force, it offered courses on base to an integrated on-base student body while the city itself was still segregated. Troy State later began offering courses off base as well. As a result, three state universities operate in Montgomery. (In the *Knight* case Troy State and its branches entered into a consent decree that calls for cooperative efforts with ASU.) In the 1980s the University of Alabama began offering two graduate degree programs on the base. One of these programs attracts students from the city's nonmilitary population.

The waste inherent when cities the size of Montgomery and Huntsville support two or more state universities scarcely requires comment.

Failed Coercion Attempts

Throughout his years as governor, Wallace repeatedly resorted to unorthodox tactics in attempts to win support for legislation that would enhance his power and authority. During the special session Wallace had diminished his legislative powers by a crude attempt to coerce the legislature into voting for HB9. The measure would have given the governor sole authority to name lawyers to handle civil rights suits, highway land cases, and other matters. This bill's patronage implications undoubtedly stirred the political loins of both its chief advocate and its opponents. Attorney General Flowers was a racial moderate whom Wallace could not trust or control in civil rights cases. Wallace wanted his own legal talent working for him. The governor already possessed the right to hire attorneys, but they had to be paid out of his funds. HB9 permitted the charging of their fees to the agency for whom they were supposedly working.

Wallace's worst mistake in pushing HB9 was ordering road construction projects halted in Jefferson, Tallapoosa, Walker, and Mobile Counties, including two Mobile interstate projects totaling $7.1 million, as a retaliation against the failure of the Senate Judiciary Committee, headed by Larry Dumas (Jefferson), to report out the bill. The withdrawing of already-promised patronage was a sanction governors rarely applied because it almost never worked. Such sanctions angered the entire body politic, because in effect the governor violated promises made to legislators and the counties they represented. Furthermore, if he cheated one set of counties, he could do it to all. The highway projects that Wallace stopped were later restarted.

Wallace reintroduced the lawyer selection bill in the regular session that started in May. A Senate filibuster against it stimulated Wallace to lobby officials from the offending senators' home counties. Like his threatened cancellation of road construction projects, this only irritated the senators, and Wallace finally abandoned the effort.

Wallace also used the regular session to propose an increase in old-age pensions. His efforts failed, and there is no evidence that he invested as much energy and political capital on this proposal as he did on education, roads, and the lawyer selection bill.

The administration's House leaders sought $7 million per year in new taxes to provide additional funding for welfare.[61] The tax proposals consisted of an increase of one cent a pack on cigarettes, a .5 percent insurance premium tax, and a 1 percent tax on contracts. They represented a mixture of regressive and progressive taxes.

Appropriations for education in the regular session mirrored the existence of new revenue sources opened in the special session. Appropriations for the 1963–64 fiscal year increased to $187 million (from $149 million) and to $192 million for the 1964–65 fiscal year. The average teacher salary increased from $3,988 to $4,600. Wallace correctly observed in his speech at the 1964 AEA annual convention that these improvements barely allowed Alabama to maintain its position relative to other states.[62] He might have added that Alabama's relative position was not very high.

During his first year in office, Wallace made no attempt to achieve property tax reform.

Civil Rights in Birmingham

Civil rights demonstrations continued, with Birmingham as their focal point. From 1957 to 1963 Birmingham was the site of more than a dozen racial bombings and over fifty cross burnings. We have already seen that when a federal court ordered city parks integrated, the city closed them. The city disbanded its professional baseball team rather than allow it to play integrated teams. Touring opera companies and other theatrical groups refused to come to the city because its municipal auditorium was segregated.

Early in 1963 Eugene "Bull" Connor ran for mayor of Birmingham against, among others, Albert Boutwell, who was, relatively speaking, a moderate. Connor began his political career in 1934 with his election to the legislature. Winning a seat on the city commission in 1937, he was reelected five times. At first he was a useful tool of the Birmingham business community, especially U.S. Steel, given his enthusiastic willingness violently to repress the civil rights movement.

Connor devoted substantial attention in his 1963 campaign to economy in government and that standby of demagogues, pornography, the sale of which he just happened to discover near election day. Resulting police raids on magazine stands generated only sparse publicity from Big Mule newspapers, which now saw him as an enemy of progress. Of course, Connor did not ignore his mainstay issue. One of his newspaper advertisements read in part: "HE WILL CONTINUE to Take ACTION About SEGREGATION."[63]

Boutwell concentrated his campaign on good government and good education and their relationship to attracting industry.[64] He responded to Connor's emphasis on using fire hoses and police dogs to continue segregation by stressing a high-road approach: "Can we maintain it [segregation] by boasts, rantings, damage suits? Or by inexperience—locally, statewide, nationally—that has never met the problem? Trust the man whose laws are now at work keeping schools segregated—(Boutwell Freedom of Choice Amendment, Alabama Pupil Placement Act; Joint Committee to Preserve Segregation in Alabama Schools)—a man who will jail agitators, enforce the law and maintain the peace."[65]

George Wallace publicly endorsed Connor's candidacy. The *Birmingham News* speculated that he did so because after Boutwell withdrew from the governor's race, he had supported the moderate Ryan de Graffenried against Wallace. Contemporary observers regarded Wallace's move as a blunder. Quite apart from the past failure of gubernatorial attempts to influence local elections, Wallace endorsed someone who had been marked for political elimination by the Birmingham Big Mules. Nor was Wallace's support needed to reinforce Connor's credentials as a segregationist. As the *Birmingham News* cleverly and elegantly phrased it, "Not even Wallace can outdo Bull on segregation ardor. The baptized require no further baptism."[66] Connor compounded Wallace's mistake by claiming that because of his ties with Wallace he would be better able to attract road construction projects than Boutwell.[67] This only reminded voters of Wallace's intrusion.

The AFL-CIO endorsed Boutwell in the April runoff. Connor attempted to turn their action into a racial matter by claiming that black labor-union members had coerced the national AFL-CIO president into suppressing the desire of Birmingham union leaders to endorse Connor.[68] The city's Big Mule civic organizations, such as the chamber of commerce, also supported Boutwell. Many wives of Birmingham's elite and professional classes assembled mass mailings, ran his campaign headquarters, and worked the telephones. The *Birmingham News* endorsed Boutwell and biased its coverage toward him.[69] The *Birmingham Post-Herald* also opposed Connor.

Predictably, Connor transformed Birmingham's Big Mule opposition to him into a racial issue. He resigned from the Birmingham Chamber of

Commerce, which he disdainfully referred to as the Mountain Brook Chamber of Commerce. (Mountain Brook is a small, affluent city where many of Birmingham's wealthier businessmen lived.) When asked why he resigned, Connor replied, "You want to integrate Birmingham. I can't work with you."[70]

Newspaper opposition to Connor became yet another excuse to raise the integration issue. One Connor advertisement read: "From the ATLANTA CONSTITUTION comes the Quisling, Ralph McGill, who integrated Atlanta to tell you how to vote. His Northern newspaper joins ours in an attempt to brainwash you! The people of Birmingham."[71]

Boutwell won the runoff 29,630 to 21,648. The *Birmingham News* quite properly described the 75 percent turnout rate as "spectacular."[72] Because of legal complications, Boutwell did not take office immediately.

Civil rights leaders targeted Birmingham for demonstrations and other pressure precisely because of its size and because its leadership, most notably Connor, could be provoked into making stupid mistakes. Their demands in Birmingham included the desegregation of stores, fair hiring practices, the dropping of charges against arrested demonstrators, and the establishment of a biracial commission with power to begin a process of complete desegregation in the city.

Protests consisted of sit-ins at downtown lunch counters as well as marches and a boycott of white merchants. The crude and brutal Connor responded by using police dogs and fire hoses against the marchers and making many arrests. In the first week of demonstrations in 1963 there were 139.[73] In mid-April Martin Luther King Jr. and Ralph Abernathy were among those taken to jail.[74] On May 2 black children and teenagers marched on downtown streets and picketed stores; 700 were arrested. The next day hundreds more demonstrated. They were greeted by police using dogs and powerful fire hoses. Confrontations between thousands of demonstrators and police continued. On May 7 George Wallace ordered 250 highway patrolmen led by Public Safety Director Al Lingo to Birmingham to assist Connor.[75]

These and subsequent attacks on peaceful demonstrators appeared throughout the country on network television news. It was not an image of America that many liked. The television pictures presented a more effective argument against segregation than any number of speeches on behalf of civil rights. Few Americans listened when the mayor-elect, Albert Boutwell, appealed for "restraint and peace" and pledged "immediate and determined attention to resolving the difficulties facing us."[76]

A May 12 article by Bill Rasco in the *Alabama Journal* compared Birmingham and Mobile.[77] Mobile struggled with its racial problems in a relatively peaceful manner and was largely ignored by the media. A biracial committee had been appointed to advise the city commission. Brookley Air Force Base, with almost fifteen thousand employees, was integrated, and the Mobile Police Department employed a number of blacks, including a detective and sergeant, although they worked primarily with other blacks. A black fire company had been in existence for a year and a half, and blacks worked elsewhere in city government. The municipal golf course was integrated, although by court order, and many other public facilities, including restaurants, were integrated.

The day Rasco's article appeared, massive riots occurred in Birmingham after the bombings of the home of Martin Luther King's brother and a black motel.[78] President John Kennedy responded by sending troops to Maxwell Air Force Base in Montgomery and Fort McClellan in Anniston. Wallace, irked that the presence of the troops suggested that law and order were not being maintained, protested that they were in the state illegally.

At the height of the violence some of Alabama's most prestigious business leaders formed a biracial committee. The committee produced a plan that included gradual desegregation of lunch counters and other public facilities, better jobs for blacks, and the creation of a permanent biracial committee. This proposal resulted in a quick reduction in violence and represented a step forward for the civil rights movement.[79] According to George Lewis Bailes Jr., a former state senator from Birmingham, many of the executives instrumental in starting the committee worked for AmSouth Bank, South Central Bell, and Alabama Power. He identifies John Woods of AmSouth as especially important in initiating and participating in the committee.[80]

Wallace and Connor tried to encourage their dispirited supporters at a poorly attended May 17 meeting of the Alabama Citizens Councils in Montgomery. Wallace promoted membership in the segregationist organization, and he flayed white moderates: "We need to organize against those who say, 'I am for segregation, but.' Evidently they are not for segregation."[81]

Wallace's biographer Stephan Lesher offers an excuse for Wallace's energetic defense of segregation. Quoting Wallace's press secretary, Bill Jones, Lesher writes that "Wallace 'felt that if he could inject himself, he could minimize violence. . . . He felt that the way to keep violence down and prepare the people to accept what they were going to have to accept was to say repeatedly—repeatedly: 'Let me do it, let me stand for you'—not only in the schoolhouse door, but in every way, such as in the courts and everything.'"[82]

Variants of this excuse are used by many surviving defenders of segregation, including John Patterson. Wallace's campaign against the civil rights
movement was too vigorous and aggressive to sustain this rationalization.
Had he been trying to serve as a safety valve, he would not have tried to
organize and encourage citizens' opposition to integration as he did at the
May 17 Citizens Council meeting and repeatedly did for a decade. It is not
the function of a safety valve to stoke the boiler.

Once again Connor attacked the business community when he complained about the minuscule showing of only about two hundred people at
the meeting: "We are too busy trying to make the almighty dollar and keep
it. We should be out here at the cow barn [State Coliseum] tonight, and it
should be overflowing with white people."[83] If it could be said that the segregationist cause surrendered at one particular point, it may have been that
night, with Bull Connor whining about the lack of idealism among white-
supremacist businessmen. Segregationists kept fighting—with Wallace's
encouragement—but it was clear that they would not win.

Alabama and the National
Civil Rights Act

By the end of May 1963 President Kennedy had been
placed in a corner by the violence in Birmingham and elsewhere. He decided to push for a strong civil rights bill. In June Wallace gave Kennedy
an opening when the governor attempted to bar the enrollment of two
black students at the University of Alabama in Tuscaloosa. In a carefully
arranged and delicately implemented charade, Wallace bowed to federal
power and permitted the students' entry.[84] That evening Kennedy gave a
nationally televised speech explaining what he had done at the university and informing the nation of his plans for civil rights legislation. Between "Bull" Connor's police-dog and fire-hose attacks on demonstrators
and George Wallace's gaudy but hollow gestures, civil rights leaders could
not have manufactured better opponents.

Kennedy's civil rights bill strengthened laws protecting black voting
rights, outlawed racial discrimination in public accommodations, gave the
U.S. attorney general the authority to file suits to bring about racial integration of schools, and extended the life of the Commission on Civil Rights.
It also allowed federal programs to be terminated wherever racial discrimination was practiced in applying them.[85]

Given the partisan and geographical makeup of Congress, civil rights
strategists realized that a bipartisan effort would be required to pass Ken-

nedy's bill. Vice President Lyndon Johnson estimated that support from twenty-seven Senate Republicans would be needed to invoke cloture, and Deputy Attorney General Nicholas Katzenbach calculated that the administration needed sixty-five House Republican votes.[86]

The Senate Judiciary Committee began hearings on July 16. The centerpiece of the hearings was the North Carolina Democrat Sam J. Ervin Jr.'s inquisition of Attorney General Robert Kennedy on the bill's constitutional ramifications. On August 23 Chairman James O. Eastland adjourned the hearings subject to the call of the chair, interring the bill as far as the Senate Judiciary Committee was concerned. Emmanuel Cellars of New York, the chair of the House Judiciary Committee, could hardly have been more different from his Senate counterpart and fellow party member. His committee's hearings were as one-sided on behalf of civil rights legislation as Eastland's had been against.

To dramatize the need for civil rights legislation, Martin Luther King Jr. staged a "March on Washington for Jobs and Freedom." It brought two hundred thousand people to the capital in the largest meeting of its kind in the nation's history. It ended with King's stirring "I have a dream" speech, which in Alabama stood in sharp, sad contrast to the "segregation forever" inaugural address that Wallace had delivered earlier the same year.

By the opening of the 1963 school year, several court orders had been issued requiring school integration in Alabama. Acting on Attorney General Flowers's advice, the Macon County Board of Education voted to open Tuskegee High School on an integrated basis, despite opposition expressed by Wallace in an executive order. On the first day of school, Wallace ordered over one hundred state troopers to surround the school and turn away the students.[87] He doubled the number of troopers a day later. Wallace characterized his actions as a necessary response to coercion by federal officials and bad advice given to the board by Attorney General Flowers.[88]

The newly elected, more moderate Birmingham City Council asked Wallace not to send troopers into Birmingham, but he did so anyway.[89] The *Birmingham News,* signaling that the Jefferson County Big Mules were bowing to the inevitable elimination of legalized school segregation, sharply criticized Wallace's attempts to dictate civil rights policy to boards of education, arguing that he had no legal right to do so. The *News* wrote: "All our people will reap a rotten harvest as one man seeks more and more power in this state. Wallace now not only defies federal courts, he defies wishes of legally-constituted local authorities. What federal court orders make inescapable still will come. But in the interval a governor so enthralled with his own sense of power will have created near-havoc."[90]

The Huntsville City Council passed a resolution similar to Birmingham's. Councilman Louis B. Lee commented, "He [Wallace] is becoming the dictator of Alabama."[91] The *Huntsville Times* blamed the governor for creating an atmosphere that encouraged "misguided hotheads" to defy the law: "Extremism breeds extremism. And the result is a shameful thing to see. Again Alabama stands before the nation and the world as a place where free men seem to be unable to govern themselves, their tempers and their territory."[92] The *Montgomery Advertiser* editorialized on Wallace's use of troops to prevent integration, writing that Wallace had "gone wild."[93] Even the Black Belt *Selma Times-Journal* argued that Wallace's troop movements would be counterproductive.[94]

In Mobile state troopers barred two black students from attending Murphy High School. U.S. District Judge Daniel H. Thomas then issued a temporary order restraining Wallace from interfering with integration. The troopers were removed, but they were soon replaced by the National Guard. The guardsmen were in turn federalized by President Kennedy and withdrawn. A federal court panel led by Judge Johnson and consisting of five judges whose districts spanned the state finally ordered Wallace to stop interfering with school districts.

Some segregationists reacted to these events with violence. Four black girls were murdered and twenty-three injured in the bombing of a Birmingham church. Later, two white youths shot and killed a thirteen-year-old black. Of course, these outrages only served to weaken segregationists and strengthen the civil rights cause. Mirroring the *Huntsville Times,* Martin Luther King Jr. blamed the bombings and shootings on George Wallace, charging that he had set a tone of lawlessness that encouraged violence. The bombings were frequently cited as additional justification for civil rights legislation.

A group of Macon County segregationists uninterested in counterproductive violence or empty symbolism considered establishing a private school. They visited three private academies in Virginia to gather information on how the schools had been organized and financed.[95] Wallace strongly supported this effort.

The inception of private primary and secondary schools received little notice from the press, but they came to have a devastating effect on school integration and support for public school funding. Their development also indicated the financial sacrifices many parents were willing to make to avoid sending their children to integrated schools—a lesson lost on civil rights advocates and the federal judiciary.

From 1939 to 1957 approximately 1.5 percent of Alabama primary and secondary students were enrolled in private schools. From 1957 to 1959 the level doubled to approximately 3.2 percent and stayed close to 3 percent until 1968. This jump was probably due to *Brown v. Board* and subsequent decisions. From 1969 to 1972 the percentage doubled again, to the 7 percent level, after which it settled down to a steady 6.5 percent. The last increase was probably caused by mandatory desegregation and forced busing.[96]

Although 6.5 percent may not appear to be an impressive figure, it represents a large proportion of the children of the state's leaders. Today in Alabama, outside of a few districts in or near the University of Alabama, the Huntsville NASA facility, wealthier Birmingham suburbs, and Auburn University, it is unusual to find a successful attorney, physician, business person, university professor, or other professional whose children have attended only public schools from kindergarten through the twelfth grade. Some idealistic professionals send their children to public elementary schools, declaring their faith in the virtues of the melting pot, only to shift them to private schools later. They justify the move with long dissertations concerning their children's particular problems and/or special needs, which can only be managed by the specialists or the smaller classes found in private school. These professionals and their spouses were the ones who in past years would have been working and voting to support public education. With their children's welfare no longer dependent on the public schools, their energies and leadership are no longer directed in full or even partial support of the public school system. The net effect on the overall quality of public education cannot be positive.

George Wallace's mail just before and during his first term overwhelmingly favored his aggressive segregationist stance, but his correspondents were far from united about tactics. Many urged that he tone down inflammatory statements and work through the legal system.[97] Wallace also received thousands of letters from out of state, including many from other countries. The vast majority of this mail was sharply critical of his segregationist stands.

Richmond Flowers

The Wallace administration employed spies in the civil rights camp. According to a report contained in Wallace's office files, one spy was a paid member of Martin Luther King's staff and a high-ranking member of the Birmingham Temple of the Black Muslims.[98] Spies reported on plans for forthcoming demonstrations and gave detailed descriptions of mass meetings. According to Richmond Flowers, Wallace also placed spies in the attorney general's office, and Flowers acknowledges doing likewise in the governor's office.[99]

Attorney General Richmond Flowers throughout this period remained the only state official openly critical of what Wallace was doing. He claimed that Wallace was holding out a "false hope of victory" to segregationists.[100] A *Montgomery Advertiser* editorial wondered why Flowers was going against popular sentiment in his pronouncements:

> To put it mildly and charitably, Flowers has been an adventurer and an opportunist. Yet in this season, as if taking keen aim and squeezing off the trigger of a rifle, Flowers has systematically fired on Alabama's emotions and convictions. Nor . . . has Flowers any illusions that the people are happy with him. . . . Flowers understands that Governor Wallace is passionately upheld by the mass of Alabamians. Yet he fiercely attacks Wallace. He tells the grim, distressed and touchy people of Macon County that their private school will fail. . . .
>
> The people of Alabama disvalue and abhor the U.S. Supreme Court. But Flowers enjoins them to obey the court as he will obey it. The people of Alabama disvalue and abhor John Kennedy. But Flowers tells them he will support Kennedy.
>
> The *Advertiser* on this occasion is not arguing with Flowers' viewpoints. We are only acknowledging bafflement over why an ambitious, opportunistic plunger like Flowers, who did not gag on the worst of Folsomism, would suddenly affront Alabama sensibilities. . . .
>
> To us this is baffling. We will pay attention in class and try to comprehend. Meanwhile, there is no hesitancy in giving Flowers credit for a virile performance.[101]

Richmond Flowers told the authors about his view of civil rights and politics during this period. In his home county of Houston, in the state's southeast corner, "hardworking, responsible blacks" were beginning to register to vote in sufficient numbers that it became clear that they would soon be a factor with which any reasonable politician would have to deal to survive. In a sense, Flowers observed, black voters did not alter conditions very much because their perspectives were not all that much different from those of hardworking, responsible whites. Nevertheless, viewed as a bloc, they represented significant voting strength in Houston County.[102] In 1963 Flowers also felt that George Wallace's activation of the redneck would repel many voters. He now acknowledges that he was mistaken.

When Flowers ran for the Alabama Senate in 1954, he was a moderate segregationist. A skilled storyteller, he was well known for jokes that he told using black dialect. In that year Jim Folsom Sr. was attempting to elect a loose-knit slate of legislators, and Flowers asked for assistance from Folsom's southeast campaign manager, who essentially took over management of Flowers's campaign. Flowers credits this man with his victory.

Flowers's transformation from a segregationist (but never a racist, he insists) to an opponent of segregation and voting discrimination puzzled and irritated many. The editor of the *Birmingham News* told him that he did not "ring true." Grover Hall Jr. believed that the change represented nothing but political opportunism. According to Flowers, soon after he had been sworn in as attorney general, Hall told him that although he was one of the most promising new figures on the scene, "I don't like your politics, and I'm going to kill your butt." As we have already noted, Hall was a strong Wallace supporter and adviser.

When the authors asked Flowers how his thinking had changed, his response was legalistic: "When the U.S. Supreme Court lays down its decisions and when Congress passes laws, what do you have left? George Wallace said, 'You've quit the fight.' I told him, 'I haven't quit it. We've lost it. Where are you going to turn?' Wallace answered, 'I'm going to turn to the people. They'll [the federal government] send troops. Let 'em bring just one soldier to the state, and I'll run for president.'" This conversation occurred as they drove to a rally for Congressman George Andrews between the 1962 primary and general election.[103]

As the civil rights movement gained ground on all fronts, voting registration of blacks grew at a rapid pace. In May 1962, 3,090 blacks were registered in Montgomery County, a year later 4,000, and by September 1963 the number reached 6,156, or 20 percent of blacks eligible to vote.[104] Approximately 50 percent of eligible whites were registered.

Wallace did what he could to stem black voting. In October he named Dr. Henry L. Lyon, pastor of the Highland Avenue Baptist Church and a vociferous opponent of integration, to the Montgomery County Board of Registrars. Lyon had delivered the invocation at Wallace's inauguration. He defended segregation as "the commandment and the law of God."[105] Lyon was also a past president of the Alabama Baptist Convention and a past president of the Montgomery Exchange Club as well as a Mason and Shriner. Lyon's appointment was symbolic of Wallace's commitment to segregation as well as an indicator of the views held by mainstream Alabama leadership.

Congressional Barriers to the
Civil Rights Bill

Meanwhile, in Washington Republican and Democratic members of the House Judiciary Committee and the Justice Department hammered out changes in the civil rights bill. The Judiciary Committee on October 29 approved the reworked legislation, which was stronger than the original Kennedy administration proposal.[106] A fight in the House Rules Committee, chaired by Howard W. Smith of Virginia, was to be the next stage, but before it could happen John Kennedy was assassinated. President Lyndon Johnson attempted to push the bill through Congress immediately thereafter, but it remained in Smith's grip.

Immediately after the Christmas–New Year's break, Smith began hearings on the civil rights bill. He tried to prolong the testimony, but the House voted on the bill a month later. It passed by an overwhelming 290-130. According to Loevy, "Only 22 Republicans and 4 Democrats from outside the South joined the Southerners in voting against the bill." [107] Eleven southern Democrats split with their colleagues and voted with the majority. Eighty percent of House Republicans voted for the civil rights bill, but only 59 percent of the Democrats supported it. No Alabama congressmen voted for the legislation.

The Senate voted to bypass the Judiciary Committee and its segregationist chairman, James O. Eastland of Mississippi. On March 30 the bill fell victim to a Senate filibuster led by the veteran Georgia senator Richard Russell. By working in shifts, Russell's team of eighteen, including Alabama's senators, Lister Hill and John Sparkman, had no difficulty controlling the Senate floor. Russell's group applied grueling pressure on the majority by requiring a quorum call every two hours, twenty-four hours a day.

The fifty-seven-day filibuster finally ended on June 10 with a cloture vote. Among those who voted against cloture was Arizona Republican Barry Goldwater, who justified his position by saying that he always voted against cloture as a way to maintain the filibuster, a tool that strengthened small states such as his own. Goldwater also voted against the civil rights bill itself, arguing that although he opposed racial discrimination and segregation, he could find no constitutional basis for the federal regulation of public accommodations or employment conditions. He further asserted that the effective implementation of the bill would require creation of a police state.[108] President Lyndon Johnson signed the legislation into law on July 2.[109]

The Civil Rights Act was a powerful and comprehensive piece of legislation. Title I (Voting Rights) barred unequal administration of registration requirements, and made a sixth-grade education in English a presumption of literacy. Title II (Public Accommodations) prohibited discrimination because of race, color, religion, or national origin in restaurants, gasoline stations, sports arenas, hotels, or other public accommodations. Title III (Desegregation of Public Facilities) permitted U.S. Justice Department suits to secure desegregation of public facilities. Title IV (Desegregation of Public Education) authorized the U.S. Office of Education to assist school systems planning or implementing desegregation and the U.S. Justice Department to enforce desegregation. Title V (Civil Rights Commission) broadened the commission's authority and extended its life four years. Title VI (Nondiscrimination in Federally Assisted Programs) prohibited discrimination because of race, color, or national origin under any program receiving federal assistance. Title VII (Equal Employment Opportunity) created the Equal Employment Opportunity Commission to assist in enforcement of rules against employment discrimination. Title VIII (Registration and Voting Statistics) directed the secretary of commerce to conduct a survey to compile registration and voting statistics based on race, color, and national origin. Title IX (Intervention and Procedure After Removal in Civil Rights Cases) authorized the attorney general to intervene on behalf of the United States whenever an action in any court of the United States sought relief from denial of equal protection based on the Fourteenth Amendment on account of race, color, religion, or national origin. The federal government in effect assumed the costs of such litigation. Title X created a community relations service to assist communities and individuals in resolving disputes related to discrimination based on race, color, or national origin.[110]

School Integration and Segregation

In January 1964 Auburn University registered its first black student, Harold Franklin. At first the university tried to deny the young man a dormitory room, but Judge Frank Johnson intervened. Governor Wallace characterized Judge Johnson's order as "shocking."[111]

In that same month, Wallace toured the newly opened Macon Academy. He praised the private school and a month later called for public contributions to support white students boycotting Macon County's integrated schools.[112] Wallace's office maintained a file of letters from individuals giving money to the Macon Academy; one contribution was for twenty thousand dollars. A woman wrote to Wallace telling him that she would like to donate seven thousand dollars toward the improvement of education in Alabama and asked him to suggest where it should go. He replied: "You may wish to contact the Macon Academy in Tuskegee, Alabama. The academy is a private school which was set up by individuals in Macon County who were not satisfied with the Federal Court order which did away with their rights to run the schools in that County as they saw fit." [113] There were many more letters like this in the one-and-a-half-inch-thick file. Wallace also supported white academies in other counties, and he pressured cabinet members to contribute to them. [114] His office maintained lists of contributors. [115]

In February 1964 the state board of education authorized financial aid to parents of Tuskegee high school students to enable them to attend private, segregated schools. It based this action on a 1957 statute that permitted such payments when children had no public school to attend. [116] Attorney General Flowers denounced the board's action.

A large percentage of letters written by Alabamians continued to express approval of Wallace's civil rights stands. Very few of the letters came from executives in major Alabama corporations. Many owners of bonding concerns, office machine companies, and other small operations dependent on the state for business wrote uncritically supportive notes. [117] Richard W. Neal, editor of the *Alabama Lawyer,* also wrote an approving letter. [118]

Only a few Alabama correspondents doubted the wisdom of Wallace's disruptive approach. For example, the pastor of one of the state's largest Baptist churches wrote in February 1964:

> This is to express my great disappointment in your continued interference in the public schools of Alabama.
>
> None of us like the integration of our public schools but there are some things infinitely worse. You have already disrupted the education of some young people and only time can tell the damage to their lives. . . . Are you determined to sacrifice our young people on the altar of political persuasion? . . .
>
> Your interference in Macon County indicates that you intend to control the local school board in every county in Alabama. We do not want this kind of attempted dictatorship in our state. [119]

A February 10, 1964, resolution by the Young Men's Business Club of Birmingham took issue with Wallace and the state board of education for "injecting themselves into the operation of local school boards." Far from protecting segregation, Wallace's "policies of interference and defiance" had quickened the pace of integration, disrupted the educational process, and created unnecessary ill will. [120]

Wallace Meets the Press

On June 2, 1963, only a few days before Wallace took his "stand" in the University of Alabama door, he appeared on the National Broadcasting Company's *Meet the Press,* a widely viewed news interview program. The response in Alabama was overwhelmingly positive. Typical was a letter from a corporate president who wrote, "I think George C., that you handled yourself extremely well on 'Meet the Press' and at Tuscaloosa. You were fighting against strong odds."[121]

The perception of even sophisticated observers was that four abrasive, liberal, citified Yankee reporters attempted to maul Wallace, and that in fighting back he demonstrated verbal acuity at least equal to that of his inquisitors. The fact that one *Meet the Press* panelist, Frank McGee, had been a reporter for the Montgomery NBC affiliate before deserting the South for New York made Wallace's victory all the sweeter. A *Montgomery Advertiser* reporter who was present at the television studio during the broadcast remembers thinking that the Yankee reporters had accidentally made Wallace's national reputation.[122]

The authors viewed a videotape of the broadcast and read the transcript of it and were amazed to find that, far from being a battle between a little knight and a four-headed dragon, the session was quite ordinary and bland. The reporters devoted roughly half their time to attempting to get Wallace to divulge the precise nature of his plans in his forthcoming confrontation with federal officials at the University of Alabama. Wallace, who wanted to maintain suspense and had no intention of revealing that he was planning to surrender without a real fight, responded to the reporters' obvious questions with evasions and legalistic rhetoric. Much of the remainder of the broadcast dealt with life in Alabama under segregation. The reporters interrupted Wallace a few times, but their behavior was routine. Lawrence E. Spivak, the program's producer and permanent panel member, was abrasive, but he was nearly always abrasive; it was his personal style.

Alabama's response to this broadcast said more about Alabama than it did about the broadcast or Wallace's performance on it. Alabamians, weary of years of criticism directed at them from the national political and media establishment, desperately wanted an outnumbered Wallace to respond brilliantly to unfair attacks, so they fantasized that the attacks had occurred and that he had defeated the enemy.

The Wallace Presidential Bid

Wallace began to view himself as having potential as a national figure even before his inauguration. At that time the Dothan banker Wallace Malone, a close friend and ally of J. Bruce Henderson, cautioned the governor-elect against becoming involved in an independent presidential campaign:

> It would take worlds of money and worlds of time and would have to have extremely widespread and active work and support. Few independent movements have ever succeeded. One reason is that they encounter the violent opposition of the vast majority of officeholders. . . .
>
> On the other hand, if we keep things like they are, we can—without doubt—and with a minimum effort, nominate electors pledged not to vote for Kennedy or anyone else on an anti-Southern platform.[123]

The decision to push for unpledged delegates to the 1964 Democratic National Convention was made sometime in 1963.

In October 1963 George Wallace flew to Chattanooga to speak to a White Citizens Council rally. Attendance was estimated as over two thousand. In November he addressed a group of twelve hundred Young Democrats at Harvard, and then other groups at Dartmouth, Smith, and the University of Pennsylvania. A two-week speaking trip throughout the West followed. His national reputation was growing quickly.

A January 1964 letter to Wallace from the experienced segregationist lawyer E. C. Boswell complimented Wallace on his speaking tours but cautioned that Wallace's "campaign for unpledged delegates to the National Convention with the idea of a third or splinter party is far doomed to failure." Boswell recommended that the governor simply run as a favorite son.[124] Wallace responded immediately: "Our efforts are not made with the purpose of forming any third party, but in an effort to secure enough electoral votes to place our region of the country in a position of determining who will be President."[125]

Boswell provided more advice to Wallace a few days later. He recommended that the governor obtain concessions from Lyndon Johnson so that Wallace could advise unpledged electors to cast their ballots for Johnson. Boswell ended the letter with a pitch to the effect that the president was a southerner who is "our best bet for any relief against Federal domination."[126] Boswell was seriously mistaken in this evaluation. By this point civil rights proponents working in Washington recognized that Lyndon Johnson was a stronger advocate of effective civil rights legislation than

John F. Kennedy had been.[127] There is no indication that George Wallace agreed with Boswell.

The *Birmingham Post-Herald* and *Montgomery Advertiser* argued that Wallace's national exposure was good for Alabama and the South.[128] The *Advertiser* maintained that Wallace's candidacy "expanded discussion of the specific provisions" of the civil rights bill pending in Congress.[129] This, the editorial continued, was important because many people were widely ignorant of its contents. The Wallace candidacy was also good for Alabama's image, according to the same editorial. Civil rights advocates would announce the approach of a "racist monster," and instead the average person would hear "a smiling, dapper little man who has come to discuss the civil rights bill and to offer a scholarly discourse on the sanctity of property rights through the ages." The *Advertiser* editors did not understand the effect that Wallace was having on northerners. Wallace's cheerful demeanor, immaculate attire, and glib patter provided a thin disguise for his segregationist policies but fooled almost no one on either side of the Mason-Dixon Line or either side of the segregation issue.

Even before his inauguration Wallace received advice regarding a potential threat to any independent presidential campaign he might decide to mount.[130] Relatively liberal members of the state Democratic party's executive committee planned to reimpose a loyalty oath committing Democratic presidential electors to support the party's nominee. In January 1964 Wallace forces turned back this proposal by a vote of forty-one to thirty. Wallace wanted the executive committee to instruct the state's convention delegates to cast their votes for Wallace for president. A motion to this effect was approved forty-six to twenty-five.

Senators Hill and Sparkman and Attorney General Flowers opposed Wallace's presidential effort. All eight congressmen refused to become involved because the 9-8 plan was still in effect for the primary and runoff elections, and they knew where their self-interest lay.

Although the *Montgomery Advertiser* liked Wallace's presidential campaign in general, it opposed the unpledged elector plan, as it had other incarnations of the same idea that had popped up through the years. Grover Hall Jr. called it "an escape from reality," and he urged Alabamians to choose between Lyndon Johnson and the Republican nominee because they were the only realistic choices available.[131]

In June 1964 the distinguished liberal Carl Elliott lost in the same kind of statewide Democratic party primary that had eliminated Frank Boykin in 1962. "Bull" Connor won the Democratic nomination for president of the Public Service Commission, which regulates Alabama's electrical power and telephone companies. Connor's opponents were Jim Folsom Sr. and a moderate named Jack Owen. Elliott was a nationally respected congressional leader who specialized in issues relating to science and technology, and Connor was a vicious bigot. Elliott's loss and Connor's victory could be interpreted as a strong indication of the electorate's attitudes concerning the directions the state and nation were moving.

A few weeks later, in the Democratic party's national convention, five Alabama delegates, five alternates, and the national committeewoman Ruth Owens signed a loyalty oath and were seated. Thirty-two of the state's delegates refused to sign and left the convention.[132]

When Wallace began his formal presidential campaign, the Kennedy-Johnson civil rights bill was still being filibustered in the Senate. Johnson and civil rights advocates feared that a Wallace victory in a Democratic primary in even a single state would strengthen the resolve of the filibusterers and perhaps even add to their support.

Wallace entered the Wisconsin, Indiana, and Maryland presidential primaries. Lyndon Johnson wisely avoided taking Wallace on directly and recruited stand-ins to run in his place. Johnson's candidate in Wisconsin was Governor John W. Reynolds. Reynolds campaigned actively with Johnson's guidance and assistance, but he made the critical mistake of predicting that Wallace would garner no more than 100,000 votes and adding that even that many "would be a catastrophe."[133] Wallace, campaigning against what he called the "civil wrongs" bill, received 266,136 votes (33.8 percent) in Wisconsin, more than two and one-half times the limit selected by Governor Reynolds. The Reynolds blunder allowed Wallace to claim victory. Wallace's claims aside, the Democratic party establishment was shocked that a southern demagogue could do so well in the North. After the Wisconsin vote he won 29.8 percent of the vote in Indiana.[134]

Wallace's strongest support came from traditionally Democratic working-class districts. The Democratic party's minority–working class alliance, molded in the 1930s, was coming apart. Money poured into the Wallace coffers. In the May 19 Maryland primary, Wallace polled 42.7 percent against U.S. Senator Daniel Brewster's 57 percent. Wallace had lost again, but the fact that this was his best showing yet permitted him to claim another victory.

The Republican presidential nominee Senator Barry Goldwater fit the southern mood of protest and policy preferences even better than Wallace did. Goldwater made the case for a strong military, an aggressive anti-Communist foreign policy, and minimal involvement of the federal government in domestic matters. The latter view led him to vote against the Civil Rights Act of 1964.

Unlike Wallace, Goldwater was a true conservative who established his credentials by writing a best-selling book, *The Conscience of a Conservative,* and by building a consistent voting record in the Senate. He was interested in a broad range of domestic and international concerns instead of a single issue. Despite the prevailing view that he was an extremist, Goldwater was a true presidential candidate in a way that Wallace, the living symbol of a single issue campaigning under the auspices of a synthetic party, never was.

In July 1964 Wallace withdrew his candidacy for president. A letter from the Black Belt planter-politician Joe Poole to Wallace may explain the reason for his decision to stand down:

> Governor, you know not many people will tell their friend, particularly if he is a very prominent man, as you happen to be, what they don't think he wants to hear. If I am not badly mistaken the people of Alabama right now are planning to vote for Barry Goldwater for President and in my judgment they are going to vote for a straight list of Barry Goldwater electors. I feel sure that if you continue in the race and make a strong plea that they stand by your proposition, you would keep a great many from voting for him, but in the end if your plan miscarried and resulted in Goldwater's defeat, a lot of Alabamians would never forgive you. Frankly speaking, I believe that Goldwater is almost as strong in Alabama today as you were on the first election when the independent electors were elected and beat their opponents 14 or 15 to 1.
>
> Your friends are appreciative of what you have done. They realize had it not been for you making the fight Barry Goldwater would not have gotten the vote he did in the convention this week. . . . They want to elect Goldwater. They want you to help elect Goldwater.[135]

Wallace met with Poole at the Jefferson Davis Hotel and responded verbally to this letter. There is no record of what was said.[136]

Virtually all the letters sent to Wallace concerning his presidential race came from rural interests, primarily Black Belt planters and small businessmen. After a thorough search, we were unable to locate a single example of a message from an urban industrialist or even an urban politician or lawyer comparable to Poole's in importance or thoughtfulness.

Goldwater supporters throughout the South applauded Wallace's withdrawal, but many Alabama Democrats were worried. Most were concerned not with the increasingly likely Goldwater victory in Alabama, but with possible Republican victories in state and county races. A former Speaker of the Alabama House, William M. Beck Sr. of the Fort Payne law firm of Beck and Beck, wrote to Wallace: "The Democrats in our County are going to need your help and we are going to need it badly. I would appreciate a letter from you, notifying and authorizing me to tell the Democrats of this County that you are standing behind them."[137] Wallace's response did not endorse the Democratic presidential nominee, but it probably allayed Beck's fears: "Let me assure you that I am standing for the Alabama Democrats who are on the ticket in November."[138]

Even the more ideologically oriented Wallace followers were pleased with his decision to leave the race. For example, one of his independent electors, I. J. (Jud) Scott, an Opelika contractor, wrote:

> I was proud of you when you got out of the race. You had awakened the people as no one else could. . . . Without saying so in words, your action said now a liberal candidate is running against a conservative, constitutional candidate. Let the people speak. . . .
>
> With you out of the race I cannot remain in longer than the day after the Democratic Convention closes. . . . It must be crystal clear so that the people can see to vote for the party of welfare statism or for the party which believes in the freedom of the individual.[139]

Wallace responded to this letter by asking the elector to meet with him after the Democratic convention before resigning.[140]

The Wallace organization cooperated somewhat with Goldwater forces during the election campaign. For example, the Independents and Democrats for Goldwater organization sought and won permission to reproduce Wallace's remarks to the Democratic platform committee in paid political advertisements.[141]

Southern Republicans spent considerable sums of money on the 1964 election. And, for the first time in many decades, Alabama Republicans ran a full slate of congressional candidates.[142] The *Montgomery Advertiser* endorsed Goldwater: "If Alabama fails to vote for Goldwater by an overmastering majority, it will signal both national parties that Alabama will submit to anything, including the civil rights bill."[143] The *Birmingham News* also endorsed him.[144]

There were ten unpledged Democratic presidential electors in the race. Bob Ingram called one, I. J. Scott: " 'How's your race going?' the press asked. 'Things look real good over here,' boomed Scott. 'We're going to get our tail beat. It could be 2 to 1 and with luck it may be 3 to 1.' 'Aren't you doing anything to get votes for yourself?' I continued. 'Not a thing in the world,' fired back Scott. 'When my friends ask me how to vote, I tell 'em to vote Republican.' "[145]

Senator Sparkman hinted that Wallace might not build a united Alabama Democratic party after the November election, but he was wrong. Grover Hall Jr. understood the situation far better than the senator: "Wallace is actively supporting all Democratic candidates at the state and local level. But unlike Sparkman, Wallace is opposed to the election of Johnson and Hubert Humphrey. Nobody, including Sparkman, is more opposed to the election of Republicans to local office than Wallace. He does not want a 2-party system at the state and local level."[146] Two days later Wallace endorsed all Democratic congressional candidates.

In Alabama there were 196,066 votes for Goldwater and 90,592 for unpledged Democrats.[147] Goldwater also carried Mississippi, Louisiana, Georgia, South Carolina, and his home state of Arizona. Goldwater's campaign strategy directly targeted the South. Although Dwight Eisenhower and Richard Nixon had received southern votes in 1952, 1956, and 1960, they assumed the South was still solidly Democratic. Their campaign strategies did not include the possibility of a southern win.

Bernard Cosman conducted a detailed analysis of the southern vote for Goldwater, comparing 1964 voting patterns with those in the Eisenhower and Nixon elections.[148] According to Cosman, Eisenhower and Nixon received Republican support from a different South than did Goldwater. They performed consistently better in the "non-Deep" South (Arkansas, Florida, North Carolina, Tennessee, Texas, and Virginia); Goldwater was strongest in the Deep South (Alabama, Georgia, Louisiana, Mississippi, and South Carolina). And the two sets of candidates attracted different types of voters:

> In the Deep South, the Goldwater candidacy enlisted the support of electoral majorities, largely composed of votes of Democrats, many of whom were casting their ballots for a Republican presidential candidate for the first time. . . . In the non-Deep South, . . . the Goldwater candidacy had the effect of alienating voters in sufficient numbers to drop Goldwater below Nixon in percentage-point terms and, most importantly, to deny him the electoral votes of the six non–Deep South states in which his immediate predecessors had enjoyed a fair measure of success.
>
> In short, change in voting preferences, rather than continuity, was outwardly the most visible component of the Goldwater outcome at the subregional level. (43–44)

Goldwater's greatest support came from the Black Belt (defined by Cosman as counties with nonwhite majorities) and non-metropolitan areas. The issue that attracted these voters was race: "Prior to 1964 the absence

of a Republican alternative on the race issue, coupled with the abandonment by the Democratic presidential party of its role as the party of the
southern white man, had served to neutralize the issue insofar as competition between the major parties was concerned" (54). Goldwater doubled
the Nixon vote in the Black Belt and non-metropolitan areas of the Deep
South (72.7 to 32.3 percent and 61.6 to 30.9 percent) and increased Nixon's
percentages in cities (60.2 to 44.4 percent) while increasing the percentages in traditional Republican areas by only 7 percent (up to 59.6 percent).
In Alabama alone, the percentage differences represented increases of 36.1
percent in the Black Belt, 35.8 percent in non-metropolitan areas, 20.6 percent in metropolitan areas, and only 13.6 percent in traditional Republican
locales (59–61, 65).

The Goldwater vote in the cities of the Deep South, particularly Jackson,
Shreveport, Birmingham, and Mobile, eliminated status polarization—the
division of the electorate along class lines: "Seemingly, racial hostility had
driven all other considerations from the minds of many lower-status whites,
causing them to rally to the Goldwater standard with greater over-all enthusiasm than voters did at the other end of the income scale" (89).

White turnout levels in 1964 exceeded the increases in black voting
and created severe problems for Democratic candidates at lower levels
on the ballot (130). Alabama elected five Republican congressmen: Jack
Edwards (59.9 percent); William L. Dickinson (61.7 percent); Glen Andrews
(58.6 percent); John Buchanan (60.6 percent); and James D. Martin (59.6
percent).[149] The Republican election gains would be temporary, but the
Democratic party would be unable to regain all of its losses. In December 1964 John E. Grenier resigned as executive director of the Republican
National Committee and rather disingenuously blamed Goldwater's defeat by Lyndon Johnson on liberal Republicans Nelson Rockefeller, George
Romney, and William Scranton.[150]

The 1964 election did not restructure the party system in the state. In
the Republican party class tensions still existed, and the country club set
still controlled the party machinery. Urban-rural divisions, like the class
divisions, were just temporarily outweighed by racial considerations. And,
given the size of the Goldwater loss nationally, the Republican party was
unlikely to nominate a similar candidate in 1968.

It is also important to remember that in 1964 Alabama, blacks could vote
for Goldwater, or they could vote for unpledged Democratic electors supporting George Wallace. They could not vote for Lyndon Johnson. Still, they
voted Democratic.[151] Between 1964 and 1968, the number of black voters
would grow tremendously as the result of federal action. For the first time

since Reconstruction, two blacks were elected to seats on the Tuskegee City Council, defeating white incumbents in a runoff.[152]

African Americans gained victories in the federal courts as well. In June 1964 the U.S. Supreme Court finally struck down the Alabama court order that John Patterson had won in 1956 barring the NAACP from operating in Alabama. Throughout 1964 integration slowly came to Birmingham lunch counters, parks, and other public places. In December 1964 the U.S. Fourth Circuit Court of Appeals ruled in Richmond, Virginia, that state tuition grants could not be used to pay the tuition of children sent to segregated schools regardless of whether they were public or private. This ruling had clear implications for Alabama.

Industrial Development

Many letters to and from Wallace show Wallace devoted substantial time and effort to attracting industry to Alabama. He personally visited Huntsville, Birmingham, and other cities.[153] Wallace also appointed a Committee of 100, modeled after the Birmingham organization of the same name, to promote state industrial growth.[154] Any rumor of a company's interest in locating in the state generated letters to company officials over Wallace's signature. Such activities probably diminished once Wallace began to make himself heard at the national level.

An Alabama Planning and Industrial Development Board pamphlet featured the Wallace and Cater Acts. The Wallace Act authorized financing the construction and equipping of industrial or business projects, and the Cater Act authorized the formation of municipal industrial-development corporations. Wallace's name on one of these statutes conveyed the sense that he had been interested in industrial growth from the beginning of his legislative career.

Wallace administration members knew that civil rights discord hurt their industry-hunting activities, but this knowledge had no apparent effect on their efforts to block progress in civil rights. A letter sent in Wallace's first year in office to Seymore Trammell from Henry C. Goodrich, vice president of the large Rust Engineering Company of Birmingham, said:

> The actions of Governor Wallace in the last few weeks have wrecked any possible major industrial expansion moves into this area. At a time when he shouts about creating jobs, his actions have scared away the responsible industrial leaders who could create new industry or move plants to this area. I have talked with hundreds of them. In all cases

they state that they do not care to argue the relative merit of segregation versus integration but that they absolutely will stay away from any possibility of violence. Governor Wallace by his recent acts has not only condoned but encouraged the violence which had its tragic conclusion here in Birmingham yesterday.[155]

Goodrich was referring to the bombing of the Sixteenth Street Baptist Church, in which four young black girls were killed, and the subsequent fatal shooting of a black youth. In the same vein a letter from the manager of Northrop Space Laboratories in Huntsville informed Wallace that Alabama's race problems were making it difficult to recruit talented technical people from such places as California.[156]

Wallace administration loyalists received substantial support for the idea that industrial development could move forward despite civil rights troubles. When Wallace appointed Royce Kershaw, president of Kershaw Manufacturing Company, to the State Planning and Industrial Development Board, Kershaw responded: "Last week when I was in Chicago, I had lunch with a prospect who has 150 employees. He told me that he is considering moving south. . . . He told me frankly that he was not considering Alabama and Mississippi because of the bad publicity we have had on our integration . . . problems. But, after I showed him that he can construct and equip a modern manufacturing plant for the same price that he is paying Cook County in taxes, he stated that he would take another look at Alabama."[157]

Through 1964 Wallace and his staff continued actively to seek industry, but a scattering of letters indicates that Wallace was out of the office when industry attraction activities occurred.[158] On the other hand, Wallace apparently visited manufacturers who might be moving to Alabama when he went on campaign trips around the country.[159]

The First Half of Wallace's First Term

In his first year in office Wallace experienced some success in bringing the fractious legislature under control. He made a noisy display of opposing integration and built a national reputation with surprising speed.

Most of the events of 1963 did not constitute critical decisions. The federal government drew the integration noose tighter. Blacks continued civil rights demonstrations. Established economic interests such as big agriculture, big industry, teachers, labor unions, and retailers fought over taxes and other aspects of public policy in the legislature. The economic blocks that made up the alliance had not disappeared. They had no difficulty working together, even after the bitter reapportionment and redistricting fights. When their interests coincided, they cooperated. Superimposed on the economic blocks in the legislature were Patterson loyalists and de Graffenried hopefuls. There was little evidence yet that geographically based divisions would change because of reapportionment. The legislative session showed Wallace as a flexible and mildly progressive but inattentive leader except for patronage matters and the area of civil rights.

The only event of 1963 that could be regarded as even close to a critical decision was the Birmingham Big Mules' turning against "Bull Connor" and ridding the city of his influence. This movement was symptomatic of their tactical shift away from extremist segregation. The Big Mules had not changed their basic attitudes, but Connor was becoming an embarrassment, and the civil rights movement was making segregation bad for business.

In 1964 Wallace fully emerged as a national figure. He probably helped make Goldwater's opposition to civil rights legislation respectable in comparison and increased the size of Goldwater's victory in the South.

There was some acceptance of integration in day-to-day life and even to a limited degree in schools. However, new private academies began to spring up. In the future they would drain public schools of crucial support from community leaders. The civil rights lag narrowed rapidly. It was clear to nearly everyone that the fight was over as far as voting rights and segregation were concerned. Of course, this lag did not narrow because of normal interest-group politics in Alabama. The states may sometimes be a source of reform and movement when the federal government is unresponsive and vice versa. In the case of the civil rights lag, the larger political system provided the responsiveness, but it was a slow process.

The urban-rural representation lag was well on its way to elimination by 1964—also as the result of actions taken by the federal government. Unlike the civil rights lag, this one might have been eliminated in Alabama without federal intervention, but it would not have happened as quickly. Again, on the national level it is possible to say that the system was responsive (but again very slowly) according to the naive interest-group model.

The sudden short movement narrowing the party lag in the 1964 general election would not have occurred at that time had it not been for civil rights activity. Here too, with both the national Democratic party and the national Republican party there was an interaction between the Alabama political subsystem and the national system.

There were hints in and around 1964 that parts of the former alliance would, or at least might, shift to the Republicans, but the Republican party seemed to offer little beyond the opportunity for protest. It was clear even then that greatly expanded black participation in the national Democratic party (there was no chance that they would become part of the GOP) would send more whites to the Republicans in national, if not statewide, races. Wallace's personal popularity would strangle the 1964 Republican gains in 1966.

What were the attitudes of industrial Big Mules toward Wallace? His files suggest that he did not communicate with them often. Most of the letters from executives representing large urban enterprises not dependent on state government business were critical of Wallace's civil rights policies. George Lewis Bailes Jr., a Jefferson County representative in George Wallace's first term and senator in Lurleen Wallace's term, was tied closely to several Birmingham banks. He observed no connections between Wallace and Birmingham's Big Mules: "They didn't believe in him. AmSouth, SouthTrust, First Alabama, everybody. They couldn't afford to deal with him. Whatever he told them, he wouldn't do."[160] They did not trust his word.

8

Wallace's Growing Popularity and Ambition

Civil rights demonstrations and black voting registration drives continued into 1965. With them came renewed violence, more demagoguery from Wallace, and additional damaging national press coverage of the state of Alabama and its leadership. These actions combined to expand Wallace's base of support within the state and feed his political ambitions.

Voter Registration

Not surprisingly, voting discrimination was especially severe in the Black Belt. It was total and absolute in Wilcox County. According to the U.S. Commission on Civil Rights, in 1961 the Wilcox County population was 78 percent black but not a single black was registered to vote. Meanwhile, 112.4 percent of the white citizens were registered.

Wilcox County was not an isolated case. Adjoining Lowndes County had an even higher percentage of blacks and no black voters, and in Dallas County (containing the city of Selma), which was 57.7 percent black, blacks represented only 1.4 percent of registered voters.

In January 1965 Martin Luther King Jr. led registration efforts in Selma. King and the Southern Christian Leadership Conference staff recognized, on the basis of their Birmingham experiences, that white attacks on blacks who were peacefully attempting to exercise their constitutional rights could provoke Congress and the Johnson administration into action. In some ways Selma represented a richer opportunity for dramatizing the civil rights cause than Birmingham. The Dallas County sheriff, Jim Clark, King realized, was potentially more vicious in the handling of civil rights demonstrators than Birmingham's police commissioner, "Bull" Connor.

As King and his staff predicted, authorities in Selma met many voting registration efforts with physical attacks. Jim Clark's brutal treatment of a black woman waiting in line to register received front-page coverage in at least one national newspaper. That night at a rally Ralph Abernathy declared the sheriff an honorary member of the Southern Christian Leadership Conference.[1]

Registration drives and the sheriff's counterattacks escalated through January. On January 25 a woman punched the sheriff. Three deputies threw her to the ground, and she snarled at Clark, "I wish you would hit me, you scum," whereupon, as the camera of a wire service photographer clicked, he appeared to smash her in the head with his billy club.[2] In February, when King and hundreds of others were arrested and jailed, King could claim in a *New York Times* advertisement, "THERE ARE MORE NEGROES IN JAIL WITH ME THAN THERE ARE ON THE VOTING ROLLS."[3] The Selma battle produced a statement from President Lyndon Johnson criticizing the slow pace of registration of qualified citizens and promising that the right to vote would be "secured for all our citizens."[4]

In February a voter registration drive in the Black Belt town of Marion attracted national media attention and more violence.[5] White toughs beat an NBC news correspondent, Richard Valeriani, and two United Press International photographers named Pete Fisher and Reggie Smith as they covered a nighttime voter registration rally. On February 19 William McAndrew, executive vice president of NBC, sent a telegram to Governor Wallace complaining that Valeriani was "the second National Broadcasting Company newsman injured in performing his duties in your state in recent months."[6]

Wallace responded by blaming the violence on rally organizers who, he argued, "scheduled it at night for the sole purpose of provoking a breach of the peace." Nighttime rallies would henceforth be banned, Wallace added. The governor noted that crime in New York City demonstrated that "there is no way to prevent a sudden, spur of the moment, act of violence."[7] Wallace repeated variants of his "crime is worse in New York" theme many more times.

As a response to the violence and continued media coverage, King began planning a massive march from Selma to Montgomery for March 7. Wallace's press secretary, Bill Jones, recommended to Wallace the leaking of fictitious plans to have police or state troopers block the marchers on the outskirts of Selma. Instead, however, the marchers would be permitted to move unhindered. Jones argued that the marchers, thinking that they would be stopped, would be unprepared for a fifty-four-mile trek that would take several days. The idea was to make King look foolish as the march disintegrated on its own. Jones also suggested blocking all traffic on the highway except for residents. Reporters and demonstrators would be denied the luxury of riding.[8]

Wallace agreed to the plan, and the next day the policy was "leaked" to the press. Later "Lowndes County State Representative Bill Edwards warned Wallace that marchers moving along the desolate route might be hit by snipers or that explosives could be planted along the roadway. Wallace reluctantly agreed with Edwards's assessment, and he and his staff together with state trooper commanders Al Lingo, John Cloud, and William R. Jones met to formulate a new plan."[9] Bill Jones described the policy on which they settled:

> Troopers stationed across the highway east of the Edmund Pettus Bridge [just outside Selma] would halt the march at that point. The troopers were to stand there. If the marchers persisted in marching, the troopers were to raise their police sticks in a protective manner. If any shoving occurred, the marchers, not the troopers, would do it. The troopers were to fall back, and again tell the marchers they must turn back. If the marchers pushed the troopers, the troopers were to fall back and use tear gas, but only enough to disperse the mob. Everyone in the Governor's office thoroughly understood the procedures to be used.[10]

There appear to be logical gaps in this narrative. The road between Selma and Montgomery with hundreds of marchers, police, and reporters on it would not be the deserted place described by Representative Edwards. Furthermore, if the marchers were as unprepared as Wallace's aides expected, they would get only a few miles. Furthermore, snipers and bombers would not be prepared because they, like everyone else, would be under the impression that the marchers would be stopped. In fact, the marchers were completely unprepared. Many were not wearing walking shoes, and they had no logistical support for water, food, and camping paraphernalia. There is no question that if, following Jones's original plan, the march had been allowed to proceed, the marchers would not have reached Montgomery.

When the six hundred marchers reached the line of troopers on the Edmund Pettus Bridge, they were ordered to disperse. When they refused, the troopers charged the marchers in a wedge formation.

> The first 10 or 20 Negroes were swept to the ground screaming, arms and legs flying. . . .

Those still on their feet retreated.

The troopers continued pushing, using both the force of their bodies and the prodding of their nightsticks.

A cheer went up from the white spectators lining the south side of the highway.

The mounted possemen spurred their horses and rode at a run into the retreating mass. The Negroes cried out as they crowded together for protection, and the whites on the sidelines whooped and cheered.[11]

Then tear gas was fired at the running crowd, and troopers and Dallas County police pursued and clubbed the dispersing marchers.

That evening the American Broadcasting Corporation interrupted the broadcast of "Judgment at Nuremberg," a motion picture about the trial of Nazi war criminals, to show footage of the violence in Selma. National newspaper and television coverage was devastating. Phrases such as "storm troopers," "pitiful line of marchers walking into the jaws of death," "the depravity of the state troopers," and "outrage against America" were the norm.[12] Meanwhile, the *Montgomery Advertiser* chose to portray the melee this way: "State troopers quietly turned back a massive right to vote march led by Dr. Martin Luther King, Jr."[13]

According to the reporter Bob Ingram, when Wallace saw the effect of the television coverage, he was furious.[14] But those at fault, Public Safety Director Al Lingo and Major John Cloud of the highway patrol, were not dismissed, some assumed because of old loyalties on Wallace's part.[15] It is more likely that he did not want to embarrass himself by admitting that mistakes had been made, nor would he have wanted to rupture his ties with constituents who viewed the attack on the marchers as appropriate. Lingo resigned in the late summer of 1965.[16]

The Tuesday after the Edmund Pettus Bridge debacle, three ministers from Massachusetts were attacked in Selma. One died of head wounds. Events in Selma encouraged Johnson administration members who were drafting voting rights legislation. Selma in 1965 would have the same effect in Washington as Birmingham had in 1963 and 1964.

Through the next week further demonstrations occurred in Selma and Montgomery. Late in the week George Wallace asked for an appointment with Lyndon Johnson in the hope of finding a way to end the demonstrations.[17] The meeting was arranged quickly, and Wallace flew to Washington. Johnson brushed aside Wallace's specious arguments that Martin Luther King Jr. was the basic cause of the violence. He then led the governor into an ambush in the Rose Garden, where he announced that a voting rights act would be sent to the Congress and cited Selma as dramatic evidence of the need for such legislation: "What happened in Selma was an American tragedy. . . . It is wrong to do violence to peaceful citizens in the streets of their town. It is wrong to deny Americans the right to vote. It is wrong to deny any person full equality because of the color of his skin." [18]

The next Monday evening Johnson appeared on network television and used much the same language to encourage popular support for his voting rights bill. Hearings began in the House of Representatives later that week.

On Sunday, March 21, a new Selma-to-Montgomery march began. Wallace asked Alabamians not to attack marchers. "Let us not play into the hands of our enemies," he said, firmly closing the barn door. [19] The march began with three thousand people. After five days they arrived in Montgomery, where twenty-five thousand people heard King and others speak.

But the violence continued. That night in Lowndes County three Klan members shot and killed a civil rights worker from Detroit named Viola Liuzzo. Because one of the Klan members present was an FBI informant, arrests came quickly. In April a bomb exploded in a black area of Birmingham, and bombs were disarmed at the homes of Mayor Albert Boutwell and city council member Nina Miglionico. [20] Similar incidents occurred in many scattered locations.

Business Leaders and Legislators Respond

The already intense anxiety in the business community over the effect of racial violence on Alabama's national image heightened still further in 1965. A full-page advertisement ran in the *Wall Street Journal, U.S. News and World Report,* and twenty-two daily Alabama newspapers. Sponsored by the Alabama Chamber of Commerce, Alabama Bankers Association, Associated Industries of Alabama, Alabama Textile Manufacturers Association, seventeen local chambers of commerce, and local business groups, it called for handling racial problems within the law: "The vast majority of the people of Alabama, like other responsible citizens throughout our nation, believe in law and order, and in the fair and just treatment of all their fellow citizens. They believe in obedience to the law regardless of their personal feelings about its specific merits. They believe in the basic human dignity of all people of all races." [21]

This advertisement should not be considered a complete surrender by the business community. Another part of it read: "We believe in the basic American heritage of voting, and in the right of every eligible citizen to register and to cast his ballot. We believe, however, that qualification of prospective voters, when properly and equitably administered, is a constitutional responsibility that must be preserved."

Not all members of the business community admired the advertisement. For example, it earned Earl Benson, president of the Mobile Chamber of Commerce, an angry letter from J. Edward Thornton. Thornton, a lawyer, referred in disbelief to "the implication in this ad that we in Alabama have not believed in the right to vote by every eligible citizen" and went on to deny that discrimination occurred![22]

In a speech the wealthy Republican businessman Winton Blount defended and praised the advertisement, and he blasted Wallace for dismissing the slaying of Viola Liuzzo by saying that it was still safer on Highway 80 in Alabama, where the murder had occurred, than in the subways of New York. Blount said, "We cannot minimize the gravity of these deeds by comparing them with similar events in other parts of the country."[23] Blount also called Wallace's remark "unbelievably callous" and charged that it "disregards the feelings of the decent people in Alabama." He went on to criticize government officials for allowing themselves to become negative symbols of defiance and thus be outsmarted by agitators. He asked the legislature to pass a law establishing equitable voter-registration tests.

The day after Blount's speech the Alabama Senate passed a constitutional amendment, sponsored by George Hawkins, that made a sixth-grade education the literacy requirement for voter registration and repealed the poll tax. The sixth-grade literacy requirement was part of the 1964 Civil Rights Act, and the poll tax had been eliminated for federal elections by the Twenty-Fourth Amendment to the U.S. Constitution, ratified in 1964. According to the *Montgomery Advertiser,* "Several senators who voted for the bill admitted privately they had done so confident it would not pass the House."[24]

Hawkins's bill was in fact indefinitely postponed in the House.[25] The House vote shows a confused and conflicted legislature. Twenty-three House members abstained or were not present. The urban delegations split their votes. In the case of the Mobile and Jefferson County delegations only pluralities voted for the bill. Montgomery's delegation split two for reform and two against. Only Madison County (Huntsville) had a united delegation in favor of reform. Rural counties in the Black Belt and the north also split their votes, although rural counties tended to oppose reform. The legislators were being pulled and hauled by changing urban Big Mule attitudes that did little but recognize reality; by diehard segregationists or their representatives, who were opposed to any easing of voting restrictions; by segregationists who hated integration but hoped to salvage maneuvering room from the Hawkins bill; and by racial moderates.

Two days after the House killed Hawkins's bill, Judge Frank M. Johnson banned literacy tests in Elmore, Bullock, and Macon Counties. The Senate and House quickly responded by passing with overwhelming majorities a constitutional amendment and an enabling act that were little different from the Hawkins measure except that they set an eighth-grade education as the literacy requirement.

In August the Alabama Senate passed a private school grant-in-aid bill that would pay the tuition of white children unwilling to attend integrated schools. The vote was twenty-two to nine. The Senate then approved a companion bill that appropriated $3.75 million (a fraction of what the cost would have been had the bill remained law) over the next two years to pay for it.[26] Wallace and most, if not all, of the senators knew that the federal courts would strike down the tuition grants.[27] The bill basically represented a symbolic encouragement of private academies.

In 1963 the legislature had created a body called the Alabama Legislative Commission to Preserve the Peace, chaired by John Hawkins Jr.[28] Its membership included Senators James S. "Jimmy" Clark and E. O. Eddins and Representatives Hugh Locke and Alton Turner, all of whom were legislative leaders and not regarded as segregation extremists. They represented the cream of governmental leadership in Alabama in the early 1960s. (Clark later became Speaker of the House in a career that stretched into the 1990s.) The commission purported to be a fact-finding body. It operated on the assumption that the civil rights movement was a conspiracy with Communist foundations.

The commission's 1965 biennial report reviewed the activities of the Student Nonviolent Coordinating Committee (SNCC), a group consisting largely of university students. It described the SNCC leadership as "deeply Marxist-oriented, tending toward the pro–Chinese Communist and pro-Castro brands of activity."[29] The report also portrayed Martin Luther King Jr. as a "false prophet of the far-left" who for ten years had been "closely advised by communists if not actually controlled by them"—a characterization that completely missed the point of what King was about.[30]

The report's analysis of the 1964 civil rights bill was equally detached from reality. It observed the following points of comparison between a Communist party document and the civil rights bill, and concluded that the similarity meant that the civil rights movement was Communist-inspired:

In the platform of the WORKERS' (COMMUNIST) PARTY OF 1928 WE READ
A MILDER FORM OF THE 1964 CIVIL RIGHTS BILL. . . .
• Abolition of the whole system of race discrimination. Full racial, politi-
cal, and social equality for the Negro Race. . . .
• Abolition of all laws which disfranchise Negroes. . . .
• Federal law against lynching and the protection of the Negro masses
in their right of self-defense.
• Abolition of discriminatory practices in courts against Negroes. No
discrimination in jury service.[31]

With thinking of this quality, it is little wonder that the civil rights movement so frequently outmaneuvered the segregationists.

Justice in Alabama

The year 1965 saw a parade of murders of blacks and
civil rights advocates, and subsequent miscarriages of justice. During the
Marion voter registration drive, state troopers assaulted blacks. Jimmie
Lee Jackson was fatally shot while trying to defend his mother from such
an attack. The trooper who killed Jackson was never publicly identified,
and no charges were brought against him.[32]

The trial of Collie LeRoy Wilkins Jr., one of three Ku Klux Klan members charged with killing Viola Liuzzo, began in May 1965 before a jury
of twelve white men in the Lowndes County Courthouse in Hayneville.
Wilkins was the first defendant tried. He was defended by a Birmingham
attorney named Matt Murphy Jr., the Imperial Klonsel of the United Klans
of America, Incorporated.

Gary Thomas Rowe Jr., a paid FBI informant, testified that he wit-
nessed Wilkins fire at Liuzzo. FBI ballistics experts tied bullets taken from
Liuzzo's body and her car to a gun recovered from the home of one of the
other two Klansmen arrested with Wilkins. Rowe testified that it was the
gun used by Wilkins to kill Liuzzo.[33]

Imperial Klonsel Murphy, unable to refute Rowe's testimony or the physical evidence, appealed to the jurors' emotions by suggesting that Liuzzo
had sexual relations with the nineteen-year-old black who was riding with
her when she was murdered. He also attacked Rowe as a "Judas Iscariot"
who had broken his oath of secrecy to the Klan. At one point in his cross-
examination of Rowe, Murphy asked whether Rowe was a paid agent of
Fidel Castro.

Much of Murphy's summation was a defense of white supremacy: "I stand here as a white man and I say we're never going to mongrelize the race with nigger blood and the Martin Luther Kings, the white niggers, the Jews, the Zionists who run that bunch of niggers, the white people are not going to run before them."[34] The Klan attorney's tirade appeared to embarrass several jurors. One, who acknowledged that he was a segregationist, observed after the trial, "I think a great many of us were insulted to a great extent and he must have thought we were very, very ignorant to be taken in by that act."[35] He added, "We can't allow murder on the highway here." The jury deadlocked ten to two in favor of conviction.

Wilkins was retried in October. This time Attorney General Richmond Flowers handled the prosecution. He attempted but failed to win an Alabama Supreme Court ruling barring jurors who expressed belief in white supremacy or bias against civil rights workers. The white male jurors finally selected included six former members and two current members of the White Citizens Council. This jury delivered a not guilty verdict after one hour and thirty-five minutes of deliberation. Later in the year Wilkins and his co-conspirators were convicted of federal civil rights violations and sentenced to ten years in prison.

On March 9, 1965, the Reverend James Reeb, a civil rights worker, was fatally beaten. Four men were arrested, tried, and found not guilty by an all-white jury that deliberated ninety minutes. Four eyewitnesses to Reeb's beating did not testify at the trial. The court ruled one mentally incompetent, two others left the state, and another refused to testify, citing his Fifth Amendment right not to incriminate himself. Two other eyewitnesses, however, positively identified the leader of the gang responsible for Reeb's injuries.[36]

On August 20 in Hayneville, Jonathan Daniels, an Episcopal seminarian, was killed and Richard Morrisroe, a Catholic priest, critically wounded by shotgun blasts. They had been jailed for participating in civil rights demonstrations and then released without explanation. They were shot soon thereafter. That same day Thomas Coleman, a highway engineer and unpaid special deputy sheriff, was arrested and charged with the shootings. Richmond Flowers assigned blame for the murder to the KKK and accused Al Lingo, a friend of Coleman's, of refusing to cooperate in the investigation.[37] Yet another all-white-male jury found Coleman not guilty. A state senator, Vaughan Hill Robison, served as his defense attorney. Many national newspaper editorials criticized the trial.[38]

In an October 2, 1965, memorandum to President Lyndon Johnson concerning Coleman's acquittal, Press Secretary George Reedy reflected that rural white southerners "believe that they have the same right to exterminate civil rights workers that a farmer has to kill rabid dogs. It is absolutely inconceivable to them that a man can be tried and convicted for such actions."[39]

The image of Alabama that emerged from national newspaper coverage of these trials could not have been worse. One editorial cartoon showed an Alabama judge plunging a dagger into the back of the figure of Justice. A *Los Angeles Times* editorial read:

> An obscene judicial travesty has just concluded in a courtroom in Hayneville, Ala., and the stench and shame of this proceeding hover over the entire nation.
>
> What kind of trial is it when the "gun" and the "knife" allegedly carried by Coleman's two victims, the slain seminarian and the seriously wounded Roman Catholic priest, are not produced?
>
> What kind of trial is it when the chief prosecution witness, the priest who was shot in the back, is too ill to testify and the judge orders the trial to proceed anyway?[40]

Accompanying this editorial was a Conrad cartoon that showed a snickering jury telling a laughing judge, "We find the ... he he he! ... defendant ... ho ho! ... git set! ... he'ah come the punch line! ... ho ho! ... NOT GUILTY!!" The governor's office was inundated with letters reflecting the kinds of sentiments expressed by the Conrad cartoon. Wallace's standard response was that Coleman and the others had been fairly tried and found innocent.

George Wallace rarely if ever denounced the civil rights murders on his own initiative, but he never missed an opportunity to condemn civil rights demonstrators and their supporters. When asked about the murder of James Reeb on the CBS interview program *Face the Nation,* he offered a feeble criticism of the murderer followed in the next sentence by a rebuke of the media: "I deplore such actions as that, but we have people in Alabama, just like they have in every state, who cannot control their feelings. President Kennedy was killed in Dallas, but I don't blame Governor Connolly or the people of Texas for that."[41]

On July 15, 1965, Willie Brewster, a black who apparently was not involved in civil rights activities, was shot and killed while driving home from work. This completely unprovoked attack elicited from George Wallace an offer of one thousand dollars for information leading to the conviction of the killer or killers. Three men were indicted for the crime on August 27. Hubert Strange, the first to be tried, was represented by the KKK attorney J. B. Stoner. (In 1980 J. B. Stoner would be prosecuted by Alabama Attorney General William Baxley and convicted of the 1963 Bethel Baptist

Church bombing in Birmingham, in which four black girls were killed.) The all-white jury returned a second-degree murder conviction, and Strange received a ten-year sentence.[42] It was the first time during the civil rights era that a white person was convicted of killing a black in Alabama. The verdict surprised everyone. While free on bond awaiting appeal, Strange was killed in a barroom brawl. The others indicted for the Brewster murder were tried and acquitted.

Early in 1966 Lowndes County was ordered to establish new jury rolls without regard to race, and the state law prohibiting women from serving on juries was struck down.

The Voting Rights Act

Alabama's U.S. senators continued their opposition to civil rights legislation, this time a voting rights bill. Their efforts and those of southerners in the House proved fruitless. The Voting Rights Act of 1965 passed by overwhelming majorities in both chambers.[43] The law guaranteed that adult citizens who wanted to vote could do so without constraint by local or state governments. Its key enforcement tool was the voting examiner, a federal official who could require registration of qualified individuals to vote in all elections.

Voting examiners could be put in place under several circumstances: by a federal court; if the U.S. attorney general certified that legitimate complaints of voting discrimination had been made by twenty or more residents of a city, county, or other state subdivision; or if a literacy test or similar device was in use on November 1, 1964, and the Bureau of the Census found that fewer than 50 percent of persons of voting age in an area were registered to vote on that date or actually voted in the 1964 presidential election. The 50 percent provision was known as the automatic triggering formula.

If a state or state subdivision fell within the automatic triggering formula, the act stopped literacy tests or similar devices. It also empowered a federal court to eliminate literacy tests or similar devices if it found that they were discriminatory. A test or device was defined as any prerequisite for registration or voting that required an individual to demonstrate educational accomplishment or moral character or to possess a voucher from a registered voter or anyone else. The act also directed the attorney general to initiate court challenges against poll taxes. In March 1966 a three-judge federal panel killed the Alabama poll tax.

George Wallace and Civic Virtue

In response to highly successful black voting regis-
tration activities, Wallace conducted a massive voter registration campaign
of his own. He sent letters to the Veterans of Foreign Wars, Masonic organizations, chambers of commerce, American Legion posts, and other largely
white civic groups asking them to run voter registration drives. Wallace
explained the action in a letter to a Birmingham Mason: "This, of course,
is not engaging in politics. Engaging in politics would be to support officially one candidate or party. However, to get good fine people who believe
in constitutional government to register to vote is in the interest of our
country."[44] While the governor engaged in a white voter registration drive,
some Black Belt employers tried to reduce the numbers of black voters. In
one instance eleven black sharecroppers were forced from their homes in
Wilcox County for attempting to register.[45]

Meanwhile, white politicians studied ways to prevent a black takeover of
the Black Belt. In February 1966 the Legislative Reference Service (LRS),
a research and bill-writing agency, completed a report to the governor
and the legislative council entitled "Legislative Control of County Government." The LRS had been charged with the task of formulating ways "of
preventing mass changes in the status of county governing bodies."[46] Its
study identified fifteen counties as likely candidates for this shift because
they had black populations of 49 percent or greater. The LRS suggested a
range of statutory changes such as educational requirements for officeholders, countywide election of all county officials, gubernatorial appointment
of county officeholders, and consolidation of counties so that whites would
be in the majority. The study explicitly ruled out the use of race-based
legislation, viewing it as certain to fall before federal court rulings.

Black political activists analyzed the structure of county government
and party organization with an eye toward capturing them. For example,
in a June 21, 1966, letter, the black civil rights lawyer Fred Gray asked
Ira Pruitt Sr. for information on the method used to select members of his
county's Democratic executive committee. Specifically, he asked whether
they were elected by "beat, countywide, or self-perpetuation."[47] In turn
Pruitt wrote to Cecil Jackson Jr., the governor's executive secretary, and
referred to the Gray letter: "The people in Barbour County had a similar
situation and they sought to remedy it by a local Bill providing that the
members would be elected on a county wide basis. . . . several candidates
who were Negroes raised the question as to the legality of the Act. . . . It is
my purpose to convene the County Committee at an early date and without
publicity for the purpose of considering this matter."[48]

Wallace and his staff paid close attention to increasing racial turmoil in northern and western cities. A riot in the Watts district of Los Angeles in the summer of 1965 resulted in 34 fatalities, 856 injuries, and $200 million in property damage.[49] Similar riots in Chicago, Detroit, and other cities outside the South served to boost their spirits.[50] They believed that these disturbances, which caused far greater destruction and more injuries than anything that occurred in the South, would cause whites throughout the country to turn against the civil rights movement.

Wallace also welcomed the rise of the black power movement. The term *black power* became popular during James Meredith's June 1966 voter registration march through Mississippi. During his march Meredith had been shot from ambush. While he recovered from his wounds, other civil rights leaders, most notably Stokely Carmichael, chairman of SNCC, took up his cause. In the course of their efforts, black power became a rallying cry. Beyond conveying a sense of pride, its meaning was never clear, but segregationists believed it split younger, more radical, and possibly more violence-prone black power advocates from the original civil rights leaders, such as Martin Luther King Jr., Roy Wilkins, Whitney Young, and A. Philip Randolph.[51] They also believed it expanded discussion of racial problems beyond the South.

In a 1966 letter to a Baptist leader, Wallace wrote: "For several years I have been trying to warn the people of this country of some of the dangers which we are facing. I notice that several of the national columnists are writing pretty much the same thing which I said some three or four years ago. . . . I am going to continue to carry this message to the people of this country."[52]

Northern urban riots and black power also cheered "Bull" Connor. In a sarcastic letter to Richard Hughes, the governor of riot-torn New Jersey, Connor wrote: "Your explanation of your delay in dispatching your letter is entirely understandable to one such as I on whom non-violent Messrs. King, Shuttlesworth, Carmichael, et al, in 1963 and 1964 practice the techniques which they now are using so successfully in Newark, Jersey City, Detroit, Cleveland and elsewhere. I notice with concern that all the leaders, or nearly so, of this revolt claim to be members of our great party. This could, I fear, cause us some trouble in the approaching elections."[53]

School Integration

One of the legal underpinnings for the desegregation of public primary and secondary schools was Title VI of the Civil Rights Act of 1964. Title VI forbade discrimination because of race, color, or national origin under programs receiving federal assistance. The most important federal agency in this regard was the Department of Health, Education, and Welfare (HEW) which quickly promulgated civil rights regulations. Printed in the *Federal Register* on December 4, 1964, they became effective one month later. The regulations applied to nearly one hundred HEW programs. In April 1965 HEW's Office of Education released a policy statement that set the beginning of the 1967 school year as the date by which all grades should be desegregated.[54]

In February 1966 Federal District Judge Frank M. Johnson Jr. ordered the Black Belt Lowndes County School District to end segregation. Judge Johnson also ordered the Lowndes County Board of Education to establish remedial programs to eliminate the effects of the segregated educational experience. Teachers and principals were to be assigned on a nonracial basis and school buses were to be supplied so that students could attend the schools of their choice.

Even where school integration occurred in Alabama, it frequently did not go smoothly. A May 1966 *Wall Street Journal* article described the situation in a small town near Montgomery:

> Many Negro students in formerly "white" schools have encountered little but bitterness, taunting and threats from white pupils. At the very best, they experience an ostracism so complete that they are totally walled off from their classmates and from normal school activity. "These colored children are the most segregated students you've ever seen," says G. A. Walters, principal of Wetumpka High, which enrolled its first Negroes this school year and which now has 16 Negroes out of a total student body of about 680. "The white students never talk to them. The other day I saw a Negro girl sit down with some whites in the cafeteria, and they just got up and moved away."[55]

This story also described the physical abuse to which black students were subjected by their white classmates.

As the public schools integrated their students and faculties under federal court orders, the governor received petitions and complaints from parents and other citizens. For example, a petition dated September 9, 1966, read, "We the undersigned would like to have the colored teacher removed from our Stevenson High School, Stevenson, Alabama."[56] A petition containing thirty-eight hundred signatures from citizens of Tuscaloosa County protesting the integration of their schools was sent to the governor's office on September 20, 1966.[57] Robert Hendrick, president of the Anniston Labor Council, AFL-CIO, sent a strong segregationist, anti-NAACP resolution from his union.[58]

Most southerners thought that school integration would culminate in a few black students and faculty entering predominantly white schools, where they would be isolated and ignored. Most northerners believed that the civil rights movement applied only to the South. Both groups were mistaken.

By 1966 civil rights strategists were planning steps that would be greeted with equal hostility by whites in both the North and the South. Harold Howe II, the new federal education commissioner, was quoted as favoring the use of federal aid "to encourage local school experiments designed to assault segregation and, in the process, to weaken or even destroy the cherished 'neighborhood school' tradition."[59] He asserted that integration efforts to this point had failed, an astounding contention given the fact that real desegregation had been ongoing for a mere three or four years. One proposal that Howe was considering would create centralized groups of schools called education plazas that would be attended by students from many neighborhoods. Another proposal called for teacher-pupil exchanges via busing. Suburban school officials in the North recognized the implications of such policies. For example, a suburban New York state senator stated: "The time is coming when the City of New York will attempt to exchange students on a forced basis with its suburbs."[60]

The 1965 Legislative Sessions

As the civil rights battles continued, the Alabama legislature carried on its normal activities. Urban-rural divisions continued to surface. The newly expanded Jefferson County delegation renewed its fight for a larger share of state monies. In a letter to Wallace, Senator Larry Dumas wrote, "Jefferson County has failed to receive a fair allocation of projects on any reasonable basis, such as highway miles travelled, per capita, or payment of gasoline tax."[61] The Wallace administration's standard response to this kind of criticism was to highlight the large dollar totals going to Jefferson County while downplaying per capita figures that nearly always showed the county in a far less optimistic light.[62]

In February 1965 the governor called a special session to act on his ambitious-looking education program. It included a 10 percent increase in teacher salaries, free textbooks, a 20 percent increase in appropriations for colleges and universities, and a $125 million school-construction bond issue. Other requested legislation would bring the number of junior colleges and trade schools to twenty-eight, a huge number for a state of Alabama's size. The House quickly passed the Wallace free textbook bill by a vote of eighty-one to thirteen and then approved a record $459 million school budget unanimously. Although Wallace and the legislature were vigorously encouraging the private school movement, they were also providing support for public schools sufficient to be satisfactory even to the AEA.[63]

The $125 million school bond issue ran into flak from Mobile school board officials who, like their Jefferson County counterparts, argued that the formula used to distribute bond monies unfairly discriminated against counties with expanding student populations. Sixty million dollars of the bond issue would be distributed directly to public schools, with $16.75 million allocated in equal $250,000 packages to each county. The remainder of the $60 million would be apportioned on a teacher-unit basis. Under this formula some rural counties would receive three times more money per pupil than Jefferson or Mobile Counties. Other funds were allocated to higher education.

On March 23 the House passed the school-construction bond issue on a seventy-four-to-twenty-four vote and sent it to the Senate. Passage came after three hours of parliamentary maneuvering involving nineteen amendments based primarily on urban-versus-rural conflict. The pivot point of the fight was a substitute bill offered by Rankin Fite. Fite's version provided prizes for select cities and reduced allocations to rural areas. The scattered opposition to this bill came mainly from rural counties and urban Tuscaloosa and Madison Counties. The latter two may have objected to extra money going to the University of South Alabama in Mobile, which was to some degree competing with the University of Alabama.

When the bond issue went to the Senate, similar urban-rural jockeying began immediately. Urban senators made proposals, rural senators made counterproposals, filibustering occurred, and compromises were reached. The core rural proposal came from Roland Cooper of Wilcox County, who wanted a fixed distribution of $250,000 per county. Bob Gilchrist and other urban senators advocated a plan based on student population. The Senate passed a compromise version that contained $150,000 per county, with the remainder distributed by student population, plus the allocation of an additional $1 million to the University of South Alabama.[64]

When the bond issue went to conference committee, the major unresolved point was that the Senate favored the universities more than the House did. The two chambers split the difference, and the conference committee version passed both chambers by unanimous votes.[65] Teachers received a 10 percent raise, and $8 million was allocated for free books.[66]

Wallace loyalists believed that his education programs constituted an enormous increase in funding. Our analyses suggest that Wallace's impact on spending in 1963 and 1965 had only a slightly positive effect.

The salaries of Alabama primary and secondary teachers, expressed in constant dollars, had experienced a strong upward trend in the 1950s. An argument can be made that Wallace had a one-time impact in his first term, abruptly raising the level of salaries, but that the rate of growth sagged thereafter. (The analysis techniques that produced this and the conclusions below are discussed fully in the Appendix.) A somewhat stronger case can be made that he had almost no impact on teacher salaries.

When Alabama teacher salaries are compared to those for the United States as a whole, it is clear that Alabama faded badly in the Patterson years. The first Wallace administration merely produced a partial recovery. In 1956, during the second Folsom administration, Alabama reached the level of 83 percent of the U.S. average. In the Patterson years it dropped to 70 percent. The first Wallace term pushed the figure to 81 percent, but then it sagged back to 75 percent in 1969. Alabama did not exceed the 1956 figure until 1974.

Per-pupil primary and secondary school operating expenditures are another index of education spending. These data suggest a somewhat stronger Wallace influence than do teacher salaries. The trend in per-pupil expenditures after the first Wallace administration was substantially higher than before it. However, a comparison of Alabama's per-pupil expenditures with those of the United States as a whole shows that the first Wallace administration's impact was to close a gap widened during the Patterson years. This was immediately followed by another gap widening in the Lurleen Wallace–Albert Brewer administration and in the second George Wallace administration, beginning in 1971.

In 1960 Alabama reached a historical peak as its percentage of U.S. per-pupil spending hit 64.3. This was followed by a drop to 56.8 percent in 1963, a sharp upward movement to 68.5 percent in 1967, and then another plunge to 55.9 percent in 1970. The 1970 figure was the lowest point from 1950 to 1985 and after. It was followed by a remarkable upward move, to 78.5 percent in 1976, and then another drop. It is difficult to make an argument for Wallace's having more than an occasional transitory effect on spending when Alabama figures are compared to those of the United States as a whole. Had Wallace been merely an ordinary one-term officeholder, this would not be a remarkable statement. But his influence was strong and lasting, for he served three four-year terms as governor during the years 1958–79 and his wife served half of another term as his surrogate.

The Succession Fight

In early May, during the regular legislative session, a filibuster led by Patterson and Sparkman forces tied up the Senate. The proximate target was an innocuous resolution concerning school boards and civil rights compliance, but that resolution was unrelated to their real objective, to consume legislative days in order to block two bills to amend the state constitution. One would permit Wallace to succeed himself as governor; the other would allow him to run against Senator John Sparkman in 1966. (Governors could not seek a U.S. Senate seat within one year of the end of the term for which they were elected governor.)

Not surprisingly, Patterson supporters, who were looking forward to a second Patterson term, opposed the succession amendment. They were joined in their opposition by supporters of Ryan de Graffenried, who still harbored gubernatorial ambitions, and by supporters of Senator Sparkman, who feared Wallace's popularity.

Three senators dubbed the "JP triplets" by Grover Hall Jr. led the opposition to succession. They were Bob Gilchrist of Morgan, Vaughan Hill Robison of Montgomery, and Sonny Hornsby of Tallapoosa. Bob Ingram identified the former Patterson House speaker Virgis Ashworth (Bibb) as the "team captain of the Patterson forces." Ashworth was now a lobbyist for the leading industrialist Big Mule organization Associated Industries of Alabama.[67] Patterson's former House floor leader, Joe Smith (Phenix City), also stood against succession. The hard core opponents were joined by others who simply opposed succession as a matter of principle or who disliked Wallace for reasons other than those related to gubernatorial or senatorial politics. Some realized that the governorship would provide him a platform and the resources required for another national campaign.

Grover Hall Jr. also opposed Wallace on succession. One of the most perceptive editorials of his career dealt with this subject:

> The adoration of the multitude for W issues from a spring deeper and sweeter to it than responsible government. It is the sense of the mechanic, farmer, truck driver, barber, waitress and clerk that W stood up for them, that he and he alone had the daring and prowess to cuff, jab and master their television tormentors and thus vindicate them as a people. They spit at the "image" of those who chide them about their image. We find a measure of satisfaction in all this because we fought, and we fought hard, for W in both 1958 and 1962. But we are against the proposition of W succeeding himself as governor. . . . it is simply good hygiene to clean the Capitol out every four years and de-louse it.[68]

Wallace's plan to run against Senator Sparkman vaporized. Wallace really wanted to be governor again.[69] In October he began in earnest to convince the legislature to pass his succession bill. He used the same theme raised in the 1990s by those opposed to congressional and state legislative term limitations—the right of the people to decide. The House passed the succession bill in the first week by a vote of seventy-four to twenty-three.

The Patterson–de Graffenried–Sparkman forces put up little struggle in the House because they held a strategic advantage in the Senate, where they were better represented. They knew Wallace supporters needed twenty-one votes to pass the constitutional amendment and twenty-four votes to invoke cloture.

A Senate filibuster began immediately. It has been described as the "filibuster with the most intense emotional impact and the most enduring consequences" in the history of the Alabama Senate.[70] Wallace's supporters attacked the filibuster itself with a Senate resolution asking the state supreme court to rule on the constitutionality of the Senate rule requiring more than an absolute majority of votes to invoke cloture. The court ruled against them.

Wallace also attacked the senators who opposed succession by withdrawing patronage, most notably three hundred thousand dollars promised to a junior college in Senator Julian Lowe's Randolph County district. The move was so generally unpopular that he reversed himself almost the next day.

Unembarrassed by his second patronage-withdrawal debacle, Wallace embarked on a speaking tour in the districts of senators who opposed him, another desperate maneuver that is rarely successful. Wallace came closer to making this tactic work than any chief executive in recent history. He changed no votes, but the unfortunate senators who tried to follow him to podiums to respond were jeered, and some felt happy to escape uninjured from the mobs that formed after Wallace's speeches.[71] Wallace also made television speeches calling the succession opponents by name. The opponents received threats and hate mail, and pickup trucks with loaded gun racks drove slowly by their homes at night.

The governor attacked on another front, again using an ancient trick. This time he asked liquor companies to stop advertising in newspapers with editorial policies against succession. The only effect this seemed to have was to antagonize the newspapers.[72]

The filibustering senators finally allowed the bill to reach a vote, but the result was eighteen to fourteen in favor, short of the twenty-one votes required for passage.[73] Vaughan Hill Robison remembered it as a "bitter" contest and "the hardest fight that ever took place in my sixteen years in the Senate."[74] He continued: "Oh, the pressure was tremendous. They'd promise you roads, and projects, and they'd threaten to cut off road building. Our position was not against succession but against succession if it included the present governor. Of course, we couldn't just say that we were against it because we were for Patterson." He later added: "During a speech I made on succession I used the line 'On what meat does this our little Caesar feed.' They tell me that Wallace heard that on the loudspeaker in his office, and it just about made him climb the walls!" At this point the tall, gaunt, now elderly Robison grinned broadly.

The most important result of the succession fight was that a disproportionate number of the senators targeted by Wallace soon suffered premature termination of their political careers. Their fate made enemies years later think carefully before pitting themselves against George Wallace. Of the fourteen who voted against succession, ten did not seek reelection. Only two—L. D. Bentley (Marshall, Blount, St. Clair) and Kenneth Hammond (Jackson, DeKalb, Cherokee)—ran for reelection; both were defeated. Bob Gilchrist (Morgan) ran for governor, and John M. Tyson (Mobile) sought the office of lieutenant governor. They also lost. Only six of the eighteen who sided with Wallace failed to seek reelection or election to some other office.[75]

A short time after the succession fight, John Patterson happened to meet former governor Folsom. Folsom suggested that opposing the succession bill had been a mistake. Patterson and de Graffenried would have been better off, argued Folsom, if they had allowed the bill to pass and then opposed it when the amendment went before a vote of the electorate. That way, the people could be seen as repudiating Wallace. Of course, this strategy carried with it the risk that the electorate would approve the amendment, but Folsom believed that this possibility was more desirable than the virtual certainty that Wallace would be strengthened by the succession fight. Patterson admits today that Folsom's estimate of the situation was correct.[76]

The succession battle represented nothing more than politicians jockeying for power. These events, however, revealed a great deal about George Wallace. They dramatized that more than anything else he wanted power and that he would do almost anything to maintain his position. In his desperate struggle he showed that he was willing to rewrite or distort rules, break his word, seek to hobble the press, and foment hatred. One of his contemporaries argued that Wallace's behavior in the succession fight was an example of how he often encouraged feelings of incivility and even lawlessness without overtly calling for riots or violence.

Redistricting and Reapportionment

In mid-April 1965 congressional districts redrawn in the 1964 legislature were declared unconstitutional on the grounds that they were insufficiently equal.[77] From the end of April into September, the Senate bickered and bargained over how Jefferson County would be divided. Little beyond the narrowest local politics was evident in this phase of the fight.[78] Finally, the legislature adopted a redistricting plan.

Toward the end of September the legislature passed a reapportionment package that ended rural domination of the state legislature. The reapportionment plan for the Senate still supported white supremacy in that only a single district, encompassing Sumter, Choctaw, Washington, and Marengo Counties, had a black majority.[79]

Less than two weeks later a three-judge federal court upheld the legislature's congressional redistricting but rejected its reapportionment of the Alabama House, characterizing the plan as "racial gerrymandering." Surprisingly, the court approved the Senate reapportionment plan.[80]

The legislature refused to deal with House reapportionment even though it was under a federal court order to do so. Most legislators, including those from the Black Belt, were tired of seemingly endless, mentally demanding dead-end struggles. They resigned themselves to allowing the federal courts to do the job, a pattern of behavior that would become a habit in several areas of policy-making.[81]

According to the *Montgomery Advertiser,* the 1965 special and regular sessions "differed principally . . . in the important area of leadership. Wallace went all out for his education program and the results speak for themselves. By contrast, Wallace has provided no leadership during the regular session. There was very little he wanted, and what he really wanted—the gubernatorial or senatorial succession bills—he knew quite well he couldn't get. . . . Wallace adopted a hands-off hurry up and go home attitude. As a result the Legislature has floundered."[82]

Another account quoted a legislator as saying, "It's hard to tell who the administration leaders really are. The leadership has been diffused. . . . One day it appears to be Senator Pete Mathews, then Roland Cooper moves to the front, then maybe Bill Nichols or somebody else. The leadership has not only been diffused, but most undistinguished."[83] Vaughan Hill Robison confirmed this characterization in an interview with the authors. These versions of Wallace's legislative leadership must be tempered somewhat with Albert Brewer's observation that "Wallace was powerful even when he didn't really try to be. Rankin Fite would introduce a bill and mutter in

his horse voice 'The Governor wants this bill. I move its passage,' and that
would be his entire justification for it. And it would pass."[84]

Attracting Industry

The 1965 Planning and Industrial Development file
in the Wallace office files suggests increased activity by Wallace and Leonard Beard, director of the State Planning and Industrial Development
Board.[85] These files seem to reflect a more vigorous attitude toward attracting industry than was evident earlier in the Wallace administration.

Wallace's staff, recognizing that Alabama's image had suffered grievously
in the past several years, organized an "editors' tour." Fifty-nine newspaper editors from throughout the country were escorted around the state,
with travel costs absorbed by a number of large businesses and business
groups.[86] The Wallace administration made sure that eight black educators
were present for the tour.[87] The editors' tour was followed in 1966 by the
"Red Carpet Industrial Tour of Alabama" for fifty executives.

The 1966 Elections

In June 1965, with gubernatorial primaries less than
a year away and the succession bill dead, the reporter Bob Ingram asked
people to forecast who the winner would be. Ingram heard many predictable names, such as John Patterson and Ryan de Graffenried. But he added,
prophetically:

> It is worth mentioning that any number of legislators, when asked
> the one question of who would get the most votes in their county, re-
> plied Wallace without hesitation. "He would get 80% of the votes in my
> county," commented a South Alabamian. "He didn't carry my county in
> 1962 but he would today," said another. Patterson is strongest in the
> very same areas that Wallace was strongest, and for the same reasons.
> He's stout on segregation, and like it or not, that remains an issue. . . .
> In reverse, de Graffenried was ruled the favorite in most of the areas
> where he ran well before—North Alabama. Patterson was given over-
> whelming leads in the Black Belt counties and in East Alabama from
> the Florida line due north to the mountains of North Alabama. This is
> where Patterson slaughtered Wallace in 1958—from Chambers north-
> ward.[88]

In January 1966 demands and counterdemands from black and Dixie-crat forces lashed the state Democratic party's executive committee. Black leaders threatened to withdraw support from the party until the committee removed the "White Supremacy" slogan from the Democratic party emblem that appeared on ballots. The emblem showed a crowing rooster with "White Supremacy" written above the rooster and "For the Right" below it.

Dixiecrats wanted primaries replaced by county, district, and state conventions similar to those then used by the Republican party. They viewed this as a way to prevent the nomination of black candidates. Dixiecrats also favored retention of the existing structure of the executive committee, which had a total of seventy-two members, eight from each of the 1960 congressional districts. Blacks and liberal whites wanted a more representative base.

The executive committee in a secret ballot went against Wallace's wishes and removed the "White Supremacy" label from the party emblem, replacing it with "Democrats." The motion to use a secret ballot for the decision had passed thirty-nine to thirty-two, a vote that can be taken as expressing sentiment on the issue itself.[89] The committee did not vote on structural changes.

Joe McFadden of the *Montgomery Advertiser* interpreted the outcome as the result of professional politicians' making decisions "based on a cold-eyed look at where the votes are. Somebody seemed to have the idea that the real purpose of a political party is to elect candidates. . . . It was perfectly clear that Negroes are going to vote in large numbers for somebody."[90] Political realities were changing rapidly.

The 1965 Republican party budget was two hundred thousand dollars, a large sum for a southern party organization at that time. The GOP recruited nearly one hundred candidates for the 1966 legislative races in the hope of winning a sizeable number of positions. John Grenier left the party chairmanship to run for governor against a Democratic nominee who would probably emerge from a tough primary campaign that everyone believed would include an expensive runoff. Congressman Jim Martin appeared ready to oppose Senator Sparkman, who, according to some, had lost contact with Alabama voters. Then, in a peculiar trade-off, Martin became the gubernatorial candidate and Grenier ran for the Senate nomination against Perry Hooper Sr. Redistricting made it unlikely that a Republican could win Martin's congressional seat.

In a speech before the Montgomery County Republican party convention in May 1966, Congressman Bill Dickinson slammed the Great Society and denounced federal integration policies. Sounding no different from George

Wallace, Dickinson said that southern resistance was "not a battle of white and black, not a racial thing as such, but a battle for human rights."[91]

White politicians nervously tracked black voter registration. Figures released in December 1965 revealed that forty thousand whites and twenty thousand blacks were registered in Montgomery County, representing a massive increase in black voters. If these electorates followed past turnout patterns of 35 percent for whites and 85 percent for blacks, there would be a sizeable black majority in Montgomery County. However, most people understood that this sort of static analysis was invalid because black voter registration drives prompted more whites to register and vote and because many believed that first-time black voters who had enjoyed a relatively easy registration procedure would probably not be as conscientious as those who had jumped much higher hurdles to win the right to vote.

In February 1966 Ryan de Graffenried was killed when his airplane crashed as he flew to a speaking engagement. He was only forty years old.

In mid-February the fact that Lurleen Wallace would run for governor became public knowledge.[92] Many viewed this as an extraordinarily risky maneuver. A week later Richmond Flowers announced his candidacy in a statement that basically guaranteed his loss against virtually any white politician of that time. He asked for the support of both black and white voters, and he promised to remove the Confederate battle flag from the capitol dome. The battle flag had been raised by George Wallace to protest a 1963 visit by Attorney General Robert Kennedy, who was trying to prevent Wallace's stand in the schoolhouse door. Black citizens viewed the rebel battle flag as a symbol of strong racist sentiment remaining in government. Potential out-of-state investors and business interests viewed the flag negatively. The rebel flag continued to fly until 1993, when the new governor, James E. Folsom Jr., ordered that only the American and state flags would fly above the capitol dome.

As attorney general Flowers had prosecuted murder cases against those accused of killing civil rights workers and had spoken out frequently against such violence and Klan activities. As a result he enjoyed strong support in the black community, especially in the Black Belt.

During the campaign, Flowers accepted speaking invitations from black groups. He was the only candidate to appear at the Bethel Baptist Church in Birmingham (site of the 1963 bombing). So many television crews covered his appearance that Flowers could not see his audience. He ended his nationally televised address with the statement: "I want to be your governor." A lonely, tired voice from near the back of the church responded, "Shore do need one."[93]

Ultimately, Lurleen Wallace faced nine opponents in 1966. In addition to Richmond Flowers, the well-known candidates were the former congressman Carl Elliott, former governors John Patterson and James E. Folsom Sr., state senator Bob Gilchrist, Folsomite A. W. Todd, and a Dothan businessman named Charles Woods.

Carl Elliott was a New Deal Democrat with close ideological and political ties to President Lyndon Johnson, who wanted to see Wallace weakened and his own ally in charge of the state and the state Democratic party. Elliott hoped to build a coalition of white liberals (including the labor unions) and blacks, but Flowers siphoned most of the latter. Elliott opened his gubernatorial campaign in Birmingham before a crowd that exhibited what Bob Ingram delicately described as "restrained enthusiasm." Elliott decried the "self-serving extremists" on both sides of the civil rights battle, arguing that the solution "lies within the framework of love and understanding, within the framework of law and order."[94] In another speech, he promised: "I will reopen the lines of communication between our state and national governments. I will talk to the leaders of Congress and the executive branch on even terms, man to man, just as the governors of all our sister Southern states are now doing."[95] Elliott lacked personal appeal and, like most former members of Congress, had little statewide name recognition. In addition, most of the state considered Elliott an outsider. Not only was he part of liberal north Alabama; he had become a Washington liberal as well.

John Patterson called for increased old age pensions and no new taxes. He observed, as so many gubernatorial candidates had before and would since, that more jobs and new markets are the keys to an improved economy.

Throughout the campaign Richmond Flowers continued his appeals for black support. He promised blacks state jobs and asserted his belief that blacks were not inferior.[96] While remaining intensely unfriendly to Flowers's candidacy, the *Montgomery Advertiser* pointed out that at the same time Flowers was promising employment for blacks, Mayor Albert Boutwell and Police Chief Jamie Moore of Birmingham were asking black ministers to assist in recruiting black applicants for city jobs.[97] The state was changing.

James E. Folsom Sr., speaking before the black Alabama State Teachers Association convention, congratulated blacks, saying, "You have struggled quietly, smoothly and peacefully and are now facing a great future."[98] Reporter and columnist Joe McFadden wrote a political obituary for Folsom: "On the race question he has been one of the most moderate men ever to reach the governor's chair in the South. Even in 1962, when segregation was considered the prime issue, he condemned the attack on the 'Freedom Riders' in the strongest terms. In 1956, he referred to the so-called interposition resolution of the legislature: 'That resolution reminds me of an old hound dog baying at the moon.'"[99] McFadden then quoted at length from Folsom's classic 1949 Christmas message. In that speech Folsom said:

Our Negroes who constitute 35 percent of our population in Alabama—are they getting 35 percent of the fair share of living? Are they getting adequate medical care . . . ? Are they provided with sufficient professional training . . . ? Are the Negroes being given their share of democracy, the same opportunity of having a voice in the government under which they live?

As long as the Negroes are held down by deprivation and lack of opportunity, the other poor people will be held down alongside them.[100]

In an editorial entitled "The Animal Fair, 1946–66" Grover Hall Jr. presented his view of the 1966 race:

In the post-war mood, the shock and marvel of J's [Folsom's] unconventional behavior provided a release. . . . It was carnival time and the weather was just right.

More than that, J had an appeal to the masses that was profound. He made a coarse class appeal and it took. And he fascinated and delighted a lot of proper people, too. . . .

J is a sorrowful sight now, but those of us who traveled with him in the '46 campaign will never forget. It is a fact—we swear it—that there was in '46 Folsom a distinct poetry. It was fresh, of the earth and of the elements. That ole mule, as he said, a-headin' fer the barn, going *clickety-clop, clickety clop*. . . .

JP [Patterson] represents an episode in Alabama political history, not an era. He was the culmination of the incredible assassination of his father, Atty. Gen.-elect Albert Patterson, and the embodiment of the purging of Phenix City. But that day is done and now he is only a scowl and a faltering, tedious speech on the tube. . . .

Richmond Flowers does not embody an era. He is a satellite flung off J and landed in the new era when there are 200,000 Negro voters. It fell to him to become the first candidate in a hundred years to say, "I want every Negro vote."

Write your own on Wallace. Be certain it is an era. When an Alabamian runs in northern primaries, offers the First Lady for governor and is one of the two best known governors in the country it has to be accounted an era.[101]

In his speeches for his wife, George Wallace made clear what everyone already knew. If she is elected, "I shall continue to speak for you." He assured voters that he would be his wife's "chief advisor." He also offered "continued progress, prosperity, and honesty," and he attacked the state's "big" newspapers, anti–Vietnam War protesters, the federal courts, and President Lyndon Johnson.[102]

Even early in the campaign it was clear to observers like Bob Ingram that the Wallaces were ahead. Crowds at Wallace rallies were enormous and their passions intense.[103] In March Ingram wrote that some were comparing Lurleen's position to that of Folsom in 1954. Though agreeing that Lurleen held a commanding lead, Ingram doubted that, like Folsom, Lurleen would win without a runoff, because she would be bucking a large new black vote. He estimated that she would need about 65 percent of the white vote to win without a runoff.[104]

In a March editorial the *Montgomery Advertiser* joined most daily newspapers in opposing the Wallace candidacy. It did so by taking the unusual step of endorsing Republican Jim Martin for governor and doing so *before* the Democratic primary. The editorial wrote off all of the Democratic opponents. Some had merit, but none could come close to defeating Wallace:

> What is wrong with the Wallace Proposition? He has achieved many splendid things for Alabama. . . .
> But it happens that Wallace is not a candidate for governor this year. . . . Mrs. Wallace would be the ornamental Queen and Wallace the prime minister.
> The arrangement is out of order of our law and propriety. . . . it is not justifiable purely because Wallace has achieved some fine things as governor and wants to run for President.[105]

This was followed by fine rhetoric about Martin—his speaking ability, sound leadership capabilities, and so forth.

Although no one doubted that Lurleen Wallace was only a satellite, she was an effective campaigner. Her first solo speech trip, required because her husband was ill, generated large crowds.[106] *Newsweek* and *Los Angeles Times* reporters attended one of the George-Lurleen rallies. Wallace asked his supporters to make the journalists welcome: "I want them to see that you are just as fine, intelligent and cultured as people anywhere in the country." Indeed, he asserted, Alabamians were better informed concerning such matters as international relations than the national media: "*Newsweek* is so smart they helped Mao Tse Tung to power . . . they were for Castro when everyone in Hueytown already knew he was a Communist." The crowd cheered appreciatively. By this point Wallace rallies were being attended by numbers on the order of ten thousand.[107]

A *Montgomery Advertiser* editorial complained that everyone was focusing on new black voters and the George-Lurleen spectacle while ignoring important issues such as bonded indebtedness, competitive bidding, and taxes: "But no Alabamian can tell what the candidates have been saying on these questions because of the fact they haven't been saying anything. Most of the candidates are running against Wallace, Flowers is running for the Negro vote, and Wallace is running against [the television news anchor] David Brinkley."[108]

Lurleen Wallace won the May 3 primary without a runoff. Her total was nearly 500,000 votes; Flowers was second with only 173,000. After him came Elliott with 46,000 and Gilchrist with 37,000. Patterson placed sixth and Folsom seventh. Most of Flowers's strength came from blacks. Lurleen Wallace carried the home counties of all opponents, and she attracted an enormous majority of white votes. The *Montgomery Advertiser* recognized "a mystical communion between Wallace and his people." And "far from handicapping Wallace, Lurleen actually added a dimension to his appeal."[109]

The reporter Joe McFadden wrote that the statewide black percentage of voters did not increase much because of increased white registration. Wallace's voter registration efforts plus expected white registration in response to the civil rights movement had had their effect.[110]

An earlier McFadden article presented a perceptive portrait of north Alabama that might explain why even that region supported the Wallace candidacy. North Alabama had few blacks. Most people in that part of the state had been "reading, writing and voting for three or four generations." Employment was high and pay good for blacks and whites. McFadden claimed north Alabamians resented the activities of federal investigators almost as much as other Alabamians because they felt that in north Alabama they had no civil rights problems.[111]

Two days after the Democratic primary, the "Stand Up for Alabama" sign was removed from the Wallace election headquarters. A "Stand Up for America" sign replaced it.

Albert Brewer, in an all-but-invisible lieutenant governor's contest, defeated state senators Neil Metcalf and John Tyson and the Huntsville attorney John Reynolds without a runoff. The former attorney general Mac-Donald Gallion, a staunch segregationist, defeated an Anniston attorney, Guy Sparks, for the office of attorney general. Senator John Sparkman did not face significant primary opposition.

Black candidates won only scattered races even in Black Belt counties where they held registration majorities. Perhaps the most notable black victory was that of Lucius D. Amerson, who was nominated for Macon County sheriff.

In the general election campaign, Republican Jim Martin shared a theme used by Wallace's many critics, that is, that the governor's efforts to fight integration, such as his "two-and-a-half minute stand in the school house door," were only empty, showy gestures that attracted federal retribution. Martin claimed he would be a more effective if less flamboyant defender of the southern way of life.

Martin was correct in his assessment of Wallace, but the electorate was in no mood to hear it. His other campaign themes were predictable and utterly ineffectual attacks on Wallace's attempt to build a political dynasty and the Wallace administration's profiteering. An excursion into foreign policy, not high on the list of voter concerns in a gubernatorial election, was as odd as it was unhelpful to his campaign. His preachments on behalf of the two-party system were met by Wallace's now famous quip that "there's not a dime's worth of difference" between national party leaders. "I'm against all of them, just like you are," he added.[112] Wallace also blasted national Republican leaders from Supreme Court Chief Justice Earl Warren to U.S. Representative Gerald Ford and the former vice-president Richard Nixon for their support of the civil rights movement.

As a Democrat, Senator John Sparkman could only benefit from Lurleen Wallace's candidacy and its potential to generate straight-ticket voting. He skillfully highlighted his record of votes against the Johnson administration's civil rights proposals while stressing the many Democratic party programs still popular in Alabama, his chairmanship of the Senate Banking Committee, and his membership on the Foreign Relations Committee.

Despite his longtime prominence in the GOP, Sparkman's opponent, John Grenier, did not enjoy widespread name recognition. Trying desperately to shake free of the double burden of the Wallaces' popularity and Sparkman's skill, Grenier attempted to attract Wallace voters and thus alienated moderate Republicans and Jim Martin. He also flailed away at the Johnson administration, which Sparkman had in large part repudiated.[113]

The Wallaces and Sparkman defeated Martin and Grenier overwhelmingly. Democrat Tom Bevill won Martin's former House seat, taking 64.6

percent of the vote, and William "Bill" Nichols defeated Congressman Arthur Andrews, a Republican, with 58.7 percent of the vote.

Unlike Barry Goldwater, who swept Alabama in 1964, neither Martin nor Grenier seemed able to differentiate the Republican party from the Wallace-Sparkman version of the Democratic party. They blindly supported Wallace's segregationist policies and tied Goldwater's honest conservatism to them. They did not make clear to majorities of Alabama voters why the Republicans were better or different. That failure continues today.

9

The Governors Wallace

Officially, Lurleen Wallace was the governor of the state of Alabama in the period January 16, 1967–May 7, 1968, but no one doubted that her chief advisor, as her husband coyly called himself, was still in power. She was widely liked and admired and never subjected to the ridicule that her actual status might otherwise have generated. When journalists tried to convey an accurate sense of who was actually making decisions, they resorted to light humor with references such as the Governors Wallace and the Wallace Administrations I and II.

The legislature that met in 1967 was the first in the state's history to be fully reapportioned on a one-person-one-vote basis. Reapportionment brought many changes, not all of them for the better. Urban-rural division became the major base of conflict. The outnumbered Black Belt delegation found new allies in other rural legislators, sometimes joining them in fights against old alliance partners from Jefferson County who now worked with other urban interests. The Governors Wallace sided with the Black Belt–rural counties.

Legislative Leadership

The governor selected the parliamentary master Rankin Fite as Speaker of the House.[1] Albert Brewer, the previous Speaker, was now lieutenant governor.

The House Ways and Means Committee chair was the crusty and able Pete Mathews, who represented Clay and Coosa, two of the most rural counties. More than half of the committee members represented rural districts. Hugh Merrill of Calhoun (rural north Alabama) became House Judiciary chair. The House Rules Committee chair was Fite by virtue of his position as Speaker.

O. J. "Joe" Goodwyn of Montgomery was selected president pro tempore of the Senate, and the "Wiley Fox from Wilcox," Roland Cooper, was named floor leader. Finance and Taxation was dominated by rural forces, including the chair Alton Turner (Crenshaw), who represented an all-rural district encompassing four Black Belt counties, Jimmy Clark (Barbour), Roland Cooper (Wilcox), Fred Folsom (Cullman), Walter Givhan (Dallas), W. Ray Lolley (Coffee), and Emmett Oden (Franklin). Urban areas were represented by Vice Chair Mylan Engel (Mobile), Jack Giles (Madison), Eddie Gilmore and Pat Vacca (Birmingham), Ollie Nabors (Etowah), and Junie Pierce (Montgomery). E. W. Skidmore (Tuscaloosa) and C. C. "Bo" Torbert (Lee) came from difficult-to-categorize counties containing the two major state universities and small towns. On this critical committee, then, seven members (four of whom were especially able and powerful) represented rural counties. The six men representing urban counties did not enjoy the personal stature of the rural members. Furthermore, the rural senators almost always supported the administration, and several of the urban senators were also pro-administration. These included Engel, Giles, Gilmore, and Vacca. Nabors, Pierce, Torbert, and Skidmore were relatively independent and could not be counted on by either side. The Senate Judiciary chair was Joe Goodwyn (Montgomery) and the Senate Rules chair Jimmy Clark (Barbour). Barbour County was George Wallace's home county.

These overwhelmingly rural leadership choices were atypical of the normal tendency of governors to distribute leadership positions evenly. The Lurleen Wallace administration's legislative leaders were the most geographically skewed of any in the post–World War II period. Their appointments helped to short-circuit much of the impact of reapportionment.

Two theories account for the heavy rural shift in legislative appointments. One, expressed by all interview accounts and borne out by the evidence of correspondence in Wallace's office files, is that Wallace's core political support came from rural areas. Interview subjects, when asked to name interest groups especially supportive of Wallace, nearly always listed the Alabama Farm Bureau Federation first. Urban newspapers were less supportive of Wallace than rural ones, and urban political and business leaders were more likely to favor moderate policies regarding segregation and voting rights.

Albert Brewer offered a second, more mechanical explanation for the shift.[2] In his view it was a product of experience levels. There were few experienced north Alabama and urban legislators in 1967, but many rural representatives had served several legislative terms. This resulted partly from the fact that many who had opposed Wallace on succession hailed from urban areas and were no longer in the legislature. It also reflected the

growth in urban districts due to reapportionment. However, after present-
ing this argument, Brewer admitted that Wallace's personal temperament
lay more with rural interests and culture.

Bases of Urban-Rural Conflict

The largest delegation in the 1967 legislature came
from Jefferson County. It consisted of twenty representatives and seven
senators. Mobile's delegation now numbered thirteen (ten House and three
Senate), Montgomery's seven (five House and two Senate), and Madison
County—Huntsville—now had four legislators (three House and one Senate). Other urban counties, such as Etowah and Tuscaloosa, also gained
representation.

The Jefferson County delegation's first attempt to utilize its new strength
was the removal of a seven-cent-per-gallon aviation fuel tax that Jefferson County had been trying to eliminate for many years. This tax was
much higher than similar ones in neighboring states. Birmingham interests argued that the tax reduced the profitability of aircraft fueling and
maintenance businesses in Jefferson County and gave airports in places
such as Atlanta an advantage in attracting airline traffic and airline hub
operations.

Before the 1967 legislative session, the entire Jefferson County delegation lobbied George Wallace to support its forthcoming attempt to repeal
or drastically reduce the tax, and he immediately agreed. Ultimately, the
tax was cut to 1.5 cents per gallon, but not before rural legislators used
it as a bargaining chip against the Jefferson County delegation in other
urban-rural tax and spending conflicts.

In January 1967 legislators from the state's larger cities held a well-
publicized meeting to plan a way to obtain a larger share of the state's
seven-cent-per-gallon gasoline tax revenue for street and road development. Urban counties, with their increased House representation in the
previous legislature, had won some concessions. Now that they enjoyed
even more strength, they planned to push again.

As matters stood, three cents of the seven-cent tax were distributed to
the state highway department and four cents to the counties. This arrangement usually made city officials dependent on rural-oriented county
commissioners for road funds.

Making matters worse from the urban perspective, by law each of the
sixty-seven counties received an equal share of the gasoline tax revenue,
not a proportional amount based on population or some other measure

of need. In 1966 each county, from the smallest to the largest, received approximately seven hundred thousand dollars from the tax.

Winston Stewart, executive secretary of the Association of County Commissioners, responded to the urban challenge by declaring that counties needed an even larger share of gasoline tax revenues. He evidently hoped that a compromise could be reached somewhere between his outrageous new position and what the cities wanted.

The Jefferson County delegation took the lead in representing urban interests. Even though it had grown, the delegation remained under Big Mule control. Jefferson County business interests actively recruited promising candidates and supported their campaigns. Each Jefferson County legislator was oriented toward a particular constellation of industries, such as steel or banking. When George Lewis Bailes Jr. was asked whether Big Mule–backed candidates opposed each other, such as the steel candidate versus the banking candidate, he replied that it had never happened as far as he could remember. Big Mule candidates ran against non–Big Mule candidates, and the former always won, according to Bailes.[3]

Albert Brewer's version of Jefferson County's power structure is very similar. It has the House members distributed geographically rather than by industry, but the result is the same. According to Brewer, Jefferson County's at-large 1966 senatorial elections produced "clones" of earlier Jefferson County Big Mule senators. They all thought alike and were selected by the largest business concerns. Later, the division of Jefferson County into single-member districts sharply reduced Big Mule power and diluted the county's impact because its diversity produced legislators with differing interests. The same thing occurred in Montgomery.[4]

Brewer maintains that single-member districts changed the legislature more substantially than reapportionment. With single-member districts it was quite possible to have a county's legislators on both sides of an issue with their votes canceling each other. Such divisions especially affected local legislation—legislation affecting a particular county or city rather than a class of counties or cities. By custom local legislation passed both houses as a courtesy to the members, but this practice applied only if the county delegation took a united position.

In the Senate, Bailes and Hugh Morrow III (a banker who was also from Jefferson County) emerged as urban leaders and Big Mule water carriers. Bailes, who was independently wealthy, had AmSouth Bank as his political patron. He made no apologies for his ties to the Big Mules: "I have always been pro-business."[5]

Bailes specialized in seeking out and eliminating bills that would damage Jefferson County. This helped make him the least-liked member of the Senate. Having his name attached to a bill almost guaranteed its demise, but since he rarely initiated legislation, this hardly mattered. On the rare occasions when he wanted a bill passed, he usually saw to it that someone else, such as his fellow Jefferson County senator, Richard Dominick, introduced it.[6]

Rudene Bailes always accompanied her husband to the legislative sessions. She watched floor deliberations from the gallery, tracking legislation important to Jefferson County. At Bailes's request the Legislative Reference Service sent him a copy of each piece of legislation it drafted. Because the LRS drafted nearly all bills of serious intent, Bailes was able to avoid missing anything. Each night during the session, he and his wife read every bill as it came from the LRS. He credits his wife with spotting many bills that would have hurt Jefferson County, noting that he could not have read all of them himself.[7]

The bills Bailes regarded as damaging to Jefferson County were primarily financial. Such measures distributed state resources disproportionately to rural counties or taxed Jefferson County unfairly or both. According to Bailes, the worst bills came from the Black Belt, and many were written by the infamous Roland Cooper of Wilcox County, who was an administration floor leader. Gone was the close cooperation between Jefferson County and the Black Belt described by James E. Folsom Sr., Albert Brewer, John Patterson, Albert Boutwell, Sam Engelhardt, and many legislators who served in the 1940s and 1950s.[8]

Governor Wallace called a special session on roads at the beginning of March 1967. In her call for the special session she asked the legislature to approve the largest bond issue in state history—$160 million for highway construction. The bond issue would be funded by using the seven-tenths of a cent then allocated to farm-to-market (rural) roads from the seven-cent gasoline tax. The governor's call also included a three-dollar increase in the state auto license fee. Proceeds would help the cities finance their own road programs. The governor also asked for passage of a competitive bid law.

According to the *Montgomery Advertiser,* neither rural nor urban forces were enthusiastic about the administration's road bond bill. The bill became entangled with a legislative pay increase that had been approved by both chambers but lay on the governor's desk unsigned.[9] In response to this suspicious holdup the House Ways and Means Committee voted eleven to three to delay the committee's business. A similar stoppage on the Senate floor was supported by a seventeen-to-twelve vote. The winning side included both urban and rural forces and the administration's floor leader, Roland Cooper.

Speaker Fite, acting for the Wallace administration, counterattacked against what the administration regarded as urban obstructionists. He assigned a package of three highly interrelated bills sponsored by the Jefferson County delegation to three different committees, thus guaranteeing that they would never be properly considered.

As March passed, the legislature split in different directions like complex geological fractures. There were pro- and anti-administration factions, rural and urban forces, those for and against the competitive bid law, and groups for and against the legislative pay increase. Roland Cooper favored the legislative pay raise (which the administration opposed), opposed the competitive bid law (he owned an automobile dealership that did a great deal of government business), opposed the administration's road bill, and opposed Jefferson County's road bill.

The urban representatives had the votes to pass their highway funding bills on the floor, but they were unable to tear them out of the rural-dominated House Ways and Means Committee. The administration finally ordered Ways and Means members to free the bills. The administration's raw power was demonstrated by an instant reversal from a solid majority against the urban bills to a thirteen-to-two vote in favor. Those opposed were Ira Pruitt and Joe McCorquodale, both representatives from rural Black Belt counties.[10] Interview subjects were unable to shed light on why this administration switch occurred, although it may have been because Wallace had plans for the House bill when it reached the Senate.

The urban-sponsored bills rocketed to the House floor, where they won quick passage. The bills changed the distribution of gasoline tax revenues in favor of the cities, substantially increased the price of auto and truck licenses, and authorized the issuance of $160 million in road bonds. Although these bills drastically changed the distribution of road money from lower- to higher-population counties, the license increases boosted the financial burden on more populous counties. The principal speakers against tax reallocation and the tag increase, in addition to Pruitt and McCorquodale, were predominantly from the Black Belt, but other rural counties were represented.

The key event in the passage of this package was a sixty-four-to-forty vote in favor of the allocation changes.[11] With very few exceptions all counties for it were urban, and all against it were rural and/or Black Belt.

The *Montgomery Advertiser* political writer Don Wasson summed up the new balance of power in one sentence: "The 44 counties which would receive less money under the reallocation plan are represented in this Legislature by only 33 Legislators, whereas the 23 counties which would receive more money are represented by 73 votes."[12]

When the road bills reached the Senate, a compromise gasoline-tax allocation bill was offered. It guaranteed each county $590,000. The House-passed bills were lodged in the rural-dominated Senate Finance and Taxation Committee. Only administration pressure could get the bills out of committee.

The administration and rural senators agreed on a version, and the bills immediately were released from the Finance and Taxation Committee.[13] In a session on Friday morning, April 21, urban senators won a twenty-one-to-eight vote adopting the House version, which was much more favorable to cities than the Senate Finance and Taxation Committee–Wallace administration version. During a lunch break rural forces regrouped.

That afternoon the House version was voted down eighteen to twelve. Nine senators switched sides, and two administration supporters absent in the morning vote were present that afternoon.[14] Some of the senators who switched sides were Albea (Calhoun), Engel (Mobile), Folsom (Cullman), Radney (Tallapoosa), Skidmore (Tuscaloosa), Stone (Cherokee), and Torbert (Lee). Except for Engel, these senators represented medium-sized "swing" counties. Albert Brewer and George Lewis Bailes Jr. agreed that George Wallace had nothing to do with this switch.[15] Bailes added that the switch occurred "because Alton Turner woke up. Alton Turner nearly collapsed when he discovered what had occurred." Albert Brewer's less dramatic version of Turner's morning vote was that Turner wanted to be able to move for reconsideration.

Brewer and Bailes also pointed to other factors that influenced the Finance and Taxation Committee vote. Mylan Engel wanted extra funding for the University of South Alabama; he was a member of the university's board of trustees. Engel and others from Mobile routinely held budgets hostage until they got what they wanted for the university.[16] This made the school strong within its first four years of operation.

Other inducements were mixtures of patronage, personality, and frivolity. Brewer and Bailes agreed that the press exaggerated the role of the Wallace administration in this and other aspects of the 1967 gasoline distribution fight and indeed all legislative matters except succession. According to Brewer, "George Wallace was very little involved in the 1967 gasoline distribution fight, as he was very little involved in anything that occurred in the legislature. His sentiments favored the rural counties, but the morning-to-afternoon changes were pushed by legislators, not Wallace."

It should be added that the Wallace legislative leaders responsible for the change drew on gubernatorial power by promising patronage that only the governor's office could deliver.

A week later, the road program passed both chambers. It included a 333 percent increase in automobile license fees (from three dollars to thirteen), a sizeable rise in truck license fees, a distribution of gasoline taxes that guaranteed each county a minimum of $550,000, and the $160 million road bond issue.[17] The drastic cut in the aviation fuel tax also passed at this time. Essentially, this package can be characterized as a compromise between urban and rural forces, with rural counties winning more than they would have had the Wallace administration not been so solicitous of their interests and so effective in meeting them.

The legislature also approved the administration's competitive bid law, which extended the existing state statute to the local level including school boards and junior colleges.[18] The governor's March call had included a request for legislation to make all county and city government purchases of five hundred dollars or more subject to competitive bid. A similar statute applying to state government had been passed in George Wallace's first term. These reforms were unusual outcroppings of good government in the Wallace years. According to interview subjects, passage was urged on George Wallace by some of his advisors to neutralize the malodorous political and financial activities of his brother Gerald. The low-bid laws were not meant to stop Gerald's dealings but just to give George a reform he could point to as evidence of his commitment to honest government if and when Gerald's activities became a public embarrassment.

To a great degree 1967 legislative politics represented an abrupt movement away from the voting patterns of the Big Mule–Black Belt alliance days to more normal patterns that often featured urban-rural splits.[19]

Property Tax Assessments

Alabama law required property to be assessed at 60 percent of market value, but assessments actually ran far lower than this amount. A state Supreme Court ruling dictated that utilities be assessed at 40 percent. In a lawsuit the Louisville and Nashville (L & N) Railroad contended that the 40 percent rate was higher than assessment rates for other property and that these differences violated the Alabama constitution's requirement that all property be taxed at the same rate. In April 1967 a Montgomery circuit judge ruled in favor of the railroad. The court noted that the average property assessment in Alabama was 15.4 percent of market value. It called the assessment of L & N property at 40 percent excessive and reduced the company's assessments to 30 percent.

Alabama property tax law and practice were only distantly related. Assessments were subject to politics, variable human judgment, and unprofessional assessment procedures. In addition, urban property was more heavily taxed than rural. The property tax worked roughly as follows: If a house was appraised for $15,000 and the county assessment rate was 25 percent, the assessed valuation for tax purposes would be $3,750. If the county tax rate was 20 mills (2 percent), the tax bill would be $75.[20]

Each county set its own millage rate. A constitutional amendment was required to increase the millage rate above 21 mills, including a state tax of 6.5 mills. Many counties had reached the 21-mill limit. The state tax of 6.5 mills was distributed in the following manner: 1 mill to the Department of Pensions and Securities for payments to surviving Confederate widows; 2.5 mills to the state general fund; and 3 mills to the Special Education Trust Fund for public schools. By law the county's 14.5 mills were divided as follows: 7 mills to schools; 2.5 mills to infrastructure; and 5 mills to the county general fund. Increases in the county millage were voted for specific purposes.[21] Public utilities were assessed by the state.

In 1967 the legislature's Joint Interim Committee on Ad Valorem Taxation issued a report that could have been written by Harry Haden and John Patterson in 1959. It recommended the establishment of a statewide reassessment program with professional qualifications required of county boards of equalization and lowering of the fictional 60 percent assessment maximum rate to a more realistic 30 percent. Timberland would be assessed at its bare-land value. Growing timber would be exempt from property taxation, as were other crops, but a severance tax would be levied on timber when marketed. There would be no exemptions for machinery or other personal property (for example, autos, boats, airplanes, trucks, and trailers) used in a business.

A report issued by a four-person minority of the interim committee recommended different percentage levels for the assessment of the various classes of property. In particular, it recommended that rural property be assessed at lower levels than other kinds. Bills reflecting this Farm Bureau Federation perspective were introduced in the Senate on Tuesday in the third week of July and assigned to the Finance and Taxation Committee. At 5 P.M. Wednesday, a notice was placed on the Senate bulletin board announcing that the committee would hold hearings at 9 A.M. on Thursday. Few were surprised when the only witnesses to appear represented the Farm Bureau, and of course they spoke in favor of the bills. In other venues urban legislators contended that the classification scheme in the rural bill was unconstitutional and that other groups besides farmers deserved tax relief.

On August 8 the Farm Bureau bill was defeated in the House because it failed to win the three-fifths vote required of a constitutional amendment. Except for a few scattered "No" votes, the division consisted of Jefferson, Mobile, and Etowah Counties against the rest of the state. Four of Montgomery's five representatives voted with the rural counties. The reporter Don Wasson cited their vote as evidence that urban interests were split concerning property tax reform because many wealthy urbanites or their relatives owned rural property.[22]

Two days later the House voted to reconsider the legislation, and the motion passed seventy-two to sixteen. In the bill that finally passed the House, personal property was assessed at 20 percent, business property at 25 percent, residential property at 20 percent, and utilities at 40 percent. Farm land was assessed at the lowest rate of all, 15 percent.[23]

The urban-rural conflict in the Senate over property tax reform was intensified by a parallel battle over the education budget, which will be discussed below. Further exacerbating the tone of debate, Alton Turner's Senate Finance and Taxation Committee met in secret executive session and gave a favorable report to the Farm Bureau property tax bills. In a scene described in the *Advertiser,* Turner arrogantly refused to reveal the breakdown of the vote: "When the closed door meeting was over, Sen. Turner was asked if he would make public the vote on the favorable report. 'Yes,' he said, taking the ballots from the committee clerk. He then folded them carefully and stuck them into his shirt pocket. 'That's as public as they will be,' he said."[24] Three committee members confirmed to the *Advertiser* that those voting for the favorable report were Turner, Engel (Mobile), Clark (Barbour), Cooper (Wilcox), Folsom (Cullman), Giles (Madison), Lolley (Coffee), Oden (Franklin), and Givhan (Dallas). The urban votes seem to substantiate Don Wasson's view regarding urban disunity on property tax policy; Engel, however, was a staunch administration team member and a strong supporter of the University of South Alabama, and Giles's vote may have resulted from logrolling agreements arrived at after he knew that his negative vote would not affect the outcome.

Before the vote the Farm Bureau's executive vice president, J. D. Hays, supported the bills. Walter Bouldin, president of Alabama Power, quite naturally opposed it, as did Dr. C. P. Nelson, who represented the Alabama Education Association. Nelson argued that the bills would undermine local property tax support for schools.

Ultimately, the legislature passed a 30 percent cap on property tax assessments plus a number of exemptions that changed virtually nothing. This outcome represented a victory for the rural counties despite the fact that the legislation did not contain property categories. Absent from all accounts of these battles is any significant involvement by the Wallace administration. Wallace did not take a public position in favor of property tax equalization, but there is also no indication that he worked behind the scenes for the rural position. Of course, his legislative leadership appointments were sufficient to assure a rural victory, and his day-to-day involvement was probably unnecessary.

In October a suit filed in U.S. District Court by a Jefferson County property owner asked that all Alabama counties be required to set assessment rates at a uniform 30 percent of valuation.[25] A three-judge panel rejected the suit in April 1968, surprising almost everyone.[26] It had been almost universally expected that the federal courts would overturn Alabama's inequitable property tax system.

The court majority's grossly inconsistent logic was that the case could not be brought under the Fourteenth Amendment to the U.S. Constitution because the case involved property rights rather than civil rights (as if the distinction could be clearly drawn), even though the impact of the decision was on education. Judge Frank Johnson wrote for the minority: "In dismissing this case, the majority of this court is judicially determining that Alabama's statutory procedure for taxation, regardless of how inequitable or illegal, is not subject to the minimal demands of the 14th Amendment. I simply do not believe this to be the law of the country."[27]

The Education Budget

Through the early months of 1967, pro-education forces publicized the need for increased spending as they had at the beginning of the Patterson and first Wallace administrations. With apparently no warning, Governor Lurleen Wallace released an education budget proposal containing cuts, the deepest of which hit teacher salaries and public school operations. Given an expected $25 million surplus in the Special Education Trust Fund at the beginning of the 1967 academic year, education forces had little choice but to interpret this as an attack on education fostered by civil rights discord and the opposition of many outspoken AEA members to George Wallace's presidential aspirations. Albert Brewer supported this view, maintaining that Wallace became angry at boards of education because they obeyed court orders requiring school integration: "He would call them names such as sissy britches."[28]

The Senate Rules Committee established a special order calendar highly adverse to urban education interests. A special order calendar is a list that allows bills to be shifted from lower to higher positions on the calendar or vice versa. The Rules Committee placed a conditional education appropriations bill ahead of the general appropriations bill and the regular education appropriations bill. Because a conditional appropriation is activated only if surplus funds exist after regular appropriations are allocated, this order was illogical except when considered in a political context. The conditional appropriation originally was set at $22 million, close to the $25 million surplus forecast for the Special Education Fund. The regular education appropriations bill had been kept artifically low to ensure that everything in the conditional appropriation bill would be funded. The conditional bill consisted almost entirely of pork for the consumption of rural counties and a few urban Wallace supporters.

On August 1 urban senators began a filibuster to protest both the location of the regular education appropriations bill on the special order calendar and the bill's lowered funding levels. By August 10 there was no movement in the Senate except that the size of the conditional education appropriations bill grew by $4 million.

Urban senators continued to oppose passage of the education budget because of the reductions it contained and because of features specific to particular cities. Jefferson County senators objected to the Finance and Taxation Committee's removal of a $1.2 million appropriation to the University of Alabama at Birmingham's College of General Studies. That appropriation was in the House version. The delegation, protecting the interests of the University of Alabama Medical School and the Alabama Medical Association, objected to the presence of a $50,000 appropriation for the establishment of a School of Optometry in Birmingham separate from the Medical School. Some suspected that the reason for the appropriation was that Alton Turner, chairman of the Finance and Taxation Committee, once represented the state optometrists and that his law partner was still their legal counsel. Another sticking point was a $100,000 appropriation to the Huntsville City Board of Education for capital construction. Other legislators objected because there were no similar appropriations for their cities.

Urban-rural conflict intensified when Senator Alton Turner responded to urban opposition by blocking a number of Jefferson County bills. Turner and the administration further angered many when they added a line item to the University of Alabama budget for a Confederate flag and staff for display at home football games as an anti–civil rights symbol.[29]

Still another problem in this confusing mix was the elimination of state funding for Tuskegee Institute. Legally, Tuskegee was a private university, but the state had given it financial support since 1945. And the state had six members on the board of trustees, a clear recognition of the school's quasi-public status. The governor's budget continued support to three predominantly white private colleges. No explanation was given, but the funding cutoff was universally interpreted as an attack against civil rights activists among the faculty and students.

The House defeated a bill putting Tuskegee Institute back into the education budget and then reconsidered and passed it, but with a $200,466 cut. These actions were part of an administration-backed charade. The institute was being warned: You were almost cut off completely, but the Wallace administration in its kindness will fund Tuskegee despite black disloyalty, although just so you don't become complacent, your budget will be reduced. The bill ultimately went to the governor with the cut in place, but Speaker Fite supposedly forgot to sign it. Because all bills going to the governor for signature must be signed by the presiding officers of both chambers, this put the governor in the position of being able to pocket veto the bill. Rankin Fite rarely forgot anything; this was undoubtedly another part of the charade to keep the institute on the hook.

The governor signed the Tuskegee bill, but, in one final twist, said that the funds would be provided only if federal courts upheld a private-school tuition grant bill (see immediately below) then under attack by civil rights groups and the federal courts.[30] Wallace never seemed to tire of this sort of crude, showy tweaking of the federal courts' nose, even though it had no chance of success. Ultimately the governor voluntarily reversed "her" decision to withhold the funds.

A bill that would pay some of the tuition for students attending private elementary and secondary schools passed the legislature with little difficulty. Similar legislation had been passed earlier and signed into law, but a federal court held it an unconstitutional device designed to evade integration. The new bill differed in that it created a state-funded commission that would actually disburse money to the students. It was on tattered legal fictions of this sort that segregationists often seemed to pin their hopes. Few attorneys seriously expected the new version to survive the federal courts' scrutiny, but symbolic activity of this sort demonstrated to the electorate that its leaders were still trying to protect them.

The governor appealed to the AEA for assistance in defending the tuition law. The AEA rejected the call for help, sidestepping civil rights implications by saying that teachers supported control of the schools by local boards of education and opposed laws that limited such control.[31]

On the last day of August 1967, the legislature passed a $562 million edu-

254 Political Power in Alabama

ation appropriation for the biennium. This was more than $5 million above revenue estimates for that time period. The bill also contained $56 million in conditional appropriations, $900,000 to build two additional junior colleges, and money for the Confederate flag and staff for the University of Alabama. These outcomes reflected no big change in the historic patterns of appropriations for education or in the substitution of symbolic action for substantive, constructive policy change.

By early July 1967 Don Wasson was arguing that the legislature had lost its independence to the administration.[32] One specific control device exercised by the administration was the so-called "hold order." A committee chairman would be ordered not to place a bill on the agenda until it had been approved "downstairs." Wasson appears to clash with those who portray Wallace as indifferent to most legislative occurrences, but there is no contradiction. Wallace files show great care and energy devoted to patronage but little attention paid to policy except in the area of civil rights. Even here his primary concern was that an illusion of authority be maintained.

At the end of the regular session, the *Advertiser* observed that urban legislators had been effective in achieving changes in the distribution of gasoline tax revenues and the reduction of the tax on aviation fuel, but after that they were overwhelmed by more skillful and experienced rural professionals who enjoyed the governor's support.

With little fanfare a bill allowing present Alabama constitutional officers, including the governor, lieutenant governor, and attorney general, to succeed themselves and serve two consecutive terms passed the Senate thirty votes to four. The House approved the Senate bill eighty-five to eight.

Tax Incidence and Tax Effort

From the Patterson administration through the beginning of Lurleen Wallace's administration, we have seen a pattern of industrial and rural interests opposing tax increases of any kind. To diminish industrial-rural opposition to tax increases, education groups and other advocates of spending growth felt obliged to favor regressive taxes. How were these tensions reflected in the state's tax structure?

Stephen E. Lile and Don M. Soule calculated interstate family tax burdens in the United States for the year 1968.[33] They sketched portraits of taxes paid by a typical family of four with $10,000 in adjusted gross income. Alabama was one of forty-five states with a state income tax. The average income tax paid by the typical family earning $10,000 was $140 per year in Alabama, $40 less than the national mean of $180 for those states with an income tax. Louisiana's rate of $40 was the lowest, and Minnesota's $410 was the highest. The average property tax in the United States was $349 per year, but the typical Alabama family paid only $150 per year in property taxes. Only West Virginia was lower at $122. New Jersey families paid the highest at $662, over four times the Alabama figure.

Alabama's reliance on the state sales tax ($158 per year for the typical family) was greater than the national average ($126) for states that had a sales tax. Families in Illinois paid the most ($223). Six states had no sales tax. The average family in Alabama paid $39 per year in local sales taxes. The average among states that had local sales taxes was $55, but thirty-eight states had no local sales taxes. Alabama at $85 was near the national average of $83 in motor vehicle taxes paid. The range was $47 to $146. Alabama relied on cigarette taxes ($40) slightly more than the national mean ($34).

When all these taxes on a typical family are combined, that family in 1968 Alabama paid $612 in taxes compared to the average of $827 for all U.S. families. On a per capita basis Alabama's state and local taxes ($61) were the fourth lowest in the nation, only $1 ahead of the three lowest, Arkansas, South Carolina, and Mississippi, which were tied at $60. The national average was $94 with the highest tax ($149) in New York. All the states had regressive tax systems, but Alabama's was somewhat less so than the national average.

Another way to examine a state's tax system is through a measure commonly called tax effort. Tax effort compares taxes with some standardized measure of income. For example, in 1968 Alabamians paid $89 in taxes per $1,000 of income. This put Alabama tenth from the bottom. Ohioans, who were at the bottom, paid $80 in taxes per $1,000 of income. The national average was $100, with the highest ($122) in California and Hawaii.

Overall, an image emerges of Alabama citizens having a tax system of average regressivity, relying on the sales tax more than average, the income tax less than average, and the property tax far less than average. Tax effort in 1968 Alabama was substantially below the national average.

Developments in School Desegregation

On February 19, 1967, the United States Commission on Civil Rights issued a report that applied the logic of *Brown v. Board* to northern schools.[34] The commission argued that the Supreme Court's reasoning that segregated schools violated a child's Fourteenth Amendment rights to equal protection was applicable whatever the cause of the segregation and that de facto segregation was widespread in the North, especially in large cities, where 75 percent of black students attended nearly all black schools. The commission advocated rigorous integration programs throughout the nation. Segregationists felt vindicated by this report. They believed that members of Congress would write and enforce civil rights laws less rigorously if those statutes covered the entire nation instead of just the South.

Since George Wallace's "segregation forever" speech in 1962, the Wallace administrations' civil rights position had changed in infinitesimal steps. In a March 1967 speech Governor Lurleen Wallace asserted that "our people will not submit to federally controlled education." She went on to say that the federal government claimed "the power to force us to act against our beliefs." Of course, by that point federally controlled education was a reality, at least as far as civil rights issues were concerned, and the federal government had asserted its power, not just claimed it. After this introductory bluster, the governor went on to admit, "We must be ever ready to adjust to change and we do not question the necessity for change."[35]

Late that month a three-judge federal court ordered the desegregation of all Alabama schools not already under court orders. The ruling placed the responsibility for enforcement on the state superintendent of education and ordered the school systems to submit desegregation plans to the superintendent for the forthcoming (1967–68) school year.

A March 23, 1967, *Montgomery Advertiser* editorial characterized the court decision as having "totally federalized" the entire public school system (a gross exaggeration). It described the new court order as "the inevitable consequence of defiance so foolish as to beggar all description." The editorial claimed that the central reason the order had been issued was George Wallace's nose thumbing at the courts even after they had granted him leniency. It reminded Alabamians of Wallace's battle cry, "If you stand up to 'em, they'll back down every time." It derided this and "countless other pure and simple frauds which persuaded Alabamians that George Wallace was an avenging angel. To date, he has lost every fight, cheerfully suffering incredible losses for the glory of the cause." Other *Advertiser* editorials continued to argue that federal courts' decisions on school desegregation would not have been as harsh as they were had George Wallace not openly challenged federal authority.[36]

Lurleen Wallace responded to the March ruling by saying that she would use the state as a shield between the federal court and the state board of education. The difficulty with this bit of posturing was that the court order placed the responsibility for its enforcement directly on Superintendent

Ernest Stone. Finally, recognizing this, she asked the legislature to give the governor the powers of the state superintendent of education! No one took the idea seriously.

Meanwhile, the Governors Wallace continued to receive advice from those who believed a guerrilla war against school integration appropriate and possibly even effective. John Kohn, a close administration advisor, held such a view. On March 24, 1967, he wrote Lurleen Wallace:

[The schools are] being slowly but surely destroyed by the Federal Government just as if our cities and towns were being bombed in war. . . . Many sincerely think and I share such view that forced integration of our schools on a more wholesale basis will not only cause a drastic and irreparable regression of our public school system but also inflict lasting trauma on innocent school children of both races. . . . To lose a battle is not to lose a war, so to speak. Orderly resistance is a must and if we are to be destroyed let them have to do it the hard way. Let us keep up the fight under law. Without presuming to invade the prerogative of the Legislature, I respectfully hope they give you complete authority to act for the school systems in this State temporarily so that a solid front may be presented. By continuous struggle we may some day win in the hearts and minds of the people of America.[37]

An earlier chapter summarized a study of education in Wilcox County performed in 1967 by a National Education Association team.[38] It represented a grim portrait of racial deprivation. In the spring and summer of 1965 Wilcox County blacks tried to correct these inequities by seeking admission to white schools. They were turned down. In August a black tenured high school teacher who requested that his sons be transferred to a white school in the county was dismissed by the county board of education. Eight more teachers were fired a month later for similar offenses. In October the Alabama Tenure Commission ruled the dismissals null and void and ordered the teachers reinstated. The Wilcox County Board of Education refused. In November the U.S. Department of Justice filed suit seeking desegregation of the county schools.

In May 1966 the Alabama congressional delegation and the Alabama Board of Education asked Alabama school officials to continue resisting federal desegregation guidelines. In August the legislature repealed the Teacher Tenure Law in Wilcox County, as the county board of education had requested. In the same month a three-judge federal appeals court ordered the Wilcox County board to begin desegregating schools for the 1966–67 school year. That September a few blacks were admitted to previously all-white schools. The Wilcox County Board of Education had to be prodded by a further court order to admit more than token numbers of blacks to white schools.

The newly admitted blacks were segregated from white students and subjected to frequent physical abuse while teachers turned their backs. Furthermore, according to the National Education Association report, "there has been no faculty desegregation in Wilcox County schools, nor as this report is being prepared, has there been evidence of any intention on the part of Wilcox County school officials to plan for faculty desegregation."[39]

Governor Lurleen Wallace responded to the NEA report by claiming it contained "biased information" and that no state's school system is perfect. Senator Roland Cooper of Wilcox County reacted with a flood of vitriol to the effect that the NEA authors should try to pay the taxes needed to fund Wilcox County schools. He and the state superintendent of education virtually admitted the validity of the study by their combination of excuses and abusive remarks.[40]

Attacks on Freedom of Choice

On March 29, 1967, the United States Court of Appeals for the Fifth Circuit upheld the Office of Education's use of numerical quotas to determine whether school systems had adequately integrated schools.[41] Freedom of choice plans that resulted in only token integration would have to be modified or replaced with more forceful measures designed to achieve full integration as defined by the Office of Education. The court decision was aimed mainly at Mississippi, Alabama, and Louisiana, where less than 3 percent of black students attended integrated schools, although it also applied to Florida, Georgia, and Texas. The U.S. Supreme Court quickly endorsed the ruling by refusing requests for a stay in its enforcement. In October the court refused to review the decision.

On the same day the Supreme Court issued its ruling, Lurleen and George Wallace hosted a meeting with the governors of Louisiana, Mississippi, and Georgia. George Wallace attempted to persuade his wife's colleagues to join Alabama in openly defying the courts. Eight other southern and border-state governors had rejected invitations to the meeting, and the three who attended refused to join the Wallace call for illegal action. Governor John McKeithen of Louisiana commented that he did not "plan to stand in school house doors or anything like that."[42]

In the South as a whole, integration progressed at a moderate pace.

Between the 1965–66 and 1966–67 school years the percentage of black students in integrated schools rose from 6 to 16. Faculty desegregation increased at a comparable rate.[43]

Peter Libassi, director of the Office of Civil Rights in the Department of Health, Education, and Welfare (HEW), attributed much of this progress to sincere efforts in some areas to make freedom-of-choice plans work. But he suggested that gains were beginning to slow because administrators and politicians in other areas (such as most of Alabama and Mississippi) abused freedom of choice by discouraging blacks from shifting to integrated schools and then claiming that blacks were happy attending all-black schools.[44]

In the educational turmoil of the mid-1960s there continued to be practically no written communication between corporate and other business leaders and the Wallace administration on any aspect of education. The Wallace administration was isolated from virtually the only power holders who might have counseled moderation.

Late in August 1967, very near the end of the regular legislative session, Governor Wallace insisted on the passage of still another hopeless civil rights law. This one would let parents determine the race of their children's teachers. In November a three-judge federal panel ruled this so-called teacher choice law and the tuition grant law unconstitutional. Both statutes violated the equal protection clause of the Fourteenth Amendment of the U.S. Constitution, according to U.S. Circuit Judge Richard Rives and U.S. District Judges H. H. Grooms and Frank M. Johnson Jr.

In mid-January 1968 the U.S. Supreme Court refused an Alabama appeal of a lower court ruling that held that the U.S. Department of Health, Education, and Welfare could block welfare funding to the state under terms of the nondiscrimination section of the 1964 Civil Rights Act. George Wallace called the threatened cutoff "another bluff."[45] Although the federal government sometimes delayed civil rights enforcement, it never bluffed. Faced with a potential loss of almost $100 million per year, the state quickly caved in.

The U.S. Court of Appeals for the Fifth Circuit in March 1968 ordered Mobile school officials to draw new school attendance zones to facilitate desegregation. Because Mobile housing patterns were relatively mixed, it was easy to adhere to the neighborhood school standard while producing a highly integrated school system. Indeed, the first plan drafted by the Mobile County Board of School Commissioners left fewer than 9 percent of black students in segregated schools.[46] The only escape for diehard segregationist parents would be to move their residences or send their children to private academies. Rallies protesting the Mobile integration plan drew crowds numbering in the thousands, levels unequaled since the meetings held to protest *Brown v. Board.* Legal jousting concerning Mobile schools continued throughout the 1970s, and the number of private schools increased rapidly.[47]

On March 19, 1968, HEW announced that the same standards that had only been applied to the South would be expanded throughout the nation. By these standards, misleadingly called "guidelines," blacks had to be assured of the same quality education as whites. This meant that blacks who were in more crowded classes than whites or received less adequate equipment or lower per-pupil expenditures must henceforth be given equal treatment. The rules also prohibited school officials from redrawing school district boundaries to increase segregation.[48]

The HEW rules left private housing patterns combined with neighborhood schools and attendance of private schools as the only remaining legal causes of racial imbalances. Requirements that students be transported from one school catchment area to another, commonly known as forced busing, were not included in the new rules because Title VI of the Civil Rights Act of 1964 as interpreted by all three branches of government outlawed only discrimination caused by official government policy.

On May 27, 1968, the U.S. Supreme Court applied increased pressure on southern freedom-of-choice plans, ruling them inadequate if they did not reduce segregation as rapidly as other methods could. That same month, the U.S. Civil Rights Commission charged that Alabama schools were failing to provide rural blacks with the skills needed to make them useful employees. William L. Taylor, the commission's staff director, observed sarcastically but accurately that some school districts were "not only failing to comply with the 1954 Supreme Court decision, but they aren't even complying with Plessy v. Ferguson,"[49] the 1896 U.S. Supreme Court decision that permitted "separate but equal" schools. The commission staff report documented great disparities between the quality of education provided in white and black schools in sixteen counties.

Academic Freedom Under Attack Again

In April 1967 legislators denounced a pamphlet that University of Alabama students had written as a program for a speaker series that included Secretary of State Dean Rusk. The lawmakers were incensed that the pamphlet, which had as its theme "World in Revolution," included excerpts from the speeches of a Communist, Bettina Aptheker, and the black power advocate Stokely Carmichael. Some also criticized the speaker series itself. University President Frank Rose defended the series and the program as educationally valuable; he treated legislators' statements as attacks on academic freedom.

Individual faculty members and even their spouses also came under fire. Senator Mylan Engel of Mobile (a member of the University of South Alabama Board of Trustees) observed on the Senate floor that six sponsors of a newspaper advertisement opposing the governor's stand on school desegregation were University of Alabama professors or their wives. "If this is the type of people who are teaching our youngsters," he said, "then I think it is time for the legislature to take another look at Alabama education."[50] Some faculty also became targets because they had taken part in the Selma-to-Montgomery march.[51] The powerful Senator Alton Turner of Crenshaw County joined Engel in his attacks. Turner opined that President Rose had "outlived his usefulness and should take another job," and he threatened to take a "close look" at University of Alabama appropriations as long as Rose remained president.[52]

Meanwhile, Senator Leland Childs of Jefferson County, the only Republican in the legislature, ensured that Democrats did not have a monopoly on abuse of freedom of speech by resurrecting a speaker ban bill that had been introduced and killed in 1965. University presidents, including Frank Rose and Auburn President Ralph Draughon, as well as the trustees and alumni associations of both institutions, the Alabama Press Association, and the Alabama Broadcasters Association had opposed the original bill, arguing that it would jeopardize university accreditations. (One requirement of the Southern Association of Colleges and Universities was that an institution of higher learning be free and independent.) Roughly the same group opposed the new version.

Senator Childs's bill banned anyone from using the facilities of a state-funded college or university if that person was "a known member of the Communist Party, . . . known to advocate the overthrow of the Constitution of the United States or the State of Alabama, [or had] pleaded the Fifth Amendment of the Constitution of the United States in refusing to answer any question, with respect to communist or subversive connections, or activities."[53]

In addition to jeopardizing the accreditation of Alabama's institutions of higher education, the bill was vague and illogical. It failed to define what a "known member" of the Communist party was and what it meant to advocate overthrow of the United States or Alabama constitutions. The bill's handling of Fifth Amendment–based actions attempted to revoke constitutional rights. Finally, it flew in the face of the need for a university to maintain an atmosphere encouraging free inquiry. The governor's office issued a statement supporting the censorship of university speakers as a general principle. Apparently Lurleen Wallace did not come out in full support of the bill itself.[54]

Senator Turner used his Finance and Taxation Committee as a vehicle for further attacks on University of Alabama President Frank Rose. Turner criticized Rose for paying some faculty members more than the $25,000 paid the governor. Turner knew and Rose explained that most faculty paid at this level were part of the outstanding University of Alabama Medical School. Not only were their salaries not especially high by the standards of other medical schools and the medical profession as a whole, but many of these faculty attracted federal grants to the school far in excess of their salaries.[55]

The Troy State College student newspaper attempted to publish an editorial entitled "A Lament for Dr. Rose," expressing support for the beleaguered president, but President Ralph Adams, a former college roommate of George Wallace, censored the editorial. Adams argued that no newspaper is free to criticize its owner and that since the student newspaper was "owned by the state . . . we have no right to criticize the state."[56] He reasoned that the governor and the legislature *are* the state. In a front-page story the *Montgomery Advertiser* reprinted the Troy State student editorial in full, thus giving it far wider distribution than it would otherwise have received.[57]

A month after this censorship incident the *Advertiser* began to publish accounts of bizarre and highly unprofessional meetings in which President Adams grilled faculty about their loyalty to Troy State and about actions taken by the American Association of University Professors. Some contract renewals were delayed until after these meetings. An *Advertiser* editorial described "professors being virtually forced to swear fealty to Queen Lurleen through her proconsul in Troy, Dr. Adams, as a condition to the renewal of their contracts." It stated that the newspaper "received many letters and telephone calls from frightened and angry [Troy] faculty."[58] The faculty of other postsecondary institutions had no need to make such phone calls.

Late in May, R. V. Hudson, a professor of English, resigned from Troy State College, apparently as a result of conflict with Adams. Hudson's department head, Dr. Phillip Wade, bravely described Hudson as "one of Troy State's finest faculty members."[59] A few days later William Munn, a creative-writing instructor and an Adams critic, was fired.

On August 1, 1967, the Senate Education Committee killed the speaker ban bill on a quick voice vote called by Chairman John Hawkins of Birmingham. The vote took the bill's sponsor, Leland Childs, by surprise, but he protested only briefly because it was clear that the majority of legislators opposed the legislation.

Party Politics and the 1968 Presidential Campaign

Although George Wallace ran for state office and president as a Democrat, he announced as the presidential candidate of his American Independent party in February 1968. At the same time he made it known that Finance Director Seymore Trammell, together with Lurleen Wallace's executive secretary (Cecil Jackson), press secretary (Ed Ewing), and recording secretary (Stan Sikes), John DeCarlo of the Banking Department, Joe Fine of the Insurance Department, and Lane Brislin of the Alabama state docks, were being removed from the state payroll, but not their offices, to join the campaign. They began active work on the Wallace campaign long before this shift occurred.[60] Wallace named Marvin Griffin, a former governor of Georgia, as his vice presidential running mate. During his 1954–58 term as governor and long thereafter, Griffin was widely known as a vehement segregationist. His gubernatorial comeback attempt in 1962 had been thwarted by the moderate Carl Sanders.

Wallace's presidential bid included large voter registration drives throughout most of the South. Unlike 1964, Wallace and his campaign were not immune from criticism by southern politicians. For example, Governor Claude Kirk of Florida blasted Wallace in November 1967, and the *Montgomery Advertiser* quoted Kirk approvingly. Wallace "cares not for the direction of America but only about his personal aggrandizement," and seeks to "raise the ugly specter of racism in a sinister attempt to force American voters to throw away their votes."[61]

In January 1968 an organization called the National Democratic party (NDP) formed in Huntsville. The NDP was an offshoot of what might be termed the ordinary Democratic party, and its charter listed as its major objective ensuring that the national Democratic presidential nominee would be on the Alabama ballot. Alvis Howard Jr. of Huntsville chaired the new party, and Robert Schwenn, also of Huntsville, served as executive director. Richmond Flowers assisted in the drafting of the NDP charter.[62]

The Alabama Independent Democratic party (AIDP) was another newly formed party and offshoot of the Democratic party. Its charter gave the naming of presidential elector candidates as the party's sole function.

AIDP's chair was David J. Vann. Joe L. Reed, executive secretary of the black Alabama State Teachers Association, filed for one of the places on the party's presidential elector slate. In March the NDP and AIDP agreed to pool their resources. The NDP withdrew its slate of presidential electors while still running candidates for other offices.

In January 1968 Lister Hill had announced that he would not seek reelection to the U.S. Senate. Because of Hill's age, his retirement was expected. The former lieutenant governor Jim Allen and Congressman Armistead Selden quickly announced they intended to run for Hill's seat. Initial thinking on the race gave Allen the advantage. Allen was perceived as closer to George Wallace, and it was said that Selden had not adequately represented Redstone Arsenal in recent defense budget reductions.[63]

Allen tried to edge closer to Wallace in the public mind by giving important campaign posts to three residents of Wallace's hometown—Murray Beasley, Tom Ventress, and Mrs. Billy Watson. Jere Beasley of Clayton served as Allen's state campaign manager. He would be elected lieutenant governor in his first election bid in 1971, defeating Senator Hugh Morrow of Birmingham in the Democratic runoff. In that race and later he closely identified himself with George Wallace.

Late in January 1968 the Alabama Democratic party's executive committee dropped the loyalty oath that obligated those participating in the Democratic primary to support all Democratic nominees in the general election. Segregationists had long opposed the loyalty oath, and this action could be mistaken for a segregationist and pro-Wallace victory, but its significance was just the reverse. In Alabama, George Wallace was running for president as a Democrat. With a Wallace victory in Alabama virtually certain, Democrats would be locked into supporting him in November if the loyalty oath remained in place.

The Democratic party primary bored everyone but the immediate participants. Allen and Selden followed the scripts that everyone expected. Both portrayed themselves as being on intimate terms with George Wallace (in fact, Wallace was not inordinately fond of either one) and as bitter opponents of federal encroachments on states' rights. The caliber of the campaign can be gauged by a Selden advertisement that read in part: "That great American Douglas McArthur said 'In war, there is no substitute for victory.' It is equally true that in Congress there is no substitute for experience."[64] Meanwhile, Allen harped on Selden's selling out to the Washington crowd. Also running were James E. Folsom Sr., Mrs. Frank Stewart, John Crommelin, and Bob Smith. None of them said anything memorable.

Allen collected more votes in the primary than Selden, but not enough to win without a runoff. In the runoff each continued to insist that he was closer to George Wallace than the other. Allen won the runoff and went on to defeat Montgomery County Probate Judge Perry Hooper Sr. in the general election. Hooper garnered only 24 percent of the vote.

Representatives Bill Nichols (Fourth District), Tom Bevill (Seventh District), and Bill Jones (Eighth District) ran unopposed for the Democratic nomination in 1968. The only other Democratic incumbent seeking reelection, George Andrews of the Third District, drew only token opposition. In a historical footnote that may have signaled voter attitudes more accurately than races for higher office, Bull Connor defeated Associate Commissioner C. C. "Jack" Owen for president of the Public Service Commission, the agency that oversees public utilities.

A Republican party committee on organization appointed by the state GOP chairman, Charles O. Smith, accurately characterized the party as at an adolescent, amateurish stage and argued the need to professionalize by appointing a state-level staff "wholly divorced from the philosophical or ideological differences within the party."[65] Little or nothing was done to correct the situation, as party attention focused on the fight between John Grenier and Jim Martin for a position on the Republican National Committee.

Except for incumbent congressmen, the Alabama Republican party was in complete disarray in the 1968 elections. The GOP's nominee for the U.S. Senate was not widely known in the state, and the party had no one running for the state supreme court. Bull Connor, now seventy-one years old and confined to a wheelchair, overwhelmed his Republican and NDP opponents to win the Public Service Commission presidency.

The *Montgomery Advertiser* reluctantly and with little enthusiasm endorsed Richard Nixon for president over the Democratic nominee, Hubert Humphrey, an old adversary of segregation and an economic liberal.[66] Richard Nixon won the presidential election; George Wallace, running nationally as a third-party candidate, received 13 percent of the popular vote.

Industrial Development

George Wallace boasted that he was highly successful in attracting new manufacturing concerns to the state. Nearly all governors make this claim, and all are able to point to at least one statistic that supports them. From 1958 to 1963, the Patterson years, Alabama experienced a 3.9 percent increase in the number of manufacturing concerns (of any size) in the state. That figure is just under the East South Central figure and substantially below Georgia's 7.8 percent, but well above the 0.3 percent decrease for the nation as a whole. From 1963 to 1967 Alabama enjoyed a 21.4 percent increase, dwarfing the regional and national trends. From 1967 to 1972 Alabama's growth was only 0.7 percent, well below the East South Central, Georgia, and U.S. results.

Percentage changes in manufacturing payrolls add perspective to the simple count of manufacturing concerns. In the Patterson years Alabama experienced a change of approximately 23 percent. This was well below the 40 percentage point change in Georgia and the east south central rate of about 27 percent, but Alabama was less than 1 percentage point behind the country as a whole. In Wallace's first term Alabama, at slightly under a 40 percentage point change, was behind both Georgia (at almost 45) and the east south central region (just over 40). The U.S. percentage change was slightly lower than the Alabama figure. During the Lurleen Wallace–Brewer administration (1967–71), Alabama's manufacturing payroll growth and that of Georgia were about equal (about a 50 percentage point change). Both states trailed slightly behind the east south central level but were substantially ahead of the rate of change in the country overall—about a 20 percentage point difference.

In terms of manufacturing value added during the Patterson years, Alabama had a change rate of slightly over 40 percent, which put the state slightly ahead of the east south central region and the United States as a whole. In the first Wallace administration the state fell slightly behind Georgia and the east south central in rate of growth, but it was slightly ahead of the nation. Its position fell substantially behind Georgia and the east south central region during the Lurleen Wallace–Brewer years (more than a 10 percentage point difference in each case).

The difference between Alabama's outstanding performance in adding numbers of manufacturing concerns and the state's mediocre results in adding payrolls and value added was probably due to the fact that the industries attracted to the state were low-tech, low-wage operations.

A Fantus report completed around April 1967 and funded by the State Planning and Industrial Development Board analyzed the state's industrial development potential. The board tried to keep the negative parts of the report under wraps. A memo to a Wallace aide, Cecil Jackson Jr., from Leonard Beard, director of the Planning and Industrial Development Board, stated, "Certain parts of this report are not to be distributed to the cities and counties but are to be closely held in this office to prevent duplications."[67]

The End of the First Two
Wallace Administrations

Lurleen Wallace, who had suffered from cancer for many months, died on May 7, 1968. Lieutenant Governor Albert Brewer became governor, and George Wallace found himself on the outside. He lost the authority, power, and patronage base of the governorship.

Over the years Wallace claimed vocally that he was far from being a do-nothing reactionary. To support his case, he pointed to education funding and the creation of great numbers of two-year institutions. The evidence for this position is not compelling. The best that can be said is that between 1963 and 1968 Wallace continued and probably accelerated trends in primary and secondary school funding that had been interrupted in the Patterson years by an economic downturn and labor disputes.

Wallace basically served the role of caretaker for a dismal public primary and secondary education system while vigorously promoting the cause of segregated private academies. The growth of these institutions weakened political support for public schools among middle- and upper-middle-class parents who could afford to send their children to private schools.

Wallace's creation of two-year institutions was hurried and educationally unsound. Location and staffing decisions for these schools were informed mainly by an unsavory combination of pork barrel and racial politics. The result was that some parts of the state had too many junior and technical colleges while others had none. The creation of the University of Alabama campus in Huntsville and the Auburn University campus in Montgomery, duplicating in many respects the efforts of existing black institutions, was cut from the same cloth. Tens of millions of dollars were wasted in the state's postsecondary education system.[68]

Wallace disrupted education at all levels with his demagogic defense of segregation. Schools were surrounded by troopers to prevent blacks from entering. The careers of university faculty were threatened when they expressed dissent against Wallace-appointed administrators or exercised their constitutional rights of free speech on their own time. Funding for black universities was threatened for political reasons. And Wallace helped to create an atmosphere in which white students felt free to intimidate and isolate newly enrolled blacks.

He also damaged the schools by inaction. He ignored property tax reform and other tax reforms as well as educational reform.

Although Wallace and his administrations made vigorous attempts to attract industry, much of this activity was intended to counter damage caused by his own actions and rhetoric. The national impact of his first term and his wife's partial term poisoned the state's reputation for at least three decades.

Blacks in Alabama and throughout the South made extraordinary progress during the years of these first two Wallace administrations. It was clear to many then, as it is obvious in retrospect, that George Wallace, assisted by Bull Connor, Al Lingo, and Jim Clark, accelerated the successes of the civil rights movement even as they contributed to the violence that resulted in the deaths of civil rights workers as well as blacks who took little or no part in civil rights demonstrations.

Blacks did not enjoy sweeping electoral victories in the 1960s, but no one doubted that the potential was there. In the 1968 Democratic primary three blacks made it into runoffs against whites for seats on the Selma City Council. That a black became Macon County sheriff that same year was clear evidence of what could be done.

10

Albert Brewer
and the Possibility
of Real Change

When Albert Brewer succeeded Lurleen Wallace as governor, he appointed Bob Ingram, a former journalist and then assistant executive director of the Alabama Medical Association, as his finance director. Robert M. Cleckler, president of the First National Bank of Childersburg and superintendent of banking under the Wallaces, became executive secretary. Ingram suggested to Brewer that reversing these appointments might better fit the talents of the two men. Brewer partly agreed but insisted that he wanted the finance director to be without ties to the financial community.[1] Besides, the executive secretary's primary responsibility was to act as the governor's legislative liaison, and Cleckler was especially adept at dealing with temperamental lawmakers.[2] Brewer remembers that he selected Cleckler partly because he was "a close personal friend." In addition, "he was a great people person and very bright—a natural for legislative relations." Ingram could be abrasive. Brewer added that Ingram knew a great deal about state finance because he had researched issues in that area as a reporter and that his "integrity had never been questioned."[3]

Herman Nelson, a widely respected Highway Department career employee, remained as highway director. Hugh Maddox became Brewer's legal adviser.

Brewer's Balancing Act

Brewer was in a delicate position. Any improvements made in administrative operations represented an implied criticism of the Wallaces. Bob Ingram was the unhappy recipient of many calls from George

Wallace complaining that even minor technical administrative changes were designed to embarrass him and make Lurleen look inadequate.

The *Montgomery Advertiser,* with Grover Hall Jr. no longer editor, enthusiastically publicized Brewer's improvements and George Wallace's failures and the inattention that had led to them. For example, Brewer formed a state motor pool that reduced by one-half the seventeen hundred state-owned automobiles. Brewer also stopped channeling auto repair work to a few favored garages and ended political bias in the operation of the Purchasing Department and in state auctions.[4] The *Advertiser* highlighted the Wallace administration's use of change orders to evade competitive bid laws. One of the seventeen questionable change orders spotted by state examiners had resulted in the purchase of a $58,000 airplane for the Hamilton Trade School. Hamilton was the hometown of Speaker of the House Rankin Fite.

These stories read like the four-year ritual of a newly elected governor sweeping into office denouncing his predecessor's dishonesty or inefficiency, instituting reforms, and then quietly beginning his own disreputable practices. There were two differences, however. All the direct criticism of the Wallaces came from the newspapers, not Brewer, Ingram, or any other member of the administration. Second, more than any governor since Frank Dixon (1939–43), Brewer was interested in the minutiae of public administration and could be expected to make the kinds of changes suggested in the *Advertiser*'s stories. Furthermore, since Wallace's times in office were marked by extreme inattention to administrative concerns except in those aspects of government that could be put to political use, any governor with a sense of professionalism would have made changes after Wallace's incumbency. A widespread administrative housecleaning and modernizing also occurred when the businessman Forrest "Fob" James became governor in 1978 after two Wallace terms.

School Desegregation

Throughout Albert Brewer's term as governor, the federal courts, the U.S. Justice Department, and the Department of Health, Education, and Welfare continued to reduce the South's ability to evade school integration. On May 27, 1968, the U.S. Supreme Court ruled that freedom-of-choice plans would be rejected if other "reasonably available" methods would provide "speedier and more effective" desegregation. U.S. Attorney General Ramsey Clark immediately began an attack on freedom-of-choice plans throughout the South, including ninety-two in Alabama.[5]

The major alternatives to freedom of choice were mandatory desegregation plans that often included forced busing.

There were obvious tensions within the federal court system between advocates of freedom of choice and mandatory plans. In September 1968 Judge Frank Johnson Jr., in a case concerning Crenshaw County, commented that he wanted to save freedom of choice partly because it was a fact of life that whites could not be forced to attend black schools. He added that forced desegregation based on zoning, pairing, consolidation, or similar plans would be a last resort for him, but if freedom of choice did not produce substantive results, he would apply more rigid devices. A *Montgomery Advertiser* editorial summarized what was to be the future of public primary and secondary education for the next quarter century, namely,

> compulsory integration by zoning or whatever would of course work faster to achieve integration—temporarily. Such plans would also insure re-segregation, since whites would move out of the areas, send their children to private schools or otherwise contrive to escape the order.
>
> The result would be, almost certainly, all-Negro schools in new locations.
>
> Another result would be the collapse of public support for public education, which would be a disaster to both races, but a far worse one to Negroes who depend heavily on white tax support and are, in the main, less able to afford private schools.[6]

In another September 1968 ruling, Judge Johnson upheld Barbour County's freedom-of-choice plan, but he substantially restricted the choices that could be made by ordering the closure of three black schools and the more complete integration of faculty according to his own detailed plan.[7] A few weeks later Johnson and U.S. Circuit Court Judge Richard Rives joined in a similar ruling. Their decision applied to seventy-six school systems.[8] By the end of September, 151 schools were closed.[9]

The members of the NEA, the major organization of primary and secondary school teachers, had voted in June 1966 to expel any "of its state or local affiliates not racially integrated by June 1, 1967."[10] In May 1969 the NEA suspended the Mississippi Education Association from national membership because of its refusal to merge with the black Mississippi Teachers Association. Louisiana lost its affiliation for the same reason.[11] A few days after the Mississippi action the Alabama Education Association (AEA), with twenty-five thousand white members, and the Alabama State Teachers Association (ASTA), with ten thousand black members, agreed to combine effective August 1.[12] This merger created an organization stronger than the sum of its original parts. In the 1970s this more powerful AEA would become one of the most effective interest groups in the state, influencing both election outcomes and legislative policy decisions. In February 1968 Paul Hubbert, superintendent of the Troy schools, had been named executive secretary-treasurer of AEA.[13] He and the ASTA head, Joe Reed, orchestrated the merger of the two organizations and assumed the number one and number two administrative leadership positions, respectively. They continue to direct AEA operations today.

On June 26, 1969, the Fifth U.S. Circuit Court of Appeals reversed a district court decision and ended freedom of choice plans in the school systems of Choctaw and Jefferson Counties and the city of Bessemer. The justification for the reversal was that freedom of choice had "not disestablished the dual school systems." The court ruled that "an all-Negro school, even if desired by the students and their parents, is just as wrong constitutionally, as an all-white school desired by white students and their parents."[14] Plans for these school districts required the elimination of all-black schools by the start of the 1969–70 term.

As federal judges tightened their control over schools, early results of newly acquired black voting rights were displayed in Black Belt Greene County in a July 1969 special election. Black candidates won majorities on the school board and county commission.[15]

In August 1969 Judge Johnson directed the Montgomery County Board of Education to develop a nondiscriminatory school system for the 1970–71 school year. Johnson told the board that the system would have to include 20 percent minority pupils and 30 percent minority teachers in all schools.[16]

Late in the summer of 1969, with the Democratic gubernatorial primary less than a year away, George Wallace called for a parental march on schools to protect freedom of choice. Albert Brewer responded between gritted teeth: "I would certainly hope and trust that no responsible citizen in Alabama would use the school children in Alabama for political purposes." He added, "I have a responsibility for maintaining law and order."[17] Some translated this statement to mean that George Wallace was irresponsible and cared nothing about law and order. Even Wallace's supporter Senator Alton Turner told the legislature that a resolution supporting the former governor's call for a parental march is "just another step down the drain," but the legislature endorsed Wallace's proposed protest anyway.

Like many conservatives, Brewer concentrated on forced busing and the resulting threat to neighborhood schools as the civil rights movement's weakest position. He proposed an antibusing resolution at the 1969 Southern Governors' Conference but was unable to secure its endorsement.[18]

As was true of nearly all southern white politicians of his age, Brewer had supported segregation in some form, but he was not personally committed to racial separation, and he was not inclined to take political advantage of racial problems. He shared with many southern and northern conservatives and moderates, including Judge Frank Johnson, a recognition of the potentially destructive nature of busing.

These moderates argued that white parents would be unwilling to send their children to poorer schools in areas with relatively high crime rates. This would even be true of those white parents who recognized that discriminatory government policies were heavily responsible for both the quality of schools and crime in segregated neighborhoods. The result would be a large-scale abandonment of public schools in which busing or other mandatory integration devices were used. Families would either move to other cities or counties or shift their children to private schools.

The migration of many middle- and upper-middle-class whites depleted city and county tax bases and helped to resegregate public schools. In places such as the Alabama Black Belt, it was the professional and small business groups that often left, further depleting the tax base. Among the middle- and upper-middle-class whites who stayed, an increasing number enrolled their children in private academies, which further reduced critical political support for public school improvements and better funding.[19] Children from less affluent families of both races suffered the most from these widely predicted changes.

Although Brewer and other southern moderates and conservatives tried to make the nonracial argument that busing and other coercive techniques would backfire, their credibility had been eradicated by the practitioners of massive resistance. Nothing a southerner like Brewer could say would have the slightest impact on the national debate about school integration. Northern conservatives and moderates who made the same criticisms of busing and other mandatory integration schemes were also ignored. Even the moderate Republican Robert H. Finch, secretary of health, education, and welfare under Richard Nixon, predicted that the Supreme Court's forced busing decisions would lead to a large-scale growth of private primary and secondary schools in the South.[20] His warning went unheeded.

In fact, the events forecast by opponents of mandatory integration occurred in most of the cities and many of the rural areas in which it was implemented. In Alabama's six largest public school districts, the percentage of white (or, more precisely, nonblack) students declined. The reduction in white enrollment in the Birmingham school district, from 58.6 percent in the 1959–60 school year to 10.6 percent in December 1993, is stark, and Montgomery's drop from 67.7 percent to 34.6 percent white in the same time period is quite dramatic. The change in the Decatur, Dothan, Huntsville, and Mobile school systems was much less severe than what could be found in many northern cities.[21]

Christine H. Rossell, a leading school desegregation analyst, compared voluntary integration systems in nine northern and western cities with mandatory systems in eleven northern, southern, and western cities.[22] The voluntary arrangements in Rossell's sample all used magnet schools, not freedom of choice as it was practiced in the 1960s. Rossell describes a model magnet system as follows: "Most or all of the predominantly minority schools that need to be desegregated would be selected to have magnet programs. . . . More money would be spent on the magnet schools in order to attract white students, and their curricula would be altered so that each magnet school's curriculum has a special theme or focus."[23]

It is difficult to squeeze the approaches taken to desegregation in Alabama into Rossell's mandatory-voluntary dichotomy. There was nothing voluntary about school desegregation in Alabama, but courts could have applied more drastic sanctions than they did.[24] With this point in mind, we will compare Alabama figures with Rossell's mandatory and voluntary desegregation cities.

In Rossell's sample five cities with greater than 30 percent minority populations used mandatory desegregation; in these cities losses in white school enrollment for three years before desegregation averaged 4.6 percent per year. Of the major Alabama urban areas with greater than 30 percent pre-desegregation minority populations (Birmingham, Mobile, and Montgomery—none of which were included in Rossell's study), pre-desegregation losses were much less than half Rossell's average of 4.6 percent per year.

During the year of desegregation, the cities in Rossell's sample lost an average of 12.7 percent of their white enrollment. For Birmingham, Mobile, and Montgomery the counterpart figure was well under 4 percent. During the next nine years white enrollment loss averaged 7.3 percent per year, a far greater rate than before mandatory integration. Among the three Alabama cities, Birmingham had the greatest post-desegregation white enrollment loss, an average of less than 3 percent per year. Rossell's sample of cities with greater than 30 percent minority population using voluntary desegregation experienced significantly less white enrollment loss after desegregation, although these losses were still much higher than those in Birmingham, Mobile, and Montgomery.[25]

The same pattern held for the eight cities in Rossell's sample with less than 30 percent minority population. In the three years preceding mandatory desegregation, white enrollments decreased an average of 2.5 percent per year. In Decatur, Dothan, and Huntsville (the three major Alabama cities with less than 30 percent minority population), white enrollments before mandatory desegregation increased slightly on a percentage basis. In the year of desegregation, the white enrollment decrease averaged 6.9 percent, and for the nine years following desegregation, the loss was 4.9 percent per year. White enrollment in Decatur, Dothan, and Huntsville barely dropped immediately after desegregation, and for nine years after desegregation the decline averaged less than approximately 2 percent per year.

Post-desegregation white enrollment losses in the two cities with voluntary desegregation plans covered by Rossell were much less severe than in the cities in her sample with mandatory desegregation. In the pre-desegregation years in these cities there was a slight white enrollment gain.[26] Decatur, Dothan, and Huntsville experienced far lower post-desegregation white enrollment losses. Indeed, in these Alabama districts percentage losses in five-year spans were comparable to losses in the Rossell cities each year.

Rossell measured integration by the percentage of white students in the minority child's school. This percentage is called interracial exposure.[27] In school districts with greater than 30 percent minority populations, she found that in the year of desegregation and for three years thereafter, interracial exposure increased more for mandatory systems than for voluntary ones. But from the fourth year on, voluntary systems significantly exceeded mandatory ones. Indeed, by the ninth year school districts desegregated by mandate were nearly back to segregated levels of interracial exposure. Voluntary desegregation plans were also superior to mandatory ones in school districts below 30 percent, although mandatory plans did not reduce interracial exposure to the levels experienced in times of segregation.[28]

Table 1 lists the percentage of students who are nonblack and interracial exposure score percentages for the six Alabama districts we have been examining and the interracial exposure scores from Rossell's samples. It should be emphasized that the interracial exposure percentage mathematically cannot be higher than the percent nonblack in the district. Thus, a different desegregation plan could theoretically increase the Huntsville interracial exposure score, but Dothan's and Decatur's are close to their maximums. Nine years after desegregation, the interracial exposure scores in Rossell's sample cities and Alabama's major cities were comparable.

In most Black Belt Alabama counties interracial exposure was zero during segregation and close to zero after mandatory desegregation. Whites with money placed their children in private academies or moved out of the Black Belt.

Many others who have studied school desegregation attempts reinforce

Table 1

Comparison Between Interracial Exposure Scores of Six Largest Alabama
Districts (1993–94) and Rossell Sample Cities

District	Percent Nonblack	Interracial Exposure
Birmingham	10.6	6.4
Montgomery	34.6	26.4
Mobile	52.3	30.3
Rossell's voluntary	>30.0*	35.0
Rossell's mandatory	>30.0*	29.4
Dothan	56.0	54.1
Decatur	74.5	72.1
Huntsville	57.3	35.7
Rossell's voluntary	<30.0*	70.6
Rossell's mandatory	<30.0*	63.6

*Exact figures not given.

Rossell's findings. For example, J. Dennis Lord described a white middle class neighborhood in Nashville with more than 250 public school students before busing that dropped to fewer than 30 students after busing. Most students switched to private schools.[29]

In his study of school desegregation in Charlotte-Mecklenburg, North Carolina, Lord discovered a strong relationship between white abandonment of public schools and family income.[30] Relatively affluent families could afford to move out of a school district or send children to private schools. Such families ordinarily were strong supporters of public school funding and often opinion leaders; their movement to private schools inevitably hurt support for the public schools.

On October 29, 1969, the U.S. Supreme Court, in an order requiring immediate school desegregation in Mississippi, observed that segregated school systems were no longer permissible anywhere in the nation.[31] In this decision the court rebuffed the Nixon administration's efforts to permit delays in the implementation of federal integration orders.

That same October the Justice Department filed suit to end school segregation in Waterbury, Connecticut, the first such action in a northern state. The head of the Waterbury school district was stunned.[32] The target of this suit was de facto segregation caused by housing patterns, not the de jure segregation that had been all but eliminated in the South.

Senator John Stennis of Mississippi sought to capitalize on the Supreme Court's widening geographic field of attention by documenting and publicizing examples of northern school segregation and demanding that federal courts and the Justice Department move against them.[33] In highlighting northern segregation, Stennis took advantage of increasingly widespread national opposition to forced busing, which resulted in public protests in such cities as Denver, Pittsburgh, Boston, Dayton, and Grand Rapids.[34]

Stennis's sauce-for-the-goose attack, advanced with cold legal logic, shook northern liberals comfortable in the role of rescuer of downtrodden southern blacks. The *New York Times* writer Tom Wicker flayed helplessly at the assertion that integration regulations had to be applied throughout the nation by arguing that if this were done, integration would not be brought about anywhere "because there is neither the manpower, the money, the knowledge nor the will to do the job."[35]

While Stennis sought to cripple federal integration programs by broadening them, some civil rights activists, such as the liberal Democratic Senator Abraham Ribicoff of Connecticut, saw the Stennis attack as an opportunity. On February 18, 1970, the U.S. Senate, under intense public opinion pressure orchestrated by Stennis, voted for an amendment to an education bill that required enforcement of school desegregation laws and court decisions throughout the country.[36] Senator Ribicoff actively supported the amendment, urging the Senate to abandon "the fiction that segregation in the South is evil while that in the North is benign." He declared, "We're just as racist in the North as they are in the South."[37]

The day after the Senate adopted the amendment, the House voted for several amendments to an appropriations bill to prevent HEW from using forced busing to bring about integration. In March all the amendments were eliminated or rendered inoperative.

On January 3, 1970, Leon Panetta, director of HEW's Office of Civil Rights, reported that 61 percent of black students and 65.6 percent of white students attended largely segregated schools. An official HEW statement said that the data "displayed a shockingly low desegregation ratio on a national basis," and HEW Secretary Robert Finch pointed up "the extensiveness of the problem on a nationwide basis and the need to provide effectively for the educational rights and needs of the disadvantaged, no matter where they may be."[38]

That same day, Mississippi's segregationist governor, John Bell Williams, told his constituents that they would not be able to evade statewide school desegregation. Williams delineated three possible courses of action: follow court rulings, defy them, or close the public schools. Unlike George Wallace, who was encouraging parents to defy court orders, Williams accepted defeat and in so doing offered an almost schizophrenic perspective. On the one hand he emphasized the importance of public schools: "I am strongly of the opinion that we must preserve our public school system as an absolute necessity for the good of all."[39] At the same time, he promised to work to build a private school system as a "workable alternative" for white children. Two weeks later he proposed that the state provide financial assistance to the parents of children in private schools.[40] By 1971, 25 percent of the white students in Mississippi attended private schools.[41]

In January 1970 the *Montgomery Advertiser* reported, "Private schools for whites only are mushrooming across the South—some in temporary facilities such as churches and basements—in the wake of each step to integrate schools. Alabama's State Education Department estimates the state has 270 private schools."[42] The same story credited Circuit Judge Jack Wallace, George Wallace's brother, with helping to organize the private schools. It reported that tuition averaged approximately thirty dollars per month for one child and diminished with each additional child.

On January 31, 1970, the executive committee of the Alabama Democratic party enlarged its membership from 72 to 111 and created new districts that ensured black representation on the committee after the next primary. The changes represented a Brewer victory over Wallace, but, more important, they resulted from pressure from the national Democratic party to give blacks a larger leadership role. Jon Nordheimer, a *New York Times* reporter, described a reception held for Brewer after the meeting at which blacks mingled with whites and Brewer greeted the blacks warmly: "It was the first time in anyone's memory that blacks who were not carrying trays were ever allowed to join a party social function."[43]

A week later George Wallace held a "Freedom of Choice" rally in Montgomery attended by over fifteen thousand people. At the rally he urged southern governors to defy the federal courts' integration orders and threatened to seek the presidency again if Nixon failed to "do something about the mess our schools are in."[44] Many interpreted this event as the kickoff of a 1970 gubernatorial run.

In February Governor Brewer, following the lead of the governors of Louisiana, Georgia, and Mississippi, called a special session of the legislature to enact a duplicate of an antibusing statute passed the previous year by the New York legislature and upheld by the New York Supreme Court. The law prohibited forced busing and granted parents freedom to decide which schools their children would attend.[45] It included the following language: "No person shall be refused admission into or be excluded from any public school in the state on account of race, creed, color, or national origin."

It is a commentary on the speed of social and political change that less than a decade before, winning the adoption of such language in the Alabama legislature would have constituted a triumph for the civil rights movement. The New York plan was approved by unanimous votes in both houses of the Alabama legislature, but the action was only symbolic. The day before a similar version in Georgia had been declared invalid by two federal judges.[46]

The Quality of Education

Albert Brewer was probably the first Alabama governor to turn his attention to the quality of classroom teaching. Governors and virtually all legislators appeared to assume that there was a one-to-one correlation between education funding and education quality. As we have seen, there is a substantial connection between these two factors, but funding explains only about one-half of the variation in education quality when comparisons are made among states.

Brewer advocated continuing education for teachers, a salary system based on professional competence, and elimination of the state's teacher tenure law. Essentially, he tried to persuade teachers to trade increased salaries for somewhat less job security. Brewer argued that tenure was a barrier to the weeding out of incompetents. When asked if existing regulations permitted the dismissal of poor teachers, he replied that they did, but that the process was too complex, involving hearings and the likelihood of court intervention. Not surprisingly, the Alabama Education Association (AEA) opposed Brewer's position on tenure. In an interview with the authors, Brewer described its opposition as ferocious.

The governor also wanted a reduction in class size, a policy with which the AEA and teachers agreed. Roughly eight hundred more teachers statewide would be needed to bring the average class size to twenty-five, which many educators regarded as ideal. Additional teachers required additional classrooms, so the budgetary implications of Brewer's program were substantial.

Faced with implacable opposition from teachers, Brewer backed away from repealing tenure. Instead he floated trial balloons about teacher evaluation. He had in mind something similar to career ladder ideas that appeared in the late 1980s, but his admittedly vague proposals took shape so close to the start of the legislative session that he was unable to formulate detailed plans, and nothing came of them.

In February 1970 the state department of education announced that 482 schools were in danger of losing their accreditation.[47] The department

granted accreditation according to standards set by the Southern Education Association. In the substandard schools 1,448 classes exceeded the
maximum allowed number of 35 students per classroom. In addition, 223
teachers did not have a college degree and 792 were teaching subjects
for which they were not trained. More than 20,000 high school students,
130,000 junior high students, and nearly 500,000 primary students attended unaccredited schools.

Near the end of March, Brewer called a special legislative session to deal
with administrative and financial problems in education. He proposed an
ambitious set of reforms including the establishment of an education study
commission and, more important, a higher education coordinating board.
He also asked for legislation to have the state board of education elected and
the superintendent appointed by the board rather than the board appointed
by the governor and the superintendent elected. He asked for election of
local boards (some already were) and local superintendents appointed by
those boards. Many superintendents were elected, and there was a widespread belief that they devoted more attention to reelection politics than
to professional school management.

Brewer's proposed postsecondary coordinating board, called the Commission on Higher Education, would oversee universities, but the bill's language was vague concerning two-year institutions. In an interview Brewer
suggested this may have been because technical schools and community
colleges were not seen as a serious problem. He said that had he been asked
he would have answered that they fell under the commission's jurisdiction,
but the issue never arose.[48] There is no indication in Brewer's office files or
in newspapers that this question ever was discussed.

The proximate cause of the creation of the Commission on Higher Education was the University of South Alabama's aggressive lobbying to expand
its programs. Closely related was Brewer's desire to create a rational budgetary process for higher education with work load indicators such as credit
hours produced tied to budgetary decisions rather than to the number of
legislators who might be serving on an institution's board of trustees or the
number of its alumni in the legislature.

All of Brewer's education bills passed, although the powers and responsibilities of the Commission on Higher Education were not specified. In later
years the commission's authority grew substantially, although it never received sufficient power over two-year institutions to keep their programs
from spreading in one of the state's worst continuing examples of pork
barrel politics.

It seems odd that the creation of the Commission on Higher Education was not in some way tied to two-year institutions, because the year before Representative Tom Gloor of Bessemer asked the board of education and Brewer for an immediate reassessment of the state's junior college and trade school program and at least a temporary halt to plans to build two more, in Fayette and Andalusia.[49] Gloor won considerable media attention when he ridiculed the building plans and observed that if the entire graduating classes of all high schools in Fayette and neighboring Lamar and Pickens Counties attended the proposed Fayette junior college, its total enrollment would be 211. He also noted that there were already six post-secondary schools within seventy-six miles of Andalusia.

Tax Reform and Education
Funding Campaigns

Earlier in this chapter we observed that in many respects the Brewer administration began as if the governor had been newly elected. John Patterson, George Wallace, Lurleen Wallace, and many governors before and after started their terms amid the drumbeats of a new campaign for education funding that was orchestrated by a few politicians, newspapers sympathetic to education concerns, the state superintendent of education, the AEA, and the universities. Albert Brewer's time in office was no exception to this pattern, even though he was completing Lurleen Wallace's term. For example, the *Montgomery Advertiser* reported the claim by Dr. Robert L. Saunders of the Auburn School of Education that one-half of the teachers graduating from Alabama's colleges and universities obtained employment out of state, especially in Georgia and Florida. By his estimates Alabama spent more than $3.7 million per year educating teachers for neighboring states.[50]

The *Auburn Bulletin* reported that over the previous eight-year period, state tax-based support of higher education in Alabama increased only 161 percent. Except for Mississippi, support for higher education in neighboring states increased more rapidly—278 percent in Florida, 323 percent in Georgia, and 329 percent in Tennessee. These rates were greater than the U.S. average of 233 percent.[51]

Published estimates indicated that an additional $100 million per year would be required to bring Alabama's public schools up to (not above) the southeastern average in per-pupil expenditures. These and similar points were no less true for having been made many times before and ignored. In this campaign, like those before it and after, the teachers and their political allies focused on the idea that more funding would solve the deficiencies in education. They steered well clear of supporting issues relating to assessing and improving the quality of instruction.[52]

The pro-education campaign promoted the usual sources of new revenue. Eliminating sales tax exemptions would raise $112 million per year, according to one estimate. A 30 percent across-the-board property tax assessment would yield an additional $63 million per year, according to another.

A new study commission on education had been created in the previous legislative session, and because the commission membership included Speaker Fite, the legislature watched its work closely. The commission attacked the method of calculating minimum funding levels for each county.[53] Specifically, it criticized the fact that a major part of the formula was based on property values as assessed in 1939.[54] (Use of these 1939 figures continued through 1993. They were cited by Circuit Court Judge Eugene W. Reese as one of the factors creating an inequitable education system that is in violation of the Alabama constitution.)[55]

The minimum funding system established in 1939 created an index of ability to pay based on property values at that time. Counties that in later years permitted their assessments to rise above the 1939 levels (which many urban counties had) paid more to the state in property taxes than was returned to them by the funding formula.

The commission recommended replacing the long-outdated formula with new penalties and newly created rewards. A county that did not levy the full property tax for education allowable under the law would be penalized by having a sum withheld by the state equal to what would be produced if the county's tax were increased to the maximum. If a county taxed above the specified rate, using property taxes and/or other taxes, the county would be rewarded with substantial additional monies beyond the minimum formula.

The commission also proposed property tax equalization at the 30 percent level, an idea identical to that championed by John Patterson and Harry Haden a decade before.[56] The commission calculated that the Special Education Trust Fund would gain $6 million from equalization and that counties would gain an additional $17.58 million. It recommended increases in income and sales taxes and the removal of all sales tax exemptions such as those on farm equipment and supplies and raw materials used in manufacturing. An estimated $50 million per year would be raised by the sales tax changes alone.[57]

Unlike Brewer, the study commission paid only slight attention to improving the quality of instruction. Its report essentially assumed that a 20 percent increase in teacher pay would automatically improve classroom teaching without exploring how this happy occurrence would come to pass.

Governor Brewer disagreed with the Education Study Commission's suggested sales tax increases, and he did not favor upping the income tax, calling both regressive.[58] (As applied, the income tax was not a true progressive tax.) Initially, Brewer lacked enthusiasm for a change in the 1939 allocation formula, arguing that the change added only $5 million a year to the Special Education Trust Fund.

Once again, education funding conflicts rested on an urban-rural pivot. Urban interests were irritated because they paid far more in school taxes to the state than they received from it. Montgomery County in 1965–66 received only $38 from the state for each $100 of state school taxes collected in the county. Madison County received only $51, Mobile $58, and Jefferson $41. At the opposite extreme, Wilcox received $252 for each $100 collected and Lowndes $259.

Near the beginning of the 1969 legislative session, Representative Quinton Bowers, chair of the twenty-member Jefferson County House delegation, announced that the delegation would stop all legislation unless the formulas for distributing school revenues were changed.[59] Rural legislators countered with their own threats.[60]

Urban-rural differences also divided the Senate. In December 1968 the *Montgomery Advertiser* counted nine urban-based senators siding with the seven from Jefferson County. Senators from Montgomery, Mobile, and a few other urban counties were missing from this list. They sometimes voted with rural interests. Still, a hard core of sixteen urban-oriented senators was just two short of a Senate majority.[61]

Meanwhile, an agriculture study commission, concerned that farmers might be asked to shoulder property taxes at rates comparable to what others were paying, proposed to change Alabama law to provide that assessments be based on current use and not the market value of property.[62] The current use notion undermines the basic principle behind property taxation—that property is taxed according to its market value, not an arbitrary figure determined by the property owner. The value of any property is the value of its best use. That use might be its current use or an alternative use such as a factory site or housing.

The Alabama Farm Bureau Federation seemed to understand the unwieldiness of the current use standard, because it offered a version of the straightforwardly discriminatory multirate plan that it had pushed through the House in 1967. (The plan had failed in the Senate.) The Farm Bureau plan assessed utilities at 40 percent of valuation, commercial and industrial property at 25 percent, personal property at 30 percent (an increase), and farm and timberland at 15 percent. To compensate for the resulting loss in revenues, the Farm Bureau suggested that others pay more through corporate and individual income tax increases and heightened taxes on beer and soft drinks.

The Alabama Farm Bureau Federation was not an organization of poor dirt farmers. It was a nonprofit tax-exempt corporation. Like its parent corporation, the American Farm Bureau Federation, the Alabama Farm Bureau issued life, automobile, and fire insurance and was involved in a wide variety of businesses. It also owned large amounts of property including shopping centers.

The education funding plan Brewer presented to the legislature represented a change in his position. He modified the Education Study Commission's reward-and-punishment tax system with one of his own while adhering to the spirit of the commission's recommendations. Brewer's approach focused on a county's tax effort and ability to pay measured by the county's mean per-capita income compared to the mean per-capita income of the state. A relatively poor county making a relatively strong effort to support its schools would be rewarded with extra state funds. A relatively wealthy county doing a below-average job of supporting its schools would be denied some funds even if it raised more taxes than the poorer county.[63] The plan gave counties two years to bring their tax systems up to the state standard and gave county commissions the power to propose tax increases to their electorates. According to Brewer, none of the commissioners desired this power.[64] The governor also wanted additional state funding from a doubling of the insurance premium tax and the imposition of a 4 percent gross-receipts tax on utilities. His entire revenue package was expected to generate $35–40 million.

Despite strong business opposition, the House Ways and Means Committee quickly approved Brewer's entire education funding program.[65] However, the rural majority in that committee amended the local-effort rewards-and-punishment bill to make the punishment less rigorous. The original bill would have eliminated state support for some counties. Many urban legislators whose counties already had high property taxes initially supported the bill, but the House Ways and Means amendment weakened urban support.[66] City representatives felt that the legislation would not help them because it failed to require a sufficient increase in the funding raised by some smaller counties. They also felt the bill lacked credibility. Although the penalty clause denied state funds to school systems that did not meet their prescribed tax effort, urban legislators predicted that no governor would actually cut off the state funds, a forecast that turned out to be accurate in its general thrust if not specific detail.

The Jefferson County House delegation submitted a bill giving urban counties a larger share of state education revenues. Speaker Fite assigned the bill to the Highway Safety Committee, a committee that since its creation by Fite in 1967 had been assigned no members. The bill's angry sponsors tried to block the governor's education funding programs in retaliation. Fite compromised and reassigned the bill to the Ways and Means Committee, which later reported it out with a positive vote.

Brewer's education package made it through the House with relatively few changes. The House also passed the education appropriations bill. The only Brewer bill entirely missing was a 4 percent tax on the sale of coal and coke, a reminder that the Big Mules still had influence.

When Brewer's education bills went to the Senate, the Finance and Taxation Committee quickly approved them. It amended his insurance premium tax, however. As passed by the committee, the total tax package amounted to $36.1 million. New tax revenues would reach $56 million if the voters approved a constitutional amendment to raise personal and corporate income tax ceilings to 7 percent.[67]

The urban bloc began a filibuster in the Senate on April 15, 1969. Its proximate target was the bill to create the postsecondary education commission, but it could have been any bill. The urban bloc had tried to wring concessions on property tax equalization out of Brewer in the House and wanted funding distribution formulas closer to a per student basis. Brewer favored property tax equalization, but he feared that it would not get through the special session and that it would probably tangle up his other bills as well.

In the course of the filibuster, a *Montgomery Advertiser* editorial that was far ahead of its time cautioned the urban filibusterers that they were in effect opposing a time-honored American tradition of the rich helping the poor. Children in poor, rural communities were not receiving educations that matched those in most Alabama cities even with the unfair distribution of state monies.[68] As the filibuster wore on, Brewer reduced his gross-receipts tax on utilities and added exemptions on sewer, garbage, taxicabs, transportation, cable television, and industrial equipment, but these changes were not a sufficient inducement to end the blockade. He also announced that in the regular session he would seek property tax reforms, including potentially important administrative changes.[69]

The Achilles' heel in the urban bloc's Senate filibuster was that urban legislators favored much of Brewer's education program. They knew or suspected that in 1970 he would be competing for reelection against George Wallace, who would not support property tax equalization. To embarrass Brewer too much with their filibuster would be counterproductive.[70]

In exchange for ending the filibuster, the Jefferson County delegation wanted an amendment to a proposed gross-receipts tax on electricity, water, telephone, and telegraph services. The amendment allowed utility firms to pass the tax on to their customers. Most, if not all, of the tax would have been paid by customers in any event, but this amendment made clear to the electorate that a tax on business was a tax on consumers and not a free ride. When Brewer gave them this point, the filibuster ended.

The administration's floor leader, Alton Turner, whose district included Black Belt counties, targeted the amendment for biting and unintentionally humorous criticism: "For 100 years the big mules have apparently run this state. If we pass this amendment, we are confessing that they still run it."[71] The vote on the amendment split along urban-rural lines. The House later passed the utilities tax bill along a similar urban-rural division.

Ultimately the legislature passed most of Brewer's tax increases, including a 4 percent gross-receipts tax on public utilities; an increase in insurance premium taxes, including 2 percent on Blue Cross–Blue Shield; a 5 percent tax on Alabama corporation dividends; a constitutional amendment to raise maximum rates on personal taxable income over five thousand dollars and on corporate income; and a use tax on TVA power identical to a public utilities tax. Overall, this was clearly a progressive package. The education appropriations bill, which included enough money to give teachers raises of seven to eight hundred dollars also passed the special session.

Despite doubts about the usefulness of Brewer's new minimum standard property tax bill with its penalty provision, urban legislators supported it. It passed the legislature and was signed into law.[72]

By 1971, when the penalty provision of the law was scheduled for implementation, few underassessed counties had acted to bring themselves up to the state norm. Some counties had tried but failed to win the taxpayers' approval. For example, the Montgomery County Board of Education asked its electorate for a 5 mill property tax increase that would have yielded $1.7 million and was turned down. Under the provisions of the 1969 act, Montgomery schools could lose $14 million.[73] In all, thirty-nine counties stood to lose funds.[74]

State Superintendent of Schools LeRoy Brown asked Attorney General William Baxley for an advisory opinion concerning the constitutionality of the act. The attorney general advised that it was unconstitutional because it denied school children in poorer districts due process and equal protection of the law under the Fourteenth Amendment of the U.S. Constitution.[75] Baxley's opinion was supported by a later federal court ruling.[76]

The removal of this disciplining device, followed as it was by the re-election of Wallace, a rurally oriented governor, served to reduce the total financial resources available to the schools. Rural and Black Belt counties had no incentives for increasing their tax rates.

The Regular Legislative Session

In the regular session that followed the special session, Brewer requested more funding to meet the state's Medicaid responsibilities. He asked for additional taxes on beer, cigarettes, and hard liquor. After the usual posturing and speechmaking, measures close to his proposals passed.

Late in the spring of 1969 a suit filed in federal court requested that state revenue officials be ordered to collect property taxes throughout Alabama at 30 percent of market value. Among the plaintiffs were the mayor of Birmingham, 7 Birmingham council members, 3 corporations, and 109 individual property owners and their children.[77] The suit contended that the state constitution required uniform property tax collection and that children were being deprived of educational opportunities because of unequal property tax collection. The state of Alabama asked for dismissal of the suit.[78] Brewer opposed the suit because he feared that it would interfere with equalization legislation and because he believed that the plaintiffs would not be successful. Fundamentally, the suit asked the court to require something contrary to explicit wording in the state constitution, that is, property taxation at 30 percent of valuation when the constitution called for twice that level. The suit later foundered on precisely that point.

In July, Senator George Lewis Bailes Jr. of Birmingham introduced a bill that provided for statewide property valuation to replace the county-based system with its wide inter- and intracounty discrepancies.[79] Analyses by the Revenue Department showed that "the average assessment is 16.1 percent, ranging from a low of 4.9 percent in Choctaw County to a high of 26.8 percent in Jefferson County."[80] The Bailes bill also provided for financing the statewide assessment process at an estimated cost of $30 million.[81] Perhaps the most important aspect of the legislation was that it allowed implementation of existing laws that would permit equalization. These were the same laws that John Patterson had preserved by backing away from Revenue Commissioner Harry Haden's attempt to bring about equalization.[82] Bailes's abrasive personal style and his habit of killing other people's legislation meant that his bill stood little chance of passage, but Brewer reluctantly endorsed the proposal as a kind of first draft. Brewer had promised his support for an equalization bill in exchange for Jefferson County's support for his education package in the special session.[83]

Meanwhile, the Alabama Farm Bureau worked to establish the property classification system that the legislature had failed to pass in 1967. By the end of the session neither urban nor rural forces produced significant changes in property tax equalization. They did enact a new statute, but like the 1967 bill, this one set the assessment rate at "not more than 30 percent" statewide, meaning that it could (and would) be well under that rate in many counties. (In 1971 the U.S. District Court in Montgomery ruled that all state property had to be valued at the 60 percent rate specified in the Alabama constitution.)[84]

The equalization battle continued in the legislature through 1971 and 1972. Finally, the Farm Bureau's classification system was enacted.[85] George Wallace was governor again, and he worked hard for its passage, but he allowed the enabling legislation to go into effect without his signature. Full enactment required the law to pass a statewide referendum. Many speculated that Wallace refused to sign the bill in order to distance himself from the legislation, because it worked against the interests of vast majorities of the state's increasingly urban electorate.[86] He would need the vote of that electorate in future election races. Wallace himself gave no explanation for his behavior.

Ethics in Government

Representative Walker Hobbie of Montgomery introduced a governmental ethics bill that Brewer favored. Rankin Fite blocked it, killing it for the year.[87] After the legislative session Brewer created an ethics commission by executive order and propounded a code of ethics. He suggested that the code also applied to the legislature.[88] Brewer's executive order created a ten-person commission composed of one senator, one representative, two merit system employees, two judges, and four members from the public at large. The commission had the power to ensure full compliance with laws and Brewer's code of ethics. It also received the power to conduct investigations based on complaints or based on its own initiative.

The code of ethics stated, "No state official or employee can accept favors, gifts, or services that might reasonably tend to improperly influence him in discharge of his duties." Further, "if an official is an officer, director, agent, or member of or owns a controlling interest in a corporation, firm, partnership, or other business entity which is subject to regulation of, or which has substantial business commitments from any state agency, he shall file a sworn statement with the Secretary of State disclosing such interest." A state official or employee was not "to use for personal profit or pecuniary gain, his official position to secure special privileges or exemptions for himself or others." Nor could confidential information be used for such purposes. Finally, holding any personal investment likely to "create a substantial conflict between private and public interest" was forbidden.[89]

Brewer's ethics provisions prodded the legislature into action. In 1973 it passed ethics legislation that set up the Alabama Ethics Commission, gave it somewhat limited authority, and wrote its own code of conduct for elected and appointed officials and public employees. Twenty years later, the legislature is still arguing over the commission's appropriate role and whether its authority, especially its investigative powers, should be strengthened.

Summing Up the Legislative and Political Scene

After the 1969 legislative session, Senator George Lewis Bailes Jr. of Jefferson County and the *Montgomery Advertiser* offered two contrasting but not inconsistent portraits of legislative operations. It was extremely unusual even for bitter legislative foes to attack one another directly or to cast aspersions on the legislature as a whole, but in October 1969 Bailes broke both taboos. In a speech delivered at the Birmingham Exchange Club he charged five legislators with conflicts of interest.[90] Bailes named Senators O. J. "Joe" Goodwyn, Roland Cooper, Ray Lolley, Mylan Engel, and Alton Turner. With the possible exception of Goodwyn, media coverage of these individuals often implied that their motives were rarely idealistic, so the Bailes charges covered little new ground.

Bailes pointed out that Goodwyn's law firm was employed by Governor George Wallace to represent the Alabama Board of Education. Goodwyn confirmed this, but he denied that the fees paid his firm amounted to the seventy-five thousand dollars cited by Bailes. Cooper and Lolley, members of the state building commission, were cited for having approved thousands of dollars in construction contracts that benefited them personally. Both denied that the commission approved contracts, a response that smacked of heavy reliance on a technicality. According to Bailes, Engel received legal fees from the governor's office for representing the state docks. Engel also had represented a Mobile taxi firm while the legislature discussed provisions exempting cab companies from education taxes. Turner was accused of attempting to reduce the beer tax from three cents to one cent while he and his law firm represented beer distributors. Bailes also claimed that Turner sought passage of a bill to allow twin trailer trucks on the state highways while his law firm represented the Alabama Truckers Association. Finally, he charged that Turner represented the Alabama Optometrists Association while as a senator he handled legislation pertinent to optometry.

Bailes's October speech presented an image of a majority of legislators narrowly focused on self-enrichment won by selling votes—government by conflict of interests. Such descriptions by close observers of the Alabama legislature are far more common than ones that portray representatives and senators working to improve the quality of life in Alabama or just honestly representing their constituents.

The *Montgomery Advertiser* described the roles played by key senators during this period. Its characterizations project a sense of the shifting forces at work in the legislature during the Lurleen Wallace and Albert Brewer administrations. It called Joe Goodwyn

> a force in the Senate, both in the 1967 session when he was on the floor and in 1969 . . . as pres pro tem. . . .
>
> [Hugh] Morrow was the leader of the urban coalition, if it can be called that, and manfully bore the brunt of the Black Belt ostracism with a stoic calm that made the Black Belters even more furious. . . . Morrow's leadership of a loosely knit band of widely diversified city slickers led to the gas tax redistribution and a meaningful beginning on more equity for urban constituents.
>
> . . . Bo Torbert was probably one of the great compromisers and worked hard at breaking deadlocks which plagued the upper house.
>
> . . . Turner huffed and he puffed and he was as unchanged at the end of a session as he was at the start. He was the champion of governor Lurleen Wallace and spent a good part of his time and his fortune in the George Wallace cause in 1968. When the torch was passed, he carried it high for his longtime friend Albert Brewer, and when the chips were down he spoke out against Wallace and stood by Brewer against all criticism. . . .
>
> It was Ollie Nabors who read Machiavelli to the Senate in one interminable filibuster and who collapsed while reading it. And it was Turner who stepped in to relieve his friend, although the Nabors filibuster was against an issue championed by Turner.[91]

During the session a bill was introduced that would have required that the Alabama ballot include the names of presidential candidates instead of just presidential electors. Wallace supporters opposed the legislation, fearing that if it became law, it would force Wallace to run for president as a third-party candidate instead of as a Democrat.[92] The bill failed.

Assessing the Brewer Administration

The urban-rural divisions that emerged in the Patterson years widened and clarified throughout the 1960s. In the days of alliance rule, Jefferson County legislators cared little about education anywhere, including Jefferson County, and they showed little concern for much else that state government did except for one thing—keeping taxes low. They viewed the fact that the Black Belt received far more in state programs than it deserved on a per capita basis as the price of maintaining Birmingham's economic and political power.

Postalliance Jefferson County legislators were far more concerned about their county's share of state government spending. They also seemed to care more about the quality of education. Their first priority, however, remained keeping taxes low and off the shoulders of their Jefferson County industrialist patrons.

The Alabama Republican party continued to lack a sense of direction and battled over its leadership. When John Grenier began his Republican party organization building in the early 1960s, he relied heavily on support from the John Birch Society. The members of this organization tended to be reactionaries given to bizarre conspiratorial theories regarding alliances of such unlikely partners as international oil companies and Communists, both of which supposedly sought world domination. Grenier's beliefs did not veer into the fever swamps occupied by the Birch Society, and he was probably too much of a pragmatist for them, so they shifted their attentions to Jim Martin.

There was no effective effort to create or support a full slate of candidates. Party leaders continued to debate about what type of voters the party should seek to attract, and more important, what type of new members to actively recruit. Grenier and Martin disagreed heatedly over whether to invite blacks to a 1968 Republican party conference. Grenier believed that some black votes would be required before the Republican party could win statewide elections; Martin wanted to continue supporting segregation. Blacks and relatively poor white Alabamians correctly read the situation as indicating that they were not wanted by most of the GOP.

During these debates Grenier and Martin competed for a position on the Republican National Committee. The election was to be held in the Republican state convention in June 1968.[93] Martin won.[94]

Albert Brewer found himself in a difficult and irksome political situation when he became governor. He inherited his position from a woman who had become a truly beloved figure. Presiding over her memory was a charismatic, skillful demagogue who continued to incite racial strife while remaining poised to launch a new campaign for the governorship. Brewer positioned himself as someone above politics, a good government reformer, and a racial moderate. He refrained from criticizing his two predecessors. This fit his personality, and it could not have represented a more stark contrast to George Wallace. A long stream of stories about Wallace administration corruption that ran in many daily newspapers accentuated their dissimilarity. The fact that a highly experienced former reporter held the critical office of finance director in the Brewer administration doubtless facilitated the journalistic search for examples of waste and political abuse.

Brewer's persona is evidenced in a speech in which he listed the major accomplishments of his administration. He cited "substantial reductions in state expenditures . . . through some simple changes."[95] He claimed savings of fifty thousand dollars per month from better administration of the state motor pool. He noted that "the state also has followed the competitive bid law, upgraded employee benefits to compete with private business and established computer centers to avoid duplication and waste." He created the Alabama Development Office for industry hunting and claimed substantial success in attracting industry. He noted that his educational program ensured "each child in each system in the state would receive the same amount of state support for his education." Brewer criticized the legislature for its failure to pass ethics legislation but pointed with pride to the ethics commission created by his executive order. He presented this list of accomplishments without direct criticism of the Governors Wallace and without the direct personal attacks that George Wallace would have used.

Brewer defended himself against Wallace's increasingly desperate and extreme civil rights pronouncements by pointing to his defense of freedom of choice and his attack on forced busing as a threat to neighborhood schools. His position was little different from that of Judge Frank Johnson.[96]

The Brewer position was well chosen. He could never "out-seg" George Wallace, but his defense of freedom of choice and opposition to busing was as convincing to many Alabamians as Wallace's pronouncements. Only those occupying nether regions of racist fantasy could believe that Wallace would succeed in maintaining freedom of choice and stopping busing.

The civil rights movement won the freedom of choice and busing battles because it held the moral high ground and the support of the U.S. Supreme Court, the U.S. Congress, and, through most of the period covered here, the executive branch of the federal government. Civil rights advocates cleverly turned the urban riots of the 1960s, in which George Wallace, Bull Connor, and their ilk placed so much hope, into an advantage. The riots, it was decided, had been caused by white racism. Only extreme civil rights policies and large, corrective federal expenditures could rectify the situation.

Brewer and other southern moderates and conservatives had no credibility in the national debate over freedom of choice and busing. Their legitimacy had been taken away by the extreme behavior of their predecessors. Northern opponents of the new directions that civil rights programs had taken were also lumped together with segregationists. "These are the people who voted for George Wallace," civil rights leaders would say of those who opposed busing. Such a charge was, by itself, almost sufficient to render an opponent harmless.

A resourceful combination of good government and good politics marked Brewer's positions on education. Brewer's novel emphasis on instructional quality was by itself a strong position. It could not be obscured by Wallace's rantings. In addition, it facilitated passage of his school finance package and suggested to voters that their tax dollars would be well spent.

His ability to achieve passage of a large set of tax increases, property tax reform, and substantial changes in educational administration with few modifications to his original proposals is very impressive. That he won while George Wallace's popularity was strong and growing even stronger, and while working mainly with Wallace legislative leaders, ranks Brewer's 1969 legislative victories with those achieved by Frank Dixon in 1939.

In an interview Brewer offered several explanations for his legislative successes. He believed that the Wallace forces did not want to be perceived as obstructionist, especially since Brewer's ideas were so reasonable and were receiving much positive press coverage. Also, even though he inherited most of Wallace's legislative leadership, Brewer was personally closer to them than Wallace. He had served in the House for two terms, one as Speaker, and as lieutenant governor he had presided actively over the Senate. Wallace rarely worked closely with legislators except for a few leaders on an ad hoc basis, and he frequently campaigned for the presidency out of state. Reapportionment also altered the numbers. On many issues the positions Brewer advocated more closely mirrored those of urban legislators. The adjustment of the tax system to benefit urban areas coincided with their own self-interests.

The 1970 Gubernatorial Election

Several candidates entered the governor's race in 1970, but only Albert Brewer and George Wallace were considered viable. After Lurleen Wallace's death George Wallace assured Brewer that he had

Wallace's support for a 1970 gubernatorial bid. According to Brewer and newspaper reporters, Wallace told others that he expected them to support Brewer as well. It is possible that Brewer was the only one who believed him.

In January 1970, when he finally realized that Wallace would run against him, Brewer began to take the offensive. He did so in his characteristically diplomatic way: "We need government free from influence of whisky agents and asphalt agents," he said, without referring to Wallace specifically.[97] Brewer took great care not to insult the memory of Lurleen Wallace.

The *Montgomery Advertiser* continued its criticism of Wallace and enthusiastically supported Brewer. A January 1970 editorial summarized the *Advertiser*'s position against Wallace:

> Singlehandedly, he brought down on Alabama the first state-wide desegregation orders. Virtually alone, he passed the Voting Rights Law. For a time, people enjoyed the wild Kamikaze attacks, hang the cost. But now, many are . . . beginning to wonder if he is not indeed a false messiah. The question for Wallace, and for the state, is whether or not he can again hornswoggle enough people into believing, as he used to say, that "if you stand up to 'em, they'll back down every time," or that if you draw magic lines in the dust, they (the feds) will really stop now. They didn't before.[98]

Democratic party professionals began to recognize that their political environment was changing. Blacks would vote in great numbers in the Democratic primary, and black votes increasingly would be needed to defeat the GOP in congressional and other general election races. As a result, on January 31, 1970, the state Democratic executive committee adopted a statement of principles welcoming "every citizen, no matter what his religion nor race nor how humble" and expanded its size in a way that would guarantee black membership.[99] Most of the Republican party leadership still felt safe in ignoring the changes in the electorate. Given their statements in support of segregation and their membership base, they would attract few black votes and even fewer black members.

In February 1970 an antibusing rally, sponsored by a group called Concerned Parents for Public Education, drew eleven thousand people in Birmingham. George Wallace was the featured speaker. The rally was held at the five-thousand-seat Municipal Auditorium, and more than half the audience stood outside listening to the speeches over loudspeakers.

Wallace's speech contained classic populist rhetoric: "This meeting here today has put the hay down where the goats can get it. The bureaucrats can call us 'rednecks' if they want to, but we're telling Democrats and Republicans alike that it doesn't make any difference what color our neck is—you're going to get off of it."[100] Wallace called on southern governors to take over school districts, something that he had somehow failed to do when he was governor. He received some of his loudest applause when he spoke about his presidential campaigns past and future: "We're going to keep the pressure on Mr. Nixon to give us back our schools." His claims that Alabamians had helped to defeat Hubert Humphrey's presidential bid by supporting Wallace's candidacy were also enthusiastically received.

Wallace cleverly played on his audience's self-image: "They used to treat us rudely and crudely because they thought Alabamians were racists and bigots like the big newspapers said we were and that we didn't know how to cross the street. Now when I appear on 'Meet the Press' or 'Face the Nation' they say 'Yes Sir Mr. Wallace.' What they really mean is 'Yes, Sir, Mr. Alabamian.'" He warned his audiences: "If I lose, it will be a signal that the people of Alabama have surrendered to the very forces I have been fighting."[101] Aside from energetic, ritualistic assaults on the federal government, Wallace had difficulty bringing his campaign into focus. He talked far too long at many of his rallies—in some instances over forty-five minutes—and lost the attention of his audiences.

Late in April Wallace charged Brewer with heaping "evil abuse on me and my wife."[102] He provided no examples, because there were none. The press ridiculed him for making such a nonsensical charge, and Wallace's aides quickly advised him that he must stop, a recommendation that he followed. Wallace also tried to connect Brewer with Republican Winton Blount. He suggested that Blount was a Vietnam War profiteer who had used some of his ill-gotten gains to build a mansion with twenty-six bathrooms, an exaggeration that made Wallace look foolish. He also offered a confusing thirty-one-point platform of promises that few took seriously. Some political observers believed that Wallace's campaign mistakes were caused by an inexperienced staff. Several longtime Wallace advisers—Seymore Trammell, Cecil Jackson, and his press secretary, Bill Jones—no longer were part of the Wallace team.

In an essentially pretelevision campaign (the first sophisticated television gubernatorial campaign was conducted by Forrest "Fob" James in 1978), both Wallace and Brewer held many large rallies throughout the state. Even in a small town such as Monroeville, fifteen hundred people attended a Wallace rally, and Brewer drew comparable numbers.[103] Both campaigns appeared to be the best financed in many years.

Brewer confined his campaign messages to vague declarations and routine criticisms of his predecessor, or, more to the point, his predecessor's husband: "I want to be your governor"; "State government is big business, and we've run it like a business. You don't see the five percenters and agents of influence who siphon off tax dollars to line their pockets. We don't have any place for them"; "My one promise is a promise I make freely. I will never make you ashamed that you voted for Albert Brewer as your governor."[104]

The state's larger daily newspapers supported Brewer. Press support for Wallace was confined primarily to smaller newspapers such as the *Dothan Eagle, Centreville Press, Linden Democrat-Reporter,* and *Andalusia Star-News.* The *Montgomery Advertiser*'s major contribution to the campaign was a long series of stories about how companies were selected for Highway Department contracts during the first two years of the first Wallace administration. These disclosures revealed that few companies received contracts unless they or their principals had contributed heavily to the Wallace campaign or hired as an agent someone who had.[105] Other stories concerned the role of George Wallace's brother Gerald as part owner of an asphalt company that was incorporated early in the first administration. The company did a good business selling asphalt to the Highway Department at prices reportedly 79 cents to $3.39 per ton higher than the average price paid at that time.[106]

Once a low bid was announced at a bid opening session, the state's competitive bid law allowed a government purchaser such as the Highway Department to award a contract to any who then presented a bid at least 5 percent under the lowest bid. These were called complimentary bids. Such bids had to be approved by the finance director and the governor. Wallace, his minions, and contractors manipulated the bidding process so that all bids but that of the business favored for that contract would be very high. Businesses that refused to participate in this charade were frozen out.[107]

It is doubtful whether stories of this sort had any effect, because most Alabamians already knew about these kinds of dealings or had their suspicions. It was widely understood that George and Gerald Wallace were far from selfless. Most Alabamians realized that the Wallace brothers were only doing what other governors and their friends and relatives had done.

The campaign tactics used against Brewer were often vicious. Someone circulated brochures using doctored photos. In one instance the original photo showed Brewer with Governors John McKeithen of Louisiana, John Bell Williams of Mississippi, and Louie Nunn of Kentucky. In the altered version one governor was cropped out and the two others were replaced with black boxer Mohammed Ali (then known as Cassius Clay) and Black Muslim leader Elijah Muhammed. Another photo of Brewer with singer Johnny Cash was modified to show Brewer with Elijah Muhammed. Other doctored photographs were used to make highly personal attacks on members of Brewer's family.

Brewer won the first primary, but he fell short of the majority required for nomination. He won most of north Alabama, representing part of the friends-and-neighbors influence, most urban areas with the exception of Mobile and Dothan, and large parts of the Black Belt. Blacks now constituted the voting majority in many Black Belt counties. According to the reporter Don Wasson, the organized groups favoring Brewer included teachers, bankers, utility interests, insurance companies, doctors, and blacks.[108]

At first Brewer and Wallace engaged in an old-fashioned out-promise-the-other-candidate runoff contest. One newspaper report described the start of Wallace's campaign as cautious and sedate.[109] Wallace mentioned but did not emphasize a so-called "bloc" vote (the southern code word for black support) for Brewer. He stressed local issues at each stop and made routine promises concerning such things as utility taxes, future investigations of insurance premium rates, and an increase in the homestead exemption for people over sixty-five. He promised to remove the sales tax from groceries.[110] Brewer pledged a $17.6 million tax reduction package including a cut in auto tags and the exemption of pharmaceuticals from the state sales tax.[111]

Near the end of the runoff campaign Wallace returned to the race issue. His official campaign newspaper carried the headline: "UNLESS WHITES VOTE ON JUNE 2, BLACKS WILL CONTROL THE STATE."[112] A newspaper advertisement read in its entirety:

> WHAT ABOUT THE 23% AND YOU!
> What about a 23% Governor? You have heard about a full time Governor. Only 23% of the white people voted for Brewer. Can any 23% of the white people and their negro friends elect the next Governor? Not if you vote for your own kind.
> VOTE RIGHT—VOTE WALLACE![113]

Wallace also spoke directly about the bloc vote: "If you want to save Alabama as you know Alabama, remember! The bloc vote—Negroes and their white friends—nearly nominated Brewer on May 5th. This black and white socio-political alliance must not dominate the people of Alabama! This spotted alliance must be defeated! This may be your last chance."[114]

The tone of Albert Brewer's campaign is captured by the following newspaper advertisement:

HERE IS WHY SOME ALABAMA VOTERS
IGNORE THIS CHART

Concerned and sensible Alabama voters who decide to vote for a man *on the basis of his proven record in office,* will be very interested in the chart, below.

Some Alabama voters will ignore it.

Which will *you* do?

It is sad, but true. Some folks can still be swayed a lot easier by political *promises,* by *smear* campaigns, by the use of *fear* techniques, by ugly *rumors.*

But, you can verify the figures shown on the chart yourself.[115]

Except for the centered headline, this material was set in extremely small type. It was followed by a table comparing state government purchases of such items as gasoline, asphalt, and tires under Wallace and Brewer and showing that the Brewer administration had paid less by substantial margins.

Wallace won the runoff with 51.5 percent of the vote. The vote distribution repeated the primary results with slight differences. Rural areas throughout the state, including north Alabama, tended to shift toward Wallace. The exceptions were twelve Black Belt counties with large black voting populations. The 1970 primary and runoff votes partly reflected the urban-rural split that divided the preceding legislature. On the other hand, the anti-Wallace Black Belt vote (and the overwhelmingly anti-Wallace Jefferson County vote) demonstrated the influence of new forces.

Few blacks ran for positions in the state legislature in 1970. One of those running was Fred Gray, a civil rights attorney. He was the only black to win.

Just as Black Belt and rural legislators were the core of the Wallace leadership base, so Black Belt and rural voters had been the core of his electoral support. As more blacks entered the electorate and the urban areas continued to grow in the 1970s, Wallace's support base eroded. Winning future elections would be more difficult.

Wallace did not have to adjust his campaign to these changes in his 1974 reelection bid. The electorate basically rewarded the politician (now confined to a wheelchair because of an assassination attempt) for his years of service in what most voters assumed would be his last campaign. When he surprised most politicians and the voters by running again in 1982, he actively sought the support of black voters in order to win the Democratic nomination and traded favors with the black political leadership. Most analysts regarded his support in the black community as crucial to his election. This was simply Wallace the pragmatic, opportunistic politician furthering his favorite cause—George Wallace.

11

... The More They Stay the Same

More than anything else the Big Mule–Black Belt alliance wanted the social, economic, and political life of Alabama to remain unchanged. From 1901 to 1961 it achieved this central objective while suffering only occasional tactical defeats. In the early 1960s rural and urban divisions within the alliance could be contained no longer as forces both inside and outside the state split the Black Belt planter–urban industrialist partnership.

For more than three decades after the alliance's dissolution over reapportionment in 1961, its components, working within a constantly shifting set of issue-specific coalitions, have been able to block change. They succeeded partly because the state's constitutional structure favored opponents of tax reform and thereby limited educational improvements. They also benefited from the financial resources supplied by the commercial elements of the old alliance and takeovers by large lumber companies in the Black Belt. In addition, these enemies of change were helped by George Wallace's rurally oriented, reactionary, racist philosophy, which he linked to a rhetoric of populism. His skillful promotion of these ideas prevented the development of a coalition among Alabama's have-nots (both white and black). Finally, fear of urban dominance tied together a loose, shifting coalition of rural counties that crossed regional lines.

The alliance also left another legacy, a tone of hopelessness and cynicism that still pervades Alabama politics. This inheritance is more difficult to document than specifics of the alliance's history, but it is no less important. The melancholy quality of Alabama politics was not designed by alliance leaders, but it has served them well. It developed partly from the presence throughout this century of legislators who regarded the alliance's corporate presidents, large landowners, and interest group directors, not the public, as their bosses. These legislators were sometimes overheard telephoning their superiors for orders before casting votes about which they had doubts. In some instances the legislators themselves were alliance leaders (especially in the Black Belt) or handpicked representatives of those leaders (as were many Jefferson County legislators).

The tone of Alabama politics also grew out of widespread corruption. The vast majority of those holding elective office were there for self-enrichment, not public service. More often than not, a politician's financial goals could be accomplished through legal, if not ethical, means.

A few idealists occasionally slipped into Alabama government intent on bettering schools or campaigning for fairer taxes. They found themselves in an environment no more hospitable than a desert. In this setting idealism quickly wilted, and these dreamers left in frustration or joined the spoils party.

Alabama was crippled by centralized power and by the fact that the power wielders believed too much in themselves and too little in their subordinates, white and black. They held a narrow vision of commerce and life. Commerce consisted of manufacturing plants with large smokestacks and sprawling plantations run by a handful of experts at the top issuing orders to large numbers of narrowly trained technicians and laborers in a chain of command. The Big Mules believed that these technicians and laborers required little education because most of them lacked the capacity to benefit from more than rudimentary training. Nor did the Big Mules believe that education would help such limited beings enrich their lives or aid them to make rational political decisions. A small middle class of store owners, clergy, attorneys, and other entrepreneurs and professionals generally could be counted on to support the system and service the large manufacturing and agriculture concerns.

The rigid, narrow vision of the alliance leaders was adequate for only a few years. In the early 1900s their sense of what was workable and appropriate in the realms of politics, economics, and social relations was little different from that of their counterparts in the rest of the country, except that northern states did not practice de jure racial discrimination. By 1930 scientific racism was dead, and among the northern elite opinion was rapidly changing. The flow of southern blacks into northern cities enhanced the political power of blacks in the national Democratic party.

At the same time, technology became increasingly important in the nation's most profitable businesses. With technological dependence came an understanding of the need for an educated work force, a work force unavailable in places like Alabama. When Alabama government sought industrial growth in the 1950s and 1960s, it attracted older mechanized industries seeking cheap labor, no labor unions, low taxes, and new markets. Only a few industries dependent on strong educational systems located in Alabama. They settled in concentrated areas such as Huntsville, where the presence of a federal facility created a demand unaffected by state-level forces.

Despite the alliance's overall poor management of the state, Alabama's economy began to improve compared to the nation as a whole because of the operation of the market economy and demographic forces. The alliance was unable and unwilling to take full advantage of the inertia-breaking power of the national market system, and by maintaining its political power (the thing it did best), no one could challenge its failing leadership.

One weakness in the alliance system was that, even in the era before enfranchisement of the black electorate, growth in the urban population meant the alliance could not always control who was elected governor. In the late 1940s President Harry Truman's civil rights programs, mild as they were, highlighted a second weakness: southern blacks were taking their fight outside the South into an arena which offered them some promise of success.

The alliance's problem with errant governors was overridden in the 1950s by its far greater vulnerability to federal action. *Brown v. Board* demonstrated that the alliance and other segregationists had lost the U.S. Supreme Court. When President Dwight Eisenhower sent federal troops into Little Rock, the alliance and other segregationists lost the support of the federal executive branch. Few expected the next president to be any friendlier to segregationists than Eisenhower was. So, as the 1960s began, the alliance was under attack from two branches of the federal government as well as urban growth and the civil rights movement.

John Patterson was only a marginally reliable ally from the alliance perspective. His position on civil rights was perfect, and he was an able protagonist on behalf of segregationist interests, but he had significant populist-liberal tendencies that made him a threat regarding education funding and property tax reform. On the other hand, the clever Big Mule tactician Albert Boutwell was lieutenant governor. With his help the alliance's control of the legislature once again prevented significant damage in these two delicate areas.

Throughout this period the Black Belt population declined and the cities grew. The fact that the planters would lose most of their political power base should the civil rights movement be successful made them increasingly abrasive and embarrassing to their allies. Younger professionals in the cities, whom malapportionment denied opportunities to participate fully in the political process, were becoming especially restive.

The federal courts hit the alliance a devastating blow with the requirement that the state legislature be reapportioned on a one-person-one-vote basis. Making matters worse, population loss relative to the rest of the nation removed one congressman. Resulting redistricting and reapportionment battles and pressure from Governor Patterson split the internally rotting alliance.

In 1963 Alabama had a partially reapportioned legislature and a new governor, but little changed. Jefferson County and other urban Big Mules were more oriented toward economic development and friendlier to education than the planters, but only marginally so. The Birmingham Big Mules still possessed virtually total control over their legislative delegation. They managed to rid themselves temporarily of the no longer useful Bull Connor by electing the moderate Albert Boutwell mayor, but Boutwell's strengths were legal strategy and parliamentary maneuvering, not the kind of innovative leadership that Birmingham needed. And the planters and many of their legislators had not disappeared. They began cooperating with other rural counties which, though not sharing the planters' total hostility toward the civil rights movement, joined with them in a general lack of enthusiasm about improving education or reforming the property tax system.

The melancholy and negative tone of Alabama politics reached full flower in the first two Wallace administrations. Wallace devoted careful attention only to the acquisition and maintenance of power through thousands of large and small patronage arrangements, gubernatorial and presidential election campaigns, and, worst of all, his self-serving orchestration of racial conflict. Little else mattered to him, and much of the political system— including, toward the end of his career, the very blacks he had so recently persecuted—seemed willing to accommodate him.

Governor George Wallace's harsh words and combative style encouraged the killing and injuring of civil rights advocates, journalists, and bystanders. He disrupted schools with troops, and he helped create and maintain an atmosphere that allowed white students to harass black students. The damage his actions did to Alabama's national image continues to be felt today.[1]

Wallace provided marginal improvements in school funding in his first term while he simultaneously built a wildly oversized and politicized system of two-year institutions and encouraged the growth of segregated private academies. In his wife's term he used the budget to punish teachers and school administrators who disagreed with his civil rights policies.

Wallace made no attempt to reform the property tax system or to expand the tax base in ways that would allow economic growth and enhance the quality of life of the populace economically, socially, or politically.

Meanwhile, a reapportioned legislature pulled money out of poor and/ or rural school districts and into the cities and wealthier districts. Rural blacks won their political rights and lost promised school funding, equal educational opportunity, and any real chance for the economic development of the communities over which they came to exercise political control.

The 1966 election demonstrated the political success of the Wallace demagoguery. The electorate was offered a choice between a continued loud, destructive, and fruitless defense of segregation on the one hand and moderation in several forms on the other. Ryan de Graffenried, the leading moderate candidate, was killed in an accident, and the focus he might have provided was dissipated. But he probably would have lost regardless. Most of the candidates were well known and relatively able leaders, and the electorate made a clear decision. Voters elected Lurleen Wallace by a landslide, and they eliminated the small number of Wallace legislative opponents with sufficient nerve to run for reelection after they dared to block George Wallace's immediate succession.

In Lurleen Wallace's term the legislature was even friendlier to George Wallace than it had been when he was officially governor. He strongly skewed committee appointments in favor of rural interests, effectively dulling the impact of reapportionment and aiding the new Black Belt–rural county partnership. George Wallace's actions extended the power of the more reactionary elements of the old alliance years beyond what otherwise could have been expected.

Upon succeeding to the governorship, Albert Brewer gave the legislature and the electorate a taste of what could be accomplished by someone interested in the state's welfare. That the previously Wallace-dominated legislature responded to Brewer's leadership as positively as it did suggests that perhaps some were beginning to bridle at Wallace's reactionary policies. Albert Brewer enjoyed the support of the most growth-oriented elements in and out of the alliance, but that was not enough to counter Wallace-spawned emotion. That Brewer came as close as he did to defeating Wallace in 1970 indicates that almost one-half of the electorate might have been tiring of Wallace or the image of Alabama that his actions helped to create, but almost half was not enough.

The alliance partnership ended because the world around it changed and because of federal court action, but its components remained. The planters were now joined by the rural counties. The forces favoring continued racial discrimination and opposing school improvement and tax reform remained strong. The alliance's objectives continued to be realized. The only difference was that day-to-day coalition building required more effort and the future appeared less and less certain.

In 1978 Wallace could not succeed himself because the constitution now permitted only two successive terms. In that year the victor was Democrat Forrest "Fob" James, a sporting goods manufacturer who had never held public office and who campaigned on the standard businessman–political outsider platform of bringing businesslike practices to state government. James's manufacturing experience did not prepare him well for interacting with experienced legislators loyal to Wallace or representing remnants of the antigrowth alliance. Aside from administrative improvements in the executive branch, his term was marked by frustration—his own and the electorate's. He wisely chose not to seek a second term in 1982.

The Wallace terms in the 1970s and the James administration saw the rising influence in the legislature of two new groups, the Alabama Education Association and blacks, who often worked together. The AEA predated this period, but under the leadership of Paul Hubbert and Joe Reed, the former head of the black teachers' organization and head of the black Alabama Democratic Conference, its power grew substantially.

Despite their considerable number and progressive public images, blacks and the AEA had little positive effect on the direction of state politics, partly because their leaders were almost as devoid of a progressive vision as alliance members or George Wallace. Once they assumed power, black leaders, whose considerable political skills had been honed fighting an entrenched power structure, did little but emulate the worst tendencies of those they had opposed. And, as the quality of public schools declined, the AEA and its black allies fought virtually every proposal for educational improvement except teacher salary increases and school building construction.

Alabama's stupor continued with yet another Wallace term (1983–87). He did not seek reelection because of the physical infirmities that plagued him after the assassination attempt against him.

In 1986 an especially uncivil Democratic primary battle between Bill Baxley (the Wallace-AEA-black candidate) and Charlie Graddick (who advocated law and order and represented bits and pieces of the alliance) accidentally resulted in a general election victory for Republican Guy Hunt, a perennial candidate largely unknown to the electorate who secured the nomination because no one else wanted it. Hunt proved to be little different from his Democratic predecessors. He represented old rural alliance groups together with increasing numbers of retirees attracted to Alabama by low property taxes, and he had little interest in developing the state. He was reelected in 1990 when he defeated AEA's Paul Hubbert in his first bid for statewide public office.

Hunt was removed from office in 1993 when he was found guilty of violating state law by converting inaugural funds to private use and was replaced by Lieutenant Governor James E. Folsom Jr. Hunt, like his predecessors, left the state little different from the way he found it.

The Civil Rights Lag

The most serious de facto civil-rights lag present in 1970 and persisting in Alabama and throughout most of the nation today is educational discrimination. Once de jure school segregation was eliminated, the major cause of de facto segregation and discrimination was housing patterns created by racial discrimination and economic disparities. In many instances the effect of segregated housing patterns on school integration could be diminished by readjusting school district lines without doing violence to neighborhood schools. But such changes left many predominantly white or black schools still operating.

In the late 1960s and early 1970s conservatives and some moderates believed that for the short term nothing more could be done to alleviate the remaining school segregation. In the long run, they felt that the elimination of racially based economic disparities would bring blacks into more affluent neighborhoods and school segregation would diminish.

Civil rights leaders and liberals, still enjoying their victories over de jure segregation and made overconfident by that success, were not satisfied with gradual economic-geographic desegregation. They demanded mandatory desegregation, often via forced busing. They dismissed the virtues of neighborhood schools and parental worries about sending children long distances into unfamiliar neighborhoods.

Mandatory desegregation often drove relatively affluent whites out of cities and counties with large black populations, or encouraged them to place their children in private schools. White flight, as it came to be known, reduced the urban tax base and eroded much-needed political support for schools. In fact, tax referenda for schools came to be voted down with increasing frequency through the 1970s. It would be difficult to prove a causal relationship between white flight and private school growth on the one hand and a reduction in support for schools on the other, but this result was widely predicted. The social and educational effects of the elimination of many neighborhood schools would be even less easily calculated, but many believe the losses to be severe. George Wallace's facilitation of white flight by using the governor's office to encourage and assist the development of white academies may have been his only anti–civil rights program that really damaged the civil rights movement rather than helping it.

Blacks had been enslaved or repressed in Alabama and the rest of the South for well over a century. It is noteworthy that their political liberation was as rapid (once the national community decided to act) and nonviolent as it was. This was due partly to the strategic skill of civil rights leaders and the quickness and decisiveness with which federal and some state and local law enforcement officials moved against those who perpetrated violence. It also resulted from the civil rights leaders' basic respect for the American system of laws.

Blacks claimed their rights as specified in the U.S. Constitution. Segregationists were violating those rights and corroding the American system of laws. The civil rights movement held the moral high ground. When the civil rights movement departed from traditional notions of common sense and equality before the law and began advocacy of mandatory school desegregation via busing and affirmative action, its support base and strength began to decline.

Urban-Rural and Regional Lags

The most important urban-rural lag was legislative malapportionment. All state legislatures were malapportioned when the United States Supreme Court ruled malapportionment unconstitutional, but in Alabama the discrimination against cities was committed by *urban* interests in partnership with the Black Belt leadership. This alliance also discriminated against non–Black Belt rural areas.

Malapportionment was at the heart of the alliance's power, but national political forces and state-level demographic and economic factors would have ended it even if the Supreme Court had not done so. The 1965 Voting Rights Act would probably have brought reapportionment to Alabama by ending the possibility of cooperation between newly elected black legislators from the Black Belt and urban Big Mules. Even without rural black votes, strains produced by the shrinkage of the Black Belt and urban expansion would have ended malapportionment, but that would probably have taken many years.

The allocation of state government dollars fit the malapportionment of the legislature. It was universally predicted that a correctly apportioned legislature would have urban forces claiming their fair share of school, road, and other funds. Since this meant that all rural areas would lose money, it was also predictable that a new conflict pivot would define legislative politics. Formerly, it was alliance counties versus the rest. Many of "the rest" were in north Alabama and a few were in the extreme south. After reapportionment a new urban-rural division formed with medium-sized counties sometimes attempting to exact tribute by siding with one group or the other. Thus Alabama shifted from its unusual system of an elite urban-rural partnership to the pattern of urban-versus-rural conflict found in most states with large cities, such as neighboring Georgia.

Ultimately, advocates of reapportionment pushed their position to imprudent extemes. They wanted mathematical equality among districts that cut coherent political communities into pieces and created legislative districts that jumbled together dissimilar interests. And because the size of the legislative bodies remained unchanged, lower population areas were placed into ever larger districts. Many of those interviewed for this book volunteered the observation that this jumbling has had a strong negative effect on the quality of legislative decision-making. They argued that a county's political culture allowed easier assessment of a constituency's preferences and easier analysis of a legislator's actions. They further argued that as a result of redistricting based on mathematical formulas, many legislators no longer represent their communities, for they have no identifiable community. Rather, they sell themselves to congeries of well-funded interest groups, often on an issue-by-issue basis.

Initially, reapportionment had little impact on the nature of public policy. This was partially the result of George Wallace's strong rear-guard action against change. Throughout the 1960s, he served as a broker between rural and urban interests and gave urban areas less than they wanted or deserved according to strict one-person-one-vote or per capita funding standards.

Wallace's natural constituents were rural. His home county was rural, and his racist-reactionary platforms of the 1960s and early 1970s appealed more to rural than urban mentalities, although there are many exceptions to this observation both in the form of populists in northern and extreme southern rural counties and segregationists in the cities.

The urban Big Mules were not suddenly overcome with revelations of racial moderation and high tech progress. Their first two reapportioned legislative delegations were little more than enlarged versions of the small pre-reapportionment ones. Most of the legislators were either Big Mules in their own right or, more commonly, their employees. Another reapportionment and three more elections were required before the diverse interests of Jefferson County were represented by their delegation in anything approaching their true proportions.

In later years, with legislatures reapportioned still further on a population basis, the distribution of state resources came to favor cities even more. Ironically, just as voting power came to the black voters in Black Belt counties in the 1960s, reapportionment took away Black Belt legislative seats. Reapportionment shifts helped to cheat many black children out of equal educational opportunity.

In 1993 Circuit Judge Eugene Reese ruled that the state had failed to provide all students with an adequate education as guaranteed by the Alabama constitution. It is a noteworthy sign of progress that this decision came from a state court, not a federal court. A major actor in the filing of the suit was one of the legislative swing voters discussed in this book— C. C. "Bo" Torbert. Torbert went from the legislature to become chief justice of the Alabama Supreme Court and upon retirement from that body, early in this decade headed a blue-ribbon task force to study the tax system and make recommendations for overhauling it. Despite considerable lobbying on his part, the reform proposals were never adopted. One of the major sticking points was increased taxation of rural land, especially timber. It remains typical of the Alabama legislature that when faced with an especially important decision, the lawmakers abandoned their responsibilities to the judicial branch.

Reese's order called for funding equalization among schools and changes in the educational system. In 1994 Governor James E. Folsom Jr. proposed legislation that responded to Reese's order. Ryan de Graffenried Jr., president pro tempore of the Senate and acting lieutenant governor, shepherded the Folsom plan through the Senate with the key assistance of Senator Fred Horn of Birmingham, a black leader. A grouping of Alfa (the old Farm Bureau Federation), the reactionary Eagle Forum, some (but not all) business leaders, some Republicans, and the Alabama Education Association (AEA) successfully blocked Folsom's reform bill from reaching the house floor.

Many liberals expressed surprise to find the AEA in the company of classic enemies of education, but we have seen that in joining with the fragments of the Big Mule Alliance, the AEA was following an old pattern. (We predicted the reestablishment of this pattern before the start of the 1994 legislative session.)[2] In this instance, the AEA appeared to be hoping that when Judge Reese or a successor responds to the legislature's inaction, he will order tax increases to support teacher pay raises without burdening the education establishment with the responsibility to improve what occurs in the classroom or bothering teachers and school administrators with parental input, both of which were included in the Folsom plan. Economic interests are gambling that no elected state judge will order tax increases. The Eagle Forum's opposition focuses on control of curriculum content.

The Lack of Party Competition

Alabama barely moved toward two-party competition in the years 1958–70, and since. Republicans enjoyed a significant victory in congressional races in 1964 because of Barry Goldwater's strong showing in the state, but George Wallace's popularity prevented the party from capitalizing on that win. In the 1970s, while the national Democratic party demonstrated a strong commitment to mandatory integration, Wallace continued to provide a release for segregationist sentiment that was sufficient to short-circuit Republican growth. John Grenier, James Martin, and other Republican leaders of the 1960s and 1970s devoted themselves to opposing one another more than the Democrats. Many party members were either satisfied with their continued receipt of Republican patronage or happy to see Alabama voting Republican in presidential and congressional races and for George Wallace for governor.

The Republican party's second great opportunity, Guy Hunt's accidental election as governor, provided the party with little advantage. Hunt, like other Republicans, was not very interested in differentiating the GOP from the Democratic party of George Wallace and the old alliance.

Despite the poverty of Hunt's leadership, the growing strength of the liberal-black wing of the Democratic party appeared to drive some conservative Democrats slowly to the Republican party, producing a small increase in the numbers of legislative positions and local offices being sought by Republican candidates. For example, in 1958 no Republicans served in the state legislature. In 1964 there were no Republicans in the Senate, and the House was less than 5 percent Republican. Both House and Senate Republican membership passed the 10 percent mark by the early 1980s, 20 percent in 1990, and 30 percent in 1994.

The 1994 general election campaign for governor pitted Governor James E. Folsom Jr. against the former governor Fob James, a Democrat turned Republican turned Democrat turned Republican. One might argue that since James turned Democrat to run in 1978 to have a chance of winning, that his 1994 switch back to the GOP is an indicator that the Republican party is now a viable minority party and Alabama a true two-party state.

We believe that James's most recent incarnation as a Republican is not an indicator of either. James ran as a Republican because he could not win the Democratic nomination. He had lost two previous attempts to do so. And since the 1990 election, Jim Folsom Jr. and Paul Hubbert were expected to be the major Democratic candidates for nomination. Governor Hunt's removal from office enhanced Folsom's stature. James shopped for a party in 1994 as he had in 1978. In addition, both he and his runoff opponent openly appealed to Democratic voters to cross over and vote in the Republican runoff even if they had voted in the Democratic primary. The political focal point remained candidate-centered and issue-centered, not party-centered.

James's opponent in the runoff was Ann Bedsole, a state senator from Mobile. Bedsole was the first woman since Lurleen Wallace to make a serious bid for the governorship. She ran on a prochoice and pro–educational reform position. Primary opponents Winton Blount III (an early advocate of education reform and son of Eisenhower's postmaster general) and the Reverend Mickey Kirkland (an antiabortion, anti–educational reform candidate) endorsed James in the runoff.

The Folsom-James campaign centered on the issues of educational reform, tax reform, and economic development, with each candidate basically taking the issue positions espoused in their nomination races. Folsom ran on the promise of improving educational quality and equity and the need to carry out Judge Reese's court order. He argued that overhaul of the state tax laws is necessary if this was to be accomplished. He also ran on his record of bringing a large Mercedes-Benz manufacturing plant to the state. He pointed to his advocacy of educational reform as well as support in this area from key state decision makers such as Ryan de Graffenried Jr. as one of the reasons the manufacturing company selected the state over other contenders.

Fob James promised a back to basics approach to education with no new taxes. He also ran against Judge Reese's order and promised an appeal of the decision if elected. For James, harder-working teachers and state employees would solve many of the problems facing the state. The interest groups behind James were many of the opponents of Folsom's education reform plan, including Alfa, the Christian right, and segments of the business community. James also inherited many of George Wallace's supporters.

Folsom's nomination occurred without a runoff election as he defeated Paul Hubbert, who had run unsuccessfully against Guy Hunt in 1990. Hubbert, identified in the public's mind as the urban-based leader of the party's liberal wing, an effective lobbyist, and a close political ally of the black leader Joe Reed, attempted to project a conservative image and emphasize his rural origins. He failed in the attempt, in part because Reed was unable to deliver the black vote.

After his defeat Hubbert agreed to support the full Democratic ticket, but in doing so he never endorsed Folsom by name. He refused to utter the governor's name even in the face of repeated questioning by reporters. Hubbert and his AEA colleagues supported the Folsom candidacy only minimally. And Hubbert indicated publicly that it was time for him and AEA to work more closely with Republican lawmakers, many of whom had joined AEA and the Eagle Forum to block the Folsom education reform package.

Folsom's election campaign was damaged by scandals involving a string of disreputable associates who held embarrassing press conferences, charges of bribery, and a family vacation in the Cayman Islands using the private plane of a gambling magnate. Folsom's responses were to deny everything except the vacation, run professionally produced but vacuous television advertisements, refuse media requests for interviews, and decline his opponent's challenge to public debate.

Fob James's campaign was a rocky affair hampered by funding shortages and, until the last few weeks, a lack of imagination. James had the advantages of a clean reputation and faded memories of his term in office (1979–83), and he was relatively open to media interviews, even though he revealed little about himself or his future policies in those sessions. His apparent openness was accentuated by a series of live statewide call-in radio programs run in the last few weeks before the election. James and many Republican legislative candidates were pushed along by the national Republican sweep that brought GOP majorities to power in both Houses of Congress for the first time in four decades.

Alabama Republicans did not experience success comparable to that enjoyed by their counterparts in many other states. Despite Folsom's many ethical and tactical mistakes, James won by less than one percentage point. Liberal Democrat Don Siegelman, the newly elected lieutenant governor, won by twenty-four percentage points, and the Democratic secretary of state was easily reelected. The state auditor's race was won by a Republican, but the victory was aided by serious questions about the Democratic nominee's work record and by the memory of the racially oriented primary and runoff campaigns he had run. The outcomes of the treasurer's and chief justice's races were so close that the results depended upon how absentee votes were counted. The results remained unknown for months as a dispute over the counting worked its way through state and federal courts.

None of the four Democratic congressmen lost their seats, and three won in excess of 60 percent of the vote. And although the Republicans gained seats in the state legislature, they still constitute a minority.

After years of fighting among themselves and alienating large segments of the electorate, Alabama Republicans seemed unprepared to run a campaign actually designed to attract votes beyond the level of governor. This was not surprising, because much of the 1994 Republican leadership and many of the 1994 Republican statewide candidates had been occupying the political landscape since the 1960s. Experience is not the best teacher if it consists of making the same mistakes repeatedly and focuses on returning to the past rather than looking to the future. Still, the Republican party's strength is growing, and the Democratic party is no longer the instrument of elite dominance. There is reason to believe that Alabama may some day be a true two-party competitive state.

Unfair Tax Structures

Alabama's regressive tax structure (especially the light burdens placed on rural landowners) changed little in the years 1958–70. John Patterson advocated progressive taxes, and he made a valiant effort to reform discriminatory property taxes, but the alliance, sometimes in concert with the AEA, deflected his most serious efforts. George Wallace had no interest in tax reform, partly because it would have alienated his Black Belt and agricultural backers.

Albert Brewer pushed for a strong property tax reform statute, and his other tax proposals were progressive. Relying on urban support, he succeeded in maneuvering most of his bills past entrenched but outnumbered rural opponents. His central property tax bill contained a provision that penalized counties that underassessed property compared to a state norm by reducing state aid they received. This feature would have gone into effect in 1971, and in the medium and long term it might have benefited rural schools, but the state superintendent of schools, frightened of the law's short-term impact, asked Attorney General Baxley to review the statute to stop its enforcement. The attorney general issued an official opinion that declared the law unconstitutional because it denied school children in poorer districts due process and equal protection under the Fourteenth Amendment of the United States Constitution. A federal court later affirmed this position.

The tax reform plan pushed by Folsom in the 1994 education reform battle contained elements very similar to those advocated in the 1950s, '60s and '70s. They in turn are similar to many tax reform positions taken by the Torbert-led blue-ribbon commission just a few years before.

Economic and Educational Gaps

The alliance and later some of its components surfed on a southern economic growth wave while doing little to take advantage of that growth to push the state further along. The southern economic development in which Alabama shared can easily be traced back to 1930. From that year to 1980, Alabama's per capita income climbed from 41.8 percent to 78.3 percent of U.S. per capita personal income. Throughout this period Alabama moved toward the national average, never meeting or exceeding it. Beginning in 1980, this trend was interrupted and either leveled or reversed, depending on which data are examined. Other indicators of economic well-being present an even less optimistic view.

Under John Patterson the percentage growth of manufacturing payrolls, a direct measure of a state's addition to its manufacturing activity, was lower than the averages for the east south central states, the United States, and the state of Georgia. By another such measure (percentage growth in manufacturing value added), Alabama exceeded the U.S. and east south central averages but was substantially below Georgia, a state frequently used for comparison by those interested in promoting Alabama's growth. (Of course, Mississippi is used by those wishing to excuse Alabama's lack of growth.)

The increase in manufacturing payrolls and value added in the Wallace years was also mediocre. Alabama's performance was greater than the U.S. average but fell below the east south central average and below Georgia on both measures. In the Lurleen Wallace–Albert Brewer years, Alabama's percentage growth in manufacturing payrolls was greater than the national average, equal to Georgia, and less than the east south central average. In terms of manufacturing value added, Alabama exceeded the national average but fell substantially below the east south central average and Georgia. In the following years Alabama's performance by these measures was never outstanding.

The most important determinants of economic growth are traditional business factors such as energy cost and availability, labor cost, land cost and availability, climate, and proximity to markets. State government can do little or nothing to affect many of these ingredients, but some state policies can attract new business and business growth. For example, in 1953

Alabama passed a right-to-work law, weakening labor unions compared to their northeastern counterparts. This change drew some industries to Alabama.

Another way to attract industry is to maintain low taxes, and Alabama has done so relative to many other states. However, low taxes are accompanied by relatively low expenditures on schools, infrastructure, public health, and other programs that can attract higher-profit businesses with better-paying jobs. Relatively high taxes do not repel high-profit businesses if the resulting revenues are efficiently and effectively spent. We are far from the first to observe that Alabama from the 1950s to the present followed a policy of attracting low-tech, low-pay industries. This policy, combined with market forces described earlier, produced healthy-looking economic growth rates until the 1980s.

Alabama never met the national average, let alone exceeded it, by any important economic growth measures. Furthermore, by selecting the low-tech, low-pay path Alabama was set farther behind. In the 1980s foreign competition won many of the jobs created that way, and the state was left with inadequate tools for attracting profitable industries. This is one more way that alliance policies of decades past continue to affect the current quality of life in Alabama. The Mercedes-Benz plant represents the first large-scale, high-tech venture successfully recruited to the state. It has been described by one economist as the opportunity of a generation, comparable in importance to the location of the NASA facility in Huntsville. And yet, segments of the old alliance and of Fob James's 1994 election coalition seek to undo portions of the legislation that made the plant siting in Alabama possible.

In the period 1958–70 only two Alabama-based institutions became truly first-rate by national and world standards, the Huntsville NASA facility and the medical complex of the University of Alabama at Birmingham (UAB). The first was entirely a federal operation. It just happened to be located in Alabama partly because of the presence in Huntsville of an Army base. A large majority of the significant developments in UAB's history derived from the federal government, with state and local government either playing a minimally supportive role or acting as a barrier to growth. Senator Lister Hill cosponsored the Hill-Ferguson and Hill-Burton Acts, which supplied the growing medical school with the massive funding it required. Congressman Carl Elliott was also highly supportive. The National Institutes of Health, which received strong appropriations support from Hill, were major sources of research grants for UAB. Assistance from private foundations also helped. The Department of Health, Education and Welfare contributed significantly to UAB's development by facilitating land condemnation and thus permitting UAB's growth. This effort, which involved the clearance of badly deteriorated structures, had the city government's support. Meanwhile, George Wallace diluted the outstanding UAB effort by adding a little-needed medical school in Mobile. He planned to place others in Dothan, Huntsville, Selma, and other cities, somewhat in the manner he had constructed junior colleges and technical schools, but others finally persuaded him that the state could not support them.

Responsive Government in Alabama

Most of the positive changes in Alabama since the 1930s have come from the federal government or market forces operating nationwide. The many federal interventions signaled a bankruptcy in Alabama state government leadership. There were exceptions—Folsom Sr. and Patterson occasionally, and Brewer most of the time. The voters have not elected a constructive and effective leader as governor since. Making matters worse, most of the positive actions taken by Folsom, Patterson, and Brewer were crushed by the alliance or its remnants.

Most of today's inheritors of the alliance's legacy are frozen in time, playing roles they fell into decades ago. Agricultural and many other rural forces remain hostile to economic and educational development and work to maintain utterly unwarranted preferential tax treatment. The Alabama Education Association still focuses almost exclusively on its members' salary concerns rather than educational quality and accountability. The state's two leading black organizations are run by civil rights–era figures (AEA's Joe Reed on one side and Birmingham's Mayor Richard Arrington on the other) whose skill as revolutionaries has not translated into an ability to govern constructively. They supported George Wallace in his last electoral bid, but in many ways they are still fighting his political ghost while emulating his worst tendencies of smallmindedness. The Republican party too remains little different from what it was in the 1960s. Jim Martin, the GOP's major standard bearer of the 1960s, was still pursuing state office in 1994.

A few corporate leaders of both parties appear to recognize, if belatedly and reluctantly, that they can no longer rely on regional economic growth to push the state along, and that synthetic incentives such as property tax breaks will attract few worthwhile new businesses and often provide unproductive subsidies for those that would have located in Alabama without such aid. The large Mercedes-Benz plant may be an exception.

Regional momentum or gimmicks will not provide an improved quality of life for Alabamians. As more in the business community have moved their companies into the service and technology sectors, they have recognized the need for a competently trained work force. With more of these business leaders born and brought up and to some extent educated in Alabama they recognize the need for educational reform and are speaking out on its behalf. But this recognition may have come too late.

Alabama will develop best and fastest if direct attention is paid to strengthening its basic institutions and infrastructure. Such an effort will require a form of leadership all too lacking in recent Alabama history.

Appendix

Applying Interrupted Time Series Analysis

Much of the discussion in chapter 10 of George Wallace's impact on education spending is based on a technique called interrupted time series analysis. An informal approach to this technique compares regression trend lines (for example, for teacher salary data) before and after an event the analyst deems important, such as George Wallace's first term in office (fig. A.1).

If the two trend lines touch to form a single uninterrupted continuous line, as the lines in figure A.1 almost do, the conclusion that the event had no impact is supported but not proven. The conclusion is not proven by the analysis because Wallace might, for example, have been fighting against deteriorating economic conditions that would have caused a decline in spending on teachers' salaries without his intervention.

If the second trend line jumps abruptly, as it does in figure A.2, the analysis suggests a one-time impact. Again, such analysis cannot prove cause and effect. This example merely provides support for the conclusion that an event such as Wallace's first term in office had an impact on spending for teachers' salaries.

The only difference between these graphs is that the second trend line pictured in figure A.2 is calculated for the years 1963–84 and the second trend line in figure A.1 is calculated for 1963–74. The former suggests a one-time Wallace impact that produced abrupt increases in salaries but a sag in the rate of growth thereafter.[1] The lower slope for the 1963–84 data is due to the sharp drop in salaries that begins in 1975. One might argue that it would be fairer to Wallace to calculate the right trend line by stopping at 1974 (he was governor again from 1971 to 1975 and from 1975 to 1979) instead of a decade later. The result, shown in figure A.1, is less flattering to Wallace than might be guessed. The 1963–74 trend line starts below the 1950–62 line, but it has a higher slope.[2] An analysis examining per-pupil expenditures in constant or inflation-adjusted dollars shows a similar pat-

Figure A.1

Alabama Teacher Salaries
Trend Lines, 1950–62 and 1963–74

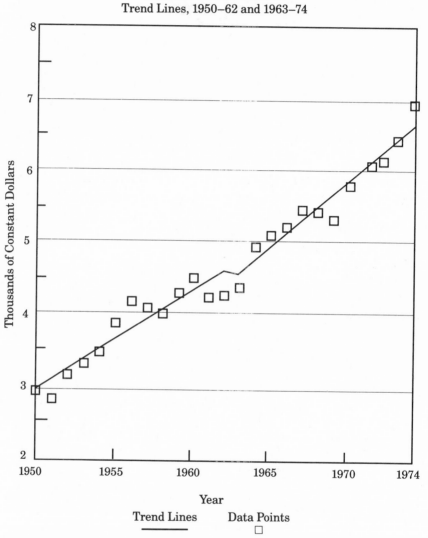

Year

Trend Lines   Data Points
                        □

tern (fig. A.3). These data suggest a somewhat stronger Wallace influence than do teacher salaries.

Our analysis follows procedures Susan Welch and John Comer describe for a rigorous version of interrupted time series analysis based on multiple regression analysis.[3] In figure A.2 the dependent variable is Alabama

Figure A.2

Alabama Teacher Salaries
Trend Lines, 1950–62 and 1963–84

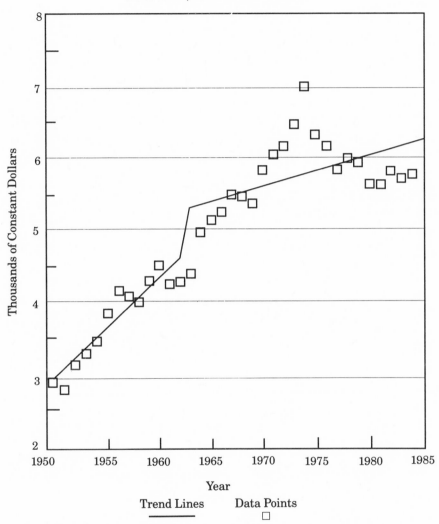

Teacher Salaries in thousands of constant dollars. The independent variables are Time, D, and P. Time runs from 1 through 35, representing the years 1950–84.

D is a dummy variable that has the value of 0 for the years 1950–62 (time periods 1–13 or the pre-Wallace years) and 1 for all years 1963 and

Figure A.3

Per-Pupil School Expenditures
Trend Lines, 1950–62 and 1963–84

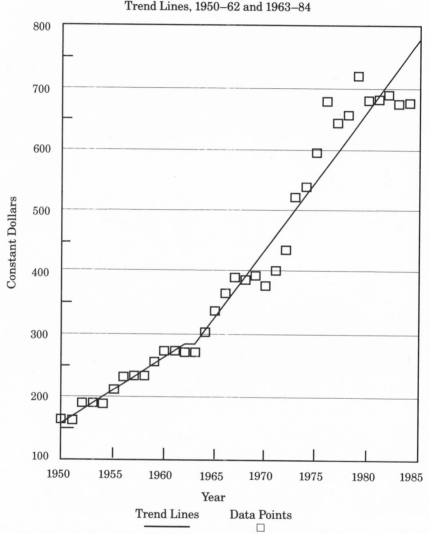

later. If a significant relationship exists between Teacher Salaries and D, there is a suggestion that Wallace's first term produced an abrupt change in teacher salaries.

P is another dummy variable, called a post–policy intervention counter variable. Like D, P takes on the value of 0 until Wallace's first term. Unlike D, however, P increases by 1 in each successive year. Thus, P takes

Table A.1
Interrupted Time Series Analysis for Figure A.2
Alabama Teacher Salaries, 1950–62 and 1963–84

Dependent Variable: Teacher Salaries
Number of Cases: 35
Multiple R: 0.934
Squared Multiple R: 0.873
Adjusted Squared Multiple R: 0.860
Standard Error of Estimate: 0.414

Variable	Regression Coefficient	Standard Error	Standardized Coefficient	T Value	Probability (Two-Tail)
CONSTANT	2.816	0.244	0.000	11.564	0.000
TIME	0.139	0.031	1.284	4.520	0.000
D	0.651	0.284	0.288	2.295	0.029
P	−0.097	0.034	−0.669	−2.890	0.007

Analysis of Variance

Source	Sum-of-Squares	Degrees of Freedom	Mean Squared	F Ratio	Probability Level
REGRESSION	36.354	3	12.118	70.717	0.000
RESIDUALS	5.312	31	0.171		

on the value of 1 in 1963, 2 in 1964, and so on. There will be a significant relationship between P and Teacher Salaries if long-term change occurs after Wallace took office. If Wallace had both an abrupt and a long-term impact on the dependent variable, we would expect to find a significant relationship between Teacher Salaries and both D and P.

The magnitude of the correlation between each independent variable and Teacher Salaries can be found by examining the regression coefficients and the standardized coefficients (also known as betas) generated by regression analysis. The sign of the coefficients will indicate whether the variables vary directly (move in the same direction) or inversely (move in opposite directions). To be statistically significant at the .05 level, the probability figure associated with the coefficients should be .05 or less. Statistical significance at the .01 level would require the figure to be .01 or less.

The statistical results generated by the regression analysis associated with figure A.2 are presented in table A.1. The relatively large and statistically significant coefficients and standardized coefficients for both D and P

Table A.2
Interrupted Time Series Analysis for Figure A.1
Alabama Teacher Salaries, 1950–62 and 1963–74

Dependent Variable: Teacher Salaries
Number of Cases: 25
Multiple R: 0.985
Squared Multiple R: 0.970
Adjusted Squared Multiple R: 0.966
Standard Error of Estimate: 0.209

Variable	Regression Coefficient	Standard Error	Standardized Coefficient	T Value	Probability (Two-Tail)
CONSTANT	2.816	0.123	0.000	22.946	0.000
TIME	0.139	0.015	0.900	8.969	0.000
D	−0.212	0.169	−0.096	−0.126	0.222
P	0.050	0.023	0.183	2.162	0.042

Analysis of Variance

Source	Sum-of-Squares	Degrees of Freedom	Mean Squared	F Ratio	Probability Level
REGRESSION	29.944	3	9.981	229.332	0.000
RESIDUALS	0.914	21	0.044		

suggest that for this data set Wallace had both an abrupt impact and a long-term effect. The fact that the D coefficients are positive and the P coefficients are negative shows what is apparent in the visual examination of figure A.2—his one-time impact was direct, but his long-term effect was negative or inverse.

Table A.2 presents the data associated with figure A.1. In both the table and figure, the time frame covered for judging impact has been reduced to the period 1963–74. This eliminates the somewhat erratic figures that appear after 1974. D, the dummy variable that signifies a one-time impact, fails the test of statistical significance and therefore suggests no one-time Wallace impact. The correlation coefficients are negative, suggesting a negative Wallace impact. P, the dummy variable that signifies a long-term effect, barely passes the 5 percent test of statistical significance. The small but positive value of the P coefficients suggest that Wallace had a slight long-term effect on the level of Teacher Salaries.

Table A.3
Interrupted Time Series Analysis for Figure A.3
Per-Pupil School Expenditures, 1950–62 and 1963–84

Dependent Variable: Per-Pupil Expenditures
Number of Cases: 35
Multiple R: 0.981
Squared Multiple R: 0.963
Adjusted Squared Multiple R: 0.960
Standard Error of Estimate: 0.914

Variable	Regression Coefficient	Standard Error	Standardized Coefficient	T Value	Probability (Two-Tail)
CONSTANT	149.589	22.307	0.000	6.706	0.000
TIME	10.499	2.810	0.569	3.736	0.001
D	−25.662	25.980	−0.067	−0.988	0.331
P	11.848	3.086	0.477	8.840	0.001

Analysis of Variance

Source	Sum-of-Squares	Degrees of Freedom	Mean Squared	F Ratio	Probability Level
REGRESSION	1170085	3	390028	271.326	0.000
RESIDUALS	44562	31	1437		

Applying rigorous interrupted time series analysis to per-pupil expenditures (table A.3) once again confirms what a visual examination of the regression plot in figure A.3 reveals. Wallace's one-time impact fails the test of statistical significance, but the analysis suggests that his long-term impact was substantial and in a positive direction.

Notes

Introduction

1. The development of this elite is discussed more thoroughly in Carl Grafton and Anne Permaloff, *Big Mules and Branchheads: James E. Folsom and Political Power in Alabama* (Athens: University of Georgia Press, 1985).

2. This follows David B. Truman's definition of an interest group as a number of people with a shared attitude who make claims on other groups. An interest group becomes a political interest group when it makes demands on government. Government, which itself consists of a multiplicity of interest groups, combines and compromises these forces and produces public policy. See *The Governmental Process* (New York: Alfred A. Knopf, 1951), 33–39.

3. See Numan V. Bartley, *The Rise of Massive Resistance* (Baton Rouge: Louisiana State University Press, 1969).

Chapter 1. Lags and Gaps in Recent Alabama History

1. Andrew C. McLaughlin, "Mississippi and the Negro Question," *Atlantic Monthly,* December 1892, 828–37.

2. C. Vann Woodward, *The Strange Career of Jim Crow,* 2d ed. (New York: Oxford University Press, 1957), 52–53.

3. Jerome Dowd, "Paths of Hope for the Negro," *Century Magazine* 61 (November 1900–April 1901): 279.

4. Francis A. Walker, "Restriction of Immigration," *Atlantic Monthly,* June 1896, 828.

5. John Hope Franklin, *From Slavery to Freedom: A History of Negro Americans,* 4th ed. (New York: Alfred A. Knopf, 1947, 1974), 323–24.

6. Ibid., 324–25. Also see Richard Young, "The Brownsville Affray," *American History Illustrated,* October 1986, 10–17.

7. Woodward, *Jim Crow,* 77.

8. Franklin, *From Slavery to Freedom,* 334.

9. Ibid., 334–35.

10. Ibid., *From Slavery to Freedom,* 480–83.

11. Thomas F. Gossett, *Race: The History of an Idea in America* (Dallas: Southern Methodist University Press, 1963), 372.

12. Ibid., 377–78.

13. Ibid., 385–86.

14. Henry Osborn, "Address of Welcome to the Second International Congress of Eugenics," New York, September 22–28, 1921. In *The Alien in Our Midst,* ed. Madison Grant (New York: Galton, 1930), 204.

15. Gossett, *Race,* 386.

16. Calvin Coolidge, "Whose Country Is This?" *Good Housekeeping,* February 1921, 14.

17. James J. Davis, *Iron Puddler: My Life in the Rolling Mills and What Came of It* (New York: Bobbs, 1922), 28, 61.

18. *Birth Control Review,* May 1919, 12, quoted in *Birth Control in America,* by David M. Kennedy (New Haven: Yale University Press, 1970), 115. For more examples of Progressive thought of a similar nature, see 113–26.

19. Michael Newton and Judy Ann Newton, *The Ku Klux Klan: An Encyclopedia* (New York: Garland, 1991), ix–x, 18–24, and 187.

20. Harvard Sitkoff, *A New Deal for Blacks: The Emergence of Civil Rights as a National Issue* (New York: Oxford University Press, 1978), 1:190–93.

21. Ibid., 193–94.

22. Philip Perlmutter, *Divided We Fall: A History of Ethnic, Religious, and Racial Prejudice in America* (Ames: Iowa State University Press, 1992), 217.

23. Franklin, *From Slavery to Freedom,* 395.

24. Newton and Newton, *The Ku Klux Klan,* x.

25. A recent history of the American and British anti-racism movements argues that the inclusion into the scientific community of outsiders (women, Jews, and leftists) facilitated the debate and the success of the movement. See Elazar Barkan, *The Retreat of Scientific Racism: Changing Concepts of Race in Britain and the United States Between the World Wars* (Cambridge: Cambridge University Press, 1992).

26. Sitkoff, *New Deal for Blacks,* 268–81.

27. Ibid., 281–82.

28. Woodward, *Jim Crow,* 105.

29. Bernard Barber, *Social Stratification* (New York: Harcourt, Brace, 1957), 501–2.

30. Ernest W. Burgess, "The Family in a Changing Society," in *Social Change,* ed. Eva Etzioni-Halevy and Amitai Etzioni (New York: Basic Books, 1973), 193, 191–92, 192.

31. Frederick W. Taylor, *Scientific Management* (New York: Harper and Row, 1911), 44–46.

32. Jeffrey D. Straussman, *Public Administration* (New York: Longman, 1990), 68–71.

33. Peter Blau and Marshall W. Meyer, *Bureaucracy in Modern Society* (New York: Random House, 1956), 133–46.

34. Melvin Kranzberg and Joseph Gies, *By the Sweat of Thy Brow* (New York: G. P. Putnam's Sons, 1975), 197–204.

35. Grafton and Permaloff, *Big Mules and Branchheads,* 53–55.

36. Arthur F. Bentley, *The Process of Government* (Cambridge: Harvard University Press, Belknap Press, 1967); Truman, *The Governmental Process.*

37. Truman, *The Governmental Process,* 520.

38. Ibid., 521.

39. David Easton, "An Approach to the Study of Political Systems," *World Politics* 9 (April 1957): 383–400. The political system is defined as the realm of authoritative allocation of values for a society.

40. Ervin Laszlo, *Introduction to Systems Philosophy* (New York: Gordon and Breach, 1972), 105.

41. Kenneth Prewitt and Alan Stone, *The Ruling Elites* (New York: Harper and Row, 1973), 163. They credit this idea to Vilfredo Pareto and Gaetano Mosca.

42. U.S. Commission on Civil Rights, *Voting,* 1961 Commission on Civil Rights Report, Bk. 1 (Washington, D.C.: Government Printing Office, 1961), 26 and 342–43.

43. Thomas R. Dye, *Politics, Economics, and the Public* (Chicago: Rand McNally, 1966), 63–64.

44. Philip H. Burch, Jr., *Highway Revenues and Expenditure Policy in the United States* (New Brunswick, N.J.: Rutgers University Press, 1962), 115, 124.

45. George H. Frederickson and Yong Hyo Cho, "Legislative Apportionment and Fiscal Policy in the American States," *Western Political Quarterly* 27 (March 1974): 5–37. The authors show that in most states reapportionment produced shifts in allocation of state monies to cities.

46. See William D. Barnard, *Dixiecrats and Democrats: Alabama Politics, 1942–1950* (University: University of Alabama Press, 1974).

47. Sarah Morehouse, *State Politics, Parties, and Policy* (New York: Holt, Rinehart and Winston, CBS College Publishing, 1981), 71.

48. Philip Converse, "Change in the American Electorate," in *The Human Meaning of Social Change,* ed. Angus Campbell and Philip Converse (New York: Russell Sage, 1972), 303–23.

49. Anne Permaloff, "Partisan Change in the American Electorate" (paper presented at the annual meeting of the Southwestern Political Science Association, Dallas, March 1974), 20.

50. Walter Dean Burnham, "The Alabama Senatorial Election of 1962: Return of Interparty Competition," *Journal of Politics* 26 (November 1964): 816–17.

51. Burch, *Highway Revenues,* 12.

52. Advisory Commission on Intergovernmental Relations (ACIR), *Regional Growth: Historic Perspective* (Washington, D.C.: ACIR, 1980), 2–4; George H. Borts and Jerome Stein, *Economic Growth in a Free Market* (New York: Columbia University Press, 1964).

53. Herman B. Leonard, *By Choice or by Chance?* (Boston: Pioneer Institute for Public Policy Research, 1992), 20–28.

54. Southern Education Reporting Service, *Southern Schools: Progress and Problems* (Nashville: Southern Education Reporting Service, 1959), 93.

55. Ibid., 136–40.

56. Brian Powell and Lala Carr Steelman, "Variations in State SAT Performance: Meaningful or Misleading?" *Harvard Educational Review* 54, no. 4 (November 1984): 392–93, 398–402.

57. National Education Association [NEA], *Wilcox County, Alabama* (Washington, D.C.: National Education Association, 1967).

58. U.S. Commission on Civil Rights, Hearing Held in Montgomery, Alabama, April 27–May 2, 1968, *Staff Report* (Washington, D.C.: Government Printing Office, 1968), 699.

59. NEA, *Wilcox County, Alabama,* 31, and *United States v. Wilcox County Board of Education,* Civil Action No. 3934-65, U.S. District Court for Southern District of Alabama.

60. *United States v. Wilcox County Board of Education, Appendices to Plaintiff's Trial Brief.*

61. Leonard, *By Choice,* 29.

62. Alabama Business Research Council [ABRC], *Skills for Progress* (Tuscaloosa: Alabama Business Research Council, 1955), 3.

63. U.S. Department of Commerce, Bureau of Economic Analysis, *Survey of Current Business* (Washington, D.C.: Government Printing Office, 1930–90).

64. See Albert Davis and Robert Lucke, "The Rich-State-Poor-State Problem in a Federal System," *National Tax Journal* 35, no. 3 (September 1982): 337–63. Davis and Lucke expand the ACIR's tax capacity measure by adding such revenue sources as fees and royalties from natural-resource extraction. They call their measure "revenue capacity." Estimates of state revenue capacity are made in dollars per capita and then indexed to the national average. In 1967, the first year Davis and Lucke cover, Nevada was the wealthiest state, with an index number of 169 (1.69 times the national average); South Carolina was in last place, with an index number of 65 (0.65 times the national average), Mississippi second from last with a 66, and Alabama and West Virginia were tied for third from last with 72. For the period 1967–80, which some measures show as a period of substantial growth for Alabama, the state's revenue capacity index improved only from 72 to 75, tying Alabama for second from last position with South Carolina. Mississippi continued to hold the bottom position with a score of 68.

65. U.S. Department of Commerce, Economics and Statistics Administration, Bureau of Economic Analysis, Regional Economic Measurement Division, *Regional Economic Information System,* CD-ROM (Washington, D.C.: Regional Economic Measurement Division, 1992).

66. Paul Brace, *State Government and Economic Performance* (Baltimore: Johns Hopkins University Press, 1993), 70.

67. ACIR, *Regional Growth,* 10.

68. Ibid., 11.

69. Grafton and Permaloff, *Big Mules and Branchheads.* Also see such works as Sheldon Hackney, *Populism to Progressivism in Alabama* (Princeton: Princeton

University Press, 1969) and Malcolm C. McMillan, *Constitutional Development in Alabama, 1798–1901* (Chapel Hill: University of North Carolina Press, 1955).

Chapter 2. Gaps and State Government Policy-Making

1. See Peter K. Eisinger, *The Rise of the Entrepreneurial State* (Madison: University of Wisconsin Press, 1988), 35–42, for simple flow chart models of state economic development.

2. Michael Barker, ed., *State Taxation Policy* (Durham, N.C.: Duke University Press, 1983), 14.

3. Gregory Jackson, George Masnick, Roger Bolton, Susan Bartlett, and John Pitkin, *Regional Diversity* (Boston: Auburn House, 1981), 3; Joseph J. Spengler, "Southern Economic Trade and Prospects," in *The South in Continuity and Change,* ed. John C. McKinney and Edgar T. Thompson (Durham, N.C.: Duke University Press, 1965), 103–9.

4. Calvin B. Hoover and B. U. Ratchford, *Economic Resources and Policies of the South* (New York: Macmillan, 1951), 4.

5. Ibid.

6. Charles W. Howe, "Water Resources and Regional Economic Growth in the United States, 1950–1960," *Southern Economic Journal* 24, no. 4 (April 1968): 477–89; August Losche, *The Economics of Location* (New Haven: Yale University Press, 1954).

7. Glenn E. McLaughlin and Stefan Robock, *Why Industry Moves South* (Washington, D.C.: Committee of the South, National Planning Association, 1949), 11–12.

8. See Thomas H. Naylor and James Clotfelter, *Strategies for Change in the South* (Chapel Hill: University of North Carolina Press, 1975), 13–20, for an excellent summary of the economic history of the antebellum South; Naylor and Clotfelter trace the rise of cotton and the plantation-slavery system.

9. Clarence H. Danhof, "Four Decades of Thought on the South's Economic Problems," in *Essays in Southern Economic Development,* ed. Melvin L. Greenhut and W. Tate Whitman (Chapel Hill: University of North Carolina Press, 1964), 9; Naylor and Clotfelter, *Strategies for Change,* 21.

10. Gavin Wright, *Old South, New South* (New York: Basic Books, 1986), 61.

11. Ibid., 62.

12. Richard Franklin Bensel, *Sectionalism and American Political Development, 1880–1980* (Madison: University of Wisconsin Press, 1984), 73–74.

13. Wright, *Old South, New South,* 62–63; Everett S. Lee, Ann Ratner Miller, Carol P. Brainerd, and Richard Esterlin, *Population Redistribution and Economic Growth: United States, 1870–1950* (Philadelphia: American Philosophical Society, 1957), 1:729–33.

14. Bensel, *Sectionalism,* 63, 69.

15. Naylor and Clotfelter, *Strategies for Change,* 23; McLaughlin and Robock, *Why Industry Moves South,* 13–14.

16. Naylor and Clotfelter, *Strategies for Change,* 23.

17. Elisabeth Sanders, "Industrial Concentration, Sectional Competition, and Antitrust Politics in America, 1880–1980," in *Studies in American Political Development,* ed. Karen Orren and Stephen Skowronek (New Haven: Yale University Press, 1986), 1:153–59.

18. Wright, *Old South, New South,* 168–70. At the time the Federal Trade Commission outlawed this practice in the mid-1940s, a Birmingham reporter named Irving Beiman quoted Tennessee Coal and Iron's charges for steel to southern customers as three dollars per ton higher than the same steel produced in Pittsburgh. See Irving Beiman, "Birmingham: Steel Giant with a Glass Jaw," in *Our Fair City,* ed. Robert S. Allen (New York: Vanguard Press, 1947), 107.

19. Danhof, "Four Decades," 46; David M. Potter, "The Historical Development of Eastern-Southern Freight Rate Relationships," *Law and Contemporary Problems* 12 (1947): 416–48; William H. Joubert, *Southern Freight Rates in Transition* (Gainesville: University of Florida Press, 1949); Ralph Gray and John M. Peterson, *Economic Development of the United States* (Homewood, Ill.: Richard D. Irwin, 1974), 377–79; U.S. National Emergency Council, *Report to the President on the Economic Conditions of the South* (Washington, D.C.: Government Printing Office, 1938), 58–59.

20. Daniel O. Fletcher, "Transportation and Communication," in *South in Continuity,* ed. McKinney and Thompson, 151, 145–66; see also Joubert, *Southern Freight Rates,* 16–21, 91–98, and 349–57.

21. Bensel, *Sectionalism,* 129–30.

22. Wright, *Old South, New South,* 223, 228–36.

23. James C. Cobb, *The Selling of the South* (Baton Rouge: Louisiana State University Press, 1982), 11–34, 64.

24. Danhof, "Four Decades," 26; Wright, *Old South, New South;* see also Albert Lepawsky, "Governmental Planning in the South," *Journal of Politics* 10 (August 1948): 536–67.

25. Richard A. Lester, "Southern Wage Differentials: Developments, Analysis, and Implications," *Southern Economic Journal* 14, no. 4 (April 1947): 386–94.

26. Bensel, *Sectionalism,* 182.

27. Danhof, "Four Decades," 51; Grafton and Permaloff, *Big Mules and Branchheads,* 244–48.

28. Alabama Business Research Council (ABRC), *Transition in Alabama* (Tuscaloosa: University of Alabama Press, 1962), 2–24; and *Statistical Abstract of the United States.*

29. Gray and Peterson, *Economic Development,* 554; see also Albert Lepawsky, *State Planning and Economic Development in the South* (Washington, D.C.: Committee of the South, National Planning Association, 1949), chap. 2.

30. *Code of Alabama,* 1958 Recompiled Edition, Title 37, Sections 815–30; John T. Reid, "Sources of Assistance for Municipal Promotion of Industry," *Alabama Municipal Journal* 23 (January 1969): 15–21; Alabama Business Research Council (ABRC),

Industrial Development Bond Financing: Business and Community Experiences and Opinions (Tuscaloosa: ABRC, 1970), 27–29.

31. Cobb, *Selling of the South,* 36; ABRC, *Industrial Development Bond Financing,* 27–29.

32. Alabama Legislature, Senate, *Journal,* 1951, 2012–13.

33. Ibid., 2013.

34. Steve Eller and Kenneth A. Wink, "The Effects of Economic Development Efforts in North Carolina Counties: An Empirical Analysis" (paper presented at the annual meeting of the Southern Political Science Association, Savannah, Ga., November 1993).

35. Eisinger, *Rise of the Entrepreneurial State,* 45–46.

36. Gray and Peterson, *Economic Development,* 549.

37. Gunnar Myrdal, *Economic Theory and Under-Developed Regions* (London: Duckworth, 1957); A. D. Hirschman, *The Strategy of Economic Development* (New Haven: Yale University Press, 1958).

38. Victor A. Canto and Robert I. Webb, "The Effect of State Fiscal Policy on State Relative Economic Performance," *Southern Economic Journal* 54, no. 1 (July 1987): 186–87; Simon Kuznets, "Economic Growth and Income Inequality," *American Economic Review* 45 (1955): 1–28; Jeffrey G. Williamson, "Regional Inequality and the Process of National Development: A Description of the Patterns," *Economic Development and Cultural Change* 13 (1965): 3–39; Robert Barro, "Eastern Germany's Long Haul," *Wall Street Journal,* May 3, 1991, A10; Merton H. Miller, "The Value of 'Useless' Research," *Wall Street Journal,* September 21, 1992, A12.

39. Gray and Peterson, *Economic Development,* 549.

40. Ibid., 550–53.

41. Richard Easterlin, "Regional Income Trends, 1910–1950," in *American Economic History,* ed. Seymore Harris (New York: McGraw Hill, 1961), 544. Easterlin discusses the difficulty of sorting out the effects on regional economic development of technological change, resource discovery and exhaustion, and transportation developments.

42. McLaughlin and Robock, *Why Industry Moves South,* 26–28; See also Henry Thomassen, "A Growth Model for a State," *Southern Economic Journal* 24, no. 2 (October 1957): 123; James Dahir, *Region Building* (New York: Harper and Brothers, 1955); Melvin L. Greenhut, *Microeconomics and the Space Economy* (Chicago: Scott Foresman, 1963), 218.

43. Martin A. Garrett Jr., "Growth in Manufacturing in the South, 1947–1958: A Study in Regional Industrial Development," *Southern Economic Journal* 34, no. 3 (January 1968): 357–63.

44. Mancur Olson, "The South Will Fall Again: The South as a Leader and Laggard in Economic Growth," *Southern Economic Journal* 49, no. 4 (April 1983): 917–32; and Robert W. Crandall, *Manufacturing on the Move* (Washington, D.C.: Brookings Institution, 1993), 37.

45. C. James Sample, *Patterns of Regional Economic Change: A Quantitative*

Analysis of U.S. Regional Growth and Development (Cambridge: Ballinger, 1974), 79–81; Garrett, "Growth in Manufacturing," 355–56.

46. This portrait of the increasing industrialization of the South is reinforced by Fletcher, "Transportation and Communication," 148–52.

47. Richard L. Simpson and David N. Norsworthy, "The Changing Occupational Structure of the South," in *The South in Continuity,* ed. McKinney and Thompson, 203.

48. Wright, *Old South, New South,* 255.

49. Gray and Peterson, *Economic Development,* 554; Mary Jean Bowman, "Human Inequalities and Southern Underdevelopment," *Southern Economic Journal* 32, no. 1, pt. 2 (July 1965): 75–76; Eisinger, *Rise of the Entrepreneurial State,* 56–62.

50. Sample, *Patterns of Economic Change,* 91; see also Jackson et al., *Regional Diversity,* 12.

51. Jackson et al., *Regional Diversity,* 4.

52. Garrett, "Growth in Manufacturing," 357–60.

53. Ibid., 359–60, 364; McLaughlin and Robock, *Why Industry Moves South;* Danhof, "Four Decades," 57.

54. Bruce J. Schulman, *From Cotton Belt to Sunbelt* (New York: Oxford University Press, 1991), 116.

55. Ibid., 117.

56. *Journal of the American Medical Association* 202, no. 5 (October 30, 1967): 39–44.

57. Schulman, *Cotton Belt,* 118–19.

58. Advisory Commission on Intergovernmental Relations (ACIR), *Regional Growth: Flows of Federal Funds, 1952–1976* (Washington, D.C.: ACIR, 1980), 12, 13, and 55.

59. Schulman, *Cotton Belt,* 139.

60. Andrew Kirby, "The Pentagon Versus the Cities?" in *The Pentagon and the Cities,* ed. Andrew Kirby (Newbury Park, Calif.: Sage, 1992), 3–4.

61. James A. Papke and Leslie E. Papke, "Measuring Differential State-Local Tax Liabilities and Their Implications for Business Investment Location," *National Tax Journal* 39, no. 3 (September 1986): 357–73.

62. Dye, *Politics, Economics, and the Public.*

63. Gray and Peterson, *Economic Development,* 15.

64. Dye, *Politics, Economics, and the Public,* 52–54; Paul Brace, *State Government and Economic Performance* (Baltimore: Johns Hopkins University Press, 1993), 114.

65. Dye, *Politics, Economics, and the Public,* 58.

66. Cobb, *Selling of the South,* 224.

67. Gary Faulkner, *A Preliminary Review of Forest Industry Development Influences: Opportunities for Alabama?* (Montgomery: Alabama Development Office, n.d.), 1; F. J. Calzonetti and Robert T. Walker, "Factors Affecting Industrial Location Decisions: A Survey Approach," in *Industry Location and Public Policy,* ed.

Henry W. Herzog Jr. and Alan M. Schlottmann (Knoxville: University of Tennessee Press, 1991), 240.

68. Corporation for Enterprise Development (CED), *Making the Grade: The Development Report Card for the States* (Washington, D.C.: Corporation for Enterprise Development, 1987).

69. Thomas R. Plaut and Joseph E. Pluta, "Business Climate, Taxes and Expenditures, and State Industrial Growth in the United States," *Southern Economic Journal* 50, no. 1 (July 1983): 100.

70. Conference of State Manufacturers' Associations, *A Study of Business Climates of the Forty-Eight Contiguous States of America* (Chicago: Conference of State Manufacturers' Associations, 1979).

71. Fantus Company, *A Study of the Business Climates of the States* (Chicago, Fantus for the Illinois Manufacturers Association, 1975).

72. Plaut and Pluta, "Business Climate," 103.

73. Plaut and Pluta, "Business Climate," 108 and 112. "Overall, the cost and availability of energy, labor-related factors, land cost and availability, and climate are strongly related to the growth of industrial output (value-added). Relatively labor-intensive industrial expansion is strongly related to climate; labor-related factors; and business climate, taxes and expenditures, while relatively capital-intensive industrial expansion is strongly related to the cost and availability of energy; the cost and availability of land; markets; and business climate, taxes, and expenditures." The following dependent variables are most strongly related to percent change in value added in order of strength of relationship: energy; labor; land; climate; business climate, taxes, and expenditures; and markets. The same variables relate to percent change in capital stock, but in different order: energy; land; markets; business climate, taxes, and expenditures; labor; and climate.

74. Ibid., 114, 112; Crandall, *Manufacturing on the Move,* 37–45.

75. Melvin L. Greenhut, *Plant Location in Theory and in Practice* (Chapel Hill: University of North Carolina Press, 1956), 273–86; E. Willard Miller, *A Geography of Industrial Location* (Dubuque, Iowa: Wm. C. Brown, 1970).

76. Plaut and Pluta, "Business Climate," 113, 113–14. See also Roy Bahl, "Regional Shifts in Economic Activity and Government Finances in Growing and Declining States," in *Tax Reform and Southern Economic Development,* ed. Bernard L. Weinstein (Research Triangle Park, N.C.: Southern Policies Board, 1979), 25.

77. Plaut and Pluta, "Business Climate," 114; Eller and Wink, "Effects of Development Efforts," 19.

78. Robert J. Newman, *Growth in the American South* (New York: New York University Press, 1984), 14–23, 74–75. The presence or absence of a right-to-work statute or constitutional amendment was taken into account as a dummy variable.

79. L. Jay Helms, "The Effect of State and Local Taxes on Economic Growth: A Time Series–Cross Section Approach," *Review of Economics and Statistics* 67, no. 4 (November 1985): 574–82.

80. Alaeddin Mofidi and Joe A. Stone, "Do State and Local Taxes Affect Economic Growth?" *Review of Economics and Statistics* 72 (November 1990): 688–89. Also see Leslie E. Papke, "The Responsiveness of Industrial Activity to Interstate Tax Differentials: A Comparison of Elasticities," in *Industry Location,* ed. Herzog and Schlottmann, 120–34.

81. Eller and Wink, "Effects of Development Efforts," 20.

82. Bruce L. Benson and Ronald N. Johnson, "The Lagged Impact of State and Local Taxes on Economic Activity and Political Behavior," *Economic Inquiry* 24, no. 3 (July 1986): 389–401. See also Timothy Bartik, "Business Location Decisions in the U.S.: Estimates of the Effect of Unionization, Taxes, and Other Characteristics of States," *Journal of Business and Economic Statistics* 3 (1985): 14–22; and Helms, "Effect of Taxes," 574–82. For even more support for the thesis that taxes inhibit economic activity, see Bernard L. Weinstein, "Tax Reform and Southern Economic Development: An Overview," in *Tax Reform,* ed. Weinstein, 2–5; and Southern Regional Education Board, *State and Local Revenue Potential, 1975* (Atlanta: Southern Regional Education Board, 1977).

83. Greenhut, *Plant Location,* 273–86.

84. E.g., Dye, *Politics, Economics, and the Public,* 81; Michael Wasylenko, "Empirical Evidence on Interregional Business Location Decisions and the Role of Fiscal Incentives in Economic Development," in *Industry Location,* ed. Herzog and Schlottman; and Mofidi and Stone, "Do Taxes Affect Growth?" 688–89.

85. U.S. Department of Commerce, Bureau of the Census, *Statistical Abstract* (Washington, D.C.: U.S. Government Printing Office, 1960, 1970).

86. Davis and Lucke, "Rich-State-Poor-State Problem," 343.

87. Brian Powell and Lala Carr Steelman, "Variations in State SAT Performance: Meaningful or Misleading?" *Harvard Educational Review* 54, no. 4 (November 1984): 389–407. We were unable to precisely replicate the results in this article, partly because it contains mistakes (specifically the Expected Score and Residual columns in table 2 on p. 399) and because the authors fail to specify their measure(s) of government expenditures for schools.

88. Dye, *Politics, Economics, and the Public,* 110.

89. Eisinger, *Rise of the Entrepreneurial State,* 37–38.

90. Stephen McDonald, "On the South's Recent Economic Development," *Southern Economic Journal* 28 (1961): 30–40.

91. Danhof, "Four Decades," 65. See also Brace, *State Government,* 118–19.

92. Ernst Swanson and John Griffing, *Public Education in the South Today and Tomorrow* (Chapel Hill: University of North Carolina Press, 1955); Patrick McGauley and Edward S. Balls, eds., *Southern Schools: Progress and Problems* (Nashville: N.p., 1959).

93. An excellent early treatment of this argument is in Beiman, "Birmingham," 103–4.

94. Brace, *State Government,* 116–21.

95. Randall W. Eberts, "Some Empirical Evidence on the Linkage Between Public

Infrastructure and Local Economic Development," in *Industry Location,* ed. Herzog and Schlottmann, 88.

96. Benjamin Bridges Jr., "State and Local Inducements for Industry, Part I," *National Tax Journal* 18, no. 1 (March 1965): 2.

97. ABRC, *Industrial Development Bond Financing,* 3.

98. Ibid., 3, 21. For a complete list of 1952–68 IDB projects, see 34–42.

99. Bridges, "Inducements, Part I," 12–13.

100. Newman, *Growth,* 42. See also Michael Kieschnick, "Taxes and Growth: Business Incentives and Economic Development," in *State Taxation Policy,* ed. Barker, 163.

101. Kieschnick, "Taxes," 163.

102. Alabama, Legislative Fiscal Office, *A Legislator's Guide to Alabama Taxes* (Montgomery: Legislative Fiscal Office, 1987).

103. William J. Stober and Laurence H. Falk, "Property Tax Exemption: An Inefficient Subsidy to Industry," *National Tax Journal* 20, no. 4 (December 1967): 386–94; see, e.g., Wasylenko, "Empirical Evidence."

104. Benjamin Bridges Jr., "State and Local Inducements for Industry, Part II," *National Tax Journal* 18, no. 2 (June 1965): 178–79, 182.

105. Ibid., 185. The present value of a stream of dollar benefits coming to someone through time is the amount of money that that person would be willing to accept or pay today that for him or her would be equal to the stream of benefits.

106. Wasylenko, "Empirical Evidence," 28–30; Eisinger, *Rise of the Entrepreneurial State,* 45–46; Robert Dvorchak, "Business Incentives Incite New Civil War," *Montgomery Advertiser,* October 4, 1992, 1A, 15A.

107. William E. Morgan, *Taxes and the Location of Industry* (Boulder: University of Colorado Press, 1967); Calzonetti and Walker, "Factors," 221–40; John R. Moore, C. Warren Neel, Henry W. Herzog Jr., and Alan M. Schlottmann, "The Efficacy of Public Policy," in *Industry Location and Public Policy,* ed. Herzog and Schlottmann, 269; Barker, *State Taxation Policy,* 249–54; Timothy J. Bartik, *Who Benefits from State and Local Economic Development Policies?* (Kalamazoo, Mich.: W. E. Upjohn Institute for Employment Research, 1991), 3–16; Dvorchak, "Business Incentives," 15A.

108. *Wall Street Journal,* October 5, 1992, A1.

109. Dye, *Politics, Economics, and the Public,* 189.

110. Ibid., 188.

111. Norman R. Luttbeg, *Comparing the States and Communities* (New York: Harper Collins, 1992), 114.

112. Advisory Commission on Intergovernmental Relations, *1983 Tax Capacity of the States* (Washington, D.C.: ACIR, 1986), 14.

113. Donald Phares, *Who Pays State and Local Taxes?* (Cambridge, Mass.: Oelgeschalager, Gunn and Hain, 1980); David Lowrey, "The Distribution of Tax Burdens in the American States: The Determinants of Fiscal Incidence," *Western Political Quarterly* 40 (March 1987): 155; Luttbeg, *Comparing the States,* 110.

114. Grafton and Permaloff, *Big Mules and Branchheads,* chap. 3.

115. *Official Proceedings of the Constitutional Convention of the State of Alabama (May 21, 1901 to September 3, 1901)* (Wetumpka, Ala.: Wetumpka Printing, 1940), 12.

116. Daniel J. Elazar, *American Federalism: A View from the States* (New York: Thomas Y. Crowell, 1966), 79–80. Subsequent citations are in parentheses in text.

117. Ibid., chap. 5; Ira Sharkansky, "The Utility of Elazar's Political Culture: A Research Note," *Polity* 2 (fall 1969): 66–83; John Kincaid, "Political Culture and the Quality of Urban Life," *Publius* 10, no. 2 (spring 1980): 89–110; Susan Welch and John G. Peters, "State Political Culture and the Attitudes of State Senators Toward Social, Economic Welfare, and Corruption Issues," *Publius* 10, no. 2 (spring 1980): 59–67; Charles A. Johnson, "Political Culture in American States: Elazar's Formulation Examined," *American Journal of Political Science* 20, no. 3 (August 1976): 491–509; Keith Boeckelman, "Political Culture and State Development Policy," *Publius* 21, no. 2 (spring 1991): 49–62; and David R. Morgan and Sheilah S. Watson, "Political Culture, Political System Characteristics, and Public Policies Among the American States," *Publius* 21, no. 2 (spring 1991): 31–48.

118. E.g., Paul Luebke, *Tar Heel Politics* (Chapel Hill: University of North Carolina Press, 1990), 70–84.

119. Beiman, "Birmingham," 110–11.

120. Hackney, *Populism to Progressivism,* 212.

121. William H. Nicholls, "Southern Tradition and Regional Economic Progress," *Southern Economic Journal* 26, no. 3 (January 1960): 191.

122. Ibid., 193.

123. Alabama Department of Revenue, *1993 Abatement Report* (Montgomery: Alabama Department of Revenue, 1993).

124. Russell L. Hanson, "Political Cultural Variations in State Economic Development Policy," *Publius* 21, no. 2 (spring 1991): 53–81.

Chapter 3. The 1958 Campaign and the Organization of State Government Under John Patterson

1. *Birmingham News,* April 24, 1958, 17.

2. Bob Ingram, *Montgomery Advertiser,* April 27, 1958, 5.

3. *Montgomery Advertiser,* March 8, 1958, 1.

4. *Greenville Advocate,* April 24, 1958, 1.

5. *Birmingham News,* March 8, 1958, 2.

6. Marshall Frady, *Wallace* (New York: World, 1968), 121–22; *Birmingham News,* April 22, 1958, 7.

7. *Birmingham News,* April 15, 1958, 6.

8. *Birmingham News,* March 8, 1958, 1.

9. *Muscle Shoals Sun,* April 12, 1958. In chapters 3 and 4, all newspaper citations without page numbers come from the clipping files maintained for the Patterson

campaign and are found in Drawer B, Patterson Personal Papers, Alabama Department of Archives and History (ADAH).

10. Personal interview with Joe Robertson, September 6, 1991, Birmingham.

11. *Birmingham News,* April 13, 1958, 6.

12. *Greenville Advocate,* May 1, 1958, 6B.

13. Personal interview with John M. Patterson, June 6, 1991, Montgomery.

14. *Montgomery Advertiser,* March 25, 1958, 1.

15. *Birmingham News,* April 28, 1958, 6.

16. *Birmingham News,* April 15, 1958.

17. *Gadsden Times,* April 15, 1958.

18. Ibid.

19. *Phenix-Girard Journal,* June 2, 1958. A detailed analysis of his speeches is in James Sheppard Taylor, "An Analysis of the Effect of John Malcolm Patterson's Campaign Speaking in the 1958 Alabama Democratic Primary" (Ph.D. dissertation, Florida State University, 1968), chap. 4.

20. *Centreville Press,* April 10, 1958.

21. Taylor, "Patterson's Campaign Speaking," 33–34.

22. *Selma Times-Journal,* April 29, 1958.

23. Stephan Lesher, *George Wallace: American Populist* (Reading, Pa.: Addison-Wesley, 1994), 111.

24. *Centreville Press,* April 10, 1958.

25. *Greene County Democrat,* April 10, 1958.

26. Quoted in *Florence Times,* April 25, 1958. A *Lee County Bulletin* editorial (April 17, 1958) reasoned that Faulkner would be most favorably inclined toward education. Lee County is the home of Auburn University.

27. *Phenix City Citizen,* April 10, 1958.

28. Personal interview with Joe Robertson, September 6, 1991, Birmingham.

29. The county base of legislators, candidates, and officials appears after their name at least on first reference. If more than one county name is given, the legislator represents a multiple-county district.

30. *Montgomery Advertiser,* February 2, 1958, 1.

31. *Greenville Advocate,* January 9, 1958, 1.

32. *Birmingham News,* May 3, 1958, 11.

33. *Huntsville Times,* May 8, 1958.

34. *Birmingham News,* May 16, 17, and 22, 1958.

35. *Birmingham News,* May 25, 1958, 1.

36. James Simpson was a three-time state senator from Jefferson County. Mayhall, chairman of the State Democratic Executive Committee, was reelected May 6, 1958, as a member of that body. He was also unopposed for renomination as circuit court judge. Clyde Anderson was also reelected to the Democratic party executive committee. McCorvey was a three-time chairman of the state Democratic executive committee and a member for twenty-four years.

37. *Mobile Labor Journal,* May 16, 1958.

38. E.g., *Tuscaloosa News* editorial, May 29, 1958; *Montgomery Advertiser,* June 1, 1958.

39. Personal interview with John M. Patterson, June 6, 1991, Montgomery.

40. Personal interview with Joe Robertson, September 6, 1991, Birmingham.

41. Bob Ingram, *Montgomery Advertiser,* May 23, 1958, 4.

42. *Montgomery Advertiser,* May 15, 1958.

43. *Montgomery Advertiser,* May 22, 1958, 1; personal interview with John M. Patterson, June 6, 1991, Montgomery.

44. Personal interview with Bob Ingram, June 4, 1991, Montgomery.

45. Personal interview with Charles Meriwether, July 1991, Mountain Brook, Ala.

46. *Birmingham News,* May 16, 1958, 1.

47. *Jackson County Sentinel,* May 15, 1958.

48. In a personal interview (January 16, 1992, Montgomery) Patterson said that the University of Alabama board had refused his offer of legal assistance.

49. *Birmingham News,* May 25, 1958, 1.

50. *Muscle Shoals Sun,* May 20, 1958.

51. Editorial, "Political Emphasis Up Here," *Huntsville Times,* February 5, 1958, 4.

52. Editorial, "Big Break for Voters," *Huntsville Times,* April 13, 1958, 4A.

53. Editorial, "Three Major Issues," *Huntsville Times,* April 15, 1958, 4.

54. *Lee County Bulletin,* May 29, 1958.

55. *Birmingham News,* October 21, 1958, 1.

56. *Birmingham News,* June 21, 1958, 1.

57. *Birmingham News,* June 22, 1958, 22.

58. *Birmingham News,* September 17, 1958, 1.

59. Research on another aspect of the Alabama conventional wisdom shows that it can be quite misleading. See Carl Grafton and Anne Permaloff, "The Politics of Highway Construction," *Southeastern Political Review* 12, no. 1 (spring 1985): 21–41.

60. See Carl Grafton and Anne Permaloff, "Regional Forces in the Southern Legislature" (paper presented at the annual meeting of the Southern Political Science Association, Atlanta, November 1988).

61. *Sylacauga Advance,* January 15, 1959.

62. Personal interview with John M. Patterson, June 6, 1991, Montgomery.

63. Recorded votes for Speaker, Speaker pro tempore, and Senate president pro tempore are usually unanimous. The political maneuvering is done behind the scenes. Two recent governors—James (1979–83) and Hunt (1987–93)—lost much, if not all, of these traditional appointment powers.

64. Personal interview with Vaughan Hill Robison, July 15, 1991, Montgomery.

65. *Birmingham News,* January 16, 1959.

66. Examples include *Walker County Times,* July 31, 1958; *Mobile Press Register,* August 3, 1958.

67. *Birmingham News,* October 15, 1958, 2.

68. E.g., see the September 29, 1959, letter from Walter Givhan to Sam Engelhardt, arranging a twenty-five-dollar-a-plate dinner, Box 3, Sam Engelhardt Personal Papers, ADAH.

69. Box 5, Sam Engelhardt Personal Papers, ADAH.

70. Personal interview with Harry Cook, August 27, 1991, Washington, D.C.

71. Speech by Harry Haden to Alabama Wholesale Tobacco Association, August 14, 1959, Mobile. Patterson Office Files, ADAH; personal interview with John M. Patterson, June 6, 1991, Montgomery.

72. Personal interview with Joe Robertson, September 6, 1991, Birmingham.

Chapter 4. The Enigmatic John Patterson and the Alliance at Work

1. *Acts of Alabama,* Regular Session, 1957, 1:496.

2. The other commission members were Representatives Hugh Kaul (a Birmingham lumberman and Big Mule Alliance member), McDowell Lee of Clio (a farmer and banker), and Hugh D. Merrill of Anniston (an attorney); Senators Lynchmore Cantrell of Tuscumbia, E. O. Eddins of Demopolis, and T. Herman Vann of Huntsville; congressional district representatives Hugh Comer (a textile manufacturer from Sylacauga), Thomas D. Russell (president of Russell Manufacturing in Alexander City), H. B. Larkins (vice president of Mutual Saving Life Insurance Company in Decatur), G. T. Walker of Kennedy, and Howell T. Heflin, an attorney from Tuscumbia (the current U.S. senator and former chief justice of the Alabama Supreme Court); and education representatives Mrs. George Yarbrough of Wedowee, Dr. David W. Mullins (executive vice president of Auburn University), and Dr. J. F. Drake (president of Alabama A & M Institute, the black state-supported university near Huntsville).

3. *Birmingham News,* August 15, 1958, 1, 2.

4. Alabama Education Commission, *Tentative Report of the Committee on Financing Education Including the Minimum Program* (Montgomery: Alabama Education Commission, 1958), 7.

5. The financing education subcommittee of the legislative interim committee included Boutwell as chair, Dawkins as vice chair, and Alabama Education Commission members Comer, Eddins, and Yarbrough.

6. Quoted in Alabama Education Commission, *Tentative Report,* 27.

7. Ira Harvey, *A History of Educational Finance in Alabama* (Auburn, Ala.: Truman Pierce Institute for the Advancement of Teacher Education, 1989), 213.

8. Ibid., 213.

9. *Montgomery Advertiser,* December 20, 1958, 1, and January 9, 1959, 1, 2; and *Birmingham News,* January 8, 1959, 1.

10. *Birmingham News,* January 8, 1959, 1.

11. *Alex City Outlook,* January 13, 1959.

12. *Centreville Press,* January 29, 1959.

13. *Huntsville Times,* July 10, 1958, 3.

14. *Huntsville Times,* October 10, 1958, 1–2.

15. *Huntsville Times,* November 24, 1958, 1.

16. Bob Ingram and Herschel Cribb, "Review of 1959," *Montgomery Advertiser,* November 15, 1959, 1.

17. The legislative efforts went back to 1953 with creation of a joint committee composed of Senators Albert Boutwell (Jefferson, the chair), J. Miller Bonner (Wilcox), and Herbert J. Byer (Hale); and Representatives Bob Kendall (Conecuh), Jack Gallalee (Mobile), and Ira Pruitt (Sumter). The joint committee was reestablished in 1955 with Senators Boutwell (chair), Sam Engelhardt (Macon), George Yarbrough (Randolph), Broughton Lamberth (Tallapoosa), Vaughan Hill Robison (Montgomery), T. Herman Vann (Madison), David M. Hall (Greene); and Representatives Bob Kendall (vice chair), Sim Thomas (Barbour), Hugh Kaul (Jefferson), James A. Branyon (Fayette), C. W. McKay Jr. (Talladega), and Joe Dawkins (Montgomery). The Alabama State Bar Association assisted both committees.

It is no coincidence that many members of both committees served on the Alabama Education Commission, and Engelhardt, Pruitt, and Robison were key members of the Patterson leadership team.

18. Personal interview with John M. Patterson, June 6, 1991, Montgomery.

19. *Montgomery Advertiser,* January 20, 1959, 1A.

20. *Montgomery Advertiser,* May 6, 1959, 1.

21. Personal interview with John M. Patterson, June 6, 1991, Montgomery.

22. Personal interview with Charles "Pete" Mathews, August 1992, Montgomery.

23. Personal interview with John M. Patterson, June 6, 1991, Montgomery. Other aspects of highway construction politics in this era are discussed in Grafton and Permaloff, "Politics of Highway Construction."

24. *Montgomery Advertiser,* June 25, 1959, 1.

25. Alabama House of Representatives, 2d Extraordinary Session of 1959, *Journal,* 10–12. In the address Patterson reiterated his opposition to a sales tax hike.

26. Personal interview with John M. Patterson, January 16, 1992, Montgomery.

27. *Alabama Farm Bureau News,* March 2, 1959.

28. Box 4, Sam Engelhardt Personal Files, ADAH.

29. Personal interview with Sam Engelhardt, August 1979, Montgomery.

30. Box 4, Sam Engelhardt Personal Papers, ADAH.

31. Personal interview with John M. Patterson, January 16, 1992, Montgomery.

32. *Mobile Register,* July 15, 1959, 1, 9.

33. *Montgomery Advertiser,* July 15, 1959, 1.

34. Alabama House of Representatives, 2d Extraordinary Session of 1959, *Journal,* 134–35.

35. Frank Dixon Personal Files, ADAH.

36. Virginia Van der Veer Hamilton, *Lister Hill: Statesman from the South* (Chapel Hill: University of North Carolina Press, 1987), 146.

37. *Montgomery Advertiser,* July 26, 1959, 1.

38. *Montgomery Advertiser,* July 23, 1959, 1.

39. The committee vote was held in executive session, but according to the *Mobile Register* (July 24, 1959, 8) the vote breakdown held no surprises. For the tax: Robison (Montgomery), Archer (Madison), Word (Jackson), Samford (Lee), de Graffenried (Tuscaloosa), Moses (Marion), Rutledge (Winston), and Turner (Crenshaw). Against: Eddins (Marengo), Givhan (Dallas), Caffey (Mobile), Kendall (Conecuh), Wilson (Hale), Dumas (Jefferson), and Graham (Chilton).

40. Alabama Senate, 2d Extraordinary Session of 1959, July 28, 1959, *Journal,* 138.

41. Personal interview with John M. Patterson, January 16, 1992, Montgomery.

42. *Montgomery Advertiser,* March 12, 1959, 4A.

43. A. F. Harman, "Frank Dixon on Education" (radio address, WSFA, May 31, 1934), in Frank Dixon Private Papers, LPR 33, Box 4, Folder 9, ADAH.

44. William H. Stewart, Jr., "Governor Frank Murray Dixon and Reform of State Administration in Alabama," in *The Public Life of Frank M. Dixon,* ed. William D. Barnard (Montgomery: Alabama Department of Archives and History, 1979), 15–30.

45. The 17-16 vote was on a motion by Dixon's Senate leader Joe Poole. The majority won a delay in consideration of the bill. The vote occurred February 10, 1939. The final 19-14 Senate vote occurred in late February.

46. March 8, 1939.

47. *Montgomery Advertiser,* June 12, 1959, 1; personal interview with John M. Patterson, June 6, 1991, Montgomery.

48. Personal interview with John M. Patterson, June 6, 1991, Montgomery.

49. *Montgomery Advertiser,* March 8, 1959, 5.

50. Letter from E. B. Haltom Jr. to the Honorable John Batts, Chairman, Limestone County Board of Equalization, June 13, 1959, 1959 Revenue Department File, Patterson Office Files, ADAH.

51. *Montgomery Advertiser,* June 19, 1959, 1.

52. Ibid.

53. Personal interview with John M. Patterson, January 16, 1992, Montgomery.

54. AEA's lack of enthusiasm is reflected in the fact that this important issue is barely mentioned in Harvey, *History of Educational Finance.* See pp. 212–18, 465.

55. *Birmingham News,* June 19, 1959, 1.

56. Personal interview with John M. Patterson, January 16, 1992, Montgomery.

57. Personal interview with John M. Patterson, June 19, 1991, Montgomery.

58. Personal interview with John M. Patterson, January 16, 1992, Montgomery.

59. *Grove Hill Democrat,* January 8, 1959.

60. *Montgomery Advertiser,* January 6, 1959.

61. *Birmingham News,* January 30, 1959.

62. *Montgomery Advertiser,* February 21, 1959.

63. *Birmingham Post-Herald,* March 11, 1959.

64. Governor John M. Patterson Office Files, ADAH.

65. *Union Labor News,* January 1, 1959.

66. *Lee County Bulletin,* January 15, 1959.

67. *Mobile Press-Register,* January 13, 1959, editorial.

68. *Birmingham News,* January 17, 1959.

69. *Mobile Press-Register,* March 21, 1959.

70. Box 3, Sam Engelhardt Personal Papers, ADAH.

71. Personal interview with Charles "Pete" Mathews, August 19, 1992, Montgomery.

72. *Montgomery Advertiser,* April 1, 1960, 4.

73. *Montgomery Advertiser,* June 26, 1960, 2B.

74. Box 4, Sam Engelhardt Personal Papers, ADAH.

75. The antiloyalist slate included former governor Frank Dixon, Birmingham; former congressman John Newsom, Birmingham; John D. McQueen Jr., Tuscaloosa; Edmund Blair, Pell City; former state representative W. W. Malone Jr., Athens; Lawrence C. McNeil, Birmingham; former state senator J. Bruce Henderson, Prairie; state senator Walter Givhan, Safford; Sam Johnston, Mobile; C. E. Hornsby, Centreville; and Frank J. Mizell Jr., Montgomery.

Several antiloyalist candidates withdrew to avoid splitting the vote against the loyalist candidates. They included former lieutenant governor Handy Ellis, Columbiana; Marion Ruston, Montgomery; Henry Sweet, Bessemer; L. D. "Lukie" Anderson, Atmore; Wilmer M. "Red" Kelly, Talladega; state representative Grady Rogers, Tuskegee; Jack Brock, Montgomery; James Sherrill, Fairfield; Offie J. Walker, Birmingham; John Eagerton III, Montgomery; and Robert A. Cummings, Cordova.

76. The loyalist slate consisted of C. G. Allen, Gadsden; state senator Dave Archer, Huntsville; C. Leonard Beard, Sheffield; J. E. Brantley, Banks; W. L. Chenault, Decatur; Milton K. Cummings, Huntsville; Karl Harrison of Columbiana; Bill Jones, Jasper; William D. Partlow, Tuscaloosa; Ben F. Ray, Birmingham; and D. Hardy Riddle, Talladega.

77. *Montgomery Advertiser,* April 15, 1960, 4.

78. Ibid.

79. *Montgomery Advertiser,* May 15, 1960, 1.

80. *Montgomery Advertiser,* May 1, 1960, 3B.

81. *Montgomery Advertiser,* June 4, 1960, 1.

82. *Huntsville Times,* July 17, 1960, 1.

83. *Huntsville Times,* September 18, 1960, 7.

84. Personal interview with John M. Patterson, June 6, 1991, Montgomery.

85. *Huntsville Times,* July 19, 1960, 1.

86. *Huntsville Times,* July 24, 1960, B10.

87. *Montgomery Advertiser,* April 24, 1960, 3B.

88. Ibid.

Chapter 5. The Alliance in Disarray

1. Alabama Legislature, House of Representatives, 1939 Extraordinary Session, *Journal,* 167–72.

2. *Birmingham News,* March 18, 1939, 2.

3. Typical were a September 18, 1947, House vote and an August 9, 1949, Senate vote.

4. Grafton and Permaloff, *Big Mules and Branchheads,* 195.

5. *Montgomery Advertiser,* June 17, 1959, 1.

6. Voting for reapportionment were Virgis Ashworth (Bibb), Tom Bevill (Walker), Fletcher Jones (Covington), Hugh Merrill (Calhoun), Hugh Rozelle (Escambia), and Pete Self (Marion). All but Rozelle represented north Alabama constituencies. Voting against: L. W. Brannan (Baldwin), A. K. Callahan (Tuscaloosa), Homer Cornett (Russell), Val Hain (Dallas), Hugh Locke (Jefferson), and Francis Speaks (Chilton).

7. For the motion: Adams, Albea, Ashworth, Bevill, Bishop, Brewer, Broadfoot, Cabiness, Camp, Casey, Cates, Cook, Copeland, Dodd, Edwards, Gilchrist, Gordon, Gross, Grouby, Guthrie, Hankins, Harris, Hawkins, Hearn, Ingram, Johnson of Elmore, Johnson of Tallapoosa, Jones of Covington, Locke, Meade, Merrill, Morrow, Murphy, Nichols, Oden, Owens, Parry, Ray, Roberts, Rozelle, Self, Sessions, Smith of Russell, Speaks, Turner. Against the motion: Avery, Bailey, Barnett, Bassett, Boyd, Brannan, Britton, Brooks, Chambers, Cornett, Daniel, Franklin, Gilmer, Glass, Goldthwaite, Goodwyn, Grant, Hain, Hardy, Harvey, Jenkins, Johnston of Elmore, Lee, Long of Perry, McClendon of Chambers, McLendon of Bullock, Martin, Nettles, Oakley, Pierce, Powell, Pruitt, Ramey, Rogers, Salter, Smith of St. Clair, Solomon, Steagall, Sullivan, Taylor, Thomas, Torbert, Trimmier, and Turnham. *Montgomery Advertiser,* October 22, 1959.

8. *Montgomery Advertiser,* May 1, 1961, 1–2A and May 2, 1961, 1–2A.

9. Box 4, Sam Engelhardt Personal Papers, Alabama Department of Archives and History (ADAH).

10. See *Montgomery Advertiser,* May 3, 1961, 1–2A.

11. Alabama Legislature, House of Representatives, 1961 Regular Session, *Journal,* 6–8; *Birmingham News,* May 1, 1961, 10.

12. *Montgomery Advertiser,* May 3, 1961, 1A; and *Birmingham News,* May 1, 1961, 10.

13. *Montgomery Advertiser,* May 3, 1961, 2A.

14. Alabama Legislature, House of Representatives, 1961 Regular Session, *Journal,* 13–14.

15. *Montgomery Advertiser,* May 4, 1961, 2A.

16. *Montgomery Advertiser,* May 3, 1961, 4B.

17. The state constitution then limited the regular sessions of the legislature to thirty-six legislative days. Any day either house met counted as a legislative day.

18. *Montgomery Advertiser,* May 7, 1961, 3B.

19. Ibid.

20. *Birmingham News,* May 3, 1961, 40.

21. *Birmingham News,* May 5, 1961, 10.

22. *Birmingham News,* May 28, 1961, 38A. See also June 15, 1961, 22A.

23. Anne Permaloff and Carl Grafton, "The Chop-Up Bill and the Big Mule Alliance," *Alabama Review* 43, no. 4 (October 1990): 243–69.

24. *Montgomery Advertiser,* May 31, 1961, 1A.

25. *Birmingham News,* May 18, 1961, 40.

26. *Birmingham News,* May 21, 1961, 18A.

27. *Birmingham News,* June 1, 1961.

28. Telephone interview with Albert P. Brewer, March 10, 1993.

29. Telephone interview with John Guthrie, January 1981.

30. Alabama Legislature, House of Representatives, 1961 Regular Session, *Journal,* 675.

31. Alabama Legislature, House of Representatives, 1961 Regular Session, *Journal,* 693–713.

32. *Montgomery Advertiser,* June 7, 1961, 2A.

33. *Birmingham News,* June 7, 1961, 2A.

34. Alabama Legislature, Senate, 1961 Regular Session, *Journal,* 1224.

35. Alabama Legislature, Senate, 1961 Regular Session, *Journal,* 1224.

36. Interview subjects suggested that de Graffenried participated in the filibuster in order to court Jefferson County voters for his 1962 gubernatorial campaign.

37. *Birmingham News,* August 3, 1961, 1A. See also August 4, 1961, 1 and 8.

38. *Birmingham News,* May 28, 1961, 38A.

39. Telephone interview with John Guthrie, January 1981.

40. Note the similarity of Folsom's view of Big Mule influence technique and John Patterson's.

41. Telephone interview with John Guthrie, January 1981.

42. *Montgomery Advertiser,* August 5, 1961, 1 and 7A.

43. Alabama Legislature, Senate, 1961 Regular Session, *Journal,* 1258–59.

44. Alabama Legislature, Senate, 1961 Regular Session, *Journal,* 1259–61.

45. *Birmingham News,* August 10, 1961, 1 and 4A.

46. *Birmingham News,* August 10, 1961, 4A.

47. *Birmingham News,* August 3, 1961, 1A.

48. *Montgomery Advertiser,* August 10, 1961, 1–2A.

49. *Birmingham News,* August 11, 1961, 11, and August 13, 1961, 4B.

50. *Montgomery Advertiser,* August 5, 1961, 1A.

51. *Montgomery Advertiser,* August 13, 1961, 1–2A.

52. *Montgomery Advertiser,* August 13, 1961, 2B; and *Birmingham News,* August 12, 1961, 1–2A.

53. *Birmingham News,* August 13, 1961, 4B.

54. Ibid.

55. Ibid.

56. Ibid.

57. *Birmingham News,* August 15, 1961, 1 and 2.

58. *Birmingham News,* August 16, 1961, 1 and 3.

59. E.g., *Birmingham News,* August 18, 1961, 1 and 4.

60. *Birmingham News,* August 20, 1961, 1 and 6A.

61. *Birmingham News,* August 23, 1961, 1.

62. *Birmingham News,* August 25, 1961, 1–2; Alabama Legislature, Senate, 1961 Regular Session, *Journal,* 2073–74.

63. Alabama Legislature, Senate, 1961 Regular Session, *Journal,* 2074–75. See also *Birmingham News,* August 27, 1961, 22A.

64. *Birmingham News,* August 26, 1961, 1 and 2, and August 27, 1961, 1 and 12A.

65. *Birmingham News,* August 26, 1961, 1–2. See also August 27, 1961, 22A.

66. *Birmingham News,* August 31, 1961, 1 and 6.

67. *Birmingham News,* September 1, 1962, 2.

68. *Birmingham News,* August 13, 1961, 1 and 8A; and Richard C. Cortner, *The Apportionment Cases* (New York: W. W. Norton, 1970), 165–66. Cortner gives an excellent detailed account of the case.

69. *Birmingham News,* August 28, 1961, 1 and 11.

70. Alabama Legislature, House of Representatives, 1962 Special Session, HB59. See *Birmingham News* (July 7, 1962, 1–2; July 9, 1962, 1, 5; July 10, 1962, 1–2; July 11, 1962, 1–2; July 16, 1962, 1, 4) for coverage of the rural-based maneuvering to create limited reapportionment.

71. Alabama Legislature, Senate, 1962 Special Session, SB29.

72. Council of State Governments, *Legislative Reapportionment in the States: A Summary of Action Since June, 1960* (Chicago: Council of State Governments, 1962); *Birmingham News,* July 21, 1962, 1–2.

73. Council of State Governments, "Legislative Reapportionment," 18A.

74. Ibid., 1A.

Chapter 6. Racial Conflict and the Politics of Race

1. *Montgomery Advertiser,* March 7, 1960, 1.

2. Grafton and Permaloff, *Big Mules and Branchheads,* 229; *Montgomery Advertiser,* March 18, 1961.

3. Grafton and Permaloff, *Big Mules and Branchheads,* 229; *Montgomery Advertiser,* May 21, 1961, 1.

4. Transcript, p. 5, Box SG14028, Patterson Office Files, ADAH.

5. Transcript, p. 12, Box SG14028, Patterson Office Files, ADAH.

6. Grafton and Permaloff, *Big Mules and Branchheads,* 230; *Montgomery Advertiser,* May 22, 24, and 28, 1961.

7. *New York Times,* May 16, 1960, 22.

8. Ibid.

9. *New York Times,* April 8, 1960, 34.

10. *New York Times,* May 16, 1960, 22.

11. *New York Times,* May 31, 1960, 20.

12. *New York Times,* July 26, 1960, 13, July 17, 1960, 18, and July 28, 1960, 27.

13. *New York Times,* August 6, 1960, 8.

14. *New York Times,* April 12, 1960, 1 and 28.

15. *New York Times,* April 13, 1960, 1.

16. *New York Times,* April 13, 1960, 33.

17. Ibid.

18. *New York Times,* April 22, 1960, 10.

19. *New York Times,* April 27, 1960, 28.

20. Ibid.

21. *New York Times,* May 4, 1960, 38.

22. *New York Times,* May 7, 1960, 9.

23. *New York Times,* May 27, 1960, 12.

24. *New York Times,* September 3, 1960, 20.

25. *New York Times,* September 7, 1960, 27.

26. Ibid., and September 10, 1960, 14.

27. *New York Times,* September 25, 1960, 87.

28. *New York Times,* November 2, 1960, 33, and November 3, 1960, 14.

29. *New York Times,* November 4, 1960, 67.

30. *"New York Times" v. Sullivan,* 376 U.S. 255 (1964).

31. Harvey, *History of Educational Finance,* 218–19.

32. Box SG14014, 1961 Education Department File, Patterson Office Files, ADAH.

33. Box SG14027, 1962–63 Education Department File, Patterson Office Files, ADAH.

34. Box SG14011, Lawrence Dunbar Reddick File, Patterson Office Files, ADAH. The telegram was dated March 2, 1960.

35. *New York Times,* March 3, 1960.

36. *Montgomery Advertiser,* June 25, 1960, quoting a *Lee County Bulletin* editorial; American Association of University Professors (AAUP), "Academic Freedom and Tenure: Alabama State College," *AAUP Bulletin* 47, no. 4 (Winter 1961): 303–9.

37. Box SG14011, Lawrence Dunbar Reddick File, Patterson Office Files, ADAH.

38. *New York Times,* December 3, 1946, 3.

39. Box SG14011, Reddick File, Patterson Office Files, ADAH.

40. AAUP, "Academic Freedom and Tenure."

41. *Dixon v. Alabama State Board of Education,* 17.

42. See AAUP, "Academic Freedom and Tenure."

43. *Huntsville Times,* July 21, 1960, 10.

44. *Alabama Journal,* June 15, 1960, 1.

45. Box SG14011, Patterson Office Files, ADAH.

46. June 18, 1960, from Dixie Klans, Inc., Kenneth Adams, Alabama Grand Dragon.

47. *Dixon v. Alabama State Board of Education,* 30 *United States Law Week* 2084, September 15, 1961.

48. Letter from John Patterson to LeCroy, February 2, 1962, Box SG14027, 1962–63 Education Department File, Patterson Office Files, ADAH.

49. Wesley C. George, "The Biology of the Race Problem," Box RC2:G319, Wallace Office Files, ADAH.

50. Ibid., 17.

51. Ibid., 19.

52. Box 4, Sam Engelhardt Personal Papers, ADAH.

53. Box 5, Sam Engelhardt Personal Papers, ADAH.

54. Ibid.

55. Memo to John Patterson from Sam Engelhardt, April 3, 1961, and attached documents, Box SG14013, File 1961, Highway Department, Patterson Office Files, ADAH.

56. Confidential personal interview, August 1992, Montgomery.

57. Box SG14014, 1961 Planning and Industrial Development File, Patterson Office Files, ADAH.

58. May 22, 1961. Box SG14014, 1961 Planning and Industrial Development File, Patterson Office Files, ADAH.

59. Letter from Marshall K. Hunter to Floyd Mann, April 12, 1961, Box SG14014, 1961 Public Safety Department File, Patterson Office Files, ADAH.

60. Handwritten letter to Mayor James W. Morgan, September 11, 1960, Morgan Files, Department of Archives and History, Birmingham Public Library.

61. Thank-you letters from Walter Craig dated late in June, Box 5, Sam Engelhardt Personal Papers, ADAH.

62. Box 5, Sam Engelhardt Personal Papers, ADAH.

63. *Birmingham News,* April 18, 1962, 14.

64. *Birmingham News,* April 26, 1962, 1, 11.

65. *Birmingham News,* April 27, 1962, 14.

66. *Birmingham News,* March 25, 1962, B1.

67. Grafton and Permaloff, *Big Mules and Branchheads,* 194.

68. *Montgomery Advertiser,* December 6, 1958.

69. See Michael Dorman, *The George Wallace Myth* (New York: Bantam, 1976), 23–24; and Tinsley E. Yarbrough, *Judge Frank Johnson and Human Rights in Alabama* (University: University of Alabama Press, 1981), 62–72.

70. *Birmingham News,* April 22, 1962, A15.

71. Ibid.

72. *Birmingham News,* April 13, 1962.

73. *Birmingham News,* April 22, 1962, B2.

74. *Birmingham News,* March 16, 1962, 2.

75. Reprinted in *Birmingham News,* March 14, 1962, 1.

76. *Birmingham News,* April 8, 1962, A27.

77. *Birmingham News,* May 27, 1962, 1.

78. *Birmingham News,* May 5, 1962, 4.

79. *Birmingham News,* April 15, 1962, 6.

80. *Birmingham News,* May 18, 1962, 6.

81. *Birmingham News,* October 21, 1962, 20A.

82. *Congressional Quarterly Weekly Report,* June 22, 1962, 1072.

83. Richard K. Scher, *Politics in the New South* (New York: Paragon House, 1992), 139.

84. *Congressional Quarterly Weekly Report,* June 22, 1962, 1072.

85. *Birmingham News,* November 11, 1962, B2.

Chapter 7. Wallace's Leap to National Prominence

1. *Birmingham News,* January 14, 1963, 1.

2. Personal interview with Richmond M. Flowers, June 17, 1991, Dothan, Ala.

3. See Bill Jones, *The Wallace Story* (Northport, Ala.: American Southern, 1968), 60–62, for a fairly complete list of Wallace appointees.

4. *Montgomery Advertiser,* June 2, 1963, 3B.

5. Personal interview with Vaughan Hill Robison, July 15, 1991, Montgomery.

6. Personal interviews with James E. Folsom, June 1973, Cullman, Ala., and Rankin Fite, July 1974, Hamilton, Ala.

7. Personal interview with Albert Brewer, June 3, 1992, Birmingham.

8. Personal interview with Vaughan Hill Robison, July 15, 1991, Montgomery.

9. Personal interview with Albert Brewer, June 3, 1992, Birmingham.

10. Box RC2:G288, Finance Department File, Wallace Office Files, ADAH.

11. Ibid.

12. Memo to Bob Weller, Finance Department, from Earl C. Morgan, executive secretary, June 7, 1963, Box RC2:G288, Finance Department File, Wallace Office Files, ADAH.

13. Letter to Richard Stone, assistant director, Finance Department, from Earl Morgan, June 19, 1963, Box RC2:G288, Finance Department File, Wallace Office Files, ADAH.

14. Letter to Bob Kendall, assistant director, Highway Department, from George Wallace, March 25, 1963, and letter to George Wallace from E. N. Rodgers, highway director, March 29, 1963, Box RC2:G288, Highway Department File, Wallace Office Files, ADAH.

15. Exact date obscured by carbon copy smudge. Box RC2:G288, Highway Department File, Wallace Office Files, ADAH.

16. July 26, 1963, Box RC2:G288, Highway Department File, Wallace Office Files, ADAH. In the same file see the letters to Bob Kendall, assistant director, Highway Department, from George Wallace, September 6, 16, and 30, 1963.

17. September 20, 1963, in Box RC2:G288, Highway Department File, Wallace Office Files, ADAH.

18. Letter from E. N. Rodgers, highway director, to George Wallace, March 29, 1963, Box RC2:G288, Highway Department File, Wallace Office Files, ADAH.

19. Box RC2:G288, Highway Department File, Wallace Office Files, ADAH.

20. Also see many memos from Wallace to finance department personnel telling them to shift business in towing and other things to particular businesses in response to legislators' requests or because those businesses had supported Wallace. Auto Parts, Auto Repair File, Box RC2:G300, 1963–64 Finance Department File, Wallace Office Files, ADAH.

21. Quoted in Robert D. Loevy, *To End All Segregation* (Lanham, Md.: University Press of America, 1990), 5.

22. Ibid., 6. Loevy cites *CQ Weekly Report,* March 8, 1963, 293.

23. *Birmingham News,* February 12, 1963, A14.

24. Ira Harvey, *History of Educational Finance,* 224.

25. *Birmingham News,* February 28, 1963, 1.

26. *Montgomery Advertiser,* April 7, 1963, 3B.

27. Harvey, *History of Educational Finance,* 224.

28. *Alabama School Journal,* February 1963, Special Section, cited in Harvey, *History of Educational Finance,* 223.

29. *Birmingham News,* March 28, 1963, 1, and April 24, 1963, 6; Harvey, *History of Educational Finance,* 227.

30. *Birmingham News,* March 28, 1963, 1; *Montgomery Advertiser,* March 31, 1963, 3B.

31. *Birmingham News,* April 3, 1963, 1, 2.

32. There was no relationship between support for Wallace in the Democratic primary and this vote.

33. *Birmingham News,* April 9, 1963, 1.

34. Ibid.

35. *Birmingham News,* April 3, 1963, 1.

36. *Birmingham News,* April 14, 1963, A12.

37. *Birmingham News,* April 19, 1963, 1, 4.

38. There was no relationship in terms of counties supporting Wallace on this vote and in the Democratic party primary.

39. Wallace's original education package, which included some of the bills passed, also suggests that his basic orientation toward tax policy was progressive. See the listing in Harvey, *History of Educational Finance,* 225.

40. Personal interview with Charles "Pete" Mathews, August 19, 1992, Montgomery.

41. Personal interview with George Lewis Bailes Jr., September 18, 1992, Montgomery.

42. Box RC2:G287, 1963 Education Department File, Wallace Office Files, ADAH.

43. Letter to C. P. Nelson, executive director, Alabama Education Association, from George Wallace, March 20, 1963, in Box RC2:G287, 1963 Education Department File, Wallace Office Files, ADAH.

44. Alabama Commission on Higher Education, *Higher Education in Alabama 1991 Directory* (Montgomery: Alabama Commission on Higher Education, 1991).

45. Regional Vocational and Trade Schools Act (Acts 1947, no. 673, p. 514).

46. Acts 1963, 2d Special Session, no. 94, p. 268.

47. Acts 1963, 2d Special Session, no. 93, p. 259.

48. The first set includes Cullman, Childersburg, Opelika, Thomasville, Eufaula, Opp, Montgomery (Negro), Jefferson County (Bessemer Cutoff-Hueytown area), Selma, Evergreen, Sumiton (Walker County). The second set includes Bay Minette, a trade school in Jefferson County, a junior college in Jefferson County, a trade school for blacks in Tuscaloosa, a trade school in Calhoun County, and Northwest Alabama

Junior College. Box RC2:G299, Gov. George Wallace, Unprocessed Administrative Records, ADAH.

49. E.g., personal interview with William "Bill" Blow of the Alabama Commission on Higher Education, February 2, 1993, Montgomery.

50. Box RC2:G299, Gov. George Wallace, Unprocessed Administrative Records, ADAH.

51. RC2:G311, Gov. George Wallace, Unprocessed Administrative Records FY 1965, ADAH. They include Alexander City, Bay Minette, Brewton, Decatur (Tennessee Valley Technical Junior College), Dothan (George C. Wallace Technical Junior College), Enterprise, Gadsden (Gadsden Technical Junior College), Jefferson (Wenonah Tech Junior College), Monroeville, northeast Alabama (Jackson-DeKalb Counties), northwest Alabama, Southern Union, and Mobile.

52. Alabama Commission on Higher Education, *Two-Year Institutions,* Preliminary Draft, 2d Version, April 2, 1980, 4.

53. 1964–65 Junior Colleges and Trade Schools File, RC2:G311, Gov. George Wallace, Unprocessed Administrative Records, ADAH. More letters of a similar nature are contained in RC2:G349, Gov. George Wallace, Unprocessed Administrative Records, ADAH.

54. Letter from J. F. Ingram to George Wallace, July 12, 1967 in RC2:G349, Gov. George Wallace, Unprocessed Administrative Records, ADAH.

55. A December 19, 1963, press release by Alabama Superintendent of Education Austin Meadows said that "the State Board of Education has located junior colleges and trade schools to blanket the State." RC2:G298, Gov. George Wallace, Unprocessed Administrative Records FY1964, ADAH.

56. *Huntsville Times,* April 13, 1958, 1–2; June 18, 1959, 4.

57. Quoted in *Huntsville Times* editorial, June 24, 1959, 4.

58. *Huntsville Times,* June 20, 1961, 1, 3; also see the June 21, 1961, editorial, p. 4.

59. Legislative Act 403.

60. John Fair, *The AUM Story* (Montgomery: Brown, 1981), 4.

61. *Montgomery Advertiser,* June 23, 1963, 1.

62. Harvey, *History of Educational Finance,* 230–31.

63. *Birmingham News,* March 2, 1963, 2. In his public statements with regard to race, Connor was not the nastiest of the four mayoral candidates. That title probably belongs to J. T. Waggoner. See *Birmingham News,* March 2, 1963, 2.

64. *Birmingham News,* March 4, 1963, 6. A small Boutwell advertisement on this page reads in its entirety: "THINK SERIOUSLY About Your Job and More Payrolls. ELECT BOUTWELL MAYOR."

65. *Birmingham News,* March 3, 1963, 4A.

66. *Birmingham News,* March 9, 1963, 5.

67. *Birmingham News,* March 26, 1963, 1. Connor announced that the state highway director had sent him a telegram promising "prompt" action with regard to highway construction.

68. The Birmingham Building Trades Council supported Connor, *Birmingham News,* March 22, 1963, 1.

69. *Birmingham News,* April 1, 1963, 1. E.g., note the placement of stories on the front page. In the two right-hand columns is a neutral story concerning the primary to be held the next day. In the center is a story about a speech given by Caldwell Marks, chair of the Committee of 100, concerning why industries often refused to locate in Birmingham. The basic reason, he argued, was the lack of "law and order," an unsubtle criticism of Police Commissioner Connor. This story continues on p. 2 with an unusually large headline: "Order Called Key to City's Growth."

70. *Birmingham News,* April 28, 1963, 1.

71. *Birmingham News,* April 1, 1963, 5.

72. *Birmingham News,* April 3, 1963, 1.

73. *Birmingham News,* April 10, 1963, 6.

74. *Birmingham News,* April 13, 1963.

75. Connor wrote Wallace, "There is no possible way I can put into mere words the feeling of gratitude we here in Birmingham have for the wonderful cooperation and assistance we have received from you and the state officers." Letter to George Wallace, May 14, 1963, Box RC2:G294, 1963 Segregation-Birmingham File, Wallace Office Files, ADAH.

76. *Birmingham News,* May 4, 1963, 1.

77. *Alabama Journal,* May 12, 1963, 3B.

78. *Montgomery Advertiser,* May 13, 1963, 1.

79. *Montgomery Advertiser,* May 5, 1963, 5F.

80. Personal interview with George Lewis Bailes, September 18, 1992, Montgomery.

81. *Montgomery Advertiser,* May 18, 1963, 1.

82. Lesher, *George Wallace,* 167.

83. *Montgomery Advertiser,* May 18, 1963, 1.

84. Jones, *The Wallace Story,* 90–91.

85. Congressional Quarterly, *Revolution in Civil Rights, 1945–1968* (Washington, D.C.: Congressional Quarterly, 1968), 50.

86. Loevy, *To End All Segregation,* 38–39. Loevy cited a memorandum to the U.S. attorney general from Norbert A. Schlei, assistant attorney general, June 4, 1963, 2, Robert F. Kennedy General Correspondence, John F. Kennedy Library, Boston; and a memorandum to the attorney general from Nicholas Katzenbach, deputy attorney general, June 29, 1963, 1, Robert F. Kennedy General Correspondence, John F. Kennedy Library.

87. *The Mobile Register,* September 3, 1963, 1, September 7, 1963, 1.

88. *Montgomery Advertiser,* September 3, 1963, 1.

89. *Montgomery Advertiser,* September 4, 1963, 1. Also note the moderate nature of the 1963 council election campaigns in Birmingham in the February and March 1963 *Birmingham News.*

90. Quoted in *Montgomery Advertiser,* September 7, 1963, 4.

91. *Montgomery Advertiser,* September 6, 1963.

92. Quoted in *Montgomery Advertiser,* September 7, 1963, 4.

93. *Montgomery Advertiser,* September 6, 1963, 4.

94. *Selma Times-Journal,* September 6, 1963.

95. *Montgomery Advertiser,* September 20, 1963, 2.

96. J. Dennis Lord, "School Busing and White Abandonment of Public Schools," *Southeastern Geographer* 15, no. 2 (1975): 81–92.

97. Letters to George Wallace from J. P. Est Jr., minister, Bellevue Methodist Church, Gadsden, Ala., October 25, 1962, and from William A. Payne, Montgomery, October 24, 1962; letter from George Wallace to Mrs. E. H. Hobbs, Selma, Ala., October 9, 1963, Box RC2:G293, Wallace Office Files, ADAH.

98. "Report on Negro Demonstration Plans for March Source: Jim—Birmingham—a Negro agent," March 6, 1964, in Box RC2:G293, Segregation-General File, Wallace Office Files, ADAH.

99. Personal interview with Richmond M. Flowers, June 17, 1991, Dothan, Ala.

100. *Montgomery Advertiser,* October 6, 1963, 3B.

101. *Montgomery Advertiser,* October 6, 1963, 2B.

102. Personal interview with Richmond M. Flowers, June 17, 1991, Dothan, Ala.

103. Personal interview with Richmond M. Flowers, June 17, 1991, Dothan, Ala.

104. *Montgomery Advertiser,* September 29, 1963, 7A.

105. *Montgomery Advertiser,* October 3, 1963, 1.

106. Congressional Quarterly, *Revolution in Civil Rights,* 52.

107. Loevy, *To End All Segregation,* 123.

108. Congressional Quarterly, *Revolution in Civil Rights,* 57 and 59.

109. It became PL 88-352.

110. The full text and an early analysis of the act's potential impact as well as its legislative history are discussed in B.A. Incorporated, *The Civil Rights Act of 1964* (Washington, D.C.: B.A. Incorporated, 1964).

111. *Montgomery Advertiser,* January 4, 1964, 1.

112. Ibid., *New York Herald Tribune,* February 11, 1964.

113. March 31, 1965, Box RC2:G299, Education–Macon County File, Wallace Office Files, ADAH.

114. Memo to cabinet members from Earl Morgan, October 16, 1963; memo to Cecil Jackson, the governor's legal advisor, from Earl Morgan, September 15, 1964: "Hugh Locke called to inquire about when they might expect the donation from the Governor's campaign fund to the Hoover Academy. I told him that it would probably be within a week" (Box RC2:G299, 1963 Private Schools File, Wallace Office Files, ADAH).

115. Box RC2:G299, Education–Macon County File, Wallace Office Files, ADAH.

116. Title 52, Sec. 61, Code of Alabama.

117. See letters to George Wallace written in November 1963, Box RC2:G293, Wallace Office Files, ADAH.

118. Letter to George Wallace from Richard W. Neal, January 23, 1964, Box RC2:G293, Wallace Office Files, ADAH.

119. Letter to George Wallace, February 6, 1964, Box RC2:G293, Wallace Office Files, ADAH.

120. Resolution of the Young Men's Business Club of Birmingham, February 10, 1964, Box RC2:G299, Education–Macon County File, Wallace Office Files, ADAH.

121. Letter from Elton B. Stephens, president, EBSCO Industries, to George Wallace, June 12, 1963, Box RC2:G288, Wallace Office Files, ADAH.

122. Personal interview, Montgomery, July 1991. See also Wallace's press secretary Bill Jones's account in Jones, *The Wallace Story,* 87–89, and the enthusiastic editorials in the *Selma Times-Journal, Dothan Eagle,* and *Tuscaloosa Graphic, Clarke County Democrat* reprinted in the *Montgomery Advertiser,* June 8, 1963, 4.

123. Letter from Wallace D. Malone to George Wallace, December 29, 1962, Box RC2:G287, File 1962–63 Democratic, Wallace Office Files, ADAH.

124. Letter from E. C. Boswell, partner in the firm of Boswell and Smith, Geneva, to George Wallace, January 17, 1964, Box RC2:G298, 1964 Presidential Election File, Wallace Office Files, ADAH.

125. Letter to E. C. Boswell from George Wallace, January 29, 1964, Box RC2:G298, 1964 Presidential Election File, Wallace Office Files, ADAH. See also Jones, *The Wallace Story,* 334.

126. Letter to George Wallace from E. C. Boswell, February 11, 1964, Box RC2:298, 1964 Presidential Election File, Wallace Office Files, ADAH.

127. Loevy, *To End All Segregation,* 32.

128. *Montgomery Advertiser,* January 12, 1964, 2B.

129. *Montgomery Advertiser,* March 10, 1964, 4.

130. Letter from Wallace Malone to George Wallace, December 29, 1962, Box RC2:G287, File 1962–63 Democratic, Wallace Office Files, ADAH.

131. *Montgomery Advertiser,* February 2, 1964, 4A.

132. Those who stayed were Roy McCord, Gadsden; Mr. and Mrs. Rueben Newton, Jasper; state senator Neal Metcalf, Geneva; and Bill Hardin, Gadsden. Alternates: Mrs. Roy McCord; Mrs. Joe Elliott, Decatur; Mrs. Ester Mannay of Hillsboro; Harold Morris, Gadsden; and Don Hawkins, Birmingham. Hardin had signed the pledge and then announced he was withdrawing his signature.

133. *Time,* April 17, 1964, 37.

134. Congressional Quarterly, *Guide to U.S. Elections,* 2d ed. (Washington, D.C.: Congressional Quarterly, 1985), 414–16.

135. July 17, 1964, Box RC2:G298, 1964 Presidential Election File, Wallace Office Files, ADAH.

136. Letter to Joe Poole from George Wallace, July 20, 1964, Box RC2:G298, 1964 Presidential Election File, Wallace Office Files, ADAH.

137. Letter from W. M. Beck Sr. to George Wallace, July 21, 1964, Box RC2:G298, 1964 Presidential Election File, Wallace Office Files, ADAH.

138. Letter to W. M. Beck Sr. from George Wallace, July 27, 1964, Box RC2:G298, 1964 Presidential Election File, Wallace Office Files, ADAH.

139. Letter to George Wallace from I. J. Scott, August 14, 1964, Box RC2:G298, 1964 Presidential Election File, Wallace Office Files, ADAH.

140. Letter to I. J. Scott from George Wallace, August 19, 1964, Box RC2:G298, 1964 Presidential Election File, Wallace Office Files, ADAH.

141. Letter to Bill Jones, George Wallace's press secretary, from Philip Clore Jr., Independents and Democrats for Goldwater, September 14, 1964, Box RC2:G298, 1964 Presidential Election File, Wallace Office Files, ADAH.

142. *Birmingham News,* July 13, 1964, 6.

143. *Montgomery Advertiser,* September 23, 1964, 4.

144. *Birmingham News,* November 1, 1964, A16.

145. *Montgomery Advertiser,* October 11, 1964, 5A.

146. *Montgomery Advertiser,* October 21, 1964, 4.

147. Grover Hall Jr., in a May 1963 editorial, foresaw Goldwater's 1964 victory and the resulting impact on congressional races.

148. Bernard Cosman, *Five States for Goldwater: Continuity and Change in Southern Voting Patterns* (University: University of Alabama Press, 1966). Subsequent citations will appear in parentheses in the text.

149. Congressional Quarterly, *Guide to U.S. Elections,* 1007.

150. *Montgomery Advertiser,* December 8, 1964, 1.

151. Cosman, *Five States for Goldwater,* 79.

152. *Montgomery Advertiser,* September 16, 1964, 4.

153. E.g., letter to William Grace, president, Fruehauf Trailer Company, from George Wallace, March 5, 1963, and letter to George Wallace from John Steger, executive vice president, Birmingham Chamber of Commerce, February 15, 1963, Box RC2:G290, 1962–63 Planning and Industrial Development File, Wallace Office Files, ADAH.

154. *Montgomery Advertiser,* December 16, 1963, 1. The story provides a full list of names.

155. Letter from Henry C. Goodrich to Seymore Trammell, September 16, 1963, Box RC2:G288, Finance Department File, Wallace Office Files, ADAH.

156. Letter to George Wallace from J. A. Barclay, manager, Northrop Space Laboratories, Huntsville Dept., May 23, 1963, Box RC2:G293, Wallace Office Files, ADAH.

157. Letter from Royce Kershaw to George Wallace, December 23, 1963, Box RC2:G300, 1963–64 Planning and Industrial Development File, Wallace Office Files, ADAH.

158. E.g., letter from Luther Little, assistant to Governor Wallace, to William Killough, judge of probate, Talladega County, March 18, 1964, Box RC2:G302, 1963–64 Industrial Relations File; letter to George Wallace from Leonard Beard, director, State Planning and Industrial Development Board, April 2, 1964, Wallace Office Files, ADAH.

159. Letter to Donald Snyder, vice president and general manager, Marathon Cor-

poration, September 30, 1964, Box RC2:G304, 1963–64 Planning and Industrial Development File, Wallace Office Files, ADAH.

160. Personal interview with George Lewis Bailes, September 18, 1992, Montgomery.

Chapter 8. Wallace's Growing Popularity and Ambition

1. David J. Garrow, *Bearing the Cross,* 2d ed. (New York: Vintage, 1986, 1988), 379.

2. Ibid., 381.

3. *New York Times,* February 5, 1965, 15.

4. Garrow, *Bearing the Cross,* 385.

5. *Montgomery Advertiser,* February 2, 1965, 1.

6. Box RC2:G319, Marion, Ala., Registration File, Wallace Office Files, ADAH.

7. Draft, probably handwritten by George Wallace, Box RC2:G319, Marion, Ala., Registration File, Wallace Office Files, ADAH.

8. Jones, *The Wallace Story,* 355–56.

9. Garrow, *Bearing the Cross,* 395–96.

10. Jones, *The Wallace Story,* 357. The specifics of this plan were confirmed by Bob Ingram in a personal interview, June 4, 1991, Montgomery.

11. Garrow, *Bearing the Cross,* 398.

12. Jones, *The Wallace Story,* 364–65.

13. *Montgomery Advertiser,* March 10, 1965, 1.

14. See also Jones, *The Wallace Story,* 368.

15. Personal interview with Bob Ingram, June 4, 1991, Montgomery.

16. Letter to Albert J. Lingo from George Wallace, September 17, 1965, Box RC2:G319, 1965 Public Safety File, Wallace Office Files, ADAH.

17. The content of Wallace's telegram to Johnson requesting the appointment is in Jones, *The Wallace Story,* 375–76.

18. Garrow, *Bearing the Cross,* 407.

19. *Montgomery Advertiser,* March 19, 1965, 1.

20. *Birmingham News,* April 2, 1965, 1.

21. *Montgomery Advertiser,* April 15, 1965, 17.

22. Wallace Office Files, ADAH.

23. *Montgomery Advertiser,* April 22, 1965, 1.

24. *Montgomery Advertiser,* April 23, 1965, 1.

25. *Montgomery Advertiser,* April 28, 1965, 1.

26. *Montgomery Advertiser,* August 7, 1965, 1.

27. Memo to George Wallace from Austin Meadows, state superintendent of education, June 16, 1965, Box RC2:G311, 1965 Education Department File, Wallace Office Files, ADAH.

28. House Joint Resolution 5.

29. "Biennial Report to the Alabama Legislature by the Alabama Legislative

Commission to Preserve the Peace," 10. For a more data-filled description of SNCC see Martin Oppenheimer, *The Sit-In Movement of 1960* (Brooklyn: Carlson, 1989); and Clayborne Carson, *In Struggle: SNCC and the Black Awakening of the 1960s* (Cambridge: Harvard University Press, 1981).

30. "Biennial Report to the Alabama Legislature by the Alabama Legislative Commission to Preserve the Peace," 14.

31. Ibid., 63.

32. *New York Times,* September 30, 1965, 2.

33. *New York Times,* May 6, 1965, 24.

34. *New York Times,* May 9, 1965, IV, 2.

35. *New York Times,* May 9, 1965, 41.

36. *New York Times,* December 11, 1965, 1, 22.

37. *New York Times,* August 22, 1965, 28.

38. Box RC2:G334, 1965 Law Enforcement—RE: Hayneville Trial of Tom Coleman File, Wallace Office Files, ADAH.

39. Memo to President Lyndon Johnson from George Reedy, October 2, 1965, from the Johnson Presidential Library, in *Civil Rights, the White House, and the Justice Department,* ed. Michael R. Belknap (New York: Garland, 1991), 465.

40. *Los Angeles Times,* October 1, 1965.

41. *Montgomery Advertiser,* March 16, 1965, 2.

42. *New York Times,* December 1, 1965, 32, December 3, 1965, 35.

43. Congressional Quarterly, *Revolution in Civil Rights,* 68–69; *Montgomery Advertiser,* May 20, 1965, 1, and May 27, 1965, 1.

44. Letter to T. H. Walker from George Wallace, September 14, 1965, Box RC2: G319, Registration of Voters File, Wallace Office Files, ADAH.

45. *New York Times,* December 22, 1965, 16.

46. Alabama Legislative Reference Service, "Legislative Control of County Government," February 7, 1966, 1.

47. Box RC2:G329, 1966 Democratic Party File, Wallace Office Files, ADAH.

48. Box RC2:G329, 1966 Democratic Party File, Wallace Office Files, ADAH.

49. Congressional Quarterly, *Revolution in Civil Rights,* 12.

50. Box RC2:G325, Civil Rights 1965–66 File, Wallace Office Files, ADAH.

51. Box RC2:G326, Black Power File, Wallace Office Files, ADAH.

52. Letter to Jesse Ray from George Wallace, July 22, 1966, Box RC2:G326, Wallace Office Files, ADAH.

53. Letter to Richard J. Hughes from Bull Connor, August 14, 1967, Box RC2:G347, 1966–67 Democratic File, Wallace Office Files, ADAH.

54. U.S. Office of Education, "General Statement of Policies under Title VI of the Civil Rights Act of 1964 Respecting Desegregation of Elementary and Secondary Schools," April 1965.

55. *Wall Street Journal,* May 26, 1966, 1.

56. Box RC2:G329, 1966 Education Department, Wallace Office Files, ADAH.

57. Box RC2:G330, Petition from Tuscaloosa County File, Wallace Office Files, ADAH.

58. Box RC2:G333, 1965–66 Labor Department File, Wallace Office Files, ADAH.

59. *Wall Street Journal,* August 12, 1966.

60. Ibid.

61. November 28, 1964, Box RC2:G311, 1964–65 Education Department File, Wallace Office Files, ADAH.

62. Letter to Bill Jones, Wallace's press secretary, from Bob Kendall, assistant director of the Highway Department, December 14, 1964. This letter supplies the statistic that the Wallace administration had apportioned $85 million in highway construction money to Jefferson County so far. Box RC2:G314, 1964–65 Highway Department File, Wallace Office Files, ADAH.

63. Harvey, *History of Educational Finance,* 233.

64. *Montgomery Advertiser,* April 9, 1965.

65. *Montgomery Advertiser,* April 28, 1965.

66. *Montgomery Advertiser,* April 2, 1965, 1.

67. *Montgomery Advertiser,* August 16, 1964, 5A.

68. *Montgomery Advertiser,* September 12, 1965, 4.

69. *Montgomery Advertiser,* September 12, 1965, 5A.

70. Albert P. Brewer, "Famous Filibusters: High Drama in the Alabama Legislature," *Alabama Review* 43, no. 2 (April 1990): 91.

71. *Montgomery Advertiser,* October 15, 1965, 1; personal interview with Albert P. Brewer, June 3, 1992, Birmingham.

72. *Montgomery Advertiser,* October 14, 1965, 4.

73. *Montgomery Advertiser,* October 23, 1965, 1.

74. Interview with Vaughan Hill Robison, July 15, 1991, Montgomery.

75. The others who voted against the succession amendment were Larry Dumas, George Hawkins, Sonny Hornsby, Ed Horton, Julian Lowe, Bill McCain, Charles Montgomery, Roscoe Roberts, Vaughan Hill Robison, and Joe Smith. Among those who voted for it, six did not run for office. They were Charles Adams, Harlan G. "Mutt" Allen, Albert Evans, H. P. James, Ed Reynolds, and Bob Wilson. Seeking renomination to the senate were Clayton Carter, Jimmy Clark, Roland Cooper, Ed Eddins, Walter Givhan, Ray Lolley, Jimmy McDow, Emmett Oden, and Gaillard Robison. Pete Mathews and L. W. Brannan ran for the Alabama House, and Bill Nichols entered the congressional race in the Fourth District and won.

76. Telephone interview with John M. Patterson, May 29, 1992.

77. *Montgomery Advertiser,* April 1, 1965, 1.

78. The *Montgomery Advertiser,* August 10, 1965, 1, reviews these actions.

79. *Montgomery Advertiser,* September 24, 1965, 1.

80. *Montgomery Advertiser,* October 5, 1965, 1.

81. Personal interview with Vaughan Hill Robison, July 15, 1991, Montgomery.

82. *Montgomery Advertiser,* August 15, 1965, 4A.

83. *Montgomery Advertiser,* May 9, 1965, 5A.

84. Personal interview with Albert P. Brewer, June 3, 1992, Birmingham.

85. Box RC2:G318, Wallace Office Files, ADAH.

86. These included the Alabama Petroleum Council, Southern Bell Telephone,

U.S. Steel Corporation, the Decatur Chamber of Commerce, Birmingham Trust National Bank, and the Mobile Chamber of Commerce.

87. They included the presidents of the Alabama Agricultural and Mechanical College, Alabama State College, and the Carver Trade School in Mobile.

88. *Montgomery Advertiser,* June 13, 1965, 5A.

89. *Montgomery Advertiser,* January 23, 1966, 1, 3.

90. *Montgomery Advertiser,* February 27, 1966, 5.

91. *Montgomery Advertiser,* May 14, 1966, 1.

92. *Montgomery Advertiser,* February 19, 1966, 1.

93. Personal interview with Richmond M. Flowers, June 17, 1991, Dothan, Ala.

94. *Montgomery Advertiser,* January 1, 1966, 1.

95. *Montgomery Advertiser,* March 15, 1966, 1.

96. *Montgomery Advertiser,* March 13, 1966, 1.

97. *Montgomery Advertiser,* March 15, 1966, 4.

98. *Montgomery Advertiser,* March 18, 1966, 1–2.

99. *Montgomery Advertiser,* April 3, 1966, 1–2.

100. *Montgomery Advertiser,* August 14, 1949.

101. *Montgomery Advertiser,* March 20, 1966, 4.

102. *Montgomery Advertiser,* March 5, 1966, 1.

103. *Montgomery Advertiser,* March 20, 1966, 4.

104. *Montgomery Advertiser,* March 27, 1966, 5.

105. *Montgomery Advertiser,* March 27, 1966, 4.

106. *Montgomery Advertiser,* April 11, 1966, 1.

107. *Montgomery Advertiser,* May 1, 1966, 1.

108. *Montgomery Advertiser,* May 1, 1966, 4.

109. *Montgomery Advertiser,* May 5, 1966, 4.

110. *Montgomery Advertiser,* May 8, 1966, 5.

111. *Montgomery Advertiser,* March 27, 1966, 5.

112. *Huntsville Times,* September 28, 1966.

113. *Huntsville Times,* November 6, 1966.

Chapter 9. The Governors Wallace

1. See the *Montgomery Advertiser,* January 8, 1967, 5, for a classic Rankin Fite story about the fast gavel.

2. Personal interview with Albert P. Brewer, June 3, 1992, Birmingham.

3. Personal interview with George Lewis Bailes Jr., September 18, 1992, Montgomery.

4. Personal interview with Albert P. Brewer, June 3, 1992, Birmingham.

5. Personal interview with George Lewis Bailes Jr., September 18, 1992, Montgomery.

6. Ibid.

7. Ibid.

8. Personal interview with Albert P. Brewer, June 3, 1992, Birmingham; and Grafton and Permaloff, *Big Mules and Branchheads,* 85–86, 96–98, 195.

9. *Montgomery Advertiser,* March 8, 1967, 1.

10. *Montgomery Advertiser,* April 9, 1967, 5.

11. A full listing of the vote and a related vote is in the *Montgomery Advertiser,* April 12, 1967, 1.

12. *Montgomery Advertiser,* April 14, 1967, 4.

13. *Birmingham News,* April 22, 1967, 1.

14. *Birmingham News,* April 22, 1967, 2.

15. Personal interviews with Albert P. Brewer, June 3, 1992, Birmingham, and George Lewis Bailes Jr., September 18, 1992, Montgomery.

16. The smaller universities often included legislators on their boards of trustees. E.g., in 1967 Florence State University had Rep. Harry Pennington, Jacksonville State University had Rep. Hugh Merrill and Rep. Pete Mathews (an extraordinarily powerful duo), Livingston State University had Rep. Ira Pruitt, Troy State University, in addition to having a president who was a close personal friend of George Wallace, had Rep. Rick Manley's wife, Senate Secretary McDowell Lee, and Sen. Jack Giles. The University of Alabama, Auburn University, and Alabama College (Montevallo) had no legislators or, as far as we can discover, legislative relations on their boards. Of course, Alabama and Auburn had many graduates in both chambers.

17. *Birmingham News,* May 2, 1967, 1, 6.

18. *Montgomery Advertiser,* April 12, 1967.

19. For a discussion of "normal" urban-rural patterns see Harlan Hahn, *Urban-Rural Conflict: The Politics of Change* (Beverly Hills: Sage, 1971), 219–67.

20. *Montgomery Advertiser,* July 10, 1967, 5.

21. Ibid.

22. *Montgomery Advertiser,* August 13, 1967, 5.

23. Rep. James Cameron (Montgomery) proposed the amendment.

24. *Montgomery Advertiser,* August 16, 1967, 1.

25. *Montgomery Advertiser,* October 7, 1967, 1.

26. *Montgomery Advertiser,* April 12, 1968.

27. *Montgomery Advertiser,* April 12, 1968, 4.

28. Personal interview with Albert P. Brewer, June 3, 1992, Birmingham.

29. *Montgomery Advertiser,* August 13, 1967, 5.

30. *Montgomery Advertiser,* September 9, 1967, 1.

31. *Montgomery Advertiser,* September 13, 1967, 1.

32. *Montgomery Advertiser,* July 2, 1967, 5A.

33. Stephen E. Lile and Don M. Soule, "Interstate Differences in Family Tax Burdens," *National Tax Journal* 22, no. 4 (December 1969): 433–49; see also Stephen E. Lile, "Interstate Comparison of Family Tax Burdens" (Ph.D. dissertation, University of Kentucky, Lexington, 1969).

34. U.S. Commission on Civil Rights, *Racial Isolation in the Public Schools,* 1967.

35. *Montgomery Advertiser,* March 19, 1967, 4.

36. See also *Montgomery Advertiser,* April 2, 1967, 4.

37. Letter to Lurleen Wallace from John Kohn, March 24, 1967, Box RC2:G348, 1966–67 Education Department File, Lurleen Wallace Office File, ADAH.

38. National Education Association, *Wilcox County, Alabama.*

39. Ibid.

40. Lurleen Wallace Office Files, ADAH.

41. *New York Times,* April 2, 1967, 74.

42. *New York Times,* April 18, 1967, 23.

43. *New York Times,* April 3, 1967, 21.

44. *New York Times,* January 12, 1968, 57.

45. *Montgomery Advertiser,* January 16, 1968, 1.

46. *New York Times,* June 10, 1968, 34.

47. In 1963 there were thirty-two private schools in Mobile, and ten years later sixty-one. Joseph W. Newman and Betty Brandon, "Integration in the Mobile Public Schools," in *The Future of Public Education in Mobile,* ed. Howard F. Mahan and Joseph W. Newman (Mobile: South Alabama Review, 1982), 48.

48. *New York Times,* March 19, 1968, 1, 20.

49. *Montgomery Advertiser,* May 2, 1968, 1.

50. *Montgomery Advertiser,* April 7, 1967, 4.

51. *Montgomery Advertiser,* May 21, 1967, 5.

52. *Montgomery Advertiser,* April 7, 1967, 4.

53. *Montgomery Advertiser,* April 9, 1967, 4.

54. *Montgomery Advertiser,* May 2, 1967, 4.

55. *Montgomery Advertiser,* May 18, 1967, 4.

56. *Montgomery Advertiser,* April 8, 1967, 1.

57. Ibid.

58. *Montgomery Advertiser,* May 18, 1967, 4.

59. *Montgomery Advertiser,* May 23, 1967, 1.

60. *Montgomery Advertiser,* November 29, 1967, 1.

61. *Montgomery Advertiser,* November 1, 1967, 1.

62. Some Alabama liberals to this day believe that Flowers's later federal indictment and conviction on conspiracy to accept a bribe charges resulted from his outspoken appeal for black votes. Flowers accepts this view but also argues that his work with the NDP together with the NDP's potential for pulling votes away from the national Democratic party in both congressional and presidential races made him a target. Personal interview with Richmond M. Flowers, June 17, 1991, Dothan, Ala.

63. *Montgomery Advertiser,* February 4, 1968, 5.

64. *Montgomery Advertiser,* April 26, 1968, 5.

65. *Montgomery Advertiser,* January 29, 1967, 1.

66. *Montgomery Advertiser,* October 27, 1968, 4.

67. Box RC2:G359, 1966–67 Planning and Industrial Development File, Wallace Office Files, ADAH.

68. In FY 1993–94 the combined appropriations for Auburn University at Montgomery, Troy State University at Montgomery, and the University of Alabama at Huntsville exceeded $45 million. Two-year colleges received annual appropriations ranging from $1.9 million to $10.8 million each. It would be a trivial matter to construct a detailed argument that tens of millions of dollars *a year* are wasted with Alabama's duplicative university branches and two-year institutions.

Chapter 10. Albert Brewer and the Possibility of Real Change

1. Personal interview with Bob Ingram, June 28, 1991, Montgomery.

2. *Montgomery Advertiser,* May 19, 1968, 5.

3. Personal interview with Albert P. Brewer, June 3, 1992, Birmingham.

4. *Montgomery Advertiser,* June 30, 1968, 5, and July 14, 1968, 5. See also the June 28, 1968, editorial, p. 4.

5. *New York Times,* July 7, 1968, 1, 52.

6. *Montgomery Advertiser,* August 11, 1968, 4.

7. *Montgomery Advertiser,* August 13, 1968, 1.

8. *Montgomery Advertiser,* August 29, 1968, 1.

9. *New York Times,* September 11, 1968, 35.

10. *New York Times,* June 28, 1966.

11. *Montgomery Advertiser,* May 7, 1969, 1.

12. *Montgomery Advertiser,* May 17, 1969, 1.

13. *Montgomery Advertiser,* February 2, 1969, 1.

14. *Montgomery Advertiser,* June 27, 1969, 1.

15. *Montgomery Advertiser,* July 30, 1969, 1.

16. *Montgomery Advertiser,* August 16, 1969, 1; a motion had been filed in U.S. District Court by plaintiffs (*Carr v. Montgomery County Board of Education*) asking the court to enter a declaratory judgment and an order finding that the freedom of choice plan of school desegregation in effect "offers no real promise of converting the dual system of segregated education to a unitary nonracial system" in the county and to order the board to "submit a plan to fully and affirmatively desegregate the student bodies of each public school in Montgomery County for school year 1969–70," to reassign the faculties of the schools so that each will have a faculty ratio of 2 Negroes to 3 whites, and to revise the transportation system to meet the needs of an assignment plan."

Solomon Seay Jr., attorney for the plaintiffs, said, "We're not asking for partial integration; we're asking for complete integration." His motion indicated that in the 1969–70 school year there were 38,329 students in the county's fifty-four public schools—22,176 white and 16,153 black (42 percent). Approximately 1,352 African Americans exercised a choice to attend a school where their race was in the minority, and no white students had chosen to attend a traditionally black school. Four schools were all white and nineteen all black, making over 42 percent of the county's fifty-four schools one-race schools. Of the traditionally white schools, seventeen had student bodies less than 5 percent black, three were 6–9 percent black, four were

10–20 percent black, three were 21–25 percent black, and only one had a student body 30 percent black. *Montgomery Advertiser,* July 23, 1969, 1.

17. *Montgomery Advertiser,* September 3, 1969, 2.

18. *New York Times,* September 16, 1969, 30.

19. See Charles S. Bullock III, "Desegregating Urban Areas: Is It Worth It? Can It Be Done?" in *School Desegregation: Shadow and Substance,* ed. Florence H. Levinsohn and Benjamin D. Wright (Chicago: University of Chicago Press, 1976), 129.

20. *Montgomery Advertiser,* November 7, 1969, 4. The Civil Rights Act of 1964 contained an antibusing provision that explicitly said that nothing in the statute would empower an official or court to issue an order seeking to achieve a racial balance in a school "by requiring the transportation of pupils . . . from one school to another or one school district to another." Courts and the Department of Health, Education, and Welfare ignored it. A 1968 appropriations bill (probably for HEW) also contained clear antibusing language. See *Montgomery Advertiser,* September 21, 1969, 4.

21. All Alabama figures reported in this chapter were taken from annual reports issued by the State Board of Education and a computer run performed for the fourth month of the 1993–94 academic year. The authors would like to thank Barbara Fanning, information specialist, and Curtis L. Cronin, coordinator of special projects, Division of Computer Services, both of the State of Alabama Department of Education, for their assistance in gathering these data.

22. Christine H. Rossell, *The Carrot or the Stick for School Desegregation Policy: Magnet Schools or Forced Busing* (Philadelphia: Temple University Press, 1990). She examines the following cities with voluntary desegregation arrangements: Buffalo; Cincinnati; Houston; Milwaukee; Montclair, N.J.; Portland; San Bernardino, Calif.; San Diego; and Tacoma, Wash. She also studies the following cities with mandatory desegregation: Boston; Dallas; Dayton, Ohio; Des Moines, Iowa; Louisville, Ky.; Montgomery County, Md.; Racine, Wis.; St. Paul; Springfield, Mass.; Stockton, Calif.; and Tulsa.

23. Rossell, *Carrot or Stick,* 20–21.

24. E.g., see the case of Montgomery, described in Jack Bass, *Taming the Storm: The Life and Times of Judge Frank M. Johnson, Sr., and the South's Fight over Civil Rights* (New York: Doubleday, 1993), 263–66.

25. Rossell, *Carrot or Stick,* 66.

26. Ibid.

27. Ibid., 71. The formula for interracial exposure in a school district used by Rossell is as follows: For each school in the district, multiply the number of blacks times the proportion of nonblacks. Then add these figures and divide the sum by the number of blacks in the entire school district. This is the percentage of nonblacks in the average minority school. See Rossell's examples, p. 35.

28. Ibid., 72–73.

29. Lord, "School Busing," 90. See also David J. Armor, "White Flight and the Future of School Desegregation," in *School Desegregation: Past, Present, and Future,*

ed. Walter G. Stephan and Joe R. Feagin (New York: Plenum Press, 1980), 187–226. Note Armor's projections of white loss rates in northern school districts without desegregation compared to actual white loss rates before and after mandatory desegregation (p. 202).

30. Lord, "School Busing," 85.

31. *New York Times,* October 30, 1969, 1, 34; *Montgomery Advertiser,* October 30, 1969, 1.

32. *Montgomery Advertiser,* October 19, 1969, 4.

33. *Montgomery Advertiser,* November 14, 1969, 4; *New York Times,* December 9, 1969, 37.

34. *New York Times,* November 3, 1969, 1, 33.

35. *New York Times,* February 19, 1970, 46.

36. *Montgomery Advertiser,* February 19, 1970, 1.

37. *New York Times,* February 10, 1970, 1, 28; February 15, 1970, IV, 2.

38. *New York Times,* January 4, 1970, 78.

39. *Montgomery Advertiser,* January 4, 1970, 1; *New York Times,* January 4, 1970, 78.

40. *New York Times,* January 14, 1970, 1.

41. Lord, "School Busing," 81.

42. *Montgomery Advertiser,* January 6, 1970, 1.

43. *New York Times,* February 1, 1970, 1, 31.

44. *New York Times,* February 9, 1970, 1.

45. *Montgomery Advertiser,* February 21, 1970, 1.

46. *Montgomery Advertiser,* February 18, 1970, 1.

47. *Montgomery Advertiser,* February 16, 1969, 5.

48. Telephone interview with Albert P. Brewer, March 10, 1993.

49. *Montgomery Advertiser,* September 12, 1968, 1.

50. *Montgomery Advertiser,* April 14, 1968, 4.

51. *Montgomery Advertiser,* December 9, 1968, 4.

52. *Montgomery Advertiser,* September 14, 1968, 4; November 10, 1968, 5.

53. Alabama Education Commission, *Financing Education in Alabama* (Montgomery, 1968).

54. *Montgomery Advertiser,* December 8, 1968, 5.

55. *Alabama Coalition for Equity, Inc., et al. v. Hunt* and *Mary Harper et al. v. Hunt* (CV-90-883-R and CV-91-0117-R).

56. *Montgomery Advertiser,* January 17, 1969, 1.

57. *Montgomery Advertiser,* January 18, 1969, 4.

58. *Montgomery Advertiser,* January 24, 1969, 2.

59. *Montgomery Advertiser,* February 19, 1969, 1.

60. *Montgomery Advertiser,* February 23, 1969, 1–2.

61. *Montgomery Advertiser,* December 15, 1968, 5.

62. *Montgomery Advertiser,* February 26, 1969, 1.

63. *Montgomery Advertiser,* March 19, 1969, 1–2.

64. Telephone interview with Albert P. Brewer, March 10, 1993.

65. *Montgomery Advertiser,* April 3, 1969, 1.

66. *Montgomery Advertiser,* April 4, 1969, 1.

67. *Montgomery Advertiser,* April 11, 1969, 1.

68. *Montgomery Advertiser,* April 27, 1969, 4.

69. *Birmingham News,* April 17, 1969, 2; April 24, 1969, 1.

70. *Birmingham News* editorial, April 28, 1969, 6.

71. *Montgomery Advertiser,* May 2, 1969, 1.

72. *Montgomery Advertiser,* May 6, 1969, 2.

73. *Montgomery Advertiser,* April 30, 1971, 1.

74. *Montgomery Advertiser,* October 8, 1971, 1.

75. *Montgomery Advertiser,* October 8, 1971, 1; Alabama, Attorney General, *Quarterly Report of the Attorney General of Alabama for the Period from October 1, 1971, through December 31, 1971,* no. 145 (Montgomery: Office of Attorney General, 1971), 7–10.

76. Bass, *Taming the Storm,* 389.

77. The corporate plaintiffs were Ken Realty Company, Vulcan Realty and Investment Corporation, and Booker T. Washington Insurance, all of Jefferson County.

78. *Montgomery Advertiser,* June 1, 1969, 1.

79. *Montgomery Advertiser,* August 5, 1969, 1.

80. *Montgomery Advertiser,* July 30, 1971, 1.

81. *Montgomery Advertiser,* November 21, 1971, 6.

82. *Montgomery Advertiser,* July 29, 1969, 2; August 8, 1971, 11.

83. *Montgomery Advertiser,* August 3, 1969, 6; August 5, 1969, 1.

84. *Montgomery Advertiser,* June 29, 1971, 1.

85. *Montgomery Advertiser,* September 22, 1971, 1.

86. *Montgomery Advertiser,* January 21, 1972, 1.

87. *Montgomery Advertiser,* June 29, 1969, 5.

88. *Montgomery Advertiser,* September 13, 1969, 1.

89. *Birmingham News,* September 12, 1969, 1, 6.

90. *Montgomery Advertiser,* October 15, 1969, 1.

91. *Montgomery Advertiser,* February 8, 1970, 5.

92. *Montgomery Advertiser,* July 27, 1969, 5.

93. *Montgomery Advertiser,* May 20, 1968, 4.

94. *Montgomery Advertiser,* June 29, 1968, 1.

95. *Montgomery Advertiser,* November 21, 1969, 1.

96. See Bass, *Taming the Storm,* chap. 19.

97. *Montgomery Advertiser,* January 9, 1970, 1.

98. *Montgomery Advertiser,* January 20, 1970, 4.

99. *Montgomery Advertiser,* February 1, 1970, 1.

100. *Montgomery Advertiser,* February 9, 1970, 1.

101. *New York Times,* April 24, 1970, 21.

102. *Montgomery Advertiser,* April 24, 1970, 4.
103. *Montgomery Advertiser,* April 2, 1970, 2.
104. *Montgomery Advertiser,* May 3, 1970, 1.
105. *Montgomery Advertiser,* April 3, 6–8, 10, 12, 14, 16, and 19, 1970.
106. *Montgomery Advertiser,* April 10, 12, 1970, 1.
107. *Montgomery Advertiser,* April 12, 1970, 1.
108. *Montgomery Advertiser,* September 26, 1971, 5.
109. *Montgomery Advertiser,* May 18, 1970, 1.
110. *Montgomery Advertiser,* May 20, 1970, 6.
111. *Montgomery Advertiser,* May 14, 1970, 1.
112. Michael Dorman, *The George Wallace Myth,* 171.
113. *Montgomery Advertiser,* May 31, 1970, 10A.
114. Dorman, *The George Wallace Myth,* 171–72.
115. *Montgomery Advertiser,* May 31, 1970, 9A.

Chapter 11. . . . The More They Stay the Same

1. E.g., *New York Times,* August 2, 1994, A1, B6.
2. Anne Permaloff and Carl Grafton, "Previous Efforts Failed to Revise Flawed Code," *Mobile Press-Register,* October 3, 1993, Perspective section, 1, 4.

Appendix

1. This slope (regression coefficient) for 1950–62 is .14, and the slope for 1963–84 is only .04. Multiple R squared for the 1950–62 trend line is .87, and for the 1963–84 line it is .24, because the line encompasses low data after 1975.

2. The 1950–62 and 1963–74 slopes are .14 and .19, respectively. The multiple R squares are .87 and .93, respectively.

3. Susan Welch and John Comer, *Quantitative Methods for Public Administration* (Pacific Grove, Calif.: Brooks/Cole, 1988), 289–95.

Selected Bibliography

Public Documents

Alabama. *Acts of Alabama.*

Alabama. *Code of Alabama.*

Alabama. Alabama Education Commission. *Financing Education in Alabama.* Montgomery: Alabama Education Commission, 1968.

———. *Report of the Alabama Education Commission.* Montgomery: Alabama Education Commission, 1959.

———. *Report of the Committee on Higher Education.* Montgomery: Alabama Education Commission, 1958.

———. *Report of the Committee on Personnel in Education.* Montgomery: Alabama Education Commission, 1958.

———. *Tentative Report to the Committee on Financing Education Including the Minimum Program.* Montgomery: Alabama Education Commission, 1958.

Alabama. Attorney General. *Quarterly Report of the Attorney General of Alabama for the Period from October 1, 1971, through December 31, 1971.* Vol. 145. Montgomery: Office of the Attorney General, 1972.

Alabama. Commission on Higher Education. *Higher Education in Alabama 1991 Directory.* Montgomery: Alabama Commission on Higher Education, 1991.

———. *Two-Year Institutions.* Preliminary Report. Montgomery: Alabama Commission on Higher Education, 1980.

Alabama. Department of Education. Division of Research and Higher Education. *Non-Residential Facilities Alabama Institutions of Higher Education Public and Private.* Comprehensive Planning Study, Publication No. 2, Alabama State Commission for the Higher Education Facilities Act of 1963. Montgomery: Alabama State Department of Education, 1969.

Alabama. Department of Revenue. *1993 Abatement Report.* Montgomery: Department of Revenue, 1993.

Alabama. House of Representatives. *Journal.*

Alabama. Legislative Fiscal Office. *A Legislator's Guide to Alabama Taxes.* Montgomery: Legislative Fiscal Office, 1987.

Alabama. Legislative Reference Service. Legislative Control of County Government. Montgomery: Legislative Reference Service, 1966.

Alabama. *Official Proceedings of the Constitutional Convention of the State of Alabama (May 21, 1901, to September 3, 1901).* Wetumpka: Wetumpka Printing, 1940.

Alabama. Senate. *Journal.*

U.S. Advisory Commission on Intergovernmental Relations. *1983 Tax Capacity of the States.* Washington, D.C.: ACIR, 1986.

——— . *Regional Growth: Flows of Federal Funds, 1952–1976.* Washington, D.C.: ACIR, 1980.

——— . *Regional Growth: Historic Perspective.* Washington, D.C.: ACIR, 1980.

U.S. Commission on Civil Rights. *Hearing Held in Montgomery, Alabama, April 27– May 2, 1968.* Washington, D.C.: Government Printing Office, 1968.

——— . *Racial Isolation in the Public Schools.* Washington, D.C.: Government Printing Office, 1967.

——— . *Staff Report.* Hearing, Montgomery, Alabama, April 27–May 2, 1968. Washington, D.C.: Government Printing Office, 1968.

——— . *Voting.* 1961 Commission on Civil Rights Report, Bk. 1. Washington, D.C.: Government Printing Office, 1961.

U.S. Congress. Senate. Committee on Banking and Currency. *Hearing on the Nomination of Charles M. Meriwether, to Be a Member of the Board of Directors of the Export-Import Bank of Washington, March 2, 1961.* Washington, D.C.: Government Printing Office, 1961.

U.S. Department of Commerce, Bureau of Economic Analysis. *Survey of Current Business.* Washington, D.C.: Government Printing Office, 1930–1990.

U.S. Department of Commerce, Economics and Statistics Administration, Bureau of Economic Analysis, Regional Economic Measurement Division, *Regional Economic Information System.* CD-ROM. Washington, D.C., 1992.

U.S. Department of Education. Office of Educational Research and Improvement. *Digest of Educational Statistics 1991.* Washington, D.C.: National Center for Education Statistics, 1991.

U.S. National Emergency Council. *Report to the President on the Economic Conditions of the South.* Washington, D.C.: Government Printing Office, 1938.

Books

Alabama Business Research Council. *Industrial Development Bond Financing: Business and Community Experiences and Opinions.* Tuscaloosa: Alabama Business Research Council, 1970.

——— . *Skills for Progress.* Tuscaloosa: Alabama Business Research Council, 1955.

——— . *Transition in Alabama.* Tuscaloosa: University of Alabama Press, 1962.

BA Incorporated. *The Civil Rights Act of 1964.* Washington, D.C.: BA Incorporated, 1964.

Barber, Bernard. *Social Stratification.* New York: Harcourt, Brace, 1957.

Barkan, Elazar. *The Retreat of Scientific Racism: Changing Concepts of Race in Britain and the United States Between the World Wars.* Cambridge: Cambridge University Press, 1992.

Barker, Michael, ed. *State Taxation Policy.* Durham, N.C.: Duke University Press, 1983.

Barnard, William D. *Dixiecrats and Democrats: Alabama Politics, 1942–1950*. University: University of Alabama Press, 1974.

Bartik, Timothy J. *Who Benefits from State and Local Economic Development Policies?* Kalamazoo, Mich.: W. E. Upjohn Institute for Employment Research, 1991.

Bartley, Numan V. *The Rise of Massive Resistance*. Baton Rouge: Louisiana State University Press, 1969.

Bartley, Numan V., and Hugh D. Graham. *Southern Politics and the Second Reconstruction*. Baltimore: Johns Hopkins University Press, 1975.

Belknap, Michal R. *Federal Law and Southern Order: Racial Violence and Constitutional Conflict in the Post-Brown South*. Athens: University of Georgia Press, 1987.

Bensel, Richard Franklin. *Sectionalism and American Political Development, 1880–1980*. Madison: University of Wisconsin Press, 1984.

Bentley, Arthur F. *The Process of Government*. Cambridge, Mass.: Harvard University Press, Belknap Press, 1967.

Black, Earl, and Merle Black. *Politics and Society in the South*. Cambridge, Mass.: Harvard University Press, 1987.

Blau, Peter, and Marshall W. Meyer. *Bureaucracy in Modern Society*. New York: Random House, 1956.

Borts, George H., and Jerome Stein. *Economic Growth in a Free Market*. New York: Columbia University Press: 1964.

Burch, Philip H., Jr. *Highway Revenues and Expenditure Policy in the United States*. New Brunswick, N.J.: Rutgers University Press, 1962.

Chester, Lewis, Godfrey Hodgson, and Bruce Page. *An American Melodrama: The Presidential Campaign of 1968*. New York: Dell, 1969.

Cobb, James C. *The Selling of the South*. Baton Rouge: Louisiana State University Press, 1982.

Conference of State Manufacturers' Associations. *A Study of Business Climates of the Forty-Eight Contiguous States of America*. Chicago: Conference of State Manufacturers' Associations, 1979.

Corporation for Enterprise Development. *Making the Grade: The Development Report Card for the States*. Washington, D.C.: Corporation for Enterprise Development, 1987.

Cortner, Richard C. *The Apportionment Cases*. New York: W. W. Norton, 1970.

Cosman, Bernard. *Five States for Goldwater: Continuity and Change in Southern Voting Patterns*. University: University of Alabama Press, 1966.

Congressional Quarterly. *Guide to U.S. Elections*. 2d ed. Washington, D.C.: Congressional Quarterly, 1985.

———. *Revolution in Civil Rights, 1945–1968*. Washington, D.C.: Congressional Quarterly, 1968.

Council of State Governments. *Legislative Reapportionment in the States: A Summary of Action Since June 1960*. Chicago: Council of State Governments, 1962.

Crandall, Robert W. *Manufacturing on the Move*. Washington, D.C.: Brookings Institution, 1993.

Dahir, James. *Region Building*. New York: Harper and Brothers, 1955.

Davis, James J. *Iron Puddler: My Life in the Rolling Mills and What Came of It*. New York: Bobbs, 1922.

Dorman, Michael. *The George Wallace Myth*. New York: Bantam, 1976.

Dye, Thomas R. *Politics, Economics, and the Public*. Chicago: Rand McNally, 1966.

Easton, David. *The Political System: An Inquiry into the State of Political Science*. 2d ed. New York: Alfred A. Knopf, 1971.

Eisinger, Peter K. *The Rise of the Entrepreneurial State*. Madison: University of Wisconsin Press, 1988.

Elazar, Daniel J., *American Federalism: A View from the States*. New York: Thomas Y. Crowell, 1966.

Fantus Company. *A Study of the Business Climates of the States*. Chicago: Fantus for the Illinois Manufacturers Association, 1975.

Faulkner, Gary. *A Preliminary Review of Forest Industry Development Influences: Opportunities for Alabama?* Montgomery: Alabama Development Office, n.d.

Franklin, John Hope. *From Slavery to Freedom: A History of Negro Americans*. 4th ed. New York: Alfred A. Knopf, 1974.

Garrow, David J. *Bearing the Cross*. 2d ed. New York: Vintage, 1986, 1988.

Gossett, Thomas F. *Race: The History of an Idea in America*. Dallas: Southern Methodist University Press, 1963.

Grafton, Carl, and Anne Permaloff. *Big Mules and Branchheads: James E. Folsom and Political Power in Alabama*. Athens: University of Georgia Press, 1985.

Gray, Ralph, and John M. Peterson. *Economic Development of the United States*. Homewood, Ill.: Richard D. Irwin, 1974.

Greenhut, Melvin L. *Microeconomics and the Space Economy*. Chicago: Scott Foresman, 1963.

———. *Plant Location in Theory and in Practice*. Chapel Hill: University of North Carolina Press, 1956.

Hackney, Sheldon. *Populism to Progressivism in Alabama*. Princeton: Princeton University Press, 1969.

Hamilton, Virginia Van der Veer. *Lister Hill: Statesman from the South*. Chapel Hill: University of North Carolina Press, 1987.

Harvey, Ira. *A History of Educational Finance in Alabama*. Auburn, Ala.: Truman Pierce Institute for the Advancement of Teacher Education, 1989.

Hirschman, A. D. *The Strategy of Economic Development*. New Haven: Yale University Press, 1958.

Hollingsworth, J. Selwyn. *Population Changes in Alabama's Black Belt, 1880–1990*. Montgomery: Center for Demographic and Cultural Research, Auburn University at Montgomery, 1993.

Hoover, Calvin B., and B. U. Rachford. *Economic Resources and Policies of the South*. New York: Macmillan, 1951.

Jackson, Gregory, George Masnick, Roger Bolton, Susan Bartlett, and John Pitkin. *Regional Diversity*. Boston: Auburn House, 1981.

Jones, Bill. *The Wallace Story*. Northport, Ala.: American Southern, 1968.

Joubert, William H. *Southern Freight Rates in Transition*. Gainesville: University of Florida Press, 1949.

Key, V. O., Jr. *Southern Politics in State and Nation*. New York: Vintage, 1949.

Kranzberg, Melvin, and Joseph Gies. *By the Sweat of Thy Brow*. New York: G. P. Putnam's Sons, 1975.

Laszlo, Ervin. *Introduction to Systems Philosophy*. New York: Gordon and Breach, 1972.

Lee, Everett S., Ann Ratner Miller, Carol P. Brainerd, and Richard Esterlin. *Population Redistribution and Economic Growth: United States, 1870–1950*. Vol. 1. Philadelphia: American Philosophical Society, 1957.

Leonard, Herman B. *By Choice or by Chance?* Boston: Pioneer Institute for Public Policy Research, 1992.

Lepawsky, Albert. *State Planning and Economic Development in the South*. Washington, D.C.: Committee of the South, National Planning Association, 1949.

Lesher, Stephan. *George Wallace: American Populist*. Reading, Pa.: Addison-Wesley, 1994.

Loevy, Robert D. *To End All Segregation*. Lanham, Md.: University Press of America, 1990.

Losche, August. *The Economics of Location*. New Haven: Yale University Press, 1954.

Luebke, Paul. *Tar Heel Politics*. Chapel Hill: University of North Carolina Press, 1990.

Luttbeg, Norman R. *Comparing the States and Communities*. New York: Harper Collins, 1992.

McGauley, Patrick, and Edward S. Balls, eds. *Southern Schools: Progress and Problems*. Nashville: N.p., 1959.

McLaughlin, Glenn E., and Stefan Robock. *Why Industry Moves South*. Washington, D.C.: Committee of the South, National Planning Association, 1949.

McMillan, Malcolm C. *Constitutional Development in Alabama, 1798–1901*. Chapel Hill: University of North Carolina Press, 1955.

Miller, E. Willard. *A Geography of Industrial Location*. Dubuque, Iowa: Wm. C. Brown, 1970.

Morehouse, Sarah. *State Politics, Parties, and Policy*. New York: Holt Rinehart and Winston, CBS College Publishing, 1981.

Morgan, William E. *Taxes and the Location of Industry*. Boulder: University of Colorado Press, 1967.

Myrdal, Gunnar. *Economic Theory and Under-Developed Regions*. London: Duckworth, 1957.

National Education Association. *Wilcox County, Alabama*. Washington, D.C.: National Education Association, 1967.

Naylor, Thomas H., and James Clotfelter. *Strategies for Change in the South*. Chapel Hill: University of North Carolina Press, 1975.

Newman, Robert J. *Growth in the American South*. New York: New York University Press, 1984.

Newton, Michael, and Judy Ann Newton. *The Ku Klux Klan: An Encyclopedia*. New York: Garland, 1991.

Perlmutter, Philip. *Divided We Fall: A History of Ethnic, Religious, and Racial Prejudice in America*. Ames: Iowa State University Press, 1992.

Phares, Donald. *Who Pays State and Local Taxes?* Cambridge, Mass.: Oelgeschalager, Gunn and Hain, 1980.

Prewitt, Kenneth, and Alan Stone. *The Ruling Elites*. New York: Harper and Row, 1973.

Rossell, Christine H. *The Carrot or the Stick for School Desegregation Policy: Magnet Schools or Forced Busing*. Philadelphia: Temple University Press, 1990.

Sample, C. James. *Patterns of Regional Economic Change: A Quantitative Analysis of U.S. Regional Growth and Development*. Cambridge, Mass.: Ballinger, 1974.

Scher, Richard K. *Politics in the New South*. New York: Paragon House, 1992.

Schulman, Bruce J. *From Cotton Belt to Sunbelt*. New York: Oxford University Press, 1991.

Sitkoff, Harvard. *A New Deal for Blacks: The Emergence of Civil Rights as a National Issue*. New York: Oxford University Press, 1978.

Southern Education Reporting Service. *Southern Schools: Progress and Problems*. Nashville: Southern Education Reporting Service, 1959.

Southern Regional Education Board. *State and Local Revenue Potential, 1975*. Atlanta: Southern Regional Education Board, 1977.

Straussman, Jeffrey D. *Public Administration*. New York: Longman, 1990.

Swanson, Ernst, and John Griffing. *Public Education in the South Today and Tomorrow*. Chapel Hill: University of North Carolina Press, 1955.

Taylor, Frederick W. *Scientific Management*. New York: Harper and Row, 1911.

Truman, David B. *The Governmental Process*. New York: Alfred A. Knopf, 1951.

Woodward, C. Vann. *The Strange Career of Jim Crow*. 2d ed. New York: Oxford University Press, 1957.

Wright, Gavin. *Old South, New South*. New York: Basic Books, 1986.

Yarbrough, Tinsley E. *Judge Frank Johnson and Human Rights in Alabama*. University: University of Alabama Press, 1981.

Articles

American Association of University Professors. "Academic Freedom and Tenure: Alabama State College." *AAUP Bulletin* 27, no. 4 (winter 1961): 303–9.

Armor, David J. "White Flight and the Future of School Desegregation." In *School Desegregation: Past, Present, and Future,* edited by Walter G. Stephan and Joe R. Feagin. New York: Plenum Press, 1980.

Bahl, Roy. "Regional Shifts in Economic Activity and Government Finances in Growing and Declining States." In *Tax Reform and Southern Economic Development,* edited by Bernard L. Weinstein. Research Triangle Park, N.C.: Southern Policies Board, 1979.

Bartik, Timothy. "Business Location Decisions in the U.S.: Estimates of the Effect of Unionization, Taxes, and Other Characteristics of States." *Journal of Business and Economic Statistics* 3 (1985): 14–22.

Beiman, Irving. "Birmingham: Steel Giant with a Glass Jaw." In *Our Fair City,* edited by Robert S. Allen. New York: Vanguard Press, 1947.

Benson, Bruce L., and Ronald N. Johnson. "The Lagged Impact of State and Local Taxes on Economic Activity and Political Behavior." *Economic Inquiry* 24, no. 3 (July 1986): 389–401.

Boeckelman, Keith. "Political Culture and State Development Policy." *Publius* 21, no. 2 (spring 1991): 49–62.

Bowman, Mary Jean. "Human Inequalities and Southern Underdevelopment." *Southern Economic Journal* 32, no. 1, pt. 2 (July 1965): 73–102.

Brewer, Albert P. "Famous Filibusters: High Drama in the Alabama Legislature." *Alabama Review* 43, no. 2 (April 1990): 83–97.

Bridges, Benjamin, Jr. "State and Local Inducements for Industry, Part I." *National Tax Journal* 18, no. 1 (March 1965): 1–14.

———. "State and Local Inducements for Industry, Part II." *National Tax Journal* 18, no. 2 (June 1965): 175–92.

Bullock, Charles S., III. "Desegregating Urban Areas: Is It Worth It? Can It Be Done?" In *School Desegregation Shadow and Substance,* edited by Florence H. Levinsohn and Benjamin D. Wright. Chicago: University of Chicago Press, 1976.

Burgess, Ernest W. "The Family in a Changing Society." In *Social Change,* edited by Eva Etzioni-Halevy and Amitai Etzioni. New York: Basic Books, 1973.

Burnham, Walter Dean. "The Alabama Senatorial Election of 1962: Return of Interparty Competition." *Journal of Politics* 26 (November 1964): 798–829.

Calzonetti, F. J., and Robert T. Walker. "Factors Affecting Industrial Location Decisions: A Survey Approach." In *Industry Location and Public Policy,* edited by Henry W. Herzog Jr. and Alan M. Schlottmann. Knoxville: University of Tennessee Press, 1991.

Canto, Victor A., and Robert I. Webb. "The Effect of State Fiscal Policy on State Relative Economic Performance." *Southern Economic Journal* 54, no. 1 (July 1987): 186–202.

Converse, Philip. "Change in the American Electorate." In *The Human Meaning of Social Change,* edited by Angus Campbell and Philip Converse. New York: Russell Sage, 1972.

Coolidge, Calvin. "Whose Country Is This?" *Good Housekeeping,* February 1921, 13–14, 106.

Danhof, Clarence H. "Four Decades of Thought on the South's Economic Problems." In *Essays in Southern Economic Development,* edited by Melvin L. Greenhut and W. Tate Whitman. Chapel Hill: University of North Carolina Press, 1964.

Davis, Albert, and Robert Lucke. "The Rich-State-Poor-State Problem in a Federal System." *National Tax Journal* 35, no. 3 (September 1982): 337–63.

Dowd, Jerome. "Paths of Hope for the Negro." *Century Magazine* 61 (November 1900–April 1901): 278–81.

Easterlin, Richard. "Regional Income Trends, 1910–1950." In *American Economic History,* edited by Seymore Harris. New York: McGraw Hill, 1961.

Easton, David. "An Approach to the Study of Political Systems." *World Politics* 9 (April 1957): 383–400.

Eberts, Randall W. "Some Empirical Evidence on the Linkage Between Public Infra-structure and Local Economic Development." In *Industry Location and Public Policy,* edited by Henry W. Herzog Jr. and Alan M. Schlottmann. Knoxville: University of Tennessee Press, 1991.

Eller, Steve, and Kenneth A. Wink. "The Effects of Economic Development Efforts in North Carolina Counties: An Empirical Analysis." Paper presented at the annual meeting of the Southern Political Science Association, Savannah, Ga., November 1993.

Fletcher, Daniel O. "Transportation and Communication." In *The South in Conti-nuity and Change,* edited by John C. McKinney and Edgar T. Thompson. Durham: Duke University Press, 1965.

Frederickson, H. George, and Yong Hyo Cho. "Legislative Apportionment and Fis-cal Policy in the American States." *Western Political Quarterly* 27 (March 1974): 5–37.

Garrett, Martin A., Jr. "Growth in Manufacturing in the South, 1947–1958: A Study in Regional Industrial Development." *Southern Economic Journal* 34, no. 3 (January 1968): 352–64.

Grafton, Carl, and Anne Permaloff. "The Big Mule Alliance's Last Good Year: Thwar-ting the Patterson Reforms." *Alabama Review* 47, no. 4 (October 1990): 243–66.

———. "The Politics of Highway Construction: A Test of the Conventional Wisdom." *Southeastern Political Review* 12, no. 1 (spring 1985): 21–41.

———. "Regional Forces in the Southern Legislature." Paper presented at the an-nual meeting of the Southern Political Science Association, Atlanta, November 1988.

Hanson, Russell L. "Political Cultural Variations in State Economic Development Policy." *Publius* 21, no. 2 (spring 1991): 53–81.

Helms, L. Jay. "The Effect of State and Local Taxes on Economic Growth: A Time Series–Cross Section Approach." *Review of Economics and Statistics* 67, no. 4 (November 1985): 574–82.

Howe, Charles W. "Water Resources and Regional Economic Growth in the United States, 1950–1960." *Southern Economic Journal* 24, no. 4 (April 1968): 477–89.

Johnson, Charles A. "Political Culture in American States: Elazar's Formulation Examined." *American Journal of Political Science* 20, no. 3 (August 1976): 491–509.

Kieschnick, Michael. "Taxes and Growth: Business Incentives and Economic De-velopment." In *State Taxation Policy,* edited by Michael Barker. Durham: Duke University Press, 1983.

Kincaid, John. "Political Culture and the Quality of Urban Life." *Publius* 10, no. 2 (spring 1980): 89–110.

Kirby, Andrew. "The Pentagon Versus the Cities?" In *The Pentagon and the Cities,* edited by Andrew Kirby. Newbury Park, Calif.: Sage, 1992.

Kuznets, Simon. "Economic Growth and Income Inequality." *American Economic Review* 45 (1955): 1–28.

Lepawsky, Albert. "Governmental Planning in the South." *Journal of Politics* 10 (August 1948): 536–67.

Lester, Richard A. "Southern Wage Differentials: Developments, Analysis, and Implications." *Southern Economic Journal* 14, no. 4 (April 1947): 386–94.

Lile, Stephen E., and Don M. Soule. "Interstate Differences in Family Tax Burdens." *National Tax Journal* 22, no. 4 (December 1969): 433–49.

Lord, J. Dennis. "School Busing and White Abandonment of Public Schools." *Southeastern Geographer* 15, no. 2 (1975): 81–92.

Lowrey, David. "The Distribution of Tax Burdens in the American States: The Determinants of Fiscal Incidence." *Western Political Quarterly* 40 (March 1987): 137–58.

McDonald, Stephen. "On the South's Recent Economic Development." *Southern Economic Journal* 28 (1961): 2–39.

McLaughlin, Andrew C. "Mississippi and the Negro Question." *Atlantic Monthly,* December 1892, 828–37.

Mofidi, Alaeddin, and Joe A. Stone. "Do State and Local Taxes Affect Economic Growth?" *Review of Economics and Statistics* 72 (November 1990): 686–91.

Moore, John R., C. Warren Neel, Henry W. Herzog Jr., and Alan M. Schlottmann. "The Efficacy of Public Policy." In *Industry Location and Public Policy,* edited by Henry W. Herzog Jr. and Alan M. Schlottmann. Knoxville: University of Tennessee Press, 1991.

Morgan, David R., and Sheilah S. Watson. "Political Culture, Political System Characteristics, and Public Policies Among the American States." *Publius* 21, no. 2 (spring 1991): 31–48.

Newman, Joseph W., and Betty Brandon. "Integration in the Mobile Public Schools." In *The Future of Public Education in Mobile,* edited by Howard F. Mahan and Joseph W. Newman. Mobile: South Alabama Review, 1982.

Nicholls, William H. "Southern Tradition and Regional Economic Progress." *Southern Economic Journal* 26, no. 3 (January 1960): 187–98.

Olson, Mancur. "The South Will Fall Again: The South as a Leader and Laggard in Economic Growth." *Southern Economic Journal* 49, no. 4 (April 1983): 917–32.

Papke, James A., and Leslie E. Papke. "Measuring Differential State-Local Tax Liabilities and Their Implications for Business Investment Location." *National Tax Journal* 39, no. 3 (September 1986): 357–73.

Papke, Leslie E. "The Responsiveness of Industrial Activity to Interstate Tax Differentials: A Comparison of Elasticities." In *Industry Location and Public Policy,* edited by Henry W. Herzog Jr. and Alan M. Schlottmann. Knoxville: University of Tennessee Press, 1991.

Permaloff, Anne. "Partisan Change in the American Electorate." Paper presented at the annual meeting of the Southwestern Political Science Association, Dallas, March 1974.

Permaloff, Anne, and Carl Grafton. "The Chop-Up Bill and the Big Mule Alliance." *Alabama Review* 43, no. 4 (October 1990): 243–69.

Plaut, Thomas R., and Joseph E. Pluta. "Business Climate, Taxes and Expenditures, and State Industrial Growth in the United States." *Southern Economic Journal* 50, no. 1 (July 1983): 99–119.

Potter, David M. "The Historical Development of Eastern-Southern Freight Rate Relationships." *Law and Contemporary Problems* 12 (1947): 416–48.

Powell, Brian, and Lala Carr Steelman. "Variations in State SAT Performance: Meaningful or Misleading?" *Harvard Educational Review* 54, no. 4 (November 1984): 389–412.

Reid, John T. "Sources of Assistance for Municipal Promotion of Industry." *Alabama Municipal Journal* 23 (January 1969): 15–21.

Sanders, Elisabeth. "Industrial Concentration, Sectional Competition, and Antitrust Politics in America, 1880–1980." In *Studies in American Political Development,* vol. 1, edited by Karen Orren and Stephen Skowronek. New Haven: Yale University Press, 1986.

Sharkansky, Ira. "The Utility of Elazar's Political Culture: A Research Note." *Polity* 2 (fall 1969): 66–83.

Simpson, Richard L., and David N. Norsworthy. "The Changing Occupational Structure of the South." In *The South in Continuity and Change,* edited by John C. McKinney and Edgar T. Thompson. Durham: Duke University Press, 1965.

Spengler, Joseph J. "Southern Economic Trade and Prospects." In *The South in Continuity and Change,* edited by John C. McKinney and Edgar T. Thompson. Durham, N.C.: Duke University Press, 1965.

Stewart, William H., Jr. "Governor Frank Murray Dixon and Reform of State Administration in Alabama." In *The Public Life of Frank M. Dixon,* edited by William D. Barnard. Montgomery: Alabama Department of Archives and History, 1979.

Stober, William J., and Laurence H. Falk. "Property Tax Exemption: An Inefficient Subsidy to Industry." *National Tax Journal* 20, no. 4 (December 1967): 386–94.

Thomassen, Henry. "A Growth Model for a State." *Southern Economic Journal* 24, no. 2 (October 1957): 123–37.

Walker, Francis A. "Restriction of Immigration." *Atlantic Monthly,* June 1896, 822–29.

Wasylenko, Michael. "Empirical Evidence on Interregional Business Location Decisions and the Role of Fiscal Incentives in Economic Development." In *Industry Location and Public Policy,* edited by Henry W. Herzog Jr. and Alan M. Schlottman. Knoxville: University of Tennessee Press, 1991.

Weinstein, Bernard L. "Tax Reform and Southern Economic Development: An Overview." In *Tax Reform and Southern Economic.Development,* edited by Bernard L. Weinstein. Research Triangle Park, N.C.: Southern Policies Board, 1979.

Welch, Susan, and John G. Peters. "State Political Culture and the Attitudes of State

Senators Toward Social, Economic Welfare, and Corruption Issues." *Publius* 10, no. 2 (spring 1980): 59–67.

Williamson, Jeffrey G. "Regional Inequality and the Process of National Development: A Description of the Patterns." *Economic Development and Cultural Change* 13 (1965): 3–39.

Young, Richard. "The Brownsville Affray." *American History Illustrated,* October 1986, 10–17.

Index